WHEN
BOXING
MATTERED

A History of Prize Fighting 1880–1980
and the Impact of Sanctioning Bodies

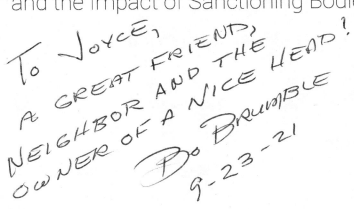

To Joyce,
A GREAT FRIEND,
NEIGHBOR AND THE
OWNER OF A NICE HEAD!
Bo BRUMBLE
9-23-21

BO BRUMBLE

PAGE PUBLISHING, INC.
Conneaut Lake, PA

First originally published by Page Publishing 2021

ISBN 978-1-6624-3151-7 (pbk)
ISBN 978-1-6624-3152-4 (digital)

Printed in the United States of America

Contents

Prologue

I have always had a love affair with boxing and especially with boxing history. The sound of the great names has always been music to my ears, especially the boxers of the classic era who were unaffected by the befuddlement of sanctioning bodies, such as the WBA, WBO, IBF, NYAC, IBC, IBO, NBA, WBF, and the mishmash of lesser sanctioning bodies. I am talking here about a ninety-eight-year span when people actually knew who the heavyweight champion of the world was, because there was only one. This is the thesis of my book.

It is my premise that the era when boxing mattered began in 1880 with the ascension of John L. Sullivan to the heavyweight throne through the time of Muhammad Ali's last title fight, his losing effort against Larry Holmes on October 2, 1980. For a time there were eight weight classes and one world champion in each class.

Although there have been great names in boxing over the last forty years many who became household names and Hall of Famers, such as Mike Tyson, Sugar Ray Leonard, Floyd Mayweather Jr., Manny Pacquiao, and Evander Holyfield, the fact is that too few of these magnificent prize fighters were ever recognized as champion of the world. That is a tragedy. These boxers belong to a different era and perhaps a different book. Perhaps that will be the follow-up to this book, which I hope is a thorough overview of one hundred exciting years of professional boxing, when the title champion of the world meant just that. Ninety-eight years when boxing mattered. It was a time when the world heavyweight championship was the biggest event in sports. Yeah, it was. Time was, when Joe Blow went walking down the street, people said, "There goes Joe Blow, the heavyweight champion of the world." Nobody doubted the fact the

Joe Blow was the heavyweight champion of the world. Today, if Joe Blow were even recognized, people might say, "There goes Joe Blow, the uh… IBC or the WBO or the IBF… Aw…forget it." So my book *When Boxing Mattered* begins.

CHAPTER I

The Eighteen Eighties
and the Great John L.

Heavyweights of the Eighteen Eighties

John L. Sullivan, 1882–1892

Modern boxing history began on February 7, 1882, in Mississippi City, Mississippi when John L. Sullivan of Boston, known as the Boston Strong Boy, bested Irish-born Paddy Ryan of Troy, New York, stopping Ryan in the ninth round for the Bare-Knuckle Championship of America. America in 1882 was still young and beginning to flex its muscle in the era known as the Gilded Age. Former Vice President Chester Arthur was in the White House following the assassination the year before of President James Garfield.

The Standard Oil Trust had just been created by John D. Rockefeller and his associates as a monopoly. The population of the United States was 50,189,209 in the 1880 census, which was an increase of over 30 percent from 1870. The New York, Chicago, and St. Louis Railroad made its maiden run between Buffalo and Chicago. Congress imposed a head tax on noncitizens of the United States who came to American ports and restricted certain classes of people from immigrating to America, including criminals, the insane, or "any person unable to take care of him or herself." But it *was* the Gilded Age. It was the time of Rockefeller, Andrew Carnegie, Cornelius Vanderbilt, Thomas Edison, and John L. Sullivan. The United States went from an agrarian, isolationist country to the world's greatest geopolitical superpower and paved the way for the next century, the American Century. On the other side of the equation, there were lynchings, diseases, Jim Crow, slums, and a huge gap between the gentrified upper class and the rest of America. One of the immigrant groups was the Irish, who became dominant in professional boxing over the next two decades.

There has always been a special relationship between boxing and immigration in the United States. I have said many times that you can tell America's story by the last names of its boxers. First, the Irish, then the Jewish, then the Italians, then the African Americans, then the Mexicans and Latin Americans, and today, we have Russian, Ukranian, South Korean, Thai, Japanese, and Middle Eastern boxers joining the earlier nationalities. It is no accident that the underclasses have always been the best boxers. Chuck Davey aside, you don't go to college to learn how to fight. You gotta be hungry to want to earn your living getting punched in the face and punching others as well. Especially in an era when bare-knuckle fights were common and champions were recognized by newspaper reports and public acclaim. There were no official sanctioning bodies, and a world champion was probably someone like John L. Sullivan, who had mass public acclaim and a lot of press. A champion in that era was a fighter who had a notable win over another fighter and kept winning afterward. I should note that boxing was then governed by the London Prize Ring Rules. A round ended when a boxer was knocked down or took a knee and resumed or stopped when the injured boxer could not come up to scratch in center ring after thirty seconds. A fight could last a few minutes or an hour or two. So a seventy-five-round fight probably had some short as well as long rounds. Irish American boxers have been well represented by such greats as Paddy Ryan, Jim Corbett, Philadelphia Jack O'Brien, Terry McGovern, Jack Dempsey, Mike McTigue, Billy Conn, and Jerry Quarry. Which brings us to the subject of this chapter: John L. Sullivan, a.k.a. the Boston Strong Boy and the Great John L.

John Lawrence Sullivan was born in the Roxbury neighborhood on the south side of Boston on October 15, 1858. From all accounts, Sullivan was a big, strapping youth, well-liked, athletic, and a good student. He most certainly played baseball in high school, because a few years later, at Boston College, he dropped out to play professional baseball. Shortly thereafter, he turned to prize fighting, where he quickly made a name for himself. As a youth, he was arrested several times for participating in illegal prize fights.[1]

John L., now being known around the fighting world as the Boston Strong Boy, had his breakout performance on May 16, 1881, on the Hudson River near Yonkers, New York. In that setting, to avoid police interfering in the illegal match, the fight took place on a barge, where illegal bouts were sometimes held under the London Prize Ring Rules. Fighting with skintight, hard gloves, Sullivan brutalized John Flood, the Bulls Head Terror, knocking him out in eight

---

[1]

rounds fought over sixteen minutes. What added a lot of drama to the affair was the motley crew of Flood's associates. "Flood was the toughest thug in the toughest neighborhood in America's toughest city." The brawler had scrapped his way around the notorious Five Points slum, and his gang ruled the rough-and-tumble streets around the Bull's Head horse market in lower Manhattan."[2] Sullivan showed no fear, and as a result, his reputation as a pugilist grew immensely. It was said that John L., spotting champion Irish Paddy Ryan in the crowd at ringside, looked at him and said, "You're next." Ryan, who won the title beating Joe Goss in his first professional fight, might have felt a little uneasy about Sullivan.[3]

The legend of John L. Sullivan was enhanced by his legendary bouts with liquor. The story goes he would often wander into a saloon and call out, "I can lick any son of a bitch in the house!" And he could. No doubt it bought him more than a few drinks. Expectations of a fight with Paddy Ryan began to swirl.

Paddy Ryan, 1880–1882

As the new year of 1882 came in, rumor had spread across much of America that Sullivan would indeed be fighting Paddy Ryan for the title sometime in February. Boxing being illegal, the site of the upcoming fight shifted from Bay St. Louis, Mississippi, to New Orleans, to a secret site outside Mississippi City. The newspaper coverage must have had a difficult time keeping up. From a reprint of an article in the *New York Times* originally written by Jose Marti:

> *When the two warriors stepped into the ring in an Oak Grove outside the Barnes Hotel on February 7, 1882 excitement must have rippled through the crowd of 5,000 who had come to see an illegal prize fight. GEORGE VECSEY Jan. 2, 1983.*

2

3

THE words in this space are more than a century old. They were written by Jose Marti in 1882 after the bare-knuckle boxing match between John L. Sullivan and Paddy Ryan in Mississippi City, Miss.

"The pen soars when it has grand things to relate, but it plods, as it does now, when it must give account of brutal things, devoid of beauty and nobility. The pen...writhes like a slave, it flees the paper like a fugitive, it swoons in the hand that holds it as though it shared in the wrong it describes.

"There are men here who fight like bulls, running together, skull against skull. They bite and claw one another during the fight, and when it is over, one of the combatants, streaming blood, his gums depopulated, his forehead bruised and knuckles raw, staggers through the crowd that swirls around him, scaling hats in the air and shouting its acclaim, to collect the purse that is his reward for victory. At the same moment, his opponent lies senseless in the arms of his handlers, his vertebrae shattered, and the women's hands arrange bouquets of flowers to perfume the crowded dressing rooms of these base ruffians.

"These fights are national holidays, setting trains and telegraphs in motion, paralyzing business for hours, and bringing together knots of laborers and bankers in the streets. Bets are laid to the clink of glasses, and the newspapers, which editorialize against the practice, fill their pages with accounts of the comings and goings, the comments, private life, training, feuds, triumphs and defeats of the rivals...

"But what of the fight itself? It was off in the South beside the sea, beneath cedars and live oak. These are not squabbles between knaves, inflamed or cooled by circumstances, and governed by caprice.

They are contests between brutes under contract, in which, as in the days of jousting, the field is divided according to the sun, and the weight of the combatants and rules of the contest are formally agreed upon in the greatest detail, as in a horse race.

"The contestants will fight on foot, without rocks or irons in their hands... It is agreed, with an eye to decorum, that this time there will be no biting or scratching, and that no blows are to be struck while an opponent has a knee and a hand touching the ground, nor while he is held by the neck against the ropes or ring posts...

"The ages of man are simply this: a transition from the man-beast to the man-man. There are moments when the beast in man gets the upper hand, and teeth feel a need to bite, a murderous thirst consumes the throat, eyes become flames, and clenched fists must find bodies on which to rain their blows. The human victory consists in restraining the beast and placing over it an angel.

"As the day of the fight draws near, the fighters keep one jump ahead of the law, for each state has different statutes, and there are many distinguished lawmakers who are strongly opposed to prize fighting. But there are states that will take them in, and their arrival touches off a general celebration. The trains come from every direction loaded with bettors, who have closed down their businesses, widowed their wives, orphaned their children, and come thousands of miles to stand in the midst of the turbulent multitude...

"At the scene of the fight...the approaches to the ring site are already filled with people. Men are roosting in trees, the curious peer from every balcony, and spectators stand embattled on the roof tops. The train unburdens itself of its human cargo.

The ring is set up, with another larger surrounding ring, within which only the privileged may come.

"Singing happily, the newspapermen take their seats at ringside in a gleeful band, when suddenly hurrahs rend the air, and every hand is waving a hat, as the scowling Sullivan enters the ring in short pants and a green jersey, and the handsome Ryan, the Giant of Troy, takes his place in the opposite corner, attired in spotless white. There are ladies in the inner circle. The ruffians shake hands and the blood that will soon stream from their wounds begins to boil. Squatted on the ground, their seconds count the money that has been bet on the two men...

"In a moment, one is down; he is dragged to his corner and feverishly sponged. They rush at each other again and deal each other mace-like blows; their skulls resound like anvils beneath the hammer. Ryan's jersey is crimson with gore, and he falls to his knees. The Strong Boy skips back to his corner, laughing. The roar is deafening. Ryan rises shakily. Sullivan moves in for the kill with his lips twisted in a smile. They clinch and maul each other's faces; they stumble back against the ropes. Nine times the assault; nine times one goes reeling to the ground. Now the Giant is staggered, now the cleated shoes no longer can help him keep his footing, now he falls like a stone from a blow to the neck, and on seeing him senseless, his second throws the sponge in the air in token of defeat.

"Some $300,000 have been wagered across the country on this fight; telegraph circuits have been set up to every corner of the nation to speed a blow-by-blow account to eager throngs that fill the streets of the great cities and receive the news of the victory with clamorous applause or angry mutterings. The victorious Bostoner has been the toast of balls *and parties, and the Strong Boy and the Giant have toured the country again to be feted and entertained in theaters and casinos. The sands by the sea are still red and trampled in the city of Mississippi. This nation is like a great tree: perhaps it is Nature's law that grubs must nestle in the roots of great trees.* "[4]

The title and the $5,000 purse were his. A new boxing era was born. Sullivan proceeded to milk his newly acquired status for all it was worth. An extrovert and a braggart, he toured the country, throwing down the gauntlet to anyone who fancied his chances of going four rounds with the champion. Some fifty men tried their hand. Only one is said to have claimed the $1,000 prize on offer, and he was a rugged pro who used his experience and every trick in the book simply to survive the allotted time. Those vanquished by Sullivan during his traveling circus days do not feature in the record books. While his victims doubtless included many no-hopers, Sullivan must have faced the roughest, toughest barroom brawlers every town had to offer. He can't be accused of being a sleeping champion, not in the early stages of his reign, at least. John L. was soon the idol of the masses. His exciting, all-action fighting style, together with his charismatic personality, endeared him to a population only too keen to embrace a new sporting hero. By 1887, Sullivan's popularity was at its height. Boxing was the number 1 sport, with Sullivan its undisputed champion and star attraction."[5] He has often been cited as America's first superstar, and he might well have been, but to be historically accurate, that title really belongs to coloratura operatic singer Jenny Lind, known as the Swedish Nightingale, who electrified America during her grand tour in the 1850s. The tour, promoted by none other than P. T. Barnum, caused a sensation in the otherwise bleak decade before the Civil War. Why this connection to boxing, you ask? This writer/historian believes that Lind woke up America to the

---

4
5

14

possibility of superstars, whether in show business or sports. And of course, Sullivan had the charisma to live up to it.

All that said, John L. Sullivan was the heavyweight champion of America since there was no such title as world champion. Yet as Sullivan's reign continued and as his legend grew, he gradually began to be recognized as the "Heavyweight Champion of the World." He was even presented with a diamond-studded championship belt from the citizens of Boston. The belt proclaimed John L. the Champion of Champions. Almost immediately, the new champ set out on his Grand Tour of America. Fights were scheduled for a set number of rounds before the contest began, and even though Sullivan was the recognized bare-knuckle champion, he actually fought most of his fights with gloves. All the exhibitions on his grand tour were fought with gloves. Few of these bouts were recorded, however, and although it has been said that Sullivan had over 450 fights, his ring record shows 38 wins, with 32 by knockout, 1 loss, and 1 no contest.[6] The Grand Tour took him from Boston to Cincinnati, to Butte, to Seattle, to San Francisco, to Davenport, to Fort Wayne, and to several other cities and towns. This is where the majority of his unreported fights occurred, although I find it hard to believe that he had the time for 450 fights.

On May 14, 1883, he met British champion Charley Mitchell in Madison Square Garden for the Heavyweight Championship of the World. Despite being knocked down in the first round for the first time in his career, Sullivan simply overpowered the Brit before stopping him in round 3. Despite the stoppage, Mitchell had shown himself the better boxer and stated that he had knocked Sullivan down and Sullivan had been unable to actually knock him, Mitchell, off his feet. This despite the fact that Sullivan outweighed Mitchell by twenty pounds.[7]

The pair fought again in Chantilly, France, on March 10, 1888, at the estate of Baron de Rothschild in pouring rain. It seems at least some of the press thought that Mitchell had bested Sullivan. The

6

7

two men fought for three hours, thirty-nine minutes, and thirty-nine rounds before exhaustion claimed both men and probably the spectators who had braved the rain for the duration. Despite the draw verdict, Mitchell was awarded a championship belt by his countrymen. This irked Sullivan and was probably instrumental in the belt given to him proclaiming him Champion of Champions by the city of Boston. It was a huge disappointment to many of Sullivan's fans and was certainly instrumental in prodding John L. to redeem himself.[8]

Against Jake Kilrain

Richard K. Fox, the publisher and owner of the *Police Gazette*, feeling he had once been insulted by John L. Sullivan, presented Jake Kilrain, who had fought a draw with Jem Smith in 1887 in what had been billed as a heavyweight championship fight, with a championship belt, which no doubt angered Sullivan.[9] On July 8, 1889, the epic John L. Sullivan-Jake Kilrain fight took place in Richburg, Mississippi. The fight had been ballyhooed and written up in newspapers for weeks, and expectations ran high. While training for the fight, Sullivan often left camp and headed to the nearest saloon. His trainer, the wrestler William Muldoon, often had to go out and get the usually drunk champion back to camp.[10] The location of the fight was kept secret until the last moment. On learning of the site, over two thousand spectators loaded onto trains and arrived early on the morning of the fight. By fight time, the July temperature had risen to over one hundred degrees. Because it was a fight, in fact the last heavyweight championship fight fought with bare knuckles, it was fought under the old London Prize Ring Rules, which I have outlined earlier. The rules used for this fight meant there were no judges and it was fight to the finish. A round ended by either contestant being knocked down, wrestled down, or taking a knee.

8

9

10

Kilrain took the early rounds, coached by Charlie Mitchell in his corner to stay outside and outbox the lumbering champion. By the middle rounds, with both men tiring, Sullivan began to take charge. He was being given liquor between rounds, as was Kilrain, and in the forty-fourth round, Sullivan vomited in the center of the ring. After that, he got his second wind and went on to stop Jake Kilrain after two hours and sixteen minutes of fighting in one-hundred-plus-degree temperature. The fight had gone on for an astonishing seventy-five rounds. Kilrain's corner threw in the sponge fearing if the fight continued, Kilrain would die. It was truly an epic, even a Homeric battle of wills between two men. Today, a plaque marks the spot where the battle took place one hundred and thirty one years ago.[11]

Credits to "Read The Plaque (readtheplaque. com), a project of 99% Invisible"

---

[11]

17

After the fight, the Boston Strong Boy was often referred to as the Great John L. He was now more or less recognized as the heavyweight champion of the world and the first linear holder of that coveted title. Now thirty-one years old and as much a wreck from alcohol as prize fighting, the champ did little more than engage in a few exhibitions over the next three years and continued his alcoholism. He even took to the stage and appeared in the drama, *Honest Hearts and Willing Hands*, by playwright Duncan B. Harrison. *Honest Hearts and Wiling Hands* was a comedy-drama written specially for Sullivan. Set in Ireland and with Sullivan in the starring role of the brawny village blacksmith who was handy with his fists, the production toured for two years and took him to theater houses in locations as far flung as Canada and Australia. Sullivan was no gifted actor, and if the observations of at least one reviewer are any guide, he appeared to care little for the "art of elocution or gesticulation" and when required to remain silent on stage he assumed a look of "high disdain for the attention of the crowd and the dramatic art in general." Still, when it came to a prize-fight scene at the end of the fifth and final act, he was deemed to have appeared "completely at home," the audiences only too delighted to roar their approval for the play's hero when he floors the play's villain with a mock knockout blow.[12]

Gentleman Jim Corbett, 1892–1897

By 1892, inactive for three years, public clamor made John L. once again return to the ring to defend the Heavyweight Championship of the World. His opponent would be a handsome young boxer out of San Francisco, California, known as Gentleman Jim Corbett. With Sullivan's rise to prominence and his international celebrity, professional boxing had now become legal with the new Marquis of Queensbury rules, the same rules that govern boxing to the present era.

---

[12]

The fight that took place on September 7, 1892, at the Olympic Sporting Club in New Orleans was part of a three-day Tournament of Champions. Lightweight champion Jack McAuliffe had previously knocked out challenger Billy Myer in five rounds, and featherweight champion George Dixon had knocked out Jack Skelly in eight rounds. But all the excitement was focused on Sullivan and Corbett.[13]

Corbett, age twenty-six and a former bank teller, had earned his right to challenge the Great John L. on the basis of his sixty-one-round draw with Peter Jackson, a black fighter from Australia whom Sullivan had drawn the color line against saying he would not fight against a black man. Betting was heavy as the two men entered the ring in New Orleans at the Olympic Sporting Club. To everyone's surprise, Corbett looked fit and confident. Sullivan, badly overweight, "looked as though he had trained for a pie eating contest."[14] For most of the fight, Sullivan pressed forward, and the younger Corbett easily outboxed him. By round 12, Sullivan was huffing and puffing, and Corbett was landing punches to the head and body, while Sullivan's offense was becoming minimal. In the twenty-first round, Sullivan hit the canvas, and the referee began his count. Sullivan arose, but a hard combination by Corbett dropped the champion again. He rolled over from his stomach to his back as he was counted out. John L. Sullivan, the Boston Strong Boy, had met his match. James J. Corbett was the new Heavyweight Champion of the World! An era had passed. Sullivan was the transitionary champion who had taken boxing from the bare-knuckled era to the modern era.

In his later life, John L. Sullivan, the ex-champion, boxed in a few exhibitions, appeared in theatrical shows, and became a temperance lecturer preaching against the evils of John Barleycorn. He was a truly great pugilist, and he was inducted into the Boxing Hall of Fame's vanguard class in 1990. He was a legend in his own lifetime.

13

14

Middleweights of the Eighteen Eighties

Nonpareil Jack Dempsey, 1884–1891

Jack Dempsey, popularly known as the Nonpareil, was born on December 15, 1862, in Curran, County Kildare, Ireland.[15] He won the middleweight title on July 30, 1884, by defeating George Fulljames. In Dempsey's first sixty-five contests, he lost only three times (to George LaBlanche, a loss he avenged, and to Billy Baker twice, both bouts were fixed to have Baker win).[16]

The Nonpareil was clearly the dominant middleweight of the 1880s. He fought and beat many of the top men of the era, including Billy McCarthy, Mike Donovan, Billy Baker, Dominick McCaffrey, and Jack Burke. He won the inaugural lineal middleweight championship of the world, beating George LaBlanche on March 14, 1886.[17] He reigned as champion for the next five years before losing the crown to future heavyweight champion Bob Fitzimmons by knockout on January 14, 1891. Nonpareil Jack Dempsey died on November 1, 1895, of tuberculosis at the young age of thirty-two. He lies buried in Portland, Oregon. He is a member of the vanguard class of the International Boxing Hall of Fame in 1990.

Welterweights of the Eighteen Eighties

Paddy Duffy was an accomplished boxer who had a good career throughout the 1880s. He came into his own in the mid-Eighties and had forty-nine fights, of which he won thirty-two, lost only one, and had sixteen draws. Draws were much more common in that long-ago era. He won the initial lineal welterweight title, beating Billy McMillian in 1888, and defended his title once successfully in March of 1889. Sadly, Paddy Duffy was dead only one year later from tuberculosis at the age of twenty-five. The crown was vacant

---

15

16

17

until Mysterious Billy Smith claimed it on December 14, 1894, but that is a little bit ahead of my story.[18]

Lightweights of the Eighteen Eighties

Jack McAuliffe was the first recognized lightweight champion. He was known as the Napoleon of the Ring and is one of only fifteen world champion boxers to retire without a loss. He made his first appearance as an amateur boxer in 1883. He turned professional soon after, fighting Jem Carney seventy-eight rounds to a draw. He fought Billy Dacey for the lightweight championship and a $5,000 purse in 1888 and knocked him out in eleven rounds. He was known as a strong two-handed fighter with catlike reflexes.[19] In 1897, he successfully defended his title against Billy Myer in a highly publicized match at the Olympic Club, New Orleans, as part of the earlier referred to Tournament of Champions. Most impressive to this writer at least was his victory over the great Young Griffo in 1894. He survived until 1937. McAuliffe was a truly great boxer of the classic era.[20]

Featherweights of the Eighteen Eighties

Boxing was still in its infancy in the 1880s, and there were fewer weight divisions than even the traditional eight. There were no recognized flyweight or bantamweight classes yet, but there was a first featherweight champion named Ike Weir, an Irish immigrant who won the generally recognized featherweight title in an eighty-round bout with one Frank Murphy on March 31, 1889. He lost the championship to Torpedo Billy Murphy, a featherweight out of New Zealand, by fourteenth-round knockout on January 13, 1890. He probably should not have taken this fight on the date. It was an unlucky thirteen for the ex-champ![21]

18

19

20

21

To summarize the 1880s boxing world, it was a time of transition between old, London Prize Ring rules, and the new, Marquis of Queensbury rules. Gloved bouts were taking the place of bare knuckles, and boxing was moving, ever so slowly, into mainstream society. By and large, boxers were still considered brutes (in some circles no doubt to the present), and boxing was still illegal in most areas of the Country as well as England and France. But a number of pugilists had become part of popular culture, especially charismatic John L. Sullivan, as well as Nonpareil, Jack Dempsey, and Jack McAuliffe. The next decade would see in addition to Gentleman Jim Corbett; the Boilermaker, James J. Jeffries; the Fighting Blacksmith, Bob Fitzimmons; Terrible Terry McGovern; the great featherweight champion, George Dixon; and Mysterious Billy Smith, among others. There were just five weight classes that would soon enough become the classic eight: heavyweight, middleweight, welterweight, lightweight, and featherweight.

CHAPTER II

The Gay Nineties

Corbett, Fitzimmons, and Jeffries

The last decade of the nineteenth century is when the Gilded Age hit its peak. Edison's electric light bulb invented in 1879 was now commonplace in most American cities and towns if not yet in rural America. In the South in the year 1890, 161 black men were lynched. The Spanish American War commenced in 1898 with the sinking of the battleship Maine and ended the same year. It made a hero of future President Theodore Roosevelt. Booker T. Washington was the head of Tuskegee Institute, which he had founded in 1881. In 1892, Thomas Edison invented the kinetoscope, and by decade's end, the movies were becoming a part of American life. Baseball had become hugely popular as a sporting event, rivalled only by professional boxing.

This was especially true in the heavyweight division. During the decade, three men became Heavyweight Champion of the World: James J. Corbett, Bob Fitzimmons, and James J. Jeffries. A new weight division had been created to accommodate smaller warriors, the bantamweight division, with a set weight limit of 110 pounds. That made six weight classes: heavyweight, middleweight, welterweight, lightweight, featherweight, and bantamweight. Let us begin with the heavyweights.

Heavyweights of the Gay Nineties

Gentleman Jim Corbett, 1892–1897

The fight which took place on September 7, 1892, at the Olympic Sporting Club in New Orleans was part of a three-day Tournament of Champions. Lightweight champion Jack McAuliffe had previously knocked out challenger Billy Myer in five rounds, and featherweight champion George Dixon had knocked out Jack Skelly in eight rounds. But all the excitement was focused on Sullivan and Corbett.[22]

The Sullivan-Corbett fight, the first heavyweight championship fight that took place under the modern rules with gloves, created quite a stir. The Great John L. had been beaten by an educated bank teller? Impossible! Not really. There were number of factors involved in the upset. The first to consider was age. Sullivan was thirty-four years old, and Corbett, by contrast, was twenty-six and in his athletic prime. The second factor was technique. It is probable that Sullivan had never met anyone quite as skilled as Corbett, with the exception of Charlie Mitchell, who had given Sullivan fits in their two encounters. Third and most obvious was conditioning. Sullivan had not fought since 1889, when he beat Kilrain. He was an alcoholic

---

who trained on whiskey. Maybe he could whip any son of a bitch in the house, but he could not compete with a younger and highly conditioned athlete. Add up these three very important factors, and a Corbett beats a Sullivan any time. So now, Gentleman Jim was the new Heavyweight Champion of the World.

Gentleman Jim Corbett might have been the face of boxing for much of the 1890s, but there were a host of other challengers waiting to take the Californian out. Corbett was not what is popularly known as a fighting champion. He scored a third round knockout victory of Sullivan's nemesis, a now past-his-prime Charlie Mitchell on January 25, 1894, and boxed a four-round exhibition with heavyweight contender Sailor Tom Sharkey in 1896.[23]

Bob Fitzimmons, 1897–1899

Fully three years since his last defense against Mitchell, Corbett was lured back into the ring against Bob Fitzimmons on March 17, 1897, at an outdoor race track in Carson City, Nevada.[24] Compared to the overwhelming public following of John L. Sullivan, interest in the Corbett-Fitzimmons fight was minimal. Photographs from the bout show a sparse attendance.

23

24

To the fight: for the first thirteen rounds, Corbett outboxed and outpunched his rival. Then in the fourteenth round, Fitzimmons suddenly switched to a southpaw stance and fired a hard straight left to Corbett's midsection, dropping the champion. This was the birth of the so-called solar plexus punch. Corbett appears to be crawling toward the ropes to pull himself up, but the soon to be ex-champion does not beat the referee's count, and Bob Fitzimmons was now the Heavyweight Champion of the World. [25]

Bob Fitzimmons was born on May 23, 1863, in Helston, Cornwall, England. When he was a child, his family moved to New Zealand. There as a teenager, he worked in his brother's blacksmith shop, developing the shoulders and arms that would give him the great punching power he later possessed as a professional boxer. He began his professional boxing career in Australia, and coming to America, he challenged the highly regarded Nonpareil Jack Dempsey for Dempsey's middleweight (160-pound) championship crown on January 14, 1891. in New Orleans, when he was twenty-eight years old. Fitzimmons knocked out Dempsey in the thirteenth round and became the middleweight champion of the world. Never really more than a middleweight, Fitzimmons weighed only 167 pounds when he challenged Corbett to win the heavyweight title, making him the lightest heavyweight champion in history.[26]

Fitzimmons only held the title for two years, before losing the crown to the much larger James J. Jeffries in 1899, but make no mistake, this man was one of the greatest boxers who ever lived.

---

[25]

[26]

The Ring magazine ranked him as the eighth hardest puncher of all time.[27] He would go on to win the light heavyweight crown in 1903. Thus, he was the first, and only one of two men, the other being Henry Armstrong to win three *undisputed* world boxing titles. There will be more to say about this great pugilist in the next chapter. Stay tuned!

The Boilermaker, James J. Jeffries, 1899–1905

Born on April 17, 1875, Jim Jeffries was a remarkable man and pugilist. Weighing in at around 225 pounds, he was the size of a modern heavyweight. But he was also the possessor of tremendous athleticism. Quick on his feet, fighting out of a crouch, with a good chin and punching power in both hands, his most powerful punch was his left hook. He was a natural southpaw, converted to orthodox, which gave him his powerful left.[28] On his way to the title in 1898, Jeffries knocked out Peter Jackson, the great boxer whom John L. Sullivan had refused to fight, in three rounds.[29] This had been only the second defeat in Jackson's entire career; his first loss was from a four-round fight over thirteen years earlier around the beginning of his career. Jackson retired shortly afterward.[30]

Jeffries won the heavyweight championship in only his thirteenth professional fight against the highly skilled and hard-punching champion, Bob Fitzimmons, by knockout in round 11 after taking a terrible battering from Fitzimmons for the first ten rounds. A right to the body followed by a left hook to the head left Fitzimmons completely unconscious and an ex-champion.[31] Jeffries was a fighting champion. After decisioning Tom Sharkey and Jack Finnegan, he was challenged by former champion James J. Corbett. The bout took place on May 11, 1900, at Coney Island in New York. Fighting the best fight of his career, Corbett took the fight to the much stron-

---

27

28

29

30

31

ger and younger Boilermaker cutting his face and swelling his eyes nearly closed. At one point, the referee nearly stopped the fight to save Jeffries from further punishment. But miraculously Jeffries rebounded and dramatically knocked Corbett out in round 23 to successfully retain the title. James J. Jeffries lived until 1953.[32] There will be more to tell about Jeffries in the next chapter.

Middleweights of the Eighteen Nineties

Middleweight boxing in the 1890s was largely dominated by two men: Nonpareil Jack Dempsey and Bob Fitzimmons. Both of these gladiators have already been previously covered.

Kid McCoy, 1895

A third great middleweight who made a name for himself in the Gay Nineties was the very colorful Kid McCoy, about whom the expression "the real McCoy" was coined. The story as I learned it at a very young age was that McCoy was on a steamship headed for England and boxed an exhibition with someone who doubted who he was. After he awoke from getting knocked out, he said, "That was the real McCoy!" There are a number of other versions of the story. I am telling it as I remember hearing it. Other versions have it set in a barroom.

He supposedly captured the middleweight championship by beating Dan Creedon in 1905. He never defended the crown and moved up to campaign as a heavyweight.

McCoy was quite a character. He was married ten times, so he must have been quite charming, and even went to Hollywood and became a minor movie star.[33]

32

33

Tommy Ryan, 1898–1907

Tommy Ryan was the fourth dominant middleweight of the era. Ryan was the standing welterweight champion when he challenged for the middleweight title. He was considered one of the greatest boxers in history, although his name and legend are largely forgotten today. Ryan reputedly had 109 fights between 1898, and when he finally vacated the championship in 1907, he won 90 fights, won 71 by knockout, lost 6, fought 11 draws, and had 2 no decisions.[34]

Tommy Ryan, a great champion, vacated the world middleweight title in 1906, making the way for one of the greatest middleweights in history.

Welterweights of the Eighteen Nineties

Mysterious Billy Smith, 1892–1900

I have always had a fondness for the welterweights, a division that tops out at 147 pounds. There are so many great and famous names in the division, among them Sugar Ray Robinson, Emile Griffith, Floyd Mayweather Jr., the original Joe Walcott, Jack Britton, Mickey Walker, Mysterious Billy Smith, Sugar Ray Leonard, Pernell Whittaker, and Thomas Hearns. Let us now take a look at the welterweight division in the era known as the Gay Nineties. The first welterweight champion of the decade was a Canadian, Amos K. Smith, known professionally as Mysterious Billy Smith. According to his profile on Wikipedia, Smith won the welter title on December 14, 1892.[35] Before the decade was finished, Smith had defended the title twice and had beaten future hall of famers Joe Walcott and Kid Lavigne, before losing his title to Rube Ferns in 1900.[36] BoxRec website differs slightly, but I am going with Wikipedia. Like Tommy

---

34
35
36

Ryan, Smith, another truly great prize fighter is largely forgotten today. He shouldn't be.

Lightweights of the Eighteen Nineties

Now as this book is being written, the majority of lightweight boxers in *The Ring* magazine ratings show an influx of pugilists from foreign countries. Ukraine, Ghana, the UK, Dominican Republic, Cuba, and France make up 60 percent of the top ten in the latest (April 2020) edition of *The Ring*. Before I go any further, I want to say that *The Ring* magazine ratings are the most honest and trustworthy ratings in boxing. No wonder it is called the Bible of Boxing. Founded by Nat Fleischer in 1922, they have been rating and ranking boxers for ninety-eight years. Well, it wasn't always this way. One hundred plus years ago, almost all the top lightweight boxers came from the good old USA.

Jack McAuliffe, 1886–1892

As the 1890 decade rolled in, Jack McAuliffe was the lightweight king. He had won the title in 1886, and he retired in 1892. After McAuliffe's retirement, the title remained inactive until 1896 when the title was won by George "Kid" Lavigne in a seventeen-round KO against Dick Burge.[37] Lavigne's victory, the first fought under the Marquis of Queensberry rules, was considered by boxing promoters of the time as the first officially recognized world lightweight championship. McAuliffe retired undefeated.[38]

---

[37]

[38]

George "Kid" Lavigne, 1896–1899

Kid Lavigne became a professional boxer in 1886 and was unde-feated with 32 wins, 11 draws, 10 no decisions, and 1 no contest in his first 54 fights over a span of twelve and a half years.[39] After defeat-ing the local talent of the area in his first twelve fights, he fought journeyman George Siddons in two battles of seventy-seven and fif-ty-five rounds in a span of two months. The first bout went five hours and nine minutes, the longest fight to date under Queensberry rules. While both were ruled draws, Siddons conceded defeat in the second bout, and with it, Kid Lavigne became lightweight champion of the Northwest. [40]

After fighting several bouts on the West Coast in the early 1890s, he landed a bout in 1894 with the lightweight champion of Australia, Albert Griffiths, a.k.a. Young Griffo. Griffo was considered by all to be the most gifted boxer of the era whose ability to avoid get-ting hit was legendary. The Kid managed to get a draw in this eight-round contest and a year later another draw over twenty rounds.

In December 1894, he fought the lightweight champion of the south, Andy Bowen, a veteran of the longest fight in the history of modern boxing, a one-hundred-ten-round, seven-hour and nine-

---

39

40

teen-minute marathon.[41] It was in the eighteenth round that Bowen, being beaten badly by Lavigne, was knocked down, hitting his head sharply on the unpadded ring surface. He never regained consciousness and died the next morning at 7:00 a.m. At first Lavigne was arrested for the death of Bowen but was later found to be innocent of any wrongdoing as a coroner's inquest ruled that Bowen's death was the result of hitting his head on the floor of the ring.[42]

With few left stateside to challenge the indefatigable Lavigne, he sailed for London to fight Iron Man Dick Burge, the English champion in June 1896. He stunned Burge with his relentless pressure and hard punches, knocking him down repeatedly in the sixteenth and seventeenth rounds before the referee called a halt and awarded the fight to Lavigne by technical knockout. He was now the first undisputed lightweight champion of the world under the Marquis of Queensberry rules.[43] He successfully defended his title six times, including a rematch with Joe Wolcott, where he punished Walcott through twelve rounds. Just prior to the beginning of the thirteenth, a sponge sailed into the ring from Walcott's corner signaling the end. Feeling somewhat invincible, the Kid decided to try his skills in a heavier weight class when he challenged his good friend and current welterweight champion, Mysterious Billy Smith. In March 1899, Lavigne fought briskly for ten rounds, getting the best of Smith. The tide turned, and Smith had him out on his feet in the fourteenth and was sizing up the knockout blow when the Kid's manager and brother, Billy Lavigne, stepped into the ring and stopped the fight. In the first loss of Lavigne's career, Smith won on a technical knockout. Lavigne finally lost the title in a twenty-round decision to Frank Erne in July 1899.[44]

41

42

43

44

Frank Erne, 1899–1902

Lavigne reigned until 1899, when he lost the lightweight title to the highly skilled Frank Erne, a Swiss-born boxer who turned professional on October 7, 1892, stopping one John Roy in round 4. He won the world featherweight title beating the great George Dixon on November 27, 1896, in New York. He held the title only four months, losing to Dixon in a rematch over twenty rounds on March 24, 1897. Next, Erne challenged for the lightweight championship.[45]

In the most important bout of his career, he took the world lightweight title from Kid Lavigne on July 3, 1899, in a twenty-round point decision before an enthusiastic home crowd in Buffalo. Looking back on Erne's critical win twenty years earlier, the *St. Petersburg Times* noted that Erne was more known for his speed and scientific skills than power, recalling that Lavigne had lost the title to "light-hitting Frank Erne."[46] This description of Erne was more accurate when he faced his most gifted opponents.

On July 16, 1900, Erne faced feather and lightweight legend Terry McGovern in Madison Square Garden in New York. Erne had superior reach and height over McGovern but, according to most boxing writers, had not demonstrated the ability to consistently connect with the power of McGovern. Erne's ring generalship with his best opponents was a slow and deliberate strategy, which took longer to end a fight. As the *Bridgeport Herald* wrote before the fight, "Erne's fights have been longer than Terry's as his record shows. He is not the finisher that Terry is. He is a point decision fighter more properly speaking and McGovern is a knocker out." (*Knocker out?* Not my term.) Though putting McGovern down in the first round, Erne was down three times in the third before his cornermen ended the fight.[47] For reasons possibly lost to the mists of time, Terry McGovern, a certifiable lightweight who had just knocked out the world lightweight champion was not generally credited with winning the title, despite

45

46

47

this impressive performance. Boxing being boxing, who knows what skullduggery took place? This fight took place one hundred and twenty years ago. That's a long time.

Featherweights of the Eighteen Nineties

Ike Weir, 1887–1890

The featherweight division, which tops out at 126 pounds, has not generally received as much attention as the heavier division, but it has had its moments. Ike Weir (February 5, 1867–September 12, 1908) was an Irish-born American boxer, credited with being the first man to take the Featherweight Championship of the World in a match against Frank Murphy on March 31, 1889, in Kouts, Indiana. The fight was billed as a World Featherweight Title, and went an astounding eighty rounds, though it was officially declared a draw. Some sources may credit Weir with taking the world title as early as 1887 in his knockout title wins over Jack Farrell in Ridgefield, New Jersey, on January 24, or Jack Williams in Westerly Rhode, Island, on March 10. Weir first claimed the title in his win over Farrell. He was recognized by most sources to have lost the title on January 13, 1890, to Torpedo Billy Murphy in a fourteenth-round knockout in San Francisco, California.

Torpedo Billy Murphy, 1890

And what a lot of great names grace this division in the 1890s! Murphy moved to the United States from New Zealand and was the first world boxing champion to come from that faraway country. Murphy lost the title to the great Young Griffo on September 2, 1890. After losing to Griffo, Murphy next took on a truly great featherweight, George Dixon, an African American boxer from Canada. In an unusual match on December 16, 1893, in Patterson, New Jersey, with George Dixon, Murphy was disqualified in the third round for a blow to the referee. Dixon had the better of the first round. Trying to break the fighters from clinching in the third round, Murphy hit referee James Stoddard with a right in the face either accidentally or distracted by the heat of the moment, and infuriated, Stoddard retaliated with two quick blows that landed Murphy under the ropes. The house became wild, but the police managed to keep order. Some papers described the fight as a knockout, though the referee, not Dixon, put Murphy on the deck.[48] Boxing can get pretty weird sometimes. His name is forgotten today, but Torpedo Billy Murphy had 220 fights!

Young Griffo, 1890–1892

Young Griffo, now the featherweight champion, basically fought the boxing hall of fame throughout the remainder of his career. During his career he defeated Abe Willis, champion Ike Weir, Horace Leeds, and Joe Harmon. He won bouts against champion Torpedo Billy Murphy a total of three times, twice in world featherweight title matches. A prolific boxer of great opponents, after coming to America, he fought champions Solly Smith, Kid Lavigne, Joe Gans, Tommy Ryan, George Dixon, Frank Erne, and featherweight contender Joe Bernstein. He was recorded as fighting over two hundred professional fights in his career. Griffo was elected to the International Boxing Hall of Fame in 2003. Young Griffo was, to put it mildly, a wild and crazy guy. He was sent to jail frequently

---

48

for assault, often against police, public drunkenness, and to a mental institution for obnoxious behavior. But he could fight like hell! He was a highly skilled boxer and a master of defense. It was said that Griffo was one of the hardest men to hit in all of boxing. He fought the legendary lightweight champ Joe Gans three times, although he lost all three. But then again, he *was* fighting one of the very greatest boxers to ever climb through the ropes.[49]

George Dixon, 1891–1897

Dixon was born in Africville, Halifax, Nova Scotia. Known as Little Chocolate, he stood five feet three inches tall and weighed only eighty-seven pounds when he began his professional boxing career. Dixon is widely credited for developing shadowboxing.[50] *Ring* magazine founder and publisher Nat Fleisher ranked George Dixon as the number 1 featherweight of all time.[51] Willie Pep, anyone? Manny Pacquiao? On May 31, 1891, Dixon beat Cal McCarthy in twenty-two rounds to win the featherweight title. On October 4, 1897, he lost the title by decision in a rematch bout with Solly Smith, who he had previously defeated by seventh round technical knock-

---

49

50

51

out. He had reigned as world featherweight champion for six years, during which there was a brief loss and regain against Frank Erne. On November 11, 1898, he regained the title from Dave Sullivan on New Year's Day, 1900.[52]

Bantamweights of the Eighteen Nineties

George Dixon

George Dixon, 1888–1891, Vacated

The bantamweight division, topping out in the modern era at 118 pounds, was first created for and by George Dixon. In rapid succession, four of the first five champions abandoned or retired their championship. So we have only three bantamweight champions in the entire decade of the Gay Nineties. The first was George Dixon, who took the crown by beating Tommy Spider Kelly at the tender young age of eighteen on May 10, 1888.[53] He abandoned the title soon afterward in 1891 after one defense to campaign as a featherweight, the division in which he reached the pinnacle of his fame.

Jimmy Barry, 1894–1899

Next up was Jimmy Barry, a very good bantamweight (actually a junior flyweight) out of Chicago. He fought more than seventy times and finally retired *undefeated* in 1899, five years after winning the crown in 1894. Understand, the various weight divisions had not yet quite settled, and Barry won his bantamweight championship at the one-hundred-pound max on February 6, 1894, over Joe McGrath, knocking him down seconds into the first round and finally stopping him in the third.[54]

52

53

54

A little confusing at best, Barry next won next won the 102-pound version of the bantamweight championship beating Jimmy Gorman on June 2, 1894. The bout was recognized as for both the United States and World championships. He wasn't done yet. By 1895, the bantamweight limit was anywhere from one hundred pounds to one hundred twelve pounds, the weight for flyweights for over the past one hundred years. On September 4, 1894, he took on Sicilian boxer Casper Leon in Lemont, Illinois, before a partisan crowd. It was a seesaw battle through the first nineteen rounds. Then in the twentieth round, Barry landed a hard right, and the fight shifted to Barry's favor. He scored a few knockdowns over the next several rounds, before knocking Casper out cold in the twenty-eighth round. The two gladiators fought again in 1895, and it was declared a draw after the police stepped in stopped the fight with Barry ahead at the time. [55]

Barry scored a knockout over British challenger Walter Croot in London on December 6, 1897, in the twentieth round. As Croot's head hit the hard wooden floor, he never regained consciousness and died soon after. Barry was charged with manslaughter, but the charges were dropped as it was ruled that the cause of death was his head striking the floor. The champion took the death hard, and although he continued boxing for two more years, he never fought with the same ferocity that had defined his earlier career.[56]

---

[55]

[56]

Terry McGovern, 1899–1900

The last man to claim the bantamweight crown was no other than Terrible Terry McGovern, the Brooklyn Terror. Possessing unbelievable punching power for a bantamweight, he won the bantam title on September 12, 1899.[57] Terry McGovern was born to Irish parents on March 9, 1880. His family moved from Pennsylvania to South Brooklyn when Terry was a year old.[58]

He began his professional boxing career in preliminary bouts at age sixteen. On September 12, 1899, at age nineteen, he took the world bantamweight title, stopping British champion Pedlar Palmer in the first round. It was the first world title bout to end in a one-round knockout in the Marquis of Queensbury Era. He abandoned the bantamweight title in 1900 to campaign as a featherweight, the division in which he gained his greatest fame in the first years of the twentieth century.[59]

Summary

The Gay Nineties were the decade when the modern Marquis of Queensbury rules of boxing replaced the old bare-knuckle London Prize Ring Rules. Beginning with SullivanCorbett in 1892, boxing

---

57

58

59

bouts were fought under three-minute-round rules with a set number of rounds. Gloves, usually six ounces, were to be worn, and some of the lighter weight boxers, such as George Dixon, Terry McGovern, Mysterious Billy Smith, and Tommy Ryan, became famous. The grand old sport of pugilism began by James Figg in England in 1719 was now poised and ready to enter the big time in the American Century, the Twentieth Century.

The Galveston Giant
And a New Weight Class

By far the most important boxing event of the new century's first decade was the rise of the first African American heavyweight champion, Jack Johnson. By force of his personality and the racism of the time, he indirectly set an example for another heavyweight champion just as controversial sixty years later. That boxer was Muhammad Ali.

As the new century rolled in, William McKinley, the twenty-fifth President of the United States, was assassinated, bringing the popular, swaggering, and colorful Theodore Roosevelt to the presidency. The Chinese Boxer Rebellion was put down, and in 1902, football's first Rose Bowl Game was played. Michigan beat Stanford, 49–0. In 1903, the first World Series was played between the Boston Americans and the Pittsburg Pirates. Boston took the best of nine series, winning five games. Also in that significant year, the Ford Motor Company was founded, and the Wright Brothers made their historic heavier than air flight on December 17, 1903, at Kitty Hawk, North Carolina. In 1904, the Panama Canal Zone was acquired, and the famous canal was built over the next several years. It was one of the greatest engineering feats ever accomplished.

This was the state of the world that professional boxing found its way into in the years 1901–1910. The standing world champions by weight were as follows:

- Heavyweight, James J. Jeffries, won title on June 6, 1899
- Middleweight, Tommy Ryan, won title on October 24, 1898
- Welterweight, Rube Ferns, won title on October 14, 1898
- Lightweight, Frank Erne, won title on July 1899
- Featherweight, George Dixon, won title on November 11, 1898
- Bantamweight, Terry McGovern, won title on September 12, 1899

(Courtesy of Boxing Wiki, lineal boxing champions)

Heavyweights of the Nineteen Hundreds

James J. Jeffries, 1899–1905

As the new century dawned, Jim Jeffries, who had won the heavyweight title from Bob Fitzimmons in 1899, gave Fitz a second chance in a rematch on July 25, 1902, in San Francisco. For several rounds, a determined Fitzimmons battered and abused the younger champion. With his nose broken and cuts over both of his eyes, Jeffries landed a hard right to the body followed by a crushing left hook that knocked poor Fitzimmons unconscious.[60]

He defended his title again, facing another ex-champion, Jim Corbett. Corbett had faded considerably since the last time the two met, and this time Jeffries dominated the entire first ten rounds of the scheduled twenty-round bout, forcing Corbett's corner to throw in the towel to save the ex-champ from further punishment in the fight on August 14, 1903. In his final defense, the undefeated champion fought Canadian challenger Jack Munroe. Jeffries stopped him

---

60

in two rounds.[61] He would make a memorable comeback against Jack Johnson in 1910.

Marvin Hart, 1905

Jeffries retired unbeaten to his alfalfa farm in 1905. He kept his finger in boxing over the next few years refereeing bouts, including the fight in which Marvin Hart bested Jack Root to claim the heavyweight crown on July 3, 1905, in Reno, Nevada. Ah, how much simpler times were back before the time of sanctioning bodies! Hart, who had beaten Jack Johnson earlier, was the underdog against the more experienced Root. Hart prevailed, however, and knocked Root out in the twelfth round. Hart is little known today, but besides beating Jack Johnson, which was no small feat, he also had wins over noted pugilists Jack Twin Sullivan and Peter Maher.[62] Then he met Tommy Burns.

Tommy Burns, 1905–1908

Sometimes known as Tiny Tommy Burns, Canadian born as Noah Brusso on June 17, 1881, was the shortest heavyweight champion at only five feet seven inches. But man, could he fight! Burns famously challenged all comers as heavyweight champion, leading to a celebrated bout with the American Jack Johnson. According to his biographer, Burns insisted, "I will defend my title against all comers, none barred. By this I mean white, black, Mexican, Indian, or any other nationality. I propose to be the champion of the world, not the white, or the Canadian, or the American. If I am not the best man in the heavyweight division, I don't want the title."[63] Burns lived up to his word, traveling all over the world defending his title a record of thirteen times. He made defenses in England, Ireland, France, and Australia. Along with Larry Holmes, the heavyweight champion

---

61

62

63

in the 1980s, Burns shares the record for the most consecutive title defenses won by knockout or stoppage. [64]

Both men had eight. He even defended his title twice in one night! While some have claimed these were exhibitions, the newspapers of the day claimed they were for the heavyweight championship. While on his world travels, Jack Johnson followed him trying to get him into the ring. Finally, after Johnson had chased him all over the world, Burns relented, and the Burns-Johnson fight took place in Sydney, Australia, on December 6, 1908. [65] Burns did his best, but he was never really in the fight against a man who some, including Nat Fleischer who had seen all the champions from Johnson through Ali, consider the greatest heavyweight champion. The fight lasted into the fourteenth round, when Johnson unleashed a torrent of blows. The police then rushed into the ring and shut off the camera filming the bout and declared Johnson the victor. Tommy Burns was elected to the IBHOF in 1996.

Jack Johnson, 1908–1915

His career was fought at the height of the Jim Crow era, and to his credit, he never backed down from who he was, a proud African American. Almost from the moment he took the heavyweight title

---

64

65

from Tommy Burns, the cry went up to find a white hope to beat Johnson. At this time, the heavyweight boxing champion of the world represented the pinnacle of masculinity. "How could a Negro be the champion of the world?" many asked. Before losing to Jess Willard in 1915, he beat them all down. Philadelphia Jack O'Brien, Tony Ross, Al Kaufman, Stanley Ketchel, James J. Jeffries, Fireman Jim Flynn, Frank Moran, and Jack Murray, all white hopes, challenged him for the title and all failed.[66]

Adding a little gasoline to the racist fire, he married three white women. Interracial couples are common today, especially in cities, but in 1910–1915, it raised the ire of white bigots to boiling. Johnson married Etta Terry Duryea, a socialite, on January 18, 1911. After a stormy year of marriage, Duryea committed suicide in 1912. He then met an eighteen-year-old prostitute named Lucille Cameron from Minnesota, whom he married on December 12, 1912. He relocated her to Chicago to work in his nightclub, a move that would come back to cause him a great deal of trouble. The couple divorced in 1924. That year, he met Irene Pineau at a racetrack in Illinois. After she divorced her husband, they married in 1925 and were together until 1946, the year Johnson died.[67]

On October 18, 1912, Jack Johnson, heavyweight champion of the world, was arrested and charged with the Mann Act for "transporting women across state lines for immoral purposes." The reason given was Lucille Cameron, a known prostitute from Minneapolis, was brought to Chicago by Johnson to be a "stenographer" in his nightclub. Johnson was convicted by an all-white jury and spent a year and as a guest of the federal penitentiary in Leavenworth, Kansas.[68] He served from September 1920 until June of 1921. The judge in the case was Kenesaw Mountain Landis, the future commissioner of major league baseball, a man who had perpetuated the baseball color line.[69] Johnson subsequently skipped bail and fled the country, masquerading as a member of an all-black baseball team.

66

67

68

69

For the next seven years, Johnson and Pineau lived in Europe, South America, and Mexico. Johnson returned to the US and was arrested by federal agents at the Mexican border.[70] I am a little ahead of my story, so it is time to return to boxing and the legendary Johnson-Jeffries fight on July 4, 1910, in Reno, Nevada, in what was then billed as the fight of the century.

First of all, the buildup. For several weeks or months, white America had been clamoring for the undefeated Jeffries to restore the so-called superiority of the white race. Johnson's do-whatever-he-pleased behavior had incensed the public who were used to a man named Gentleman Jim, Bob Fitzimmons, who never made a lot of headlines, and practically hero worship of James J. Jeffries. Sullivan had been very colorful, a drunk and a bully, but he was white. Ken Burns, the filmmaker who chronicled a documentary about Johnson, called it *Unforgivable Blackness*.[71] That nailed it. Novelist Jack London, who had written the best seller *Call of the Wild*, wrote about the upcoming fight. London wrote, *"Jim Jeffries must now emerge from his alfalfa farm and remove that golden smile from Jack Johnson's face. Jeff, it's up to you. The White Man must be rescued."*[72] Well, that was America in the year 1910.

The day dawned warm and sunny and promised to be hot by afternoon, when the so-called fight of the century would take place. Twenty thousand fans filled the stands for the fight to watch the great white hope James J. Jeffries hopefully thrash the cocky champion. Jack Johnson, in the prime of his career, entered the ring first, as a superstition. Jeffries then entered, and the expectation built. For the first four rounds, both men were cautious and just felt each other out. Then Johnson got more aggressive, and it was soon apparent that Jeffries, who had ballooned up to over 330 pounds in his retirement and had to shed 100 pounds to get down to his fighting weight of 226 and who had lost muscle mass, was going to get beaten. Badly. At times, the superbly conditioned champion taunted Jeffries and

---

70

71

72

more or less in response to Jack London, who was at ringside made a point of frequently smiling.[73] For the next several rounds, Johnson had his way in the fight, which had been scheduled for 45 rounds. In the 15th, he suddenly upped the tempo and went after Jeff with a vengeance, dropping him for a short count. At the time, a boxer scoring a knockdown did not have to go to the farthest neutral corner, and Johnson stood over Jeffries ready to knock him down as soon as he arose. He did just that and knocked Jeffries through the ropes and partially on the ring apron. He was helped back into the ring by the timekeeper and a fan, and now Johnson was the attack dog after his prey. Even after Jeffries's seconds had come into the ring, he kept on punishing the old champion until it was totally evident that the fight was over.[74]

Well, facts are facts. Jim Jeffries, despite a heroic effort at a comeback and who had not had a fight in five years, simply was not in Johnson's league. This was hard for a lot of people to accept, and the films of the fight shown soon after sparked race riots across America. Jack Johnson would continue to rule the heavyweights for the next five years. [75]

73

74

75

Light Heavyweights of the Nineteen Hundreds

Jack Root, 1903

In 1903, a new weight class was formed between the heavy-weights, unlimited weight with some weighing in over two hundred pounds (champion Jeffries came in around 220) and the middle-weights, at the time one hundred sixty-five pounds. The light heavy-weight division was created in 1903, the brainchild of Chicago jour-nalist Lou Houseman, who was also a boxing manager and promoter. The new weight class, now called light heavyweight, topped out at 175 pounds. He matched his own fighter Jack Root with Kid McCoy and announced the fight as being for the light heavyweight cham-pionship of the world. Root beat the Kid and was crowned the first champion of the new division.[76]

George Gardner, 1903

He wasn't champion for long. In his first title defense against George Gardner, he lost by a twelve-round knockout and also the light heavyweight crown. George Gardner was born in County Clare, Ireland, on St. Patrick's Day in 1877, and he lived until 1954. At one time, he was considered one of the best boxers in the world. He had a remarkable career and had at least a claim to the middle-weight title before winning the undisputed light heavyweight title in Ontario, Canada on July 4, 1903. In November of 1904, he chal-lenged Marvin Hart for the heavyweight crown in a nontitle fight that ended in a draw. He challenged Hart for the title a second time but was once again denied. He even fought the great Jack Johnson in 1902 and lost after twenty rounds. Johnson had Gardner down twice, but Gardner made it to the final bell. I find it strange that he is all but forgotten today. More remarkable still is that he is not in the International Boxing Hall of Fame. [77]

76
77

On November 25, 1903 in San Francisco, California, he lost the title to forty-one-year-old Bob Fitzimmons, who had previously held the world middleweight crown as well as the world heavyweight crown.

Bob Fitzimmons, 1903–1905

He is the first three-division champion, and he beat Garner on a closely disputed decision. He is also the only heavyweight champion to go down to the light heavyweight division and win a world title. Gardner tried to get a rematch, but Fitz was not interested.

Fitzimmons did not rule for long. After losing the title to Philadelphia Jack O'Brien, he went back to fighting heavyweights. He challenged the much younger Jack Johnson in 1907 at the tender age of forty-four and was KO'd in two rounds.

Philadelphia Jack O'Brien, 1905, Abandoned Title

Nat Fleischer, founder and editor of *The Ring* magazine, rated Philadelphia Jack Obrien as the number 2 light heavyweight of all time.[78] He was agile, quick, and limber, a two-handed puncher who landed often but not a particularly hard hitter. His best punches were a left jab and a hard overhand right, and he was a good defensive fighter who blocked punches well and counterpunched accurately. On December 20, 1905, he won the light heavyweight title from Bob Fitzimmons by a thirteenth-round knockout in San Francisco, California, but abandoned the title without ever defending it. He challenged world heavyweight champion Tommy Burns on November 28, 1906, in Los Angeles, and got a twenty-round draw.[79] The referee was former world champion James J. Jeffries. O'Brien challenged Burns again in Los Angeles on May 8, 1907, and this time Burns won the twenty-round decision. He fought the fearsome middleweight champion Stanley Ketchel in a ten-round

---

78

79

No Decision on March 26, 1909, in which O'Brien was saved by the bell at the end of the tenth round. He fought heavyweight champion Jack Johnson in a six-round No Decision on May 19, but on June 9 he faced Ketchel again and was beaten in three rounds.[80] On December 20, 1905, O'Brien relinquished the crown and it was vacant for the next nine years.

Middleweights of the Nineteen Hundreds

Tommy Ryan, 1898–1906

The first middleweight champion of the twentieth century was Tommy Ryan, who held the middleweight championship from 1898 until he retired in 1907. Ryan was a great fighter, who apparently cemented his claim to the middleweight crown on December 23, 1898, beating Dick O'Brien by KO in fourteen rounds when the police intervened, halting the contest.[81] He defended his title against Jack Root in Chicago, stopping the future light heavyweight champion in three rounds. This further enhanced his claim as middleweight champion. He next defended against Tommy West in Louisville, Kentucky, on March 4, 1901. The champion then traveled to London, England, where fought Johnny Gorman, scoring a third-round knockout. He beat Kid Carter in Canada and boxed some exhibitions with heavyweight champion Jim Jeffries.[82] He retired in 1906 and gave the middleweight title to Hugo Kelly. The public did not accept Kelly as champion, and the title was vacant until Stanley Ketchel, a former runaway and boy hobo, took the crown.

Stanley Ketchel, 1908–1910

Make no mistake about it, Stanley Ketchel was one of the very greatest boxers at any weight who ever entered the ring. He began

80
81
82

his professional career in Butte, Montana, knocking out Kid Tracy in one round. Ketchel gained universal recognition as world middleweight champion on February 8, 1908, against Mike Twin Sullivan, knocking him out in the first round. His reign didn't last for long. After beating Mike Sullivan's twin brother, by a twenty-round knockout, he lost the title to another great, Billy Papke, by KO in round 12. He had decisioned Papke in an earlier bout. There was an immediate rematch in which Ketchel regained the crown, knocking Papke out in eleven rounds.[83]

In 1909, Stanley Ketchel figured he could win another title by fighting the reigning light heavyweight champion Philadelphia Jack O'Brien. Ketchel survived a terrible beating at the hand of the slick, quick O'Brien in the early rounds, only to mount a terrific comeback and score four knockdowns in the ninth and tenth rounds. When the final bell rang at the end of the tenth round, O'Brien was lying unconscious on the mat, his head in a resin box in his corner. Under New York rules at the time, though, O'Brien had been saved by the bell, and because official decisions were outlawed in New York boxing, the fight was declared a no decision. A few weeks later, Ketchel had a rematch, knocking out Philadelphia Jack in three rounds. [84]

Ketchel won a third fight with Billy Papke, and then on October 16, 1909, he challenged the great heavyweight champion Jack Johnson for the heavyweight crown. Ketchel's 1909 battle with Jack Johnson has been called by many a modern-day David and Goliath. Ketchel and Johnson were rumored to have been friends and to have gone gambling, as well as hit the brothels, together. They shared a love for women.[85] Ketchel and Johnson planned to fight together. Because Ketchel was shorter than Johnson, he wore long coats to conceal the platform shoes he had worn to make him look taller at a publicity event.[86] They set up a script for their fight to stretch it to twenty rounds, as a twenty-round fight would guarantee boxing fans would pay to go to local theaters to watch the replay of the fight.

83

84

85

86

After twelve rounds, Ketchel swung a surprise punch that knocked Johnson down. Angered by the apparent betrayal and regaining his feet, Jack Johnson knocked out Ketchel with a swift combination to Ketchel's head and jaw. Ketchel did not wake up for many minutes, and some of his teeth were knocked out by the blow, some embedded in Johnson's glove.[87]

Following the Johnson fight, he fought a newspaper decision draw against Frank Klaus over six rounds and then the feared African American Sam Langford. The Ketchel versus Langford fight was close, and it was ruled a draw by newspaper decision. I should add here that newspaper decisions were often used to judge fights in this era. The reports might have leaned slightly toward Langford, but were disputed by those who felt Ketchel had won.[88] At any rate, it was a hard-fought battle between two all-time great warriors. Langford, an all-time great, is covered in detail in chapter 17.

Stanley Ketchel fought three more times in 1910 against Willie Lewis, Porky Flynn, and Jim Smith. All three fights ended by knockout. He was the middleweight champion of the world, but fast living and unsavory friends had worn him down. Hoping to regain his vigor, he moved into a ranch owned by a friend of his, near Conway, Missouri. There, so the story goes he scolded a ranch hand named

87

88

Walter Dipley for beating a horse. Bent on revenge, Dipley vowed to rob the champion. Instead, Dipley shot Ketchel, who died a few hours later. Dipley and his wife were charged with the murder, and both went to prison. Stanley Ketchel, one of the greatest middleweight champions, was dead. He was twenty-four years old. His funeral was the most attended of any celebrity in the twentieth century up to that point. His final record stands at 51 wins with 48 by knockout, 4 losses, 4 draws, and 4 newspaper decisions. He was inducted as part of the inaugural class in 1990 to the International Boxing Hall of Fame[89](IBHOF).

Billy Papke, 1909

Billy Papke was a middleweight boxer out of Spring Valley, Illinois, born on September 17, 1886. He is primarily remembered for his four-bout series with Stanley Ketchel. Papke comes into popular history of the middleweight division with his win over Hugo Kelly on October 16, 1908, at the Hippodrome in Milwaukee. This win over a top contender put Papke in line for a shot at middleweight champion Stanley Ketchel. The first of four meetings between the man known as the Michigan Assassin, Stanley Ketchel, and the Illinois Thunderbolt, Billy Papke, took place on June 4, 1908. Ketchel beat Papke on a ten-round decision in Milwaukee. He fought Ketchel again, this time in Los Angeles on September 7, 1908. The Spring Hill native beat Ketchel on a twelfth-round TKO. The story I have always heard was when Ketchel reached out his right hand to shake before the bout, Papke let loose with a powerful sucker punch that hurt Ketchel before the fight even started. Papke opened the first round aggressively and had Ketchel down three times in the first round. Ketchel never fully recovered, and the fight was stopped by the referee in the twelfth round, giving the middleweight championship to Billy Papke. There are some who dispute this story, but it is a good yarn, nevertheless.

89

The two fought their third battle on November 26, 1908, in Colma, California. Ketchel, bent upon revenge, gave Papke a terrible beating and finally knocked him out in eleven rounds to regain the title. The fourth and final meeting of the two took place in San Francisco on July 5, 1909. From the reports of the battle, it was hard fought and competitive. At the end of twenty grueling rounds, Ketchel had won and retained his crown. After Ketchel's murder, Papke again claimed the middleweight championship but was never really recognized as such. The title was in a mishmash for the next three years, before it was solidified by Frank Klaus in 1913, who defeated Papke at France's Cirque de Paris. [90]

Papke died on November 27, 1936, by suicide, after first killing his wife. The violent incident might have been a result of undiagnosed brain dementia suffered from years of trauma in the ring.

Welterweights of the Nineteen Hundreds

Joe Walcott, 1901–1906

On December 18, 1901, a boxer known as the Barbados Demon became the welterweight champion of the world. Joe Walcott was a formidable pugilist with great power in both hands. He reigned as welterweight champion from 1901 until 1906. The future heavy-

---

[90]

weight champion Jersey Joe Walcott (Arnold Cream) idolized Barbados Joe and adopted his name.

Walcott was born on March 13, 1873, in Demerara, Guyana, according to several sources, though he spent most of his youth in Barbados. As a youngster, he set out to see the world and got a job as a cabin boy on a ship sailing to Boston that arrived around 1887. He soon settled in Boston as a piano mover and porter and took other odd jobs as well. Later, he landed a job in a gym and became popular with even the best of the boxers as an able opponent before turning professional. His amateur boxing and wrestling years spanned roughly from 1887–89.[91]

On December 18, 1901, on a cold day in Buffalo, New York, Joe Walcott beat welterweight champion Rube Ferns by TKO in the fifth round of a scheduled twenty-round bout, thus becoming the new welterweight champion of the world. Ferns, the taller man, held his own throughout the first four rounds, but Walcott dropped him twice in the fifth round before the referee stopped the fight.

The new champion then took on a very good welterweight named Young Peter Jackson. The bout, which would be followed by at least three others between the two, took place in Philadelphia on January 13, 1902, in the city of brother love, Philadelphia. Walcott won by a newspaper decision. Exactly two months later, the two met again, this time in Baltimore, resulting in a ten-round draw. He lost a couple of nontitle bouts against Philadelphia Jack O'Brien and George Gardner, both of whom were legitimate light heavyweights and considerably larger than Walcott, and took a decision win over Mysterious Billy Smith. He successfully defended the welterweight title in a draw with Young Peter Jackson and defended against Dixie Kid on April 4, 1904. He was winning the fight handily when the referee disqualified Walcott for no apparent reason in the final seconds of the twentieth round. Duck Sullivan, the referee, was a last-minute replacement, and Walcott protested the choice before the bout began. In the one-sided contest, Walcott appeared to have a clear advantage in all but the seventh round. Many in the crowd were shocked with

---

91

the decision, and Walcott himself was immediately angered at referee Sullivan who made the call. The match was disregarded as a title bout when it was discovered, not surprisingly, that referee Sullivan had bet on Dixie Kid to win the match.[92]

Worth noting between these bouts Walcott fought two nontitle affairs with two of the greatest boxers who ever lived. On September 15, 1904, he fought Sam Langford to a fifteen-round draw and lost a newspaper decision to the great lightweight Joe Gans.

William Honey Mellody, a welterweight out of Massachusetts, finally ended Walcott's championship tenure on October 16, 1906.[93] Walcott quit the bout in the eleventh round, claiming he had injured his arm in the ninth round. Joe Walcott retired on November 2, 1911. He died October 4, 1935.

Harry Lewis, 1908–1911

In the next three years, the welterweight crown changed hands three times. After Honey Mellody, Mike "Twin" Sullivan briefly held the title from April 23, 1907, when he beat Mellody, until 1908, when he vacated the crown. When Sullivan relinquished his title for being over the welterweight limit, Harry Lewis, a very good Jewish welterweight out of New York City decided to lay claim to it. On January 23, 1908, he defeated the top world championship welterweight claimant Frank Mantell at Edgewood Athletic Club in New Haven, Connecticut, in a third-round TKO, giving real substance to his claim to the title.[94] At the zenith of his career, Lewis secured the Welterweight Championship of the World, defeating William "Honey" Mellody, the most recent holder of the title, on April 20, 1908, at the armory in Boston in a fourth-round TKO. Lewis held the title until January of 1911 when he decided to campaign as a middleweight. [95]

92

93

94

95

Lightweights of the Nineteen Hundreds

Joe Gans, 1902–1904, Abandoned Title

Joe Gans (born Joseph Gant, November 25, 1874–August 10, 1910) was an American professional boxer. Gans was rated the greatest lightweight boxer of all time by boxing historian and *Ring* magazine founder, Nat Fleischer. Known as the Old Master, he became the first African American World Boxing Champion of the twentieth century, reigning continuously as World Lightweight Champion from 1902 to 1908. He was inducted into the International Boxing Hall of Fame in 1990. I don't know if I would agree with Fleischer. I believe Roberto Durán, Floyd Mayweather Jr., and Manny Pacquiao would all have made life very difficult for Gans, but then, who knows. One thing is for sure, Joe Gans was *the* dominant lightweight boxer during the years 1900–1910, the subject of this chapter. And let's face it. Anybody who is known as the Old Master had to be pretty doggone good. Fleischer died in 1972, and he was the founder and editor of *The Ring* magazine for fifty years. So I have to cut him some slack. Durán, Mayweather Jr., and Pacquiao all came to prominence after Fleischer's death.

On May 12, 1902, Gans knocked out champion Frank Erne in one round. He had lost to Frank Erne a year earlier, but this time he convincingly made it clear that he was *The Man.* Gans was a busy champion. During his reign, he defended against Steve Crosby and

Gus Gardiner. There was also Charley Sieger, Kid McPartland, Rufe Turner, Charles "Elbows" McFadden, and Frank Erne.[96] The biggest and most important fight, the one with the longest lasting fame took place in Goldfield, Nevada, on September 6, 1906. On that memorable day, Joe Gans, the world lightweight champion, took on one Battling Nelson, the Durable Dane. In a bout that lasted an unbelievable forty-two rounds, the longest fight in the history of Marquis of Queensbury rules, Gans had beaten Britt on a disqualification a few months earlier in San Francisco, but as the days passed, attention turned to a big promotion in Goldfield. The town's promoter was Northern Saloon owner and future Madison Square Garden promoter George "Tex" Rickard. More than $30,000 was put up for a championship match, an arena was built of pitchy pine, and soon enough word went out far and wide that a lightweight championship bout pitting Gans against the bruising Nelson was on. Nevada political powerhouse George Wingfield and stock hustler George Graham Rice helped promote the event with an eye on increasing their list of investors in mines of undetermined worth. The image of the black man fighting the white man was irresistible to sports writers of the era and captured the public's fascination. Joe Gans would do most of his talking in the ring.

On fight day, with the weather sweltering and President Teddy Roosevelt's son Kermit at ringside, referee George Siler brought the men together at center ring. Despite holding the world lightweight title, Gans was set to receive just $11,000 for the fight, with Nelson grabbing the greater share of the purse at $22,500. Gans didn't quibble much. A recent divorce had left him nearly penniless. He needed the money.

It was said that the top sportswriters in the country made the trip to Nevada for this lightweight championship fight. The Nelson fight in Goldfield would be the 31-year-old Gans's 187th as a professional. Nelson, at 24, was in his tenacious prime.

And they were off. Nelson was indeed durable and peppered his punches with the occasional low blow and errant elbow. Gans

---

96

was by far the more skilled practitioner, but his sojourn was complicated when he broke his right hand in the 33rd round. He fought the rest of the fight almost one handed, still kept Nelson on his heels, and at one point even helped the Dane to his feet after a knockdown. Nelson returned the favor with another low blow, and by the 42nd round, Siler had seen enough. Gans won on a disqualification. One hundred and four years after this historic encounter, the Gans-Nelson fight is still remembered by diehard boxing fans.

Jimmy Britt, 1904–1905

Jimmy Britt (born on October 5, 1879, in San Francisco, California, died on January 21, 1940) was a boxer from 1902 to 1909. He fought Joe Gans twice for the world lightweight title but lost both bouts. In a career spanning twenty-three bouts, Britt met six different hall of famers for a combined total of ten fights, going 4-4-2. After retiring from boxing in 1909, Britt toured the United States as a vaudeville performer and later worked as a WPA superintendent. He died of a heart attack in his San Francisco home on January 21, 1940, and was interred at Holy Cross Cemetery (Colma, California). Britt was elected to *The Ring* magazine hall of fame in 1976.[97]

Battling Nelson, 1905–1906

97

The Durable Dane, Oscar "Battling" Nelson was born June 5, 1882, the year that John L. Sullivan bested Paddy Ryan to become the first modern heavyweight champion. So one could say he was born to be a boxer. And what a boxer he was! He might have been born in Denmark, but he was raised in the south side of Chicago. Nelson became a professional boxer at the tender age of fourteen in 1896. He fought for the lightweight title in 1904, losing in twenty rounds to the more experienced Jimmy Britt. He lost to Abe Attell but got another chance, and this time he beat Jimmy Britt for the vacant title. He defended the title against Terry McGovern but then faced a greater challenge against former champion Joe Gans on September 3, 1906, in Goldfield, Nevada. Gans dropped Nelson repeatedly during the bout, but could not knock him out. Finally, in the forty-second round, Nelson hit Gans below the belt, receiving a disqualification, and lost his title. As discussed in the section about Joe Gans, this was a fight for the ages.[98]

Nelson and Gans fought two more times. On July 4, 1908, Nelson knocked out Gans in the seventeenth round, and again two months later he knocked the old champion out in the twenty-first round. In 1909, the Durable Dane lost the lightweight title to Ad Wolgast on February 22, 1910, in the forty-second round. [99]

Featherweights of the Nineteen Hundreds

Young Corbett II, 1901–1904

Young Corbett II, born William J Rothwell, in Denver, Colorado, challenged reigning champion Terry McGovern on November 28, 1901. In the fight held at Hartford Connecticut Corbett, who often trash-talked his opponents before a fight, burst into McGovern's dressing before the fight, shouting all kinds of insults about not only McGovern but McGovern's mother to unsettle the Brooklyn, New York, champion. No doubt McGovern had

---

98
99

to be restrained. The ploy seemed to work, however, as Corbett II knocked out Terrible Terry in the second round to become the new featherweight champion of the world in 1901.[100] He defended the title four times, including a rematch against McGovern, which Corbett also won by knockout. Unable to make the featherweight limit, which was 122 pounds at the time, he relinquished the title. Abe Attell, the outstanding featherweight at the time, claimed the featherweight title.

Abe Attell, 1903–1912

Abe Attell is one of the most fascinating characters in boxing history. Attell was born in San Francisco, California, the son of Jewish parents. Many sources give his year of birth as 1884, but in an article published in the October 1961 issue of *Cavalier* magazine, he stated that he had turned seventy-eight that year. A copy of his passport also gives his birth year as 1883, and the 1900 US census gave his age as seventeen. Growing up in a mostly Irish neighborhood, he was often involved in fights with neighborhood boys. He said as a kid, he sometimes had up to ten bouts each day. After his father abandoned the family when Attell was thirteen, he sold newspapers to earn money. Selling at the corner of Eighth and Market, near the Mechanics Pavilion, a frequent venue for important boxing matches, Attell watched the fight between Solly Smith and George Dixon for the world's featherweight championship. With that, Attell and his brothers Caesar and Monte became convinced they might have futures in boxing. [101]

In 1901, Attell fought George Dixon and beat him on a fifteen-round decision to win the world featherweight title. He lost the crown to Tony Sullivan in 1904, but regained it February 1906, with a win over Jimmy Walsh. From there until 1912, Attell successfully defended the world featherweight championship eighteen times,

---

100

101

a record that stood for decades. He finally lost his title to Johnny Kilbane in 1912.

His name was later linked to the infamous Black Sox baseball scandal of 1919. He was alleged to have been the bag man for gambler Arnold Rothstein and to have given $10,000 to several Chicago White Sox players. They had in return agreed to throw the World Series with Cincinnati. When the scandal broke in 1920, Attell went to Canada for a year to avoid being subpoenaed. Rothstein was never convicted of the crime.[102]

Bantamweights of the Nineteen Hundreds

When Terry McGovern abandoned the bantamweight title in 1901, Harry Harris and Danny Dougherty both laid brief claims to the title. On November 11, 1901, Harry Forbes took the championship by beating Danny Dougherty by knockout in two rounds in St. Louis, Missouri. Forbes held the crown until August 13, 1903, when he was knocked in San Francisco in two rounds by Frankie Neil. Neil subsequently lost to Englishman Joe Bowker on a close twenty-round decision October 17, 1904. Bowker abdicated the bantamweight throne one year later. [103]

Jimmy Walsh, 1905–1909

Walsh was one of the more outstanding bantamweights of the first decade of the twentieth century. He claimed the World Bantamweight Championship on March 29, 1905, when he defeated Monte Attell, in a controversial six-round bout at the National Athletic Club in Philadelphia. The controversy stemmed from his claim that was recognized by the World Boxing Association, at the time known as the National Boxing Association. The fight ended in a disqualification called by the referee when Walsh sent a low right hook that landed below the belt of Attell. Most sources believed

102

103

Walsh had led throughout the fight and that the blow should have been considered legal, which might be why Walsh was credited with the title by the National Boxing Association. Walsh attempted to win the featherweight title but was beaten by Abe Attell three times and Johnny Kilbane once. Having held the title into 1909 and then losing to Jimmy Reagan, he fought until 1914 and then retired, having attained an exceptional record with only ten losses by decision in roughly 150 matches. Reagan only held the title one month before losing it to Monte Attell. According to one source, Jimmy Walsh worked as a head salesman for a cigar firm in Boston after retiring from boxing and sent a son to the US Naval Academy. He died on November 23, 1964. [104]

Now the crown passed in rapid succession from Jimmy Reagan to Monte Attell to Frank Conley, to close out the decade 1900–1910.

To summarize, the decade was when America flexed her muscles. Whether in industry, science, or prize fighting, America ruled the world and would continue to do so for the twentieth century. The great prize fighters Jack Johnson, James J. Jeffries, Stanley Ketchel, Barbados Joe Walcott, Joe Gans, and Battling Nelson are all known to this day.

CHAPTER IV

The Great War and the Great Transition

Add Flyweights

The new decade that began on January 1, 1911, and ended on December 31, 1920, was a transition. It was a time of change. Change from the Victorian Era into the twentieth century. True, a lot of change happened between 1900 and 1910—Teddy Roosevelt and the Square Deal, the invention of the airplane and the automobile assembly line at Ford Motor Company, the Great Migration of African Americans from the Southern United States to cities like Chicago, Philadelphia, and Detroit, the invention of motion pictures and phonograph records and the growth of the railroads that crisscrossed the continent were all important advancements that began the transition. But the decade of the Great War sealed it. The decade came in with high button shoes and went out with jazz and flappers.

The Great War, which we now know as World War I, changed America and the world forever. It began in 1914, with the assassination of Archduke Franz Ferdinand of Austria, and it lasted until 1918. By the war's finish, more than sixteen million people, soldiers and civilians alike, were dead. As a result of the war's technology, better aircraft, the first aircraft carrier, flamethrower, machine gun, poison gas, hand grenades, and who knows what else came into existence to make this war truly hellish.

The term *movie star* came into popular usage. African Americans were still rock bottom, just a bit above slavery, because of the Jim

Crow laws in the Southern United States. The increase of African American boxers points out the desperation that hung over Black America. It was a great decade for professional boxing.

These were the world champions on January 1, 1911.

- Heavyweight, Jack Johnson
- Light heavyweight, vacant
- Middleweight, vacant due to death of Stanley Ketchel
- Welterweight, Harry Lewis
- Lightweight, Ad Wolgast
- Featherweight, Terry McGovern
- Bantamweight, Harry Harris
- No Flyweight division existed in 1910

(Boxing Wiki, lineal boxing champions)

Heavyweights of the Nineteen Tens

Jack Johnson, the Saga Continues

Jack Johnson, the heavyweight champion of the world, was fresh off two of his biggest victories, the twelve-round knockout of Stanley Ketchel in 1909 and his epic battle with James J. Jeffries in 1910, the fight of the century. Because Johnson felt he could make more money against white opponents than black, he was accused of drawing the color line against his own people. Feeling the pressure, he finally consented to defending his championship against an African American, Battling Jim Johnson on December 19, 1913, in Paris, France. The fight was more of an exhibition than a fight, as neither man put up much of a fight. Some spectators left early, not even bothering to see the ending. Because it was called a draw, Jack Johnson kept his title.

Jack Johnson's reign as heavyweight champion ended in 1915, even as the war raged on in Europe. On April 15, 1915, he took on challenger Jess Willard, a former cowboy from Kansas. The bout was scheduled for forty rounds. Johnson won almost every round, but by the twentieth, he was tiring. Videos of the fight show an intense Willard stalking Johnson. In round 26, he knocked the great champion out. Johnson took the count on his back with his knees raised from the hot canvas. As the camera rolled, he lowered them to the canvas. He was out. He claimed to have taken a dive in the fight and offered the video of his legs raised and his eyes shaded by his arms as evidence of the dive. Willard was widely regarded as having won the fight outright. Many people thought Johnson purposely threw the fight because Willard was white, in an effort to have his Mann Act charges dropped. Later videos of the fight seem to show Jess the legitimate winner. Willard said, "If he was going to throw the fight, I wish he'd done it sooner. It was hotter than hell out there."[105]

After losing his world heavyweight championship, Johnson never again fought for the heavyweight crown. His popularity remained strong enough that he recorded for Ajax Records in the 1920s. Johnson continued fighting, but age was catching up with him. He fought professionally until 1938 at age sixty, when he lost seven of his last nine bouts, losing his final fight to Walter Price by a seventh-round TKO. Johnson made his final ring appearance at age sixty-seven on November 27, 1945, fighting three one-minute exhibition rounds against two opponents, Joe Jeanette and John Ballcort, in a benefit fight card for US War Bond. [106]

Jess Willard, 1915–1919

Kansas-born Jess Willard was an unlikely candidate to be a world heavyweight champion. At 6 feet, and 6 and a half inches, and weighing around 235 pounds, Willard was an imposing physical specimen, but shy, countrified, and not the most graceful of boxers.

Jess Myron Willard was born on December 29, 1881, at Saint Clere, Kansas. In his teenage years and twenties, he worked as a cowboy. He was of mostly English ancestry, which had been in North

---

105

106

America since the colonial era. The first member of the Willard family arrived in Virginia in the 1630s.

Willard first began boxing at the age of 27. Despite his late start, he proved successful, defeating top-ranked opponents to earn a chance to fight for the championship. He said he started boxing because he did not have much of an education, but thought his size and strength could earn him a good living. He was a gentle and friendly person and did not enjoy boxing or hurting people, so often waited until his opponent attacked him before punching back, which made him feel at ease as if he were defending himself. He was often maligned as an uncoordinated oaf rather than a skilled boxer, but his counter-punching style, coupled with his enormous strength and stamina, proved successful against top fighters. His physical strength was so great that he was reputed to be able to kill a man with a single punch, which unfortunately proved to be a fact during his fight with Jack "Bull" Young in 1913, who was punched in the head and killed in the 9th round. Willard was charged with second-degree murder, but was successfully defended by lawyer Earl Rogers. [107]

Before winning the title from Jack Johnson, Willard engaged and beat a number of top heavyweights of the era, among them Arthur Pelkey, Luther McCarthy, and Carl Morris. Following his loss of the title to Jack Dempsey in 1919, he made a comeback after four years and faced contender Floyd Johnson. Sixty-three thousand people jammed the newly opened Yankee Stadium on May 12, 1923. Willard received quite a beating from Johnson, but then knocked him down in the ninth and eleventh rounds to earn a TKO victory. His last fight was against the Argentinian "Wild Bull of the Pampas" Luis Angel Firpo on July 12, 1923. After being knocked out by Firpo, Jess Willard permanently retired. He died on December 15, 1968. He was eighty-seven years old, the longest living ex-champion up to that time. He was inducted posthumously into the International Boxing Hall of Fame in 2003.[108]

107

108

Jack Dempsey, the "Manassa Mauler," 1919–1926

The first book I ever read about boxing, I was about thirteen or fourteen years old, and I had just begun boxing. The book was called *Dempsey, by the Man Himself* as written by Bob Considine. I devoured this book. I was nuts about boxing. Sixty years later, I still remember one quote from the book. I hope get this right. "*They called me Jack the Giant Killer. They said I feared no man. The hell I feared no man! There was one man; he was even smaller than me. I wouldn't fight him because I knew he would flatten me. I was afraid of Sam Langford.*"[109]

Sam Langford was perhaps the greatest boxer never to win a world title.

William Harrison Dempsey was born on June 24, 1895. The Manassa Mauler was an Irish American professional boxer who competed from 1914 to 1927 and reigned as the world heavyweight champion from 1919 to 1926. Along with Babe Ruth, Mae West, Charlie Chaplin, and Louis Armstrong, Jack Dempsey was a cultural icon of the 1920s. That is beyond the scope of this chapter, and he will be covered more in the next chapter. In the decade 1911–1920, he came roaring out of the hobo jungles and barrooms, a savage, take-no-prisoners, early-day Mike Tyson to a shot at Jess Willard on

July 4, 1919, in Toledo, Ohio. That day, a legend began. He was Mike Tyson's hero.

Jack Dempsey left an impoverished home in Colorado at sixteen. He was already a pretty tough cookie who soon took the moniker Kid Blackie. He became a boxing hobo, riding the rods underneath rail cars going from town to town, looking for fights. I seem to remember another quote from so long ago. Sixty years is a long time to remember quotes from a book. Even if the book is about Jack Dempsey. *"I had a high voice. I would walk into a bar and like a high voiced John L. Sullivan say 'I can't sing and I can't dance but I can lick any son of a bitch in the house.' It got me a lot of fights."*[110] This is at best paraphrasing what he actually said. Dempsey almost always won these fights. As Kid Blackie, he turned professional on August 8, 1914, in a fight in Colorado Springs fighting a six-round draw against one Young Herman. He won his next three by knockout and then fought another draw. By 1917, Dempsey was fighting contenders. That year he beat Gunboat Smith and Carl Morris, both serious contenders. As 1918 came in, Dempsey was on fire! In February, he beat Carl Morris and Fireman Jim Flynn,[111] who had beaten Dempsey earlier. He beat Bill Brennan in the same month. The excitement about Dempsey, now being known as the Manassa Mauler, grew, and he had a national following. A matchup with champion Jess Willard seemed inevitable. First he had to get past Fred Fulton, Battling Levinsky, Billy Miske, and Gunboat Smith.[112] Now, he was ready to challenge Jess Willard, the "Pottowami Giant," for the heavyweight championship of the world. This fight is on YouTube, and I have watched it many times. Willard towers over Dempsey, and it looks like a mismatch from the start. But Willard look soft and Dempsey, with a deep tan, looks rock hard. For the first minute of round 1, Willard stocks a rapidly moving Dempsey. Then twelve seconds after the one-minute mark, Dempsey explodes! Willard goes down for the first of seven knockdowns. This is not

---

110

111

112

only before the three knockdown rule. It is before the farthest neutral corner rule. Every time Willard tries to get up, Dempsey is there to beat him down again. Thinking that the fight is over, Dempsey's seconds come into the ring. But the fight will go on. Willard managed to make it to the bell. Oddly, Dempsey has left the ring. Why? His seconds yell at him to return, because the fight is still on. Willard finally retires on his stool at the end of round 3. Dempsey appears to have punched himself out and is tired and winded from the incredible volume of punches he threw in round 1. Willard suffered a horrible beating. His jaw and nose were broken. Six teeth were knocked out. There were cuts above and below both eyes. He was unable to answer the bell for round 4. Now on his death bed forty-four years later, Dempsey's manager supposedly confessed that Dempsey's gloves had become loaded. In other words, as he claimed his hands were wrapped with plaster of Paris that when hardened became like cement. Now, Jack "Doc" Kearns, Dempsey's manager, was no boy scout. He did not have a lot of credibility, and people did not want to believe that Dempsey had cheated. Okay, back to Dempsey leaving the ring. It has always been a tradition for both combatants to remain until the official announcement of the result. As soon as his seconds entered the ring, Dempsey jumped out of the ring and was on his way to the dressing room when Kearns called him back. You can see this on the YouTube video of the fight. I believe that from the incredible physical damage inflicted on Willard by a much smaller man and the fact that he left the ring in such a hurry points a lot of suspicion that Dempsey's gloves were indeed loaded. This is just my opinion. Others might differ.

Light Heavyweights of the Nineteen Tens

Jack Dillon, 1914–1916

Shortly after Philadelphia Jack O'Brien defeated Bob Fitzimmons in 1905, he abandoned the light heavyweight title, and it remained vacant until April 14, 1914, when Jack Dillon beat Battling Levinsky to claim the crown. Dillon beat Battling Levinsky again on May on May 29, 1914, to further cement his claim to the light heavyweight crown. He proved to be a fighting champion. He defeated Bob Moha on June 15, taking the scalp of another title claimant. He then beat Sailor Ed Petoskey, George "KO" Brown, Frank Mantell, and Fireman Jim Flynn. He continued fighting and defending the light heavyweight title until October 24, 1916, when he lost to archrival Battling Levinsky.[113] He is in the top tier of light heavyweight boxing champions. He was inducted into the IBHOF in 1995.

Battling Levinsky, 1916–1920

      Barney Lebrowitz (June 10, 1891–February 12, 1949), better known as Battling Levinsky, was the world light heavyweight champion from 1916 to 1920. Statistical boxing website BoxRec lists Levinsky as the number 12 ranked light heavyweight of all time, while *The Ring* magazine founder Nat Fleischer placed him at number 9. The International Boxing Research Organization rates Levinsky as the twentieth best light heavyweight ever. He was inducted into *The Ring* magazine Hall of Fame in 1966, the International Jewish Sports Hall of Fame in 1982, and the International Boxing Hall of Fame in 2000.[114] On October 12, 1920, fifty-nine bouts later, and almost four years to the day after he took the title, he lost his championship in a fourth-round knockout to France's enormously popular Georges

---

113

114

Carpentier in Jersey City, New Jersey. Before a crowd of fifteen thousand, after a series of rights and lefts from Carpentier, Levinsky lost his title as he fell from a heavy right to the jaw, one minute and seven seconds into the fourth round. Levinsky received his largest purse of $25,000 for the fight.[115] Carpentier had dominated the battle and sent Levinsky down twice for counts of eight. Struggling to rise after being counted out, the vanquished Levinsky had to be brought to his feet and partly carried to his corner by Jack Britton, who had assisted him with the bout.[116]

Georges Carpentier, 1920

Georges Carpentier, a French boxer who once fought Jack Dempsey for the heavyweight championship of the world, might have been boxing's first (only?) matinee idol. He was handsome, debonair, and charming, and he could fight like hell. Appropriately, he was nicknamed the Orchid Man. Carpentier was a French Air Force aviator during World War I and was awarded two of the highest French military honors, the Croix de Guerre and the Médaille Militaire.[117] This served to heighten his already exceptional popularity not only in France but in the United States and England as well.

After winning the European heavyweight title, he dropped down in weight (although he was never really more than a light heavyweight) to challenge Battling Levinsky for the world light heavyweight championship. The fight took place on October 12, 1920, in Jersey City, New Jersey. He knocked the old battler out in the fourth round to become light heavyweight champion.[118] He became the seventh man to hold that title.

115
116
117
118

Middleweights of the Nineteen Tens

Frank Klaus, 1913

Frank Klaus (born on December 30, 1887 in Pittsburgh, Pennsylvania, died on February 8, 1948) was an American boxer from 1904 to 1918. Klaus claimed the vacant World Middleweight Championship in 1913 and was elected to the Ring Boxing Hall of Fame in 1974. Gifted with a strong punch, he lost exceptionally few fights in his nine-year career and was knocked out only once. Nat Fleischer ranked Klaus as the number 6 all-time middleweight. His manager was George Engel. Following the murder of Stanley Ketchel, the middleweight title was vacant for three years. There were claimants, but no lineal champion had been recognized. Accounts vary as to when Klaus was officially champion, but Klaus himself first claimed the title after defeating Sailor Ed Petrosky in a twenty-round points decision in San Francisco on February 22, 1912. His victories over Jack Dillon, and later fellow claimant Georges Carpentier and former champion Billy Papke in France cemented his claim to the title on March 5, 1913.[119] His win over Papke came in the fifteenth round after the referee disqualified Papke for repeated fowls. Klaus lost the championship only a few months later to George Chip on October 11.

George Chip, 1913–1914

George Chip was born on August 25, 1888, in Scranton but was raised in New Castle, Pennsylvania, in what is today the Pittsburgh metropolitan area where most of his matches occurred. He was of Lithuanian descent. His manager was Jimmy Dime. [120]

He was active in both baseball and football in his youth and later worked in the coal mines in Madison, Pennsylvania. In January 1909, realizing his athletic gifts at the age of twenty, he decided to

---

119
120

try boxing on the advice of L. B. Lewis, a mining superintendent he knew. He won his first match when Billy Manfredo received a second-round disqualification in Greensburgh, Pennsylvania. The following month he knocked out George Gill and John Chew. He continued to fight through 1910 with only one recorded loss. [121]

Chip claimed the middleweight crown with an upset knockout victory or Frank Klaus. He defended against Tim O'Neill, and then against Klaus in a rematch, knocking the former champion out in the fifth round to further cement his claim as middleweight champion. In 1914, he defended successfully against Gus Christie on January 12 and two days later defended it again against Tim O'Neill. [122]

Al McCoy, 1914–1917

On April 7, 1914, only six months after winning the title from Frank Klaus, Chip lost the title in a major upset to Al McCoy by a one round knockout. McCoy has been unfairly criticized as a "cheese champion", but how many of his detractors have ever climbed through the ropes to fight? McCoy may not be IBHOF material, but he knocked out George Chip. His successful defense of the title for forty-two consecutive bouts would prove he deserved the honor of Middleweight World Champion. In fact, at forty-two bouts, according to Ken Blady, McCoy had the longest undefeated streak of any boxer to ever hold a title.[123] While holding the championship, he allowed most of the world's top contenders to challenge him for it. He fought Soldier Bartfield twice on November 10, and 22, 1914, in Brooklyn losing by the decision of newspapers in ten-round bouts. Though not gaining a decided edge in the two well fought bouts, the exceptional Bartfield was unable to land a knockout, and so McCoy retained the title. He took on top contenders Willie Lewis, Willie "KO" Brennan, Jewish contender Emmit "Kid" Wagner, and Italian Joe Gans, losing only to Brennan by the decision

---

121
122
123

of newspapers in their middleweight matchups. His bout with Lewis on October 13, 1914, at the Broadway Sporting Club in Brooklyn, resulted in a near knockout of Lewis, once a top welterweight contender, in the fourth round. New London's *The Day* noted, "*The bell saved Lewis in the fourth round. He was tottering, incapable of defense, when the bell rang. He came up for the final round (fifth) groggy, and McCoy consequently knocked him out, using his left to deliver the telling blow in the prior round.*" [124]

McCoy even took on the great Harry Greb, but Greb, trying to the last round to knock McCoy out, the champion survived and kept the title. Since championships could only be gained by knockout or foul, Al McCoy was still champ even though Greb won every round.

Every boxer has his day, and every boxer has his due. On November 14, 1917, McCoy met his match against Irish American boxer Mike O'Dowd in a war of a fight. This was something I read about many years ago, perhaps *The Ring* Magazine? I know that both fighters went toe to toe, and both men were knocked down until O'Dowd finally prevailed in the sixth round. Mike O'Dowd became the new middleweight champion of the world. [125]

Mike O'Dowd, 1917–1920

Michael Joseph O'Dowd (born on April 5, 1895 in St. Paul, Minnesota, died on July 28, 1957) was an American boxer who held the World Middleweight Championship from 1917 to 1920. He won the title on November 14, 1917, by knocking out Al McCoy in the sixth round after dropping him six times.[126]

O'Dowd was the only active boxing champion to fight at the front during World War I (1918, while serving in the US Army).[127] During his career he claimed victories over hall of famers Jack Britton, Mike Gibbons, Kid Lewis, and Jeff Smith. On February 25, 1918, he

---

124

125

126

127

held the legendary Harry Greb to a draw. On May 6, 1920, he lost the world middleweight title in Boston to Johnny Wilson. O'Dowd was knocked out just once in his career, his last fight on March 16, 1923.[128] He was inducted into the Minnesota Boxing Hall of Fame in 2011 and the International Boxing Hall of Fame in 2014.[129]

Johnny Wilson, 1920–1923

Johnny Wilson was born Giovanni Francesco Panica on March 23, 1893, in Harlem, New York City. He was a professional boxer who fought from 1911 until 1926. He won the world middleweight title from Mike O'Dowd on May 6, 1920, and lost it on August 31, 1923, against Harry Greb after making one successful defense in a rematch with Mike O'Dowd.[130]

Welterweights of the Nineteen Tens

Jack Britton, 1915; Second Reign, 1916–1917; Third Reign, 1919–1922

When Harry Lewis abandoned the welterweight title in 1911 that he had won in 1908, the title became vacant until 1915, when it was claimed by Mike Glover. Glover only held the title for three weeks, before losing it to Jack Britton, who earned universal acclaim as world champion. He lost it on his next outing on August 31, 1915, to his archrival Ted "Kid" Lewis. He regained the title from Lewis on April 24, 1916, from Lewis, lost it again to Lewis, and regained for the third time on March 17, 1919. He would then hold the title until 1922.[131] From his bio on Wikipedia, we have the following information.

Jack Britton (October 14, 1885–March 27, 1962) was three-time world welterweight boxing champion. Born William J. Breslin

---

128

129

130

131

in Clinton, New York, his professional career lasted for twenty-five years beginning in 1905. He holds the world record for the number of title bouts fought in a career with thirty-seven; eighteen of which ended in no decisions, many against his arch-rival Ted "Kid" Lewis, against whom he fought twenty times. Statistical boxing website BoxRec lists Britton as the number 6 ranked welterweight of all time while *The Ring Magazine* founder Nat Fleischer placed him at number 3. He was inducted into *The Ring Magazine* Hall of Fame in 1960 and the International Boxing Hall of Fame as a first-class member in 1990. [132]

So from the first time Britton won the welterweight title in 1915 until he lost it for the last time the welter crown was monopolized by Britton and Ted "Kid" Lewis. The rivalry was not only competitive between two evenly matched warriors, there was a lot of animosity between them. They exchanged threats and refused to speak to each other. They also refused the customary handshake before the start of their bouts. The two fought each other a remarkable twenty times![133]

Ted "Kid" Lewis, 1915–1916; Second Reign, 1917–1919

He became a professional boxer in 1909. On October 6, 1913, Lewis won the British Featherweight Championship with a seventeenth-round knockout of Alec Lambert at London's National Sporting Club. A year later, on February 2, 1914, at London's Premierland (in Whitechapel), he won the European Featherweight title from the French boxer Paul Til via a twelfth-round foul. Still in 1914, campaigning as a lightweight and welterweight, Lewis left London and toured Australia. In 1915, Lewis traveled to the United States, fighting Phil Bloom in New York's Madison Square Garden and winning by a decision. [134]

In Boston's Armory, on August 31 of that same year, he fought the man known as the Boxing Marvel, Jack Britton, for the wel-

132
133
134

terweight title. Lewis won in a twelve-round decision, becoming world welterweight champion and beginning an historic rivalry. Lewis became the first English boxer to cross the Atlantic and beat an American for a world title. [135]

The fights between Lewis and Britton for the world title were particularly notable. Their relationship has been described as one of the greatest rivalries in boxing history, and it was said that *"they winced and ducked every time they heard the other man's name."* From 1915 to 1921 Lewis and Britton fought 20 times, a total of 224 rounds. [136]

On April 24, 1916, in New Orleans, Lewis lost the title to Britton. He reclaimed it on June 25, 1917, at Westwood Field, Dayton, Ohio. He lost the title for the last time on March 17, 1919, in Canton, Ohio, when Britton knocked him out in the ninth round, the only knockout of the series. The roundup of his matches with Britton: Lewis won three, lost four, and had one draw. There were twelve no decisions. After his last loss to Britton, Lewis returned to England. [137]

Lewis is often ranked among the all-time greats, with ESPN ranking him forty-first on their list of the 50 Greatest Boxers of All Time and boxing historian Bert Sugar placing him forty-sixth in his Top 100 Fighters catalogue. Statistical boxing website BoxRec ranks Lewis as the seventeenth best welterweight of all time and the seventh best UK boxer ever. He is a member of the International Jewish Sports Hall of Fame, the *Ring* magazine Hall of Fame, and the International Boxing Hall of Fame. [138]

Amazingly, he fought 303 professional fights. His record forever stands at 234 wins with 80 knockouts, 46 losses, and 23 draws. Ted Kid Lewis, welterweight champion of the world, died in London on October 20, 1970, at the age of 75. [139]

135
136
137
138
139

Lightweights of the Nineteen Tens

Ad Wolgast, 1910–1912

On February 22, 1910, the great lightweight Battling Nelson, lost his world lightweight title to Ad Wolgast. Nelson, known as the Durable Dane, was most famous for his forty-two-round victory of another great, Joe Gans.

Ad Wolgast turned professional in 1906, and on February 22, 1910, he won the world lightweight title with a technical knockout (TKO) during the fortieth round against Battling Nelson.[140] In 1909, Nelson fought Ad Wolgast in a fight held over the lightweight limit. Wolgast beat him, and Nelson gave Wolgast a chance at his title on February 22, 1910. Eventually unable to see due to the accumulation of punches, Nelson lost the title when the referee stopped the fight in either the fortieth or the forty-second round.[141] After the California bout, both fighters were arrested and charged with violating the anti-prizefighting law. Wolgast would later defend the title against Mexican Joe Rivers in 1912, a bout that caused controversy. Delivering simultaneous blows, they knocked each other out. Referee Jack Welch counted to ten and the bout was over. However, he awarded the win to Wolgast, claiming that Ad had started to rise before the fatal ten. Rivers's fans let out a roar, believing he had been fouled. To add to the confusion, the timekeeper insisted the round had ended when Welch reached the count of four. But Welch's ruling became the official verdict.[142] Wolgast ultimately defended the belt five times before losing it to Willie Ritchie in 1912.

Sadly, as is too often the case, Wolgast suffered from pugilistic dementia, the medical term for brain damage that has affected many boxers and football players over the years.

140

141

142

Even at 61, the broken-nosed, greying little battler was more than a match for most men. It took two husky hospital attendants to handle him when they decided to get him under control. He got a chestful of broken ribs during the mauling, but he recovered quickly enough. He was used to beatings. It was a long series of beatings that had put Adolph ("Ad") Wolgast into the psychopathic ward of California's Stockton State Hospital in the first place.[143]

Willie Ritchie, 1912–1914

Willie Ritchie was born Gerhardt Anthony Steffen February 13, 1891, in San Francisco and became a professional boxer in 1907. He changed his name to Willie Ritchie so that his mother, who did not approve of boxing, would not know it was Gerhardt. Evidently it worked, and young Gerhardt went on to become a famous world lightweight champion. [144]

Ritchie's first title shot was with reigning lightweight champion Ad Wolgast on November 28, 1912, in San Francisco. Ritchie dominated the fight, and after Wolgast landed two blows below the belt in the sixteenth round, the referee called the fight for Ritchie. [145]

Ritchie held the title until July 7, 1914, when he lost the title in London to Welshman Frederick Hall Thomas, known professionally as Freddie Welsh. [146]

Freddie Welsh, 1914–1917

Born in Wales in 1886, boxer Freddie Welsh turned professional in Philadelphia and fought most of his battles in either the United States where he won the world lightweight title or Great Britain, where he won the prestigious Lonsdale Belt. He beat Willie Ritchie

---

143
144
145
146

to become lightweight champion on July 7, 1914. Throughout his career, Welsh fought the top men of the era beating Leach Cross, Matty Baldwin, Mexican Joe Rivers, Ad Wolgast, and Charley White and finally losing the championship on May 28, 1917, to Benny Leonard.[147] Primarily a clever boxer, he was sometimes criticized for not being a hard puncher. During the time Welsh boxed, scoring resulted in a large number of no-decision fights. However, newspapers commonly reported a winner in the case of no-decision bouts. With that adjustment, Welsh's final record would be 110-25-15, with 32 KOs and 16 no decisions. He was inducted into the IBHOF in 1997.[148] He is surely one of boxing's all-time greats.

Benny Leonard, 1917–1925

Prior to the modern era, the era of Roberto Duran, Pernell Whittaker, Manny Pacquiao, and Floyd Mayweather Jr., Benny Leonard was usually at the top of great all-time lightweight polls. Joe Gans also often got the nod. Born Benjamin Leiner, On April 7, 1896, he grew up in the Jewish Ghetto on New York City's Lower East Side. His parents were devout Jews who disapproved of professional boxing but wanted young Benny to be able to defend himself in a tough neighborhood. He got pretty good at it. Leonard began his professional career in 1911 at age fifteen. He took the Americanized name Benny Leonard to prevent his parents from discovering he had taken up professional boxing to earn extra money for them and himself.[149]

Leonard was known for his speed, lightning reflexes, excellent boxing technique, and ability to think fast on his feet. Equally important, he taught himself to be a powerful hitter, who scored seventy knockouts from his eighty-nine wins. He was defeated only six times in his career and was held to a draw on few occasions. As was common in the era in which he fought, he engaged in many no-deci-

---

147

148

149

sion matches and was believed to have engaged in around ninety-six bouts. He most distinguished himself by decisively winning over 90 percent of his career matches in his prime between 1921–32, and all his matches decided by judges and based on points.[150]

Leonard lost his share of early bouts, losing six of his first ten fights, probably because of his youth and inexperience, but by his third year, when he would have been eighteen, he was regularly fighting top men. He seemed to have found his mojo by the spring of 1914. By now, with added self-confidence, he was winning the vast majority of his fights. He went undefeated in seventeen fights before losing to the great lightweight Johnny Dundee followed by another loss to another great, Johnny Kilbane. Both of these outstanding boxers are hall of famers. He beat both in return matches.[151]

He got his first shot at lightweight champion Freddie Welsh on July 28, 1916. Welsh took the newspaper decision. Leonard kept trying. He beat Johnny Dundee in November, and on May 28, 1917, he faced the great Freddie Welsh in a rematch. It was a close fight as to be expected between two excellent scientific boxers. By round 9, Welsh appeared to be fading, and was knocked down three by Leonard, the last time hanging over the ropes and unable to defend himself. With that Benny Leonard was the new lightweight champion of the world.

150

151

He would hold his title nearly eight years, defending it several times, including two victories over the great southpaw Lew Tendler. Tendler was/is arguably the greatest southpaw. Tell that to Pernell Whittaker or Manny Pacquiao. He also bested Rocky Kansas, Soldier Bartfield, and Charlie White.[152]

The great champion announced his retirement after almost eight years as world lightweight champion on January 15, 1925. He announced his retirement because of his mother's failing health. He was a good Jewish boy. He lost most of his considerable fortune from real estate investments, boxing, and his work as an actor in the stock market crash of 1929. As a result, between 1931–2, he made an ill-advised comeback, defeating a total of nineteen handpicked opponents who were unlikely to end his comeback hopes. But he needed money. The Great Depression had not been good for him. He needed a big payday. [153]

He got it against an all-time great, Jimmy McLarnin, on October 7, 1932, in Madison Square Garden, New York City. A capacity crowd filled the Garden to witness young McLarnin take on the aged and faded, retired lightweight champion. In the first round, the crowd rose to its feet as Leonard landed a hard right that made one of McLarnin's knees touch the canvas. That was Leonard's only moment. McLarnin took charge in the second and knocked the old champion down. He continued to dominate Leonard until the sixth round when the referee mercifully stopped the bout to save Leonard from more punishment. It was Benny Leonard's final fight.[154]

On April 18, 1947, while refereeing a bout at St. Nicholas Arena, during the seventh bout of the night, Benny Leonard had a massive heart attack and died in the ring.[155]

152
153
154
155

Featherweights of the Nineteen Tens

Abe Attell, 1904–1912

The great featherweight champion Abe Attell, who won the title way back in 1904, and had defended it eighteen times, finally met his match on February 22, 1912, in Vernon, California, to Cleveland, Ohio, featherweight Johnny Kilbane in a decision over twenty rounds. Attell had been a great champion, despite the infamy of his later life.

Johnny Kilbane, 1912–1923

When Kilbane took the feather title from Abe Attell, he would go on to become the longest-reigning featherweight world champion in history, continuing his reign until June 2, 1923, losing it to Eugene Criqui when he was stopped by the Frenchman in the sixth round. Between 1904 and 1923, there were only two featherweight champions. Following his great victory over Abe Attell, upon his return to his home town of Cleveland, on St. Patrick's Day, he was given the greatest welcome ever given to a native Clevelander, with more than one hundred thousand people turning out.[156] One could say in the year 1923 that boxing mattered. In October 1917, while still world featherweight champion, Kilbane became a lieutenant in the US Army, assigned to Camp Sherman located near Chillicothe, Ohio, training US soldiers in self-defense during World War I.[157]

Bantamweights of the Nineteen Tens

Monte Attell, 1909–1910

The younger brother of featherweight champion Abe Attell, Monte Attell was born in San Francisco on July 28, 1895. Like his

---

156

157

older brother, being Jewish and small in a primarily Irish neighbor-hood, Monte Attell learned to fight at an early age. On June 19, 1909, Attell defeated Frankie Neill to win the World Bantamweight Championship by eighteenth-round knockout in Colma, California. In the seven months following his winning the title, Attell success-fully defended it seven times. Among those he successfully defended against to keep his championship were Phil McGovern and John Daly. He lost to Frankie Conley in 1910 by a forty-second-round knockout. Conley held the title barely a year, before succumbing to Johnny Coulon, a top bantamweight out of Chicago.[158]

Johnny Coulon, 1911–1914

Johnny Coulon was a tough kid from turn of the twentieth-cen-tury Chicago. Coulon won twenty-six of his early bouts before losing a ten-round decision to Kid Murphy. In a rematch with Murphy in 1908, Coulon reversed the decision and earned recognition as the American bantamweight champion, though the title was billed as the paperweight world title and not recognized as the world bantam-weight title by all sanctioning bodies.[159]

Many sources consider Coulon's twenty-round points deci-sion over Frankie Conley on February 26, 1911, in New Orleans, Louisiana, as bestowing the World Bantamweight Title for the first time at age twenty-two. In the historic bout at the West Side Athletic Club, both men gave equal punishment throughout the bout, with Conley still able to throw punches in the final twentieth round. Believing Coulon still a clear winner of the bout, the *Indianapolis Star* gave eighteen of the twenty rounds to Coulon, though not by wide margins.[160]

On February 18, 1912, he took a hard won fought close-deci-sion win over Frankie Burns in a world bantamweight title fight in New York City. It would be his last fight as champion.

158

159

160

Coulon lost the title when Kid Williams stopped him in a lop-sided victory ending in a third-round knockout on June 9, 1914, in Vernon, California. Coulon made "only a feeble resistance" in the June title bout with Williams, before a crowd of 10,700, and as he lost the bout in less than nine minutes of total fighting, New York's *Evening World* wrote that "he slid into obscurity with barely a protest."[161]

Coulon was not only a topnotch trainer but living boxing history. He was a close friend of Jack Johnson, had frequented Johnson's restaurant, the Café de Champion, and served as a pallbearer at the great champion's funeral. He knew every heavyweight champion since the Great John L. Sullivan, trained hundreds of fighters, and was a revered celebrity in Chicago during the 1960s. At seventy-six, he could leave a ring by jumping over a top rope, landing softly on his feet. He celebrated a birthday by walking the length of the gym on his hands.[162] He died at eighty-four in 1973 in Chicago and was buried in St. Mary's Cemetery along with his wife. He was a very colorful man and a great champion.

Kid Williams, 1914–1917

World bantamweight champion Kid Williams Williams was born in Copenhagen, Denmark. He traveled with his parents to the United States in 1904 where they ended up in Baltimore, Maryland. He took to boxing early, and on June 9, 1914 he won the world bantamweight championship by knocking out Johnny Coulon in the third round in Vernon, California.[163] He defended often, going up against the best men in the division. Between 1914, when he won the title, and 1917, when he lost the title, he fought the great Pete Herman three times, Memphis Pal Moore, Johnny Kilbane, and

---

161

162

163

Frankie Burns.[164] Along with Battling Nelson, he is one of the two greatest Danish boxers in history.[165]

Pete Herman, 1917–1920

A smooth boxer and a good body puncher, Pete Herman, a.k.a. Kid Herman, came out of New Orleans in 1912 to establish himself in the bantamweight division of professional boxing. Over the next several years, he did just that, facing some of the greatest small men boxing has ever known. On May 14, 1917, he faced Johnny Coulon and knocked him out in the third round to become bantamweight champion of the world.[166] On November 5, 1917, one day after he was married, Herman beat Frankie Burns in twenty rounds. Hmm… after his wedding night? Twenty rounds? This guy was one tough mutha. I mean, Frankie Burns was no slouch. On December 14, 1917, Herman won with a third-round technical knockout against Frankie Mason, in Fort Wayne, Indiana. In the second round, Mason was knocked to the canvas for the first time in his career.[167]

On May 23, 1919, he defeated Johnny "Kewpie" Ertle in Minneapolis, Minnesota, in a fifth-round technical knockout. The deciding blow was a strong left to the jaw. Ertle had previously been down for a count of eight in the fourth but was saved by the bell. He defeated Chicago bantamweight Johnny Ritchie on January 7, 1920, in an eighth-round technical knockout at Tulane Stadium in New Orleans. After a knockdown in the eighth, Ritchie arose still staggering, and the fight was stopped by the referee. Herman had won the bout with ease. [168]

On December 22, 1920, Pete Herman lost the bantamweight title to Joe Lynch by unanimous decision after fifteen rounds.[169]

164
165
166
167
168
169

Flyweights of the Nineteen Tens

Jimmy Wilde, 1916–1923

I must state unequivocally here that Jimmy Wilde, who won universal recognition as the first world flyweight champion, who reigned from December 18, 1916, until June 18, 1923, is the greatest boxer to ever hold the world flyweight title. When Wilde defeated American flyweight champion, the Young Zulu Kid, by an eleven-round KO, for the title in London on December 18, 1916, he was recognized in both Europe and America as the World Flyweight Champion.[170]

Wilde was a freak of nature, with unnatural power. His officially listed debut was on December 26, 1910, when he fought Les Williams to a no-decision in three rounds. His first win came on January 1, 1911, when he knocked out Ted Roberts in the third round. At one point in his career, Wilde had a streak of an amazing 103 victories without a loss. The most of all flyweight champion.[171]

The record books often show that Wilde started boxing professionally in 1911, but it is widely assumed (and later confirmed by boxing analysts) that he had been fighting professionally for at least four years before that. His claim that he had at least 800 fights is

170

171

probably greatly exaggerated, but it was certainly more than the 152 shown in BoxRec and elsewhere. He was boxing in the fairground booths taking on men as large as 200 pounds and knocking them out.[172] One could say Wilde was a pretty good puncher. All these bouts took place in England. This has to be one of the most amazing records in sports. Today, in 2020, if you asked a thousand people who the first flyweight champion of the world was, I doubt there would be more than a dozen who would respond "Jimmy Wilde."

Wilde held the title until June 18, 1923, when he lost to Pancho Villa.

With the longest unbeaten streak in boxing history, he went 103 fights before his first loss. Wilde had a record of 139 wins, 3 losses, 1 draw, and 5 no-contests, with an impressive 99 wins by knockout. *Ring* magazine, named him both the third greatest puncher of all time and the greatest flyweight of all time, and rated him as the thirteenth greatest fighter of the twentieth century. [173]

Summary

The decade of the Nineteen Tens was a truly remarkable decade in the history of professional boxing. Boxing and baseball were the two most important professional sports in America at that time. The heavyweight championship was celebrated as the greatest prize in sports. From Jack Johnson all the way down to Jimmy Wilde, the decade produced great and in some cases legendary fighters. In the decade, fighters such as Benny Leonard, Freddie Welsh, Jack Britton, Battling Levinsky, Jack Dempsey, and Pete Herman all gave a lustrous finish to a decade dominated by World War I.

172

173

CHAPTER V

Jack Dempsey and the Roaring Twenties

Like the 1960s, the 1920s was a breakout time for youth, a time of jazz, flappers, frolic, speakeasies, bathtub gin, F. Scott Fitzgerald, Hemmingway, Gertrude Stein, the lost generation, Babe Ruth, and the '27 Yankees, the charleston, the radio, Jack Dempsey, and million-dollar gates. The Eighteenth Amendment to the United States Constitution had been ratified just one year before, and now Prohibition was the law of the land. This opened the door to gangsters, bootleggers, and moonshine. It also led to speakeasies, illegal nightspots (wink-wink, nod-nod) where the booze flowed and the dancers danced. It was a time of great prosperity across the land. It was also a time of racial prejudice, the KKK, no Social Security, and for a lot of people, poverty.

Heavyweights of the Nineteen Twenties

Jack Dempsey, 1919–1926

The controversial knockout over Willard now passed, Jack Dempsey now ruled the boxing landscape, but controversy followed him. Dempsey had not served in World War I. He did do a photo shoot working in a shipyard in work clothes. But somebody with sharp eyes looked at the picture and noticed the patent leather shoes the then heavyweight contender was wearing. Immediately the outrage spread. Dempsey was branded a slacker, a term used then for what was later called a draft dodger. Dempsey went on with his career and became champion after the war ended. But there would always be those who regarded Jack Dempsey as less than patriotic.[174]

Dempsey versus Billy Miske

Dempsey took over a year before defending his title for the first time. The fight between Billy Miske and Jack Dempsey took place on September 6, 1920, in Benton Harbor, Michigan.

Unbeknown to the fans at ringside, Billy Miske was suffering from terminal Bright's disease and would be dead within two years. Dempsey took him on as a challenger because he knew that Miske was ailing and needed the money. He knocked Miske out in the third round.

Miske's enduring legacy is that of an underappreciated fighter. It is argued that Miske deserved, but never received, title matches against Jack Dillon, Battling Levinsky, and Georges Carpentier. His three recorded losses are against Hall of Famers Jack Dempsey, Kid Norfolk, and Tommy Gibbons, while his list of defeated opponents boasts some of the most storied names in boxing history. Miske's final professional record was 72-15-14, with 33 wins by knockout. On December 8, 2009, it was announced that Miske would be inducted into the International Boxing Hall of Fame in 2010. On September 28, 2012, Miske was inducted into the Minnesota Boxing Hall of Fame.[175]

Dempsey versus Bill Brennan

Two months later on December 14, 1920, at New York's Madison Square Garden, Dempsey defended against a seasoned heavyweight contender named Bill Brennan. If the fans were expecting another blowout, they and Dempsey were in for a surprise. Brennan was

---

174

175

in much better shape than he had been when he lost to Dempsey before he won the title. He took the first few rounds and even hurt Dempsey in the second. The two fought on evenly from the fourth round on. After ten rounds, Dempsey's ear was bleeding, and blood was also coming out of the champ's mouth. Brennan was ahead in the scoring. Then in the twelfth round, Dempsey once again found his inner tiger and dropped the challenger with a right body shot under the heart and a left hook to Brennen's right side. Dempsey retained the title with a twelfth-round TKO.[176]

Brennan had two more fights after Dempsey. He fought the feared Argentinian Luis Angel Firpo on March 24, 1923, and suffered a brutal knockout in the twelfth round. His handlers discussed retirement for Brennan, but he went through with another fight, losing by knockout to Billy Miske.

Brennan was shot to death outside a bar he owned on June 24, 1924, by someone for buying the beer for his establishment from the wrong source. This was pretty common in the era of prohibition.[177]

Dempsey versus Georges Carpentier and the Million-Dollar Gate

On July 2, 1921, Jack Dempsey and Georges Carpentier stepped into a boxing ring surrounded by ninety-one thousand people at Boyle's Thirty Acres in Jersey City, New Jersey. It was the largest crowd up to that point to ever attend a sporting event.[178] The draw was simple. The beetle-browed, unshaven, ex-hobo and slacker against the handsome, debonair war hero who was a popular in the United States as he was in his native France. Boxing mattered. When Dempsey and Carpentier came into the ring, the expectation rose to a fever pitch. Then the bell. Both men moved in to attack. There was no cautious feeling out. The fight quickly took a pattern, Dempsey bobbing and weaving and stalking Carpentier, boxing from the out-

176
177
178

side to avoid Dempsey's power and showing the champ his right. In the second round, Dempsey learned that the Orchid Man had some power as he was rocked by a right. But Dempsey's body attack began to take its toll on Carpentier. Dempsey dropped him in the fourth for a six count and then immediately dropped him a second time, and Carpentier could not beat the count. Dempsey won by fourth round knockout.[179]

Tommy Gibbons and the Fiasco in Shelby

The Jack Dempsey-Tommy Gibbons fight story is so surrealistic I decided to use the entire Wikipedia article to describe it. If I had written this myself, no one would believe it. But it really happened this way.

Because of the California economy and the influence of the Hollywood film industry, many people traveled west with dreams of becoming rich and famous. Shelby, Montana, had a train service, and the town's officials thought it would be wise to try to make the city an economic and tourist center. The money would be provided by revenues that the oil found in the area would bring. Multiple bank branches had opened there since the discovery, and many families would move in, or at least pass by, and spend their money as tourists, according to plans.

The first stage on this plan, which failed in great part because of the Dempsey versus Gibbons fight, was to bring a fight for the world heavyweight boxing title to town. Dempsey was a member of the *Big Five*, alongside Red Grange, Bobby Jones, Bill Tilden, and Babe Ruth. Being an idol all over the United States made Dempsey an attraction. The fact that his manager, Jack Kearns, and his promoter, Tex Rickard, to whom many refer today as the Don King of his era, were also famous, made city officials even more convinced that a large crowd would visit Shelby for the fight, in hopes of seeing Kearns and Rickard as well as the fight. Shelby also figured people would be attracted to running into Dempsey in town, or maybe

---

179

another member of the big five, should they make it to Montana to see the fight. There were no television networks, so whomever wanted to see the fight live would have to go to Shelby.[180]

Officials chose Tommy Gibbons, whose brother Mike was better known as a former world champion, to challenge Dempsey. But Gibbons proved the plan's first failure, as he was unknown except to boxing fans. Gibbons was strong, but not on Dempsey's level.

Thinking patriotism would play a part in the promotion, the city chose July 4, the United States' Independence Day. A large arena was built over a farm. The area is now known as Champion's Field.[181]

Kearns asked Shelby officials to guarantee him and the champion an advance for their traveling costs, as airplanes were available at the time but not safe, and train travel to Montana from the more populated areas of the United States took up to a week (it is said that Dempsey and Kearns took a week to get there by train). He also asked for the champion to have a guaranteed purse. So Kearns convinced Shelby to commit money or lose the fight to somewhere else. [182]

While Gibbons was not a champion, he was a professional and he needed money as well. He reportedly took 150,000 dollars to fight Dempsey.[183]

Shelby officials, again believing they would be the beneficiaries, agreed to every demand by both boxers and their management and promotional teams. Area banks were to provide the money to stage the event. Dempsey was received at the train station by thousands of residents, which gave the city officials even more hope that the fight would be a success.[184]

The fight was scheduled for the then almost regular distance of fifteen rounds. Dempsey was considered an aggressor: he had dropped Jess Willard seven times in the first round before winning the title from Willard by stopping him in round 3, retaining the title with

---

180

181

182

183

184

knockouts over Bill Brennan and Georges Carpentier, among others. Because of this, the fight was thought to be a possible action bout, but instead it was quite strategic. Dempsey constantly threw punches to Gibbons's head, with Gibbons trying to attack Dempsey's body. As a consequence, Gibbons was able to duck many of Dempsey's shots. Dempsey's mobility, however, made it hard for Gibbons to punch Dempsey's stomach and ribs.

There were some isolated moments of action: Dempsey is said to have had Gibbons hurt in round 7, but he could not score a knockout. Gibbons landed hard punches to Dempsey's chin once in a while, but Dempsey shrugged the punches off. In the end, Dempsey retained the title with a fifteen-round unanimous decision.

The aftermath was worse than the fight for Shelby: a large arena, the size of a football field, had been built. Since most of Shelby's residents and those of nearby cities could not afford ticket prices set so that the city could come up with the money guaranteed to the participants, only 7,702 paying fans showed up, making the fight one of the biggest economical disasters in boxing history. An estimated 13,000 people got to see the fight free.

Four banks in Shelby went bankrupt in the months following the fight. The town's dreams of prosperity went away with them.

Luis Angel Firpo

The last successful title defense for Dempsey was in September 1923 at New York City's Polo Grounds in Dempsey versus Luis Angel Firpo. More than eighty-five thousand, with another twenty thousand trying to get inside, filled the arena. In one of the wildest opening rounds ever, Firpo was knocked down seven times in the first round by Dempsey, yet continued to battle back, even knocking Dempsey down twice. On the second knockdown, Dempsey flew headfirst through the ring ropes, landing on a ringside reporter's typewriter. Ouch! At this point he was out of the ring for approximately fourteen seconds, less than the twenty-second rule for out-of-ring knockouts. As eighty-five thousand people screamed, he was helped back into the ring by the writers at ringside. He took out the typewriter, and when he went back into the ring, he had scrapes and cuts on his back, courtesy of the aforementioned typewriter. He knocked Firpo out and down in the second round, and the challenger was counted out. Jack Dempsey had defended his title in the wildest slugfest the heavy division may have seen since the days of the Great John L.

Dempsey's heavyweight title-defending fights, exhibition fights, movies, and endorsements made Dempsey one of the richest athletes in the world, putting him on the cover of TIME on September 10, 1923.[185] Following the Firpo fight, the champion took a three-year hiatus from the rigors of training, roadwork, and fighting. Instead, he made a movie called *Daredevil Jack*.

While there, he partied and generally had a great time with his celebrity. There he met a lovely movie star, Estelle Taylor, and they married. There was talk of matching him against the top African American boxer of the era, Harry Wills, but the match never came off. It is still debated whether Dempsey drew the color line. He claimed he wanted the fight, but no promoter would do it.

Finally, after three years of dissipation, the great heavyweight agreed to defend his title against a former Marine and a very smart boxer, Gene Tunney, on September 23, 1926, at Philadelphia's Sesquicentennial Stadium. There on a rain-soaked night, Tunney outboxed the ring-rusty champion, who had held the title since 1919. Returning home after the fight, his wife, Estelle, asked him, "Honey, what happened?" Jack replied, "Honey, I forgot to duck."[186] This rather endearing comment was plagiarized by President Ronald Reagan after he was shot in 1981. Admittedly, he had just taken a bullet, but what about later? He must have known Dempsey had said it, being a very sports-minded young person in 1926, and he had lots of opportunities to tell the world who thought it originated with him to say he got it from Jack Dempsey. He went to his grave without coming clean on the plagiarization. Other than that, I guess he wasn't a bad guy.

Dempsey-Jack Sharkey

Perhaps feeling that his long layoff had been a factor in his title loss, Dempsey decided he needed a tune-up fight before challenging Tunney again. In those simpler times, a boxer had to fight to earn a rematch. Jack Sharkey was a rapidly rising contender, with a good jab a good right uppercut and ring savvy. The two met on July 21, 1927, at Yankee Stadium. The house that Ruth built was filled with eighty-two thousand fans. At the bell for the seventh round, Dempsey stepped up his attack on Sharkey's body. If you look closely at the film, you can see Sharkey was being bothered by those blows. With about thirty seconds gone in the round, Sharkey complained of a foul, and as he turned to the referee, Dempsey nailed him with a left hook, and the fight was over. Dempsey got his second match with Gene Tunney. Jack Sharkey would go to beat Max Schmeling and become heavyweight champion on June 21, 1932.[187]

Dempsey retired after the second loss to Tunney, and though he boxed a few exhibitions here and there, he never fought again. In 1935, he opened his famous restaurant on Eighth and Fiftieth Street in New York City. He recounted an incident where he was assaulted while walking home at night, telling the press in 1971

186

187

that two young muggers attempted to grab his arms, but he broke free and laid them both out cold on the sidewalk. The story of the encounter appeared in the *Hendersonville Times-News* and reported the incident had taken place "a few years [earlier]." After a full and exiting life, Jack Dempsey passed away on May 31, 1983. He was eighty-seven years old. He was embedded in the inaugural class of the IBHOF in 1990.[188]

Gene Tunney, 1926–1928, Retired

Irish American James Joseph Tunney was born in Greenwich Village, New York City, on May 25, 1897. Tunney was an educated cultured man, often misunderstood by the boxing public, and an ex-Marine Corp boxing champion, as well as American light heavyweight champion and world heavyweight champion. While in many ways a man's man (US Marine veteran, heavyweight champion of the world), he was often viewed as a snob by the boxing public. Like Jim Corbett, who followed American icon John L. Sullivan, Larry Holmes had the misfortune to follow Muhammad Ali, but he was not a sophisticated intellectual like Corbett and Tunney, who had once lectured on Shakespeare and who had the nerve to beat Jack Dempsey.

188

Before he met Jack Dempsey, Tunney already had an amazing career beating the best world-class boxers of his era, the teens and the twenties of a century ago. He defeated Battling Levinsky, literally outclassing him, Georges Carpentier by TKO, and the greatest middleweight ever, Harry Greb, whom he beat three times out of five, with one loss and one draw. All his fights with Greb were fought in the light heavyweight division.[189]

First Dempsey Fight

On September 23, 1926, at Philadelphia's Sesquicentennial Stadium, Jack Dempsey met Gene Tunney in a ten-round rain-soaked bout for the heavyweight championship of the world. It was Dempsey's first fight since Luis Angel Firpo in 1923. Among the many events at the Sesquicentennial, perhaps none drew as much attention and publicity as the world's heavyweight title fight between defending champion Jack Dempsey and challenger Gene Tunney. Held at the Sesquicentennial Municipal Stadium on September 23, 1926, the boxing match drew a crowd of over 120,000 people and became one of the best known fights of the 1920s.[190] From almost the opening bell, the pattern of the fight was set. Dempsey would rush, throwing haymakers, and Tunney would tie him up. The referee would then break the fighters, and Tunney would fight from the outside, using a great left jab to continually poke Dempsey's face, followed by a right cross that landed as often as not. The pattern would be repeated over and over for ten rounds. As the fight wore on, Dempsey appeared to tire, and Tunney coasted to victory.[191] I want to repeat this: over 120,000 people watched this fight through pouring rain. Boxing Mattered.

189

190

191

Dempsey-Tunney 2
The Long Count

September 22, 1927, was the date of the second meeting between champion Gene Tunney and challenger Jack Dempsey. The fight took place at Soldier Field in Chicago before a crowd of 104,934 boxing fans.[192]

For the first six rounds, the fight was a virtual repeat of the first encounter. Dempsey bent low in his familiar crouch, while Tunney used lateral movement on the outside, scoring with sharp jabs and hard rights. Then it happened. In round 7, Dempsey caught Tunney along the ropes and fired a flurry of leather soaked bombs at the champion, dropping Tunney for the first time in his career. A new rule had recently been adopted, one that was not especially suited to Jack Dempsey's killer instinct. The new rule stated that the boxer scoring the knockdown must go to the farthest neutral corner before the count began. In the heat of the moment, Dempsey did not move, waiting to batter the rising Tunney again despite the referee's ordering Dempsey to the neutral corner. By the time he got Dempsey there, already several seconds had elapsed while Tunney was down. When the referee picked up the count over Tunney, he got to "Nine," and Tunney was back on his feet. He had been down for fourteen seconds. He lasted out the round and took charge again in the eighth, dropping Dempsey for a short count. At the final bell, the win for Tunney was a foregone conclusion.[193], [194]

Light Heavyweights of the Nineteen Twenties

Georges Carpentier 1920–1922

As the Twenties rolled in, the light heavyweight champion, the great French boxer Georges Carpentier had just taken the title from

---

192

193

194

Battling Levinsky, a ring-worn, tough, old battler whom Carpentier knocked out in the fourth round. After losing his heavyweight title bid to Jack Dempsey at Boyles Thirty Acres, he dropped back down to the light heavyweight division and defended successfully against Ted "Kid" Lewis in Paris by first-round knockout. He lost his world light heavyweight title and his European heavyweight and light heavyweight titles the following year, on September 24, 1922, in a controversial bout with Senegalese fighter Battling Siki. Carpentier died October 28, 1975.[195]

Battling Siki, 1922–1923

Louis Mbarick Fall (September 16, 1897–December 15, 1925), known as Battling Siki, was a French Senegalese light heavyweight boxer born in Senegal who fought from 1912 to 1925, and briefly reigned as the world light heavyweight champion after knocking out Georges Carpentier.[196]

When World War I erupted, Siki joined the French army, serving in the Eighth Colonial Infantry Regiment. During the war, he was decorated for bravery in battle with the Croix de Guerre and the Médaille Militaire, before being honorably discharged.[197] From

---

195

196

197

November 1, 1919, until he faced Georges Carpentier for the world light heavyweight championship in 1922, Siki compiled the impressive record of forty-three wins in forty-six bouts (twenty-one KOs), suffering just one loss (on a decision) and two draws. Carpentier, the reigning world and European champion, agreed to fight Siki for the title, and they met in Paris, France, on September 24, 1922. It was an auspicious day for Battling Seki, who knocked Carpentier out in the sixth round. As was typical in fights of this era, there was controversy. Siki claimed he had agreed to take a dive, but when he suffered a knockdown by Carpentier, he got mad and subsequently knocked the great French boxer out. Siki then went on a rampage of partying, drinking, and carousing. He would walk his pet lion down the Champs-Élysées while wearing his top hat and tuxedo. Siki was known to fire his revolvers in the air in public as a means of prompting his two Great Danes to do tricks. He was constantly reported drinking champagne in nightclubs and spent freely on flashy clothes and partying. He was fond of white women, and both his wives were white.[198]

Offers began pouring in for Siki to appear in the United States against middleweight champion Harry Greb, Harry Wills, Johnny Wilson, and even Jack Dempsey. He instead chose to go to Dublin, Ireland, and fight an Irishman, Mike McTigue, on St. Patrick's Day. His dissipation was apparent as he lost the fight, and the world championship by a unanimous decision on, you guessed it, March 17, 1923. He pretty much fell apart mentally, physically, and spiritually after losing his championship. Even in the States, Siki continued to carouse and train on booze and street brawls. Often, he would get drunk in speakeasies, refuse to pay the tab, and fight his way out.

It ended too soon for the once-mighty Siki. On December 15, 1925, he was stopped by a policeman, who saw him staggering drunk on Forty-Seconnd Street, not far from his apartment in New York City. Siki stated that he was on his way home and walked off. Later he was found lying facedown, shot twice in the back at close range, dead at the age of twenty-eight. [199]

198

199

Mike McTigue, 1923–1925

Mike McTigue was born in Ireland in 1892. After winning the light heavyweight championship of the world, McTigue largely fought in America, against the top men in the light heavyweight division. He defended his title against Young Stribling, Tommy Loughran, and Mickey Walker, all IBHOF boxers, before losing the title to Paul Berlenbach on May 20, 1925, a reign of a little over two years. He fell into poverty and possibly pugilistic dementia in his later years and died in Queens, New York City, on August 12, 1966.[200]

Paul Berlenbach, 1925–1926

On the twentieth day of May in the year 1925, Paul Berlenbach became light heavyweight champion of the world. Described by writer Paul Gallico as "untutored, unlettered, slow-witted, slow-moving, and wholly lacking in animation or imagination,"[201] Berlenbach was, nevertheless, a formidable fighter. As Gallico noted, he possessed "a numbing, paralyzing body punch that caused his opponents suddenly to crumple up," as though shot. His weaknesses were his non-existent defense and slow movements, which enabled sharp shooting opponents, such as Jack Delaney, to hit him at will. Despite Gallico's rather cruel assessment of Berlenbach, he was a world champion and a 2001 inductee into the IBHOF. He won the world title from Mike McTigue in 1925 and lost it fourteen months later to Jack Delaney of July 17, 1927. He was also an AAU champion wrestler before becoming a professional boxer. He died in 1985 at age eighty-four.[202]

Jack Delaney, 1926–1927

Jack Delaney, French Canadian born light heavyweight champion from from July 16, 1926, until July 17, 1927 was a smooth box-

---

200

201

202

ing prize fighter who won the title from Paul Berlenbach and vacated his title a year later to campaign as a heavyweight.

Delaney's stepped into the big time in 1924 when he decisioned Georges Carpentier on September 24. He followed it up in same year, knocking Paul Berlenbach down twice in the fourth round to win a TKO victory on July 16, 1926. The fight was held in Brooklyn's Ebbets Field and spurred on by his loudly cheering female fans, known as Delaney's screaming mamies, Delaney dropped Berlenbach, controlled the fight, and won the light heavyweight title.[203]

Delaney always prepared for fights in secluded training camps, in idyllic settings where no liquor was allowed on the premises. Unknown to the fans and sportswriters of the day was the reason for the no-liquor rules: Delaney drank. He just didn't drink socially but would disappear on benders lasting days. Before the Maloney fight, Delaney disappeared on a three-day drunk. Unknown to his manager, sometime during the three days, Delaney threw a punch at a railroad porter. The porter ducked, and Delaney hit the steel side of the rail car, breaking his hand. He told no one of his injury and fought Maloney anyway. Unable to throw his right, Delaney dropped the ten-round decision. [204]

By this time, Delaney's drinking had become a major obstacle in his career. In his last big fight he was matched with future heavyweight champion Jack Sharkey. Once again, the possibility of a crack at the heavyweight crown, and a big gate with Tunney, was in the balance. This time Delaney entered the ring flabby, bloated, and listless. When the bell rang for the opening round, he was unable to move. Apparently intoxicated to the point of virtual paralysis, Delaney stood staring at his corner as Sharkey came across the ring. Sharkey paused momentarily in disbelief and then knocked Delaney to the canvas. The fight ended with Delaney on his hands and knees, crawling around the ring like a man looking for a lost button, while the referee counted him out. The emotional Sharkey, his mouthpiece

203
204

hanging halfway out of his mouth, clung to the top ring rope crying in joy as the furious spectators cried fix.[205]

Delaney abdicated the light heavyweight crown on July 17, 1927, to campaign as a heavyweight. His alcohol problem rampant, he retired soon after. His final boxing record consisted of 77 wins (44 KOs), 12 losses, and 2 draws, 2 No Decisions and 2 No Contests.[206] After his boxing career, he operated a number of businesses, ran a tavern in New York, and refereed.[207]

Tommy Loughran, 1927–1929, vacated crown

Tommy Loughran was born in Philadelphia, the city of many champion boxers and contenders, on November 29, 1902. Loughran fought many middleweight, light heavyweight, and heavyweight champions in his career, including Gene Tunney, Jack Sharkey, and Georges Carpentier. Loughran even achieved a newspaper decision over fistic phenom Harry Greb, whom he first met at age nineteen. As a light heavyweight, he defeated two future world heavyweight champions: Max Baer and James J. Braddock. Loughran finally fought Primo Carnera for the heavyweight title but lost a decision.[208]

Loughran was primarily a slick boxer more than a slugger. He relied on good footwork, fast punches, and good defense. Loughran vacated the crown in 1929 to campaign as a heavyweight. He had 169 fights, but he only scored 14 knockouts. He passed away on July 7, 1982, in Altoona, Pennsylvania. He was a 1991 inductee into the International Boxing Hall of Fame.[209]

205
206
207
208
209

CHAPTER VI

The Roaring Twenties Part 2

Middleweights of the Nineteen Twenties

Harry Greb 1923–1926

The Roaring Twenties were off and rolling not only with Jack Dempsey but a truly great (some would call the greatest) middleweight champion of the world. What a remarkable guy Harry Greb was! He fought a recorded 298 times and was only stopped on two occasions. He won 261 of those fights, often against the crème de la crème professional middleweights, light heavyweights, and even heavyweights. He fought some of the greatest fights of his career, blind in one eye, the result of a thumbing in a match with hall of famer Kid Norfolk.[210]

Greb would fight 37 times in the sole year 1917 (a record), winning 34 of those fights either officially or unofficially. Among his victims that year were the reigning light heavyweight champion Battling Levinsky (in a nontitle fight), former light heavyweight champion Jack Dillon, middleweight George Chip, and heavyweight Willie Meehan, who had beaten future heavyweight champion Jack Dempsey earlier in the year.[211] Despite all these great results, Greb was still denied a chance to fight for a title. A February 1918 newspaper loss to Mike O'Dowd, who would go on to win the middleweight title during the year, didn't help in his effort.[212] After that setback, though, Greb would go unbeaten for over two years. During that stretch, he would beat future light heavyweight champion Mike McTigue, heavyweight contenders Gunboat Smith, Billy Miske, and Bill Brennan, and defeat Battling Levinsky no less than five times in newspaper decisions. Levinsky was the reigning light heavyweight champion at the time.

Harry Greb was many a fighter's worse nightmare. He was called the Pittsburg Windmill because of his swarming all-out attack style of fighting. Never a great puncher, he nevertheless, battered, beat, cut, bruised, and won 261 fights.[213]

Gene Tunney

On May 23, 1922, Harry Greb was matched with Gene Tunney, the undefeated American light heavyweight champion (the world title was then in the hands of Frenchman Georges Carpentier) in what would arguably end up being the defining bout of his career. In the first round, Greb immediately fractured Tunney's nose in two places and then proceeded to open a deep gash over the reigning champ's left eye. According to eyewitness reports, Greb was subse-

210
211
212
213

quently forced to commission the referee to intermittently wipe off his bloodstained gloves with a towel. Throughout the bout, Greb would repeatedly petition the referee to stop the fight, while a determined Tunney concurrently implored him to allow the contest to continue. Round after round, the beating continued, with Tunney refusing to submit and even smiling during the bloodshed to keep the referee from halting the match. At the end of fifteen brutal rounds, Tunney was a bloody mess, and Greb was crowned champion via unanimous decision. This was the first and only professional loss in Tunney's career, with the bout being hailed as the "Fight of the Year" for 1922 by the fledgling *Ring* magazine.[214] Harry Greb and Gene Tunney met again, in February of 1923, at New York's Madison Square Garden. This time, Tunney won, but the decision was controversial and was met with boos when announced.

The two men would meet three more times, with Tunney successfully defending his regained title in another fifteen-round bout and then splitting a pair of no-decision battles. The fifth battle was reminiscent of the first fight in their series, except this time it was Tunney bludgeoning Greb for the duration of the bout. According to Tunney, near the end of the match, while the two fighters were locked in a clinch, Greb straightforwardly asked Tunney not to knock him out. Tunney reputedly acquiesced to this request and later acknowledged the incident as the highest tribute he received in his career, stating, "Here was one of the greatest fighters of all time laying down his shield, admitting defeat and knowing I would not expose him."[215]

On August 23, 1923, Greb took the world middleweight title from Johnny Wilson by a workmanlike fifteen-round decision. Of course workmanlike in a Greb fight met a lot of fouling and eye gouging. When referee Jack O'Sullivan stepped in to separate the fighters during a particular rough clinch, he incredulously asked Greb what he thought he was doing, to which Greb responded, "Gouging Johnny in the eye, can't you see?" Greb would grant Wilson a rematch

---

214

215

on January 18, 1924, in Madison Square Garden, winning another fifteen-round decision.[216]

Probably the fights most people associate Harry Greb with are his fights with the great Mickey Walker, the Toy Bulldog. On July 2, 1925, Greb successfully defended his title in a fifteen-round decision over Walker. Following is one of my favorite boxing stories. It seems that after their fight, both men were in a speakeasy, and Walker, a great fighter who would win the middleweight title the following year, stumbled upon Greb at the nightclub after their fight, and according to the legend, the two fought an impromptu rematch there. According to some reports, Greb easily won the spontaneous rematch, while the general consensus maintains that Walker landed a sucker punch on Greb that knocked him out cold. According to Walker himself, the two sat discussing their fight over a drink when Walker made a comment stating that he felt had it not been for Greb thumbing him in the eye, he would have won the fight. The heavily intoxicated Greb took great offense to this and jumped to his feet to fight. As he was struggling to take off his jacket, Walker seized the moment and landed a vicious uppercut that put him down for the proverbial count. Booze and testosterone, bad combination.

By 1926, Harry Greb was thirty-two and a little on downside of his career. He had already had well over two hundred professional fights and had given and received punches with the top boxers in the world. His days were numbered. Greb died on the operating table December 22, 1926 while undergoing surgery to repair his nose. He was thirty-two.[217] Less than a year later, in November 1927, Tiger Flowers died while undergoing an operation to remove scar tissue from around his eyes. He was thirty-two.[218]

---

[216]

[217] Google. "How Did Harry Greb Die?"
[218] Google. "How Did Tiger Flowers Die?"

Tiger Flowers, 1926

On February 26, 1926, Greb stepped into the ring at Madison Square Garden to defend against a smart and tricky southpaw named Tiger Flowers. Coming out of Camilla, Georgia, to Philadelphia, where he became a professional boxer at the age of twenty-three. A natural southpaw, he had exceptional quickness and a very good right jab. Flowers outpointed Greb in fifteen rounds to become the new middleweight champion. To two fought again August 19, 1926, and Flowers won a highly disputed decision. This would be Harry Greb's last fight. [219]

Tiger Flowers was a deeply religious man. He was known as the Deacon because he always carried a Bible into the ring. He would always recite a part of Psalm 144 before the fight began:

Praise be the Lord my Rock
Who trains my hands for war
My fingers for battle
He is my loving God and my fortress,
My stronghold and my deliverer
My shield in whom I take refuge
Who subdues peoples under me[220]

Mickey Walker, the Toy Bulldog, 1926–1931, vacated

On December 3, 1926, Mickey Walker won the world's middleweight title with a controversial ten-round decision over world champion Tiger Flowers. He kept that title for five years, defending it three times during that period. He beat Mike McTigue and former world champion Paul Berlenbach. He fought future heavyweight champion Jack Sharkey to a draw and was badly beaten by Max Schmeling and knocked out in the eighth round. That ended his sojourn into the heavyweight ranks. Walker opened a restaurant in

---

219

220

New York City after retirement that became a popular landmark. He became an accomplished painter, with many of his works exhibited at New York and London art galleries.[221] During his boxing career, he found golf to be a suitable distraction to his training regimen, and he often dragged his manager, Doc Kearns, and his kids to golf courses to play golf.

Mickey Walker said on the January 13, 1955, *You Bet Your Life* show that he was married and had two daughters. He also said he "fought a draw for the heavyweight title."

Walker was found by police in 1974 lying on a street in Freehold, New Jersey, and taken to a hospital, where he was admitted with doctors initially thinking he was just a drunk lying on the street. But further tests revealed that Walker was suffering from Parkinson's syndrome, arteriosclerosis, and anemia. He was admitted to Marlboro Psychiatric Hospital for treatment.[222] He died on April 28, 1981, in Freehold, New Jersey.[223]

Welterweights of the Nineteen Twenties

Jack Britton, 1919–1922

After Britton won the welterweight title for the third time, he defended against the great lightweight Benny Leonard in a bout that smelled like fish rotting in a dumpster. As the story goes, and as I remember it, from reading about it many years ago, the two world champions fought on June 26, 1922, in Brooklyn, New York. For ten of the first twelve rounds, Britton had clearly outboxed Leonard. Then in the thirteenth, Britton went down from a clearly legal, above-the-belt punch, claiming foul. Almost nobody there believed it was a foul, even the referee. As he started counting over Britton, who clearly was not in pain, Benny Leonard ran around him and threw a sweeping right at Britton while he was down. At

---

221

222

223

this, the referee declared Britton the winner on a foul.[224] The record forever stands on Britton's record as WDQ, as in "win by disqualification." Did Benny foul Jack to keep him from losing his title? Was the end prearranged? It sure seemed that way to contemporary accounts.

Five months later, on November 1, 1922, Britton took on the much younger Toy Bulldog Mickey Walker in the Garden and lost the welterweight title. He had been a great champion.

Mickey Walker, 1922–1926

Mickey Walker, discussed in the middleweight section, became world welterweight champion on November 1, 1922, by fifteen-round decision over the great welterweight Jack Britton in Madison Square Garden. He was a fighting champion who held the title until 1926, defending against Pete Latzo and Jimmy Jones, Lew Tendler, Bobby Barrett, and Jock Malone.[225]

After winning two fights to start 1925, he went up in division to challenge World Middleweight Champion Harry Greb on July 2 but failed to win the Middleweight crown at that time, losing a fifteen-round decision to the 160-pound division champion. He went back to the welterweight division, defending his title against Dave

224
225

Shade and retaining it by decision. He won three bouts, lost one, and had three no decisions that year. [226]

Pete Latzo, 1926–1927

Pete Latzo was born in coal mining country, in Pennsylvania, in 1902. He made his professional boxing debut on October 3, 1922, winning a newspaper decision over Frankie Schoell. Schoell was already an accomplished welterweight, having been a professional boxer since 1918 with a winning record. Latzo got his shot at Mickey Walker's welterweight title on May 20, 1926, in Latzo's fourth year as a pro.

In an impressive upset, Latzo defeated Mickey Walker to take the world welterweight championship before a crowd of twelve thousand on May 20, 1926, in a ten-round unanimous decision in Scranton, Pennsylvania.[227] The bout was marred somewhat by frequent clinching, holding, and covering up, and it lacked haymakers and knockdowns, but Latzo brilliantly executed his win after previously losing to Walker, a 3–1 favorite to win the match. The Associated Press gave Latzo five rounds, with three to Walker, and two even, and both judges ruled in his favor.[228]

He lost the welterweight crown to Joe Dundee on June 3, 1927, in a fifteen-round majority decision before one of his largest audiences, an impressive crowd of thirty thousand, at the New York City's Polo Grounds.[229] After losing the title, Latzo went after bigger game and fought some of the marquee name fighters of the late twenties and early thirties. Among those he fought were Tiger Flowers, Maxie Rosenbloom, Tommy Loughran, future heavyweight champion Jim Braddock, and Jimmy Slattery.[230]

---

[226]

[227]

[228]

[229]

[230]

Joe Dundee, 1927–1929

Joe Dundee was born Samuel Lazzaro in Palermo, Sicily, Italy, on August 16, 1903. He was tutored at St. Mary's Industrial School in Baltimore, where his family moved when he was a young boy.[231] A far more famous alumni of St. Mary's was Babe Ruth, the Sultan of Swat, the greatest baseball player of all time.

Dundee became a professional boxer in Baltimore at age sixteen. Before winning the welterweight title, he fought important bouts against Lew Tendler, Tommy Freeman, and George Levine.[232] On June 24, 1926, Dundee beat and battered Mickey Walker to an eighth-round TKO victory. He got his big chance on June 3, 1927, before thirty thousand people at New York's Polo Grounds, beating Pete Latzo in a majority split decision and becoming the new welterweight champion of the world. On July 25, 1929, he faced Jackie Fields in defense of his welterweight title. Fields dominated, scoring four knockdowns in the second round. Fields then went down from a low blow, and the referee ruled it a foul and awarded the championship to Jackie Fields, who was winning the fight before the referee stopped the contest.[233]

Jackie Fields, 1929–1930

Jackie Fields was born Jacob Finkelstein in Chicago in 1908. He was a Jewish boxer in an era of great Jewish boxers that included the Attell brothers, Abe and Monte, Ruby Goldstein, Battling Levinsky, and Benny Leonard. He was an outstanding amateur and the winner of a gold medal at the 1924 Olympic Games.[234]

He must have been in the right place at the right time, because one of his early trainers/tutors was the great old-time lightweight

---

231

232

233

234

boxer Jack Blackburn, who became famous later on as the trainer of the Brown Bomber, Joe Louis. [235]

Fields suffered an early defeat and learned a powerful lesson when he took on future hall of fame lightweight and welterweight champion Jimmy McLarnin. Oh! He took such a pounding from McLarnin! He was stopped in the second round. But Fields was tough and full of *chutzpah*. He also lost pre-title fights against Louis "Kid" Kaplan and lightweight champion Sammy Mandell, both future IBHOF inductees.

After defeating Joe Dundee for the title, Fields lost and regained the welterweight title in the next decade. To be continued. He lost the title for the first time to Young Jack Thompson on May 9, 1930.[236] About this time, the National Boxing Association (now the WBA) started getting their fingers involved in boxing, creating havoc and split titles. This writer wishes they would just go away. Boxing would be a lot better off without them.

Lightweights of the Nineteen Twenties

Benny Leonard, 1917–1925, retired

When the nineteen twenties came in, Benny Leonard had already been world lightweight champion for three years. He would fight some of his greatest battles in the next five years. Before a capacity crowd, Leonard scored a victory over Willie Loughlin on the evening of November 12, 1920, at the Camden Sporting Club in Camden, New Jersey, in a ten-round newspaper decision. Leonard began cautiously wary of the skills and two-inch-longer reach of Loughlin, whom he had met previously. In the last three rounds, Leonard used his punching power, though it was met with frequent but less effective blows from Loughlin. In the fourth, Leonard's jabs to Loughlin's face were frequent, but Loughlin continued his defense and never retreated. In the fifth, Leonard scored more punches and

---

235
236

began to take a point's margin, but not without receiving a few blows from his opponent. In the ninth, Leonard tried to end the fight with uppercuts, but could not deliver a knockdown blow to Loughlin, who remained on his feet even through the exchange of blows in the tenth. Leonard knocked Loughlin across the ring and staggered him at times, but Loughlin's ability to take punishment repeatedly saved him from a knockout.[237], [238]

The Benny Leonard-Richie Mitchell fight was a battle for the ages. In the fight that took place in Madison Square Garden, Leonard defeated Ritchie Mitchell in six of fifteen rounds on January 14, 1921, in a tough world lightweight championship bout. Atypically, Leonard was down in the first round, when his alarmed seconds and probably Jewish underworld figure Arnold Rothstein, who had bet on Leonard to win, freaked out. Leonard pulled himself up at "Seven" and, to the surprise of everyone, dropped both of his hands and beckoned Mitchell to come in. Fearing a trap, Mitchell hesitated, and Leonard escaped. In an incredible first round, Mitchell was down as well for a count of nine from a right to the stomach by Leonard and down twice more before the bell. With a hook to the stomach and a right to the jaw, Mitchell went down for a count of 9 in the sixth. Mitchell was up before Leonard with a flurry of punches put him down again. On his third trip to the canvas, the referee called the bout.[239] Whew! I first read about this fight in a Nat Fleischer biography called *Leonard the Magnificent*.

As the decade rolled on, Leonard successfully defended against Sailor Friedman, Tim Droney, Rocky Kansas, Soldier Bartfield, and hall of famer Lew Tendler. The Tendler match was one of Leonard's most memorable. On July 27, 1922, Leonard defeated fellow Jewish boxer Lew Tendler in a twelve-round newspaper decision in Jersey City in a lightweight world title match, which might have been the most remarkable bout of his career. Before a record audience of seventy thousand enthralled fans, Leonard won five rounds, Tendler

---

237

238

239

four, with three even. Tendler may have led in the first five rounds, as Leonard could not adjust to or penetrate his unique Southpaw stance, style, and defense. In the eighth, Tendler crashed a terrific left to his opponent, but Leonard distracted him by mumbling a few words and then going to a clinch to slow Tendler down. Tendler never delivered the follow-up knockout blow, and Leonard, getting time to recover, dominated the next seven rounds. [240]

In their last meeting on July 24, 1923, Leonard won a unanimous fifteen-round decision at Yankee Stadium before an extraordinary crowd of fifty-eight thousand. The bout took place in the Bronx in another lightweight world title match. Leonard excelled in the speed and precision of his attack, while still managing to ward off most of his opponents blows, particularly Tendler's strong left. Leonard demonstrated his mastery of ring tactics against an opponent who became sluggish and was unable to mount the offensive he had shown in their bout the previous July. By one account, Leonard managed to land three blows for every one of Tendler's, demonstrating his speed and mastery of tactics. With the huge crowd, Leonard's take home pay exceeded $130,000, an extraordinary sum for the era. [241]

From there, Leonard defeated Pinky Mitchell, Andy Hart, and Johnny Mendelsohn. On January 15, 1925, Benny Leonard announced his retirement, at the request of his mother, who was ailing. He had been unbeaten as lightweight champion for just under eight years. With the stock market crash of October, 1929, Leonard lost most of his earnings as a boxer, actor, vaudevillian, and his real estate interests. Forced to make a comeback in 1932, the great champion, now softened up and fighting as a welterweight, beat nineteen handpicked opponents, drew some fairly large crowds for Depression-era America, and finally got his big payday against the very formidable Irish American welterweight Jimmy McLarnin. Leonard, now balding, seemed stiff and slightly perplexed by McLarnin, as he tried to box him from the outside with left jabs and an occasional

---

240

241

right. McLarnin could not be denied. In round 6, he was punishing Leonard, who was not fighting back, being so busy covering up, and the referee stepped in to rescue the former all-time great lightweight champion.[242]

Jimmy Goodrich, 1925

While Jimmy Goodrich, who held the lightweight title briefly in the Twenties, might not have had the greatest record, with eighty-five wins (only twelve by KO), thirty-four losses, and twenty-one draws or newspaper decisions, but he fought a lot of great fighters and did win the lightweight tournament to determine Benny Leonard's successor on August 13, 1925, beating Stanislaus Loayza to claim the lineal world lightweight championship. His reign was brief. He was dethroned less than four months later by Rocky Kansas on December 7, 1925.[243]

Rocky Kansas, 1925–1926

Rocky Kansas was a tough, short (five foot two tall) world lightweight champion. He was born Rocco Tozzo on April 21, 1893, in Italy and came to America in 1898. He died on January 10, 1954.[244] He came from a fighting family with two brothers who were also professional boxers.

Kansas turned pro in 1911 and won all but two of his first seventy-five fights. One of those losses was to Benny Leonard in 1916. Kansas went the distance, but received a boxing lesson from Leonard for the full ten rounds. In 1921, in his tenth year as a professional boxer, Rocky finally got the attention he deserved by scoring a one-round knockout over Richie Mitchell, who had not lasted past the sixth round against champion Benny Leonard. After Leonard retired in 1925, Rocky Kansas beat Jimmy Goodrich to win the world light-

242
243
244

weight championship. After fourteen years as a professional boxer, he finally was the champion of the whole world.[245]

He wasn't champ for long. On July 3, 1926, at Comiskey Park in Chicago, Rocky Kansas lost the lightweight title to Sammy Mandell. Kansas retired after the loss to Mandell. Like many other people, the stock market crash of 1929 wiped him out. He went to work for the City of Buffalo.[246]

Sammy Mandell, 1926–1930

Mandell developed his fighting skills at the Camp Grant barracks in Rockford, Illinois. He was too young and underweight to join the army, weighing 105 pounds. Despite this, his persistence in hanging around the wrestling and boxing training areas saw him gain permission to join in with the military personnel. The camp boxing instructor at the time was Fred Dyer, the Singing Boxer, who recalled in a 1926 interview how Mandell beat every soldier in the bantamweight class and was able to best men ten pounds heavier than him. Dyer also stated that he advised Mandell to turn professional.[247]

He was a highly skilled professional boxer who was trained by the great trainer Jack Blackburn. He won the world lightweight title from Rocky Kansas on July 3, 1926, and retained his title until July 17, 1930. In that time span, he defeated besides Rocky Kansas, Billy Petrolle, Jimmy McLarnin, Tony Canzeroni, and Jackie Fields, all of whom are in the IBHOF. In a shocking upset, Mandell was knocked out in the first round by Al Singer. He was inducted into the International Boxing Hall of Fame in 1998. Mandell's final record stands at a very respectable 120 total bouts, with 88 wins, 22 losses, 10 draws, and 5 no contests. He fought the very best men in his class, and he fought a number of them several times.[248]

245
246
247
248

Al Singer, 1930

Dubbed the Bronx Beauty for his smooth boxing and good looks, Al Singer briefly held the world lightweight title. Singer was born in a tenement on Broome Street, part of the Jewish section in New York's Lower East Side on September 6, 1909. He was one of four sons and a daughter born to an ambitious ladies' garment entrepreneur who would keep his large family in America's middle class. Singer was a good athlete and played basketball besides boxing. He had a very strong amateur career before turning professional.[249]

Though Singer was young and had stayed far distant from crime, his exceptional winning record caught the eye of the New York mob, who hoped to bring him to a championship as quickly as possible. Most reference books on Singer noted that in 1928, two men came to his training camp and asked to meet with his manager, Harry Drucker. Accepting a ride with the men, Drucker was never heard from again, and Singer came under the influence of the mob, whom many believed fixed a few of his early fights.[250] He performed exceptionally well against Lou Moscowitz at Madison Square Garden and Pete Zivic at St. Nicholas in late 1928, knocking them out in five and six rounds respectively. In his first real feature match on September 14, 1928, Singer and the exceptionally skilled Tony Canzoneri, former holder of the featherweight world title, battled to a ten-round draw, satisfying an impressed audience and spotlighting Singer as a potential feather or lightweight contender. In his career, Singer won 61 of 72 pro fights (25 by KO), drawing twice, and losing nine.[251]

Singer captured the World Lightweight Championship on July 17, 1930, before a crowd of thirty-five thousand at Yankee Stadium, with a first-round knockout (1:46) of champion Sammy Mandell. Though both boxers started the match boxing cautiously, Singer dropped Mandell with a left hook to the jaw in less than a minute

---

249

250

251

of fighting. Three more times Mandell went down to the mat for short counts, scarcely able to raise his hands in defense. The final knockdown came with a crushing one two punch to the jaw. Mandell had defended his four-year claim to the lightweight crown only a few times and claimed that the weight loss required to make weight had sapped his strength.[252] Singer held the lightweight title until November 14, 1930, losing it to Tony Canzoneri by a first-round knockout, thus becoming the first and only man until John Mugabi to both win and lose a world championship by one-round knockouts.

Featherweights of the Nineteen Twenties

Johnny Kilbane, 1912–1923

(For the first part of this section, please see chapter 4 under "Johnny Kilbane.") As the 1920s came in, Johnny Kilbane had been the world featherweight champion since he had beaten Abe Attell on February 22, 1912, eight years before. In the time between, he had met and beaten a stellar group of featherweight and lightweight boxers, including Frankie Burns, Tommy Dixon, Monte Attell, Johnny Dundee, and Jimmy Walsh, a rare loss to Patsy Brannigan, Rocky Kansas, Benny Leonard, and George "KO" Chaney. Now, eight years into his reign, his title defenses became less frequent. There were two successful defenses in 1921 and then on June 2, 1923, at the Polo Grounds in New York, the great champion lost the featherweight crown to a French challenger, Eugene Criqui, by a stunning sixth-round knockout. Criqui had become the aggressor in the round and then landed a crushing right hand. Kilbane went down for the count.[253]

Eugene Criqui, 1923

Eugene Criqui, born in Paris, France on August 15, 1893, was a French WWI war hero, whose jaw was shattered by a sniper's bullet and had to be reconstructed. His reign was short. On July 26, 1923, just fifty four days after winning the title from Kilbane, Criqui was beaten in fifteen rounds in New York City by Johnny Dundee. Criqui retired soon after. His record reads 130 fights, 98 wins, 53 knockouts, 17 losses, and 14 draws. He was inducted into the IBHOF in 2005.[254]

Johnny Dundee, 1923–1924, vacated title

The great boxer known as Johnny Dundee, "the Scotch Wop," was born in Sciacca, Sicily, Italy as Giuseppe Corrara on November 19, 1893. His family immigrated to America in 1909, and young Giuseppe was raised on New York City's West Side, where his father owned a fish market. Corrara was given his ring name in 1910 by his manager, Scotty Montieth. [255]

Johnny Dundee has to be considered one of the most remarkable pugilists in history. Just the basic fact of his sheer number of professional fights, 334 from the time he beat Skinny Bob at the Sharkey Athletic Club in New York in 1910 until his last fight in 1932 against Mickey Greb, a little arithmetic averages a little over 15 fights a year for 22 years! At one time he was the featherweight and junior lightweight champion both at the same time.

253

254

255

"Scotty saw me scrapping in front of my old man's fish place. He convinced me I could make a living fighting and gave me my name, Scotch, to go with his name."[256]

Dundee lost a lot of fights, around 73 of them, but considering he won 201 fights, that is just a little over twenty percent.[257] Not counting newspaper decisions, this man won 201 fights! There were 46 draws (newspaper decisions in many cases), and no doubt many of these were victories by decision.

In 1913, Dundee earned a world title fight in his 87th fight. He fought 20 rounds against World Featherweight champion, Johnny Kilbane in Vernon, California. The fight ended in a draw. Dundee would not be afforded an opportunity to fight for the 126-pound featherweight title again for another 10 years when on July 26, 1923, he lifted the featherweight title from Eugene Criqui on a fifteen-round decision at the Polo Grounds in New York, a fight he had to shed twenty-eight pounds for.[258] While the majority of Dundee's fights were at the junior lightweight division, I have made it clear that this book is about the era when boxing really mattered, and there were eight, and only eight legitimate divisions, and yes, there have been a lot of great fighters at cruiserweight, junior middleweight, junior welterweight, and so on, but again, that is for another book, maybe my next. Dundee vacated the crown almost as soon as the final bell rang and the title would be vacant for two years, until Louis "Kid" Kaplan won a tournament to succeed him. Johnny Dundee died in New Jersey on April 9, 1965.

Johnny Dundee was strictly a product of a generation that has long since passed and will not return. He was a fighter in the era when boxing was in full flower, a superior craftsman among a lot of other superior craftsmen. Although he was once the featherweight champion of the world, he gained far more

---

256

257

258

fame than fortune. When he died the other day, at the age of 74, the main legacy he left was the enduring friendships that this popular and amiable little guy collected over the years.[259], [260] (San Antonio Express, 1965)

Louis "Kid" Kaplan, 1925–1926, vacated

Things get a little complicated here, so I am taking this from Wikipedia. By late 1924, world featherweight champion Johnny Dundee vacated his title, and a tournament was arranged to determine a successor. Kid KO'd Angel Diaz in three rounds, outpointed Bobby Garcia over ten rounds, and then halted Joe Lombardo in four rounds to advance to the finals. On January 2, 1925, he knocked out Danny Kramer in nine rounds at Madison Square Garden to become the new champion. His first two defenses were against the familiar Babe Herman (D15 and W15) in late 1925. Kaplan next decisioned hall of famer Billy Petrolle over twelve rounds in a nontitle bout. Unlike his predecessors, Johnny Dundee and Johnny Kilbane, the Kid was not champion for long. By 1927, he decided he could no longer make the featherweight weight limit of 126 pounds and abdicated, moving up to the lightweight (135 pounds) and campaign in that division. He had some success, beating stellar performers Jackie Fields, Battling Battalino, and Sammy Mandell. He retired soon afterward, leaving a 108-17-13 D-12 ND (26 KOs) record. The Kid died in 1970.[261]

Benny Bass, 1927, NBA, 1928, World

Bass was born in Kiev, Russia, on December 4, 1904, the second son to Jewish parents Jacob and Pauline, and was brought to America three years later. His father first came to Philadelphia to earn

---

259

260

261

enough money to send for his five sons and wife in Kiev. They sailed to America but were first rescued from a shipwreck on their way, spending five weeks in Queenstown, Ireland. By then, he was making living selling newspapers at a busy street corner in Philadelphia. In his early teens, Benny held down a job at Curtis Publishing Company, who published the *Saturday Evening Post*. From age twelve to sixteen, Bass won 95 of 100 bouts as an amateur. Impressively, he qualified for the Olympic Trials in the flyweight class in 1920, where he lost a decision to the future Gold Medal winner Frankie Genaro. Turning pro the following year, he was managed by Phil Glassman. By 1926, he was rated the number 1 featherweight contender.[262]

On September 12, 1927, Bass defeated Jewish boxer Red Chapman (Morris Kaplan) before an extraordinary crowd of thirty thousand in Philadelphia for the NBA featherweight championship in a ten-round unanimous decision. In the fourth through seventh, Bass managed to fight from a distance using his long game to prevent Chapman from opening a swollen cut on his eye opened in the third round. Bass led a two fisted-slugging attack in the seventh, eighth, and ninth, which gained him a points margin and won him the decision of all three judges. In the early ninth, an unusual sight occurred, when both boxers charged each other, landing rights to their jaws and were knocked to the canvas simultaneously.[263] One can only assume that Bass got up first.

Bass lost the world featherweight title to Tony Canzoneri on February 10, 1928, at Madison Square Garden in a fifteen-round split decision and went on to campaign as a junior lightweight with considerable success. Retiring from the ring in 1940, he worked as a liquor and beer salesman for Penn Beer Distributors in the Philadelphia area until 1960, when he became a clerk in Philadelphia Traffic Court. On June 25, 1975, Bass died at seventy at Rolling Hills hospital in Philadelphia, where he had been a patient for several months.[264]

262

263

264

Tony Canzoneri, 1928

Tony Canzoneri is one of the very greatest boxers that ever lived. Canzoneri fit the mold of the typical American boxer of the era: he could box up to three or four times in one month and up to twenty-four or twenty-five times in one year, and he would seldom fight outside New York City, considered to be boxing's mecca at the time. Of his first thirty-eight bouts, only one was fought west of New York City, and that was in New Jersey. Canzoneri won his first title, the world featherweight title, with a fifteen-round decision over Benny Bass on February 10, 1928.[265] Canzoneri was also a world lightweight and junior welterweight champion, and his career will be covered more extensively in the next chapter.

Andre Routis, 1928–1929

On September 28, 1928, French challenger Andre Routis beat Tony Canzoneri on a split decision in New York City's Madison Square Garden. Following his victory, he lost two nontitle fights, one against Canzoneri. He defended his title successfully once against Buster Brown, winning a third-round TKO. On September 2, 1929, following four nontitle losses, he surrendered his featherweight crown to Battling Battalino. In his career, he fought eighty-six times

265

between 1919 and 1929, winning 54 (12 by knockout), losing 25 and drawing 7.[266]

Battling "Bat" Battalino, 1929–1932

Christopher Battaglia was born on February 18, 1908, to an Italian family in Hartford, Connecticut. The son of Italian immigrants, he never attended high school but worked in a typewriter factory and labored in the tobacco fields.[267]

As a professional boxer, Battalino would become known as a courageous and rugged fighter with good inside boxing abilities. He was not known for a disciplined and studied boxing technique but rather a strong and relentless attack. On September 23, 1929, Battalino outfought Andre Routis over fifteen rounds in his hometown of Hartford, Connecticut, and won all fifteen of the fifteen rounds to become featherweight champion of the world.[268]

Bantamweights of the Nineteen Twenties

Joe Lynch, 1920–1921

Bantamweight champion Joe Lynch was my kind of fighter. He was an aggressive, come-at-you, in-your-face fighter who made you fight every second of every round. And he was durable. He was never knocked out in 156 fights. He was born in New York City on November 30, 1898, and he died in Brooklyn, New York, in 1965. He won the world bantamweight title in 1920, defeating Pete Herman. Herman defeated him to regain the title the following year. Lynch regained the title from Johnny Buff after Buff defeated Herman, defended it successfully against Midget Smith, but lost in 15 rounds to Abe Goldstein in 1924. He retired in 1926 and died in 1965. In 1965, he drowned in an accident in Sheepshead Bay, Brooklyn. He

---

266

267

268

was found floating in a New York City bay and died en route to the hospital. Foul play was suspected. His boxing record, while not exactly stellar, was respectable. Hey, anybody who has 156 fights is respectable. He won 99, lost 36, and had 19 draws and 2 no contests.[269]

Pete Herman, 1921

Having written extensively about Herman earlier, I will try to make this as brief as possible without doing disservice to this great champion. He was one of the all-time great bantamweight champions.

Herman's most memorable match was fought against Jimmy Wilde, the legendary Welsh flyweight world champion.

The Wilde-Herman fight was staged on January 13, 1921, at Royal Albert Hall in London and resulted in a seventeenth-round technical knockout for Herman. The former bantamweight champion used his weight advantage and body punching to wear down Wilde, the still reigning flyweight champ. Herman hurt Wilde in the fifteenth, when the fighting was fierce against the ropes, and knocked him through the ropes three times in the seventeenth round to end the fight. The classy Wilde made no excuses. He stated after the fight, "I can sincerely say that Herman beat me because he was the better boxer." Many gave Wilde the first five rounds, but Herman came back particularly strong in the fifteenth, until he ended the bout in the seventeenth.[270] The exciting match brought an impressive crowd of around ten thousand, including the Prince of Wales.

On July 25, 1921, Herman fought Joe Lynch in a rematch for the world bantamweight title in New York's storied Ebbets Field. Both boxers weighed in at 116 3/4 pounds. The *Scranton Republican* and other sources gave Herman 13 of the 15 rounds, with only the eleventh to Lynch and the second even. Herman's decisive win on points fueled speculation that he had thrown the first fight. Herman forced the fighting, taking the lead from the opening bell using both

269

270

left and right effectively. At the time, Herman was one of the few fighters ever to regain a lost title.

He didn't hold it for long. On September 23, 1921, just two months after regaining the title, he lost it to fast boxing Johnny Buff. Earlier in 1921, Herman began going blind. Sadly, the great champion went completely blind. He died on April 13, 1973.[271]

Johnny Buff, 1921–1922

Six months after taking the American flyweight championship, on September 23, 1921, Buff won the World Bantamweight Championship by defeating Pete Herman in Madison Square Garden in a fifteen-round points decision. Buff took ten of the fifteen rounds, with only four given to Herman and one even. By the fifteenth round, Herman was exhausted, and Buff reigned blows on him without Herman putting up an effective defense. Buff was remarkable for taking a world title at the advanced age for a boxer of thirty-two.[272]

Buff had a noteworthy defense of the title at Madison Square Garden against Jackie Sharkey on November 10, 1921, in a fifteen-round points decision.[273]

On July 10, 1922, Buff lost the championship to Joe Lynch at the Velodrome in New York in a fourteenth-round TKO. After six seconds of fighting in the fourteenth, Lynch having taken three strides toward Buff at the sound of the bell delivered a left hook to the jaw that ended the fight. One source gave Lynch fourteen of the fifteen rounds, in a victory he could have easily won on points, gaining a considerable advantage by the late rounds. Buff was unable to get past the defenses of Lynch and landed comparatively fewer blows. Lynch's three-inch advantage in height and reach might have been a factor in his victory. A few ringside felt that facing Lynch so soon after taking the bantamweight championship was poor match-

---

271

272

273

making on the part of Buff's handlers. In an advantageous prefight negotiation, Buff made $30,000 on the results of the fight, while Lynch technically made nothing due to the house receipts given to Lynch amounting to only around $20,000.[274]

Joe Lynch, 1922–1924

After Joe Lynch defeated Johnny Buff, he had two newspaper decisions against a very good bantamweight, Memphis Pal Moore. He won the first and lost the second. He lost his title for the second time to Abe Goldstein on March 21, 1924, at Madison Square Garden. He fought a couple more newspaper decisions in 1926, a draw and a loss to his nemesis, Memphis Pal Moore. He retired soon after in 1925.[275]

Abe Goldstein, 1924

The *News* noted that the capacity crowd of 14,900 at Madison Square Garden witnessed a "*stirring, hard fought battle with Goldstein assuming the lead almost from the start, and continuing to pile up points throughout the fifteen rounds.*" The *News* gave only the tenth round decisively to Lynch, who for the first time in the battle landed his signature right hand to the chin of Goldstein. The result of the fight was not a foregone conclusion in the minds of most fans, as Wilmington's *Evening Journal* noted that Lynch had been the big favorite on the night of the match.[276]

Goldstein successfully defended the title twice the year he took it, against Charles Ledoux and Tommy Ryan, before losing to Eddie "Cannonball" Martin in a fifteen-round decision on December 19, 1924. The fight was razor-thin close, and many thought Goldstein won, but more people felt Martin had earned the victory.

274

275

276

On April 23, 1926, Goldstein beat Hall of Fame Black Panamanian boxer Panama Al Brown in ten rounds in New York. The fighting was described as fast-paced. As a result of a reach disadvantage, Brown being four inches taller at five feet nine inches, Goldstein fought at long distance, which improved his chances at defense. Though Brown had the advantage during in-fighting, Goldstein seemed to have a points advantage from the early rounds, and his lead was never in question throughout the bout. Brown, a black Panamanian, would become the first Latin American to hold the NYSAC world bantamweight title three years later in 1929.[277]

Goldstein retired in 1927. By 1929, after the collapse of Wall Street, he was forced to drive a cab to make a living. His professional record, according to BoxRec, counting newspaper decisions, for 135 bouts, was 101 wins, 24 losses, 9 draws, and 1 no contest. He had an impressive thirty-five knockouts among his wins.[278]

He died February 12, 1977, in New York.

Eddie "Cannonball" Martin, 1924–1925

On December 19, 1924, Eddie Martin, with the ring name Cannonball, took the World Bantamweight Championship from Abe Goldstein by a narrow majority decision.

Eddie Martin lost the title to Jewish boxer Charlie "Phil" Rosenberg in a fifteen-round unanimous decision on March 20, 1925, in Madison Square Garden. In the sweeping victory, the *Lincoln Evening Journal* wrote, "*Rosenberg had a clean margin in eleven of the fifteen rounds, and three were even.*" Martin appeared to have held a slight lead only in the early rounds. The *Palm Beach Post* noted that Rosenberg won using a "*tantalizing left jab and a right uppercut, outboxing Martin at every turn and at the latter part of the match, holding his own in a furious toe-to-toe skirmish.*"[279]

277

278

279

Eddie Martin retired from boxing around 1932. He had a wife, Emmy, and a son, Martin, Jr.

He died on August 27, 1966, at his home in Brooklyn, New York, though some sources erroneously give his year of death as 1968. He had been suffering from a heart condition.

Charlie "Phil" Rosenberg, 1925–1927, Vacated

He was born on New York City's Lower East Side on August 15, 1902, as Charles Green. Later, his widowed mother moved to Harlem, where Charlie grew up.[280] Rosenberg was working as an errand boy for a millinery shop when coworker Phil Rosenberg had to pull out of a scheduled match.

He won his bout substituting for Phil Rosenberg and subsequently took his name as his ring moniker. He retained his real first name of Charlie. He didn't exactly set the bantamweight universe on fire, losing most of his early bouts. Charlie's manager, Harry Segal, frustrated with Charlie's poor record in his early fights, might have intentionally overmatched him with Olympic flyweight champion Frankie Genaro around that time. Although losing the twelve-round points decision at the Commonwealth Sporting Club against Genaro on May 23, 1922, the close fight could have gone either way, and Charlie's manager was impressed with his young boxer's ability to learn. Rosenberg had picked up pointers on bobbing, ducking, and effectively using his left, from Jewish boxing great Benny Valgar, while training at his gym. He would meet Genaro again on October 21, 1922, in another close twelve-round bout. Rosenberg would become known for his speed, hard-hitting ability, and cleverness in the ring.[281]

Through 1922 and 1823, Rosenberg kept fighting and kept improving. In 1925, he challenged Eddie "Cannonball" Martin on March 20, 1925, winning a unanimous fifteen round decision to win

---

280

281

the bantamweight title. He had won nine fights in a row to get the title shot, and he made the most of it, outboxing Martin for eleven of the fifteen rounds.[282]

Rosenberg vacated the bantam title on February 2, 1927, as a result of no longer being able to make the bantamweight 118-pound limit. He later served jail time for racketeering in the Bronx. In the late thirties, he became an insurance salesman and was in the insurance business for the next thirty years. He also managed restaurants. He died on March 12, 1976.[283]

Panama Al Brown, 1929–1935

Alfonso Teofilo Brown (July 5, 1902–April 11, 1951), better known as Panama Al Brown, was a Panamanian professional boxer. He made history by becoming boxing's first Latin American world champion and is widely regarded as one of the greatest bantamweight boxers in history. Alfonso Teofilo Brown was born on July 5, 1902, to Afro-Caribbean immigrants in the City of Colón, Panama. His first exposure to boxing came while working as a young adult clerk for the United States Shipping Board, at the Panama Canal Zone, witnessing American soldiers boxing.[284]

282

283

284

Freakishly tall for a bantamweight, Brown stood 5 feet 11 inches and weighed less than 118 pounds. This was a plus for him, giving him a reach advantage over his opponents and leverage in his punches. Panama Al Brown's final record is believed to have been 123 wins, 18 defeats, and 10 draws, with 55 knockouts, placing him in the exclusive list of boxers who have won 50 or more wins by knockout. He was the recognized bantamweight world champion for 6 years and over that time made 11 title defenses against the best bantamweights and featherweights of his era.[285] The bulk of Brown's career was fought in the 1930s and will be covered in the following chapter. Stay tuned.

Flyweights of the Nineteen Twenties

Jimmy Wilde, 1916–1923

Wilde, who is widely recognized as the greatest flyweight champion of all time, was born in Wales on May 15, 1892. Known throughout his career as the Mighty Atom and Ghost with a Hammer, he started boxing in British fairground booths at age sixteen. By the time he won the universal lineal flyweight championship of the world, beating Young Zulu Kid on November 9, 1916, he had already garnered European and British titles. By the time he fought great bantamweight Pete Herman in 1921, his record stood at 131 wins, 1 loss, and 1 draw. Herman gave him his second loss, stopping him in 17 rounds. Outweighing Wilde by 14 pounds, Herman wore the great flyweight champion down.[286]

After a win over Young Jennings, Wilde announced his retirement. With the public clamoring over the Philippine sensation Pancho Villa, Wilde decided to fight one more time. The younger man knocked Wilde out in the seventh round at the Polo Grounds in New York City on June 18, 1923, and Wilde never fought again.

285

286

He ended his career at 131-3-1 with an astonishing, for a flyweight, 99 knockouts.[287]

Pancho Villa, 1923–1925, Died

Pancho Villa was born August 1, 1901, as Francisco Guilledo in Ilog Negros, Philippines. He was the world flyweight champion from June 18, 1923, until his untimely death on July 14, 1925. He and Wilde were the two greatest flyweights up to the modern era. After defeating Jimmy Wilde, he defended his championship several times, his lone defeat coming in a nontitle match against bantamweight Bud Powell (not the late jazz pianist) on March 6, 1924.[288]

Villa returned to the United States to prepare for his next match, a nontitle fight against Jimmy McLarnin scheduled for July 4, 1925, at Ewing Field in San Francisco. In the days leading to the fight, Villa's face became swollen due to an ulcerated tooth. According to contemporary newspaper accounts, on the morning of the fight, Villa went to a dentist to have the tooth extracted. Despite the pain and swelling, Villa insisted on going ahead with the fight with McLarnin. Villa ended up spending most of the fight using one hand to protect his afflicted face. Given these circumstances, Villa naturally lost, though he managed to stay the distance. It was to be Villa's last fight.[289]

Two or three days after the McLarnin fight, he had three more teeth extracted after an infection was discovered. Against his dentist's prescription of bed rest, Villa spent the next few days carousing with friends. His condition worsened, and by July 13, 1925, he had to be rushed to the hospital. It was discovered that the infection had spread to his throat, resulting in Ludwig's angina. Villa was rushed into surgery, but he lapsed into a coma while on the table and died the following day, July 14, 1925. Tragically, his death occurred only seventeen days before his twenty-fourth birthday.[290]

287

288

289

290

Fidel LaBarba, 1927, vacated

Pancho Villa's death on July 14, 1925, following a loss to Jimmy "Baby Face" McLarnin on July 4, caused the title to be vacated. A bout on August 22, 1925, between Fidel La Barba and American flyweight champion Frankie Genaro saw the title go to La Barba who defeated Genaro in a ten-round decision.[291]

LaBarba was a great amateur boxer, winning a Gold Medal at the 1924 Olympic Games. He might have been the first of a number of Olympic champions to win a world professional title. Other noteworthy Olympians to achieve this distinction would be Floyd Patterson in 1952, Cassius Clay (Muhammad Ali) in 1960, Joe Frazier in 1964, George Foreman in 1968, and Lennox Lewis in 1988. Each of these men became undisputed world heavyweight champions.

Fidel was born in New York City and grew up in Los Angeles. He began boxing at age thirteen or fourteen, and while still in high school, he turned professional. He defeated Frankie Genaro and Elky Clark to claim the Flyweight Championship of the World. In 1927, he retired to attend Stanford University.[292] Less than a year later, however, he returned to the ring as a featherweight. He won his first five fights and in 1931 split two decisions with Kid Chocolate. On May 22, 1931, he was given an opportunity to win the world featherweight title but was out pointed by Battling Battalino. He returned to Stanford and received a degree in journalism. Later in his life, he worked as a sportswriter and as an advisor for boxing films in Hollywood. LaBarba died of heart failure in Los Angeles in 1981.[293] There would be several title claimants in the next few years, but it was not until 1935 that the flyweight title became unified again.

291

292

293

CHAPTER VII

Hard Times Part I

On October 29, 1929, the stock market crashed, and the United States, as well as the world, fell into what became known as the Great Depression. Millions of people lost jobs and income, without unemployment security and Social Security. Bread lines and soup kitchens formed to feed the poor and unemployed. Hooverville's named for Republican president Herbert Hoover were made-on-the-fly shanties in large cities where the unfortunate victims of the Depression lived. A terrible time of drought fell across much of the American Southwest, which combined with poor farming techniques and windstorms, created the Dust Bowl, the ruin of many a farmer. Despite all this, literature, music, and art thrived. John Steinbeck published *The Grapes of Wrath*, which some consider the great American novel. Steinbeck often wrote about poor, working-class people and their struggle to lead a decent and honest life. Pearl S. Buck published *The Good Earth* and William Faulkner published *As I Lay Dying*. In desperation, people called Okies loaded up jalopies and trekked to the promised land of California to hopefully find work. Folk singer Woody Guthrie (1912–1967), the unofficial chronicler of the Dust Bowl, wrote memorable songs about the era. Margaret Mitchell wrote *Gone with the Wind*, another important book of the decade of the Thirties. In 1932, Democratic president Franklin Delano Roosevelt was elected, and soon after, he enacted the New Deal, putting unemployed men back on the job.

The following were the boxing champions as the decade began:

- Heavyweight, Max Schmeling
- Light heavyweight, Jimmy Slattery
- Middleweight, Ceferino Garcia
- Welterweight, Young Jack Thompson
- Lightweight, Tony Canzoneri
- Featherweight, Battling Battalino
- Bantamweight, Panama Al Brown
- Flyweight, Frankie Genaro

(Courtesy of Boxing Wiki, lineal boxing champions)

By now, the eight standard weight classes had been established, boxing was pretty much as it would be for the next few decades, and some of the greatest names in pugilism were active in these years. Let us now begin our journey through the decade.

Heavyweights of the Nineteen Thirties

Max Schmeling, 1930–1932

In 1928, German heavyweight Max Schmeling came to the United States to make a name for himself. Nobody took him seriously until he beat top-ranked Spaniard Paulino Uzkudun in fifteen rounds at Yankee Stadium. Following that win, Schmeling was regarded as the foremost young contender in the division. With the world heavyweight champion Gene Tunney having recently retired, promoters arranged a matchup between the German and veteran contender Jack Sharkey to fill the vacancy. It amazes this writer that everyone could suddenly agree to this fight and make it for the championship. Today, uh-uh. No way. All the sanctioning bodies would have their own claimant, and it would eventually despoil into chaos. On June 12, 1930, at Yankee Stadium, in a fight billed as the Battle of the Continents, Schmeling, known as a slow starter, fell slightly behind on points going into the fourth round. He was trying to corner his opponent when Sharkey let loose with a very fast, clear hit to the groin. Schmeling fell to the canvas, claiming to have been fouled. When manager Jacobs ran into the ring, prompting chaos, the referee disqualified Sharkey and declared Schmeling the victor and the first man to win the world heavyweight championship on a foul. The New York State Athletic Commission (NYSAC), reviewing the call, agreed.[294]

This did not make Schmeling either popular or legitimate. He was derided as the "foul champion". Nevertheless, Max Schmeling of Germany was now the Heavyweight Champion of the World. He gained more legitimacy on March 7, 1931, in a successful defense in Cleveland over Young Stribling, whom he TKO'd in the fifteenth round of a fight that garnered *The Ring* Fight of the Year.[295]

One year later, on June 21, 1932, he fought a rematch with Jack Sharkey in Long Island Bowl, Queens, New York, and Sharkey won a highly disputed decision to become the new champion. Now an ex-champion, he fought some of his most famous battles.

On September 26, 1932, Schmeling fought the great former welterweight and middleweight champion Micky Walker, who had recently fought a fifteen round draw against Sharkey. He dealt a terrible beating to the smaller man. The fight was stopped in the eighth

294

295

round when Walker's manager Jack Kearns told the referee to stop the bout.[296]

Public opinion took a sharp turn in 1933 when the Nazi Party became the most powerful political party in Germany and Europe. Schmeling was sort of found guilty by association simply because he was German. He was matched against Max Baer, a future heavyweight champion who had a Jewish father. Baer, not a practicing Jew, wore the Star of David on his trunks. The public bought into it. Jack Dempsey, the promoter, played up this angle, and suddenly the fight was viewed as Baer defending his faith against the prejudice of the Nazis, represented reluctantly by Schmeling. The German, thrown off his game by all the negative press, received a sound thrashing from the younger, stronger Baer and was stopped in the tenth round.[297]

Versus Joe Louis

Looking to advance their fighter on his climb to the big prize, Louis manager John Roxborough, feeling that Schmeling was now over the hill as a boxer, sought to match him against the man now being called the Brown Bomber. To the utter shock and amazement of all, Schmeling knocked Joe Louis out in the twelfth round on June 12, 1936, in their meeting at Yankee stadium. Schmeling had studied movies of Louis very carefully and noticed the Joe had a habit of dropping his left after throwing a jab. "I seez something," he said to his manager and trainer. Well, he did, and in the fourth round, he caught Joe with a hard right that put him on the canvas and from which Louis could not recover. Schmeling outfought him over the next several rounds and dropped him again in the twelfth. Joe Louis was counted out and now Schmeling was the top contender. Meanwhile the title had gone from Max Baer to Jim Braddock to Joe Louis. [298]

296

297

298

Braddock, a proud Irish American, felt that he had to beat the best in the world to be considered champion and that man was Joe Louis.

Joe had taken the crown from Braddock, knocking him out in the eighth round at Comiskey Park in Chicago.[299] Louis won, and the world accepted him, but he felt he could not call himself the heavyweight champion of the world until he beat the only man to defeat him, Max Schmeling. That fateful meeting would take place on June 22, 1938.[300]

Jack Sharkey, 1932–1933

In the meantime, the heavyweight title would change in quick succession between Jack Sharkey, Primo Carnera, Max Baer, and Jimmy Braddock.

Jack Sharkey was still a teenager when he tried to enlist in the Navy during World War I and was turned down because of his age. He was finally allowed to enlist after the war. Born Joseph Paul Zukauksas, he was a strapping lad who first took to boxing while in the Navy. He soon distinguished himself as the best boxer in the Navy and turned professional before his discharge. His first pro fight took place in Boston on January 24, 1924, against one Billy Muldoon who he knocked out in the first round.[301]

He took his name from two of his idols, heavyweights Tom Sharkey and Jack Dempsey. In 1927, he defeated Harry Wills, Mike McTigue, and Jim Maloney! These wins put him in line for a match against Jack Dempsey, the winner to face champion Gene Tunney. The Dempsey-Sharkey fight was already covered in the Jack Dempsey segment of this book. To repeat, Dempsey hit Sharkey low. Sharkey dropped his hands and turned to the referee to complain. Remember that old boxing rule "Protect yourself at all times"? Well, Sharkey forgot it, and Dempsey knock him cold with a left hook. We

---

299

300

301

already know what happened: Dempsey lost to champion Tunney in the Battle of the Long Count.

On June 21, 1932, Jack Sharkey won the heavyweight championship of the world by a split decision over Max Schmeling and returned the title to America. Sharkey held the title until June 29, 1933, when he was knocked out by Italian Primo Carnera.[302]

Primo Carnera, 1933–1934

So Jack Sharkey was the first man to win the heavyweight championship from a foreigner a German and lose it to a foreigner an Italian. Carnera held the world heavyweight championship from June 29, 1933, until June 14, 1934. He was the biggest man, at six feet six inches, since Jess Willard, who stood six feet seven inches. Carnera was heavier, though, usually around 275 pounds and more muscular than Willard.[303]

Carnera was born a Scorpio in Sequals, Italy, on October 26, 1906. He enjoyed a sizable reach advantage over most rivals, and when seen on fight footage, he seems like a towering giant compared to many heavyweights of his era, who were usually at least sixty pounds lighter and seven inches shorter. One publicity release about him read in part, "*For breakfast, Primo has a quart of orange juice, two*

302

303

quarts of milk, nineteen pieces of toast, fourteen eggs, a loaf of bread and half a pound of Virginia ham." [304]

He turned professional on September 12, 1928, winning by knockout in round 2. He won his next several fights against questionable opposition and came to the United States in 1930 and won his first seventeen fights by knockout. His streak was ended by George Godfrey, who lost by disqualification in the fifth round. From TIME Magazine, *"Since his arrival in the US, backed by a group of prosperous but shady entrepreneurs, Carnera's career has been less glorious than fantastic. His first opponents—Big Boy Peterson, Elzear Rioux, Cowboy Owens—were known to be incompetent but their feeble opposition to Carnera suggested that they had been bribed to lose. Suspicion concerning Carnera's abilities became almost universal when another adversary, Bombo Chevalier, stated that one of his own seconds had threatened to kill him unless he lost to Carnera. Against the African American George Godfrey (249 lbs.), he won on a foul. But only one of 33 US opponents had defeated Carnera—fat, slovenly Jimmy Maloney, whom Sharkey had beaten five years earlier. In a return fight, at Miami last March, Carnera managed to outpoint Maloney."* [305]

After winning the title from Jack Sharkey, he successfully defended against Paulino Uzcudun and light heavyweight champion Tommy Loughran. Both of these men took Carnera to the fifteen round distance. On June 14, 1934, he lost the crown to Max Baer. Nat Fleischer of *The Ring* magazine reported Baer knocked Carnera down twelve times before stopping him in eleven rounds. [306]

In 1945, he temporarily returned to boxing and won two fights. But the next year, after three losses against Luigi Musina his talent for wrestling was discovered. In 1946, he became a professional wrestler and was immediately a huge success at the box office. For several years, he was one of the top draws in wrestling. Carnera continued to be an attraction into the 1960s. Max Baer attended at least one of

---

304

305

306

Carnera's wrestling matches. Carnera won his debut on August 22, 1946, when he defeated Tommy O'Toole in California. On October 23, 1946, Carnera won his forty-first consecutive wrestling match by defeating Jules Strongbow. On November 19, 1946, Carnera beat Harry Kruskamp to remain undefeated at 65-0-0.

Primo Carnera went 120 straight wrestling matches undefeated (119-0-1) before suffering his first loss to Yvon Robert in Montreal, Quebec, Canada, on August 20, 1947. Carnera's greatest victory took place on December 7, 1947, when he defeated former world heavyweight champion Ed "Strangler" Lewis.

In May 1948, Carnera took a 143-1-1 record against world heavyweight champion Lou Thesz. Thesz defeated Carnera in a world title defense.[307]

Carnera died on June 29, 1967.

Max Baer, 1934–1935

I was a thirteen-year-old beginning amateur boxer on November 21, 1959, when I heard over the radio that Max Baer had died at age fifty. I knew he was once the heavyweight champion of the world, but I knew little else about him. For that matter, this was before *The Beverly Hillbillies* television show, so I did not even know about his also-famous son.

Maximilian Adelbert Baer was born on February 11, 1909. He was the heavyweight champion of the world from June 14, 1934, when he knocked out Primo Carnera until June 13, 1935, when he

---

307

clowned his way to a loss to James J. Braddock. His title reign lasted exactly one year.[308]

His family moved from Nebraska to Livermore, California, in 1926. Livermore was cowboy country, and his family had a ranch, raising cattle. In later years, Max claimed that working on the ranch, doing the hard labor, gave him his broad shoulders and punching power. He claimed to stun the steers before slaughter by punching them.[309]

He became a professional boxer in 1929. Sadly, he knocked out and killed Frankie Campbell in 1930, a fight that affected him so deeply he strongly considered never fighting again.

There was more. On August 31, 1932, at a fight in Chicago, he knocked out Ernie Schaaf, and the damage suffered in his bout with Baer stayed with him. He next fought Primo Carnera, who knocked him out with a left jab. Schaaf died. It has been assumed that the punches he took from Baer were the cause of death.[310]

On June 14, 1934, at the outdoor Madison Square Garden Bowl at Long Island, New York, Baer defeated the huge reigning world champion Primo Carnera of Italy, who weighed in at 267 pounds. He knocked Carnera down in in rounds 1, 2, 10, and 11. Carnera was down either 11 or 12 times (disputed).[311]

On June 13, 1935, one of the greatest upsets in boxing history transpired in Long Island City, New York, as Baer fought down-and-out boxer James J. Braddock in the so-called Cinderella Man bout. Baer hardly trained for the bout. Braddock, on the other hand, was training hard. "I'm training for a fight, not a boxing contest or a clownin' contest or a dance," he said. "Whether it goes one round or three rounds or ten rounds, it will be a fight and a fight all the way. When you've been through what I've had to face in the last two years, a Max Baer or a Bengal tiger looks like a house pet. He might come at me with cannon and a blackjack and he would still be a picnic compared to what I've had to face."[312] Baer, ever the showman, "brought

---

308

309

310

311

312

gales of laughter from the crowd with his antics" the night he stepped between the ropes to meet Braddock. As Braddock "slipped the blue bathrobe from his pink back, he was the sentimental favorite of a Bowl crowd of 30,000, most of whom had bet their money 8-to-1 against him."[313]

They should have betted for him. Baer clowned his way throughout and lost 8 of the 15 rounds. Jim Braddock, the Cinderella Man was the new heavyweight champion of the world. The fact that 30,000 boxing fans showed up and paid during the lowest financial time in American history says boxing mattered.

Baer fought on for a few more years, including a losing bout with Joe Louis, and then retired to go into films and nightclub performance. He even teamed up with light heavyweight champion Maxie Rosenbloom as the Two Maxies. Baer often performed at Rosenbloom's club Slapsie Maxie's.[314]

The Cinderella Man, James J. Braddock, 1935–1937

Fighting under the name James J. Braddock (ostensibly to follow the pattern set by two prior world boxing champions, James J.

313

314

Corbett and James J. Jeffries), Braddock was known for his spoiling, counterpunching style, powerful right hand, and iron chin. He had lost several bouts due to chronic hand injuries and was forced to work on the docks and collect social assistance to feed his family during the Great Depression. He made a comeback, and in 1935, he fought Max Baer for the heavyweight title and won. For this unlikely feat he was given the nickname Cinderella Man by Damon Runyon. Braddock was managed by Joe Gould.[315]

If you saw the movie *Cinderella Man*, you pretty much know the story. Born James Walter Braddock, he chose the name James J. Braddock. He was more or less an ordinary club fighter when he took on highly regarded Tuffy Griffiths on November 30, 1928, and scored a major upset knocking Griffiths out in the second round at Madison Square Garden. Brittle hands and hard times severely curtailed Braddock, who had started with a thirty-one-win, two-loss, four-draw record through the summer of 1929.[316] When the stock market crashed, so did a lot of people, among them Jim Braddock. He took a job as a longshoreman and for a time he had to go on relief (welfare) to feed his family. This was always a source of shame to this brave warrior. On July 18, 1929, he got his title shot, losing a very close decision to master boxer Tommy Loughran for the light heavyweight championship of the world in Yankee Stadium. Depressed by the loss to Loughran and having broken his hand in several places, 1929 through 1932 were hard times for Braddock who went on a losing streak, with a paltry 11 wins, 20 losses, 2 draw record. But the boxing gods were smiling at Jim Braddock!

He caught fire in 1934. In a bout with highly rated Corn Griffin, a bout in which he was regarded as a mere stepping stone for Griffin, Braddock pulled off another major upset and knocked Griffin out in the third round. He quickly followed that up with a decision win over future light heavyweight champ John Henry Lewis on November 16, 1934. In his third Madison Square Garden appearance in a row, he beat top heavyweight contender Art Lasky.

315

316

These three important wins put him in line for the fight of his life, a shot at heavyweight champ Max Baer. Considered little more than a journeyman fighter, Braddock was handpicked by Baer's handlers because he was seen as an easy payday for the champion, despite his recent impressive victories. Instead, on June 13, 1935, at Madison Square Garden Bowl, Braddock won the heavyweight championship of the world as the 8-to-1 underdog in what was called the greatest fistic upset since the defeat of John L. Sullivan by Jim Corbett.[317]

Max Schmeling's people began trying to get a fight with champion Braddock, but Braddock knew he would make a lot more money by giving the up and coming contender Joe Louis the first crack at the title. Louis, who had been knocked out by Schmeling in 1936, had been considered invincible prior to his loss to Schmeling, and now seemed vulnerable. The two met at Comiskey Park in Chicago on June 22, 1937. To the surprise of almost everyone, Braddock dropped Louis in the first round. Joe got up though and, from that point on, proceeded to give Braddock a Brown Bomber beating, eventually knocking him out cold with a hard right cross.[318] Braddock was out for several minutes, and Joe Louis was now the heavyweight champion of the world.

Joe Louis, 1937–1949

Joe Louis Barrow, born May 13, 1914, is of course, one of the major players in this book. Along with John L. Sullivan, Jack Johnson, Jack Dempsey, Sugar Ray Robinson, Benny Leonard, and Muhammad Ali, Joe Louis, known as the Brown Bomber, had an indelible effect on the sweet science.

Louis was born in a ramshackle shack in Chamber County, Alabama. He weighed eleven pounds at birth. In 1926, shaken by a gang of white men in the Ku Klux Klan, Louis's family moved to Detroit, Michigan, forming part of the post-World War I Great Migration. Joe's brother worked for Ford Motor Company (where

---

317

318

Joe would himself work for a time at the River Rouge Plant and the family settled into a home at 2700 Catherine, now Madison Street in Detroit's Black Bottom neighborhood).[319]

The Great Depression hit the Barrow family hard, but as an alternative to gang activity, Joe began to spend time at a local youth recreation center at 637 Brewster Street in Detroit. His mother attempted to get him interested in playing the violin. A story about the young Louis is that he tried to hide his pugilistic ambitions from his mother by carrying his boxing gloves inside his violin case.[320]

Violin, schmiolin, Joe had a great amateur career winning the Chicago Golden Gloves and National AAU championship. By the time he turned professional, he had compiled an amateur record of 50 wins and 3 losses with 43 knockouts.[321]

On July 7, 1934, Joe Louis made his professional debut scoring a one round knockout over Jack Kracken.[322] His climb up through the heavyweight ranks was spectacular. By 1936, he had accumulated twenty-seven wins and no defeats, including wins over King Levinsky, Lee Ramage, Primo Carnera, and Max Baer.[323]

With the backing of major promotion, Louis fought thirteen times in 1935. The bout that helped put him in the media spotlight occurred on June 25, when Louis knocked out 6-foot-6-inch, 265-pound former world heavyweight champion Primo Carnera in 6 rounds. Foreshadowing the Louis-Schmeling rivalry to come, the Carnera bout featured a political dimension. Louis's victory over Carnera, who symbolized Benito Mussolini's regime in the popular eye, was seen as a victory for the international community, particularly among African Americans, who were sympathetic to Ethiopia, which was attempting to maintain its independence by fending off an invasion by fascist Italy.[324]

Then came his fateful meeting with Max Schmeling. In front of a sellout crowd at Yankee Stadium, Max Schmeling knocked Louis

319
320
321
322
323
324

out in the twelfth round. This was an incredible shock on both sides of the Atlantic. The first few rounds were mostly Schmeling using his jab and an occasional sneak right over Louis's jab. Then in the fourth round a hard right dropped Louis. The fight went on, but now Louis was out of it. He was counted out eight rounds later in the twelfth and much of the world wept. A quote from Langston Hughes, the great writer of the Harlem Renaissance, "*I walked down Seventh Avenue and saw grown men weeping like children, and women sitting in the curbs with their head in their hands. All across the country that night when the news came that Joe was knocked out, people cried.*"[325] Hitler of course trumpeted Schmeling's win as proof of Aryan superiority.

Louis versus Schmeling, 1936

Louis went right back to work. Champion Jim Braddock, possibly thinking that Joe was now mortal after his knockout loss to Max Schmeling, signed to fight him on June 22, 1937. In Braddock's first defense, he had dispatched Welsh boxer Tommy Farr, who had gone the distance with Louis. Joe Louis might have been mortal, but he knocked the Cinderella Man out and became the new and the first African American since Jack Johnson, to claim the title of heavyweight champion of the world.

Joe Louis, now being called the Brown Bomber, was everything Jack Johnson wasn't. Where Johnson was loud, proud, and flashy, Louis was humble, decent, and always a gentleman. Where Johnson was more or less vilified by the white press, Louis became an American hero and icon. His managers saw to it that Joe was never seen photographed with a white woman. He never spoke despairingly of his opponents. They made sure that the Bomber was practically a Boy Scout. Decades later, in an era marked by Black Power, and radical leaders like Malcolm X, Stokely Carmichael, and Eldridge Cleaver, Louis was castigated as an Uncle Tom. Among those who criticized Joe during this era was heavyweight champ Muhammad Ali.

Helping the white press to overcome its reluctance to feature a black contender was the fact that in the mid-1930s boxing desperately needed a marketable hero. Since the retirement of Jack Dempsey in 1929, the sport had devolved into a sordid mixture of poor athletes, gambling, fixed fights, thrown matches, and control of the sport by organized crime. *New York Times* columnist Edward Van Ness wrote, "*Louis…is a boon to boxing. Just as Dempsey led the sport out of the doldrums…so is Louis leading the boxing game out of a slump.*"[326] Likewise, biographer Bill Libby asserted that "*the sports*

326

world was hungry for a great champion when Louis arrived in New York in 1935."[327]

Despite his championship, Louis was haunted by the earlier defeat to Schmeling. Shortly after winning the title, he was quoted as saying, "I don't want to be called champ until I whip Max Schmeling." Louis's promoter Mike Jacobs attempted to arrange a rematch in 1937, but negotiations broke down when Schmeling demanded 30 percent of the gate. When Schmeling instead attempted to arrange for a fight against British Empire champion Tommy Farr, known as the Tonypandy Terror, ostensibly for a world championship to rival the claims of American boxing authorities, Jacobs outmaneuvered him, offering Farr a guaranteed $60,000 to fight Louis instead. The offer was too lucrative for Farr to turn down.[328]

On August 30, 1937, after a postponement of four days due to rain, Louis and Farr finally touched gloves at New York's Yankee Stadium before a crowd of approximately 32,000. Louis fought one of the hardest battles of his life. The bout was closely contested and went the entire 15 rounds, with Louis being unable to knock Farr down. Referee Arthur Donovan was even seen shaking Farr's hand after the bout, in apparent congratulation. Nevertheless, after the score was announced, Louis had won a controversial unanimous decision. *Time* described the scene thus, "*After collecting the judges' votes, referee Arthur Donovan announced that Louis had won the fight on points. The crowd of 50,000…amazed that Farr had not been knocked out or even knocked down, booed the decision.*"[329]

It seems the crowd believed that referee Arthur Donovan had raised Farr's glove in victory. Seven years later, in his published account of the fight, Donovan spoke of the mistake that might have led to this confusion. He wrote the following:

> *As Tommy walked back to his corner after shaking Louis' hand, I followed him and seized his glove.*

327

328

329

"Tommy, a wonderful perform," I began... Then I dropped his hand like a red-hot coal! He had started to raise his arm. He thought I had given him the fight and the world championship! I literally ran away, shaking my head and shouting. "No! No! No!" realizing how I had raised his hopes for a few seconds only to dash them to the ground... That's the last time my emotions will get the better of me in a prize fight! There was much booing at the announced result, but, as I say it, it was all emotional. I gave Tommy two rounds and one even— and both his winning rounds were close."[330]

Speaking over the radio after the fight, Louis admitted that he had been hurt twice.

In preparation for the inevitable rematch with Schmeling, Louis tuned up with bouts against Nathan Mann and Harry Thomas.[331]

Second Schmeling Fight

Along with the Jack Johnson versus Jim Jeffries, Jack Dempsey's second fight with Gene Tunney, and the first fight between Muhammad Ali and Joe Frazier, the second Louis fight with Max Schmeling will always be remembered as one the most important, some would say *the* most important boxing match of all time. It had by now clearly become a bout between Hitler's Aryan superiority and an African American who now found himself in the role of savior of western civilization. The Nazi Party had trumped after the first fight, proof that no African American, or to use the language of the era, no Negro could beat an Aryan. Boxing really mattered!

The stage was set, and the two boxers met at Yankee Stadium in New York City before a crowd of more than seventy thousand people

---

330

331

on June 22, 1938. President Franklin Roosevelt had told Louis, "We need muscles like yours to beat Germany."[332]

The fight lasted two minutes and four seconds. Watch in on YouTube. I have watched this fight since YouTube came into existence. I have seen it at least twenty times. Schmeling throws a total of two punches, one being the right that had vanquished Joe in their first fight. This time, uh-uh. The punch barely lands on Joe's left shoulder, and Louis knocks the German down a few seconds later with a hard right. Schmeling is up almost without a count, and Joe is back on him immediately. He lands a left hook followed by another right, and Max is down again. There is a third knockdown and Schmeling's corner throws in the towel. Ah, YouTube!

Following the dramatic fight, Joe Louis became an instant American icon. His popularity was as great with white Americans as black Americans. Joe Louis, the Brown Bomber, became a symbol of American might. So great was Louis's popularity now that he had what became known as the Bum of the Month Club. In other words, Joe Louis was a fighting champion, and he nearly defended his title if not every month, almost every month, as follows:

- John Henry Lewis, January 25, 1939, KO, 1;
- Two Ton Tony Galento, February 28, 1939, KO, 4 (Galento has Louis down in the third);
- Arturo Godoy, February 9, 1940, split decision;
- Arturo Godoy, June 6, 1940, KO, 8;
- Al McCoy (not the same one as former middleweight champ), June 16, 1940, KO, 6;
- Clarence "Red" Burman, January 31, 1941, KO, 5;
- Gus Dorazio, February 17, 1941, KO, 2;
- Abe Simon, March 21, 1941, TKO, 13;
- Tony Musto, April 8, 1941, TKO, 9;
- Buddy Baer, May 31, 1941, W. DISQ, 7;
[333]

332
333

Despite the disparaging name, most of the boxers listed above were top ten ranked contenders as listed by *The Ring*. The relatively easy pickings came to an end when Louis faced the light heavyweight champion Billy Conn on June 18, 1941, in front of a crowd of 54,487 fans at the Polo Grounds in New York City. The fight turned out to be one of the greatest heavyweight boxing fights of all time.

Conn would not gain weight for the challenge against Louis, saying instead that he would rely on a hit-and-run strategy. Louis's famous response was, *"He can run, but he can't hide."* [334]

I will continue the story of Joe Louis and Billy Conn in the next chapter. Stay tuned!

Light Heavyweights of the Thirties

Maxie Rosenbloom 1932–1934

Ah, Slapsie Maxie Rosenbloom, a former world light heavyweight champion, known to as many people as a radio comic, television actor, and film actor, whose resume includes over sixty motion pictures as a professional boxing champion who had 298 professional fights and is a member of the IBHOF.[335] He got the moniker Slapsie from Damon Runyon for his often open gloved slaps. [336]Rosenbloom was born in Leonard's Bridge, Connecticut, on November 1, 1907. He won the NYAC version of the title August on August 5, 1931, by unanimous decision over Jimmy Slattery and then took the lineal world championship on November 16, 1933, defeating NBA champ Bob Godwin in Madison Square Garden on March 24, 1933, in a unification bout for the world championship.[337] During his championship reign, a little less than two years, he reputedly had 106 bouts, only 8 of which were for the title. Going down the BoxRec list of his fights, there are victories over many top fighters of the thirties. Some of the men he beat include Lee Ramage, King Levinsky, John Henry Lewis, Mickey

---

334

335

336

337

Walker, Leo Lomski, Jimmy Slattery, and Jim Braddock.[338] He might have been Slapsie, but he was also a helluva fighter, even though he lacked knockout power only scoring nineteen knockouts in 298 fights.

He won 223 of those 298 fights and was inducted into the IBHOF in 1993. He died on March 6, 1976, and was interred at Valhalla Memorial Park Cemetery.[339] This was a man who lived life to the fullest. I, for one, am glad he was who he was, Slapsie Maxie Rosenbloom.

Bob Olin, 1934–1935

Lower East Side born and Brooklyn raised, Bob Olin defeated Maxie Rosenbloom at Madison Square Garden before a relatively small Depression Era crowd of 7,400 people. The fight was listless and dull for fifteen rounds. Rosenbloom seemed lackadaisical about the whole thing, and at the end of the boring contest, Bob Olin was the new Light Heavyweight Champion of the World. Apparently it was so bad, some fans thought it was a fix, though it was never proven.[340]

Olin made one successful defense of his title against one Henry Firpo on September 30, 1935, at the Convention Center is Asbury Park, New Jersey, stopping the challenger by knockout in round three.[341]

Bob Olin was outclassed by John Henry Lewis on October 31, 1935, in a fifteen-round unanimous decision at the Arena in St. Louis.[342] Due to the depression and a lack of interest in the light heavyweight class, Olin's manager had a difficult time finding a promoter or an audience for the fight, finally settling on a payment of $15,000 to fight Lewis in St. Louis. The meager audience of 9,219 that showed on fight day could not provide enough in receipts to pay Olin half of what he was promised.[343]

338

339

340

341

342

343

John Henry Lewis, 1935–1935, retired

Lewis was born in Los Angeles in on May 4, 1914, to Mattie Drake Foster and John Edward Lewis. The family settled in Phoenix, Arizona, where he grew up and was taught to box at an early age by his father, a former lightweight who ran a Phoenix gym. Lewis claimed a great-uncle was the noted bare-knuckle brawler Tom Molineaux. Lewis battled in exhibition midget boxing matches at the age of five. Turning professional as a welterweight at fourteen, he gained a reputation for speed and rapidly improving scientific boxing skill. He made steady progress through to professional ranks and in 1935 took the world light heavyweight championship in a fifteen-round decision over Bob Olin. He then lost a dull ten-round decision to Maxie Rosenbloom in a nontitle affair in San Francisco.

He retained the title on March 13, 1936, against Jock McAvoy in Madison Square Garden in a fifteen-round unanimous decision. Though few people know his name today, McAvoy was a first-rate English boxer who won 118 of 132 fights.[344] Not exactly chopped liver.

Bob Godwin fell to Lewis at New York's Madison Square Garden in a technical knockout only 1:27 into the first round on May 29, 1936. Before a tiny crowd of 2,988, Lewis batted Godwin to the mat with a stunning right cross, and after he rose unleashed a flurry of blows that forced the referee to call the fight. Godwin

---

344

had been an NBA light heavyweight champion in 1933.[345] The small crowd testified to the hard times of the Depression. Not many people could afford to go to Madison Square Garden to watch a prize fight, but boxing still mattered.

On July 28, 1938, the New York State Athletic Commission stripped Lewis of his title for failing to accept the challenge filed by Tiger Jack Fox.[346]

On October 28, 1938, he won a fifteen-round National Boxing Association (NBA) world light heavyweight title decision against Al Gainer in New Haven before a crowd of only 2,486, the smallest ever assembled for a title bout in any weight class. The fight was recognized as an NBA light heavyweight title and was sanctioned by the state of Connecticut. Lewis claimed his refusal to fight Tiger Fox, the reason he was stripped of the NYSAC light heavyweight title was an economic necessity, as he knew Fox would not draw a significant audience. Lewis won decisively, but Gainer made a stronger showing in the first twelve rounds, visibly shaking Lewis with a few of his blows. Lewis took the decision, with a strong finish in the last three heats. The local Courant gave Lewis six rounds, Gainer, four, with five even. Gainer's sluggishness in the last three rounds was the result of an illness he suffered the week before the fight. There were no knockdowns in the bout.[347]

On January 25, 1939. he challenged Joe Louis for the heavyweight title. The bout was one-sided as a prime Joe Louis knocked John Henry Lewis down three times in the first round as the fight, and John Henry's heavyweight challenge ended.[348]

He was next scheduled to meet Len Harvey in a rematch but he failed his prefight physical. The reason? He was going blind. He was already blind in his left eye and had impaired vision in his right eye. He retired with an admirable record of 103 wins, 9 losses, and 6 draws with 60 wins by knockout.[349] He died in 1974.

345

346

347

348

349

After John Henry Lewis retired, the NBA light heavyweight crown passed in rapid succession between 1938 and 1939 to Tiger Jack Fox, Melio Bettina, Len Harvey, and Billy Conn.[350] The last named, Billy Conn, will be covered in the next chapter.

Middleweights of the Thirties

After Mickey Walker vacated the middleweight title in 1929 the crown was vacant until Vince Dundee unified the world title on October 30, 1933, beating Lou Brouillard on September 11, 1934. Before Dundee unified the title, it passed between NBA champions and NYSAC champions in the early Thirties. The partial crown went from Gorilla Jones to Marcel Thil to Ben Jeby to Lou Brouillard in the brief span of January 1932 to August 1933.[351] All of these boxers were legitimate good, world-class fighters, but the emphasis of this book is on the men who were champions of the world.

Vince Dundee, 1933–1934

Having unified the middleweight title in a closely fought battle with Brouillard, he next set about defending his crown. Vince Dundee defended his world middleweight title on December 8, 1933, against southpaw Andy Callahan, winning in a fifteen-round split decision before eleven thousand two hundred in Boston. Dundee dominated the last five rounds, though Callahan frequently tried to force the fighting which was particularly close in the first ten rounds. The *Boston Globe* gave Dundee nine rounds with only the first, seventh, eighth, and ninth to Callahan.[352]

Before a crowd of eight thousand, Dundee mounted his second successful defense of the world middleweight title against Al Diamond on May 3, 1934, in Patterson, New Jersey, winning in a fifteen-round points decision.

350

351

352

Dundee lost his claim to the middleweight crown when he was outpointed by Teddy Yarosz in a fifteen-round decision on September 11, 1934, before a crowd of twenty-eight thousand at Forbes Field in Pittsburgh. The bout was close but somewhat dull due to too much wrestling and clinching, though Yarosz seemed to hold the lead in all but the late rounds when he looked visibly exhausted. Yarosz was awarded eight rounds to Dundee's four, with three even. He scored well with long range blows to the head of Dundee, who seemed to focus more on Yarosz's midsection. Dundee was down three times during the bout, once falling out of the ropes in round three.[353]

Dundee retired with a record of 118 wins (28 knockouts), 20 losses and 13 draws.[354]

Teddy Yarosz, 1934–1935

Teddy Yarosz was born Pittsburg on June 24, 1010. His family moved to Pennsylvania when he was ten. He won the world middleweight championship from Vince Dundee on September 11, 1934, by a close decision over Vince Dundee and held the title until September 19, 1935, when he lost the title to Eddie "Babe" Risko. In his career, he defeated Archie Moore, Billy Conn, Lloyd Marshall, Pete Latzo, Solly Krieger, and Lou Brouillard.[355]

Yarosz lost the both the NBA and NYSAC middleweight title to Eddie Babe Risko, who defeated him on September 19, 1935, in Pittsburgh in fifteen rounds before a crowd of twenty-five thousand. Risko knocked Yarosz to the mat twice for counts of nine in the sixth and seventh rounds, and several judges gave Yarosz only the first round.[356] Yarosz made his best showing in the eighth but did not appear to win any other round on points. In the ninth, Yarosz was

353
354
355
356

stunned by a blow beneath his heart which caused him to clinch, and after the third had received frequent pounding to his midsection.[357]

Teddy Yarosz died on March 29, 1974. He was inducted into the IBHOF in 2006.[358]

Eddie "Babe" Risko, 1935–1936

Risko was born Henry Pylkowski on July 14, 1911, in Syracuse, New York, the son of a struggling Lithuanian family of five. He attended school in Syracuse. He had a long and impressive amateur boxing career in the United States Navy, which he joined at only 16 in 1927, and fought around 125 matches as Sailor Puleski. Risko won the Navy Middleweight Title in a Panama Bullring in 1931 and was undefeated in his fights with the Navy.[359] From personal experience I know that some military boxers are world-class amateurs and some are career servicemen who are literally professional boxers.

Risko won the unified world middleweight championship with a win over Teddy Yarosz on September 19, 1935. Risko knocked Yarosz to the mat twice for counts of nine in the sixth and seventh rounds, and several judges gave Yarosz only the first round.

Risko lost the belt on July 11, 1936, to Freddie Steele via a 15-round unanimous decision in Seattle, Washington, before an impressive crowd of 25,000. Steele scored the only knockdown in the bout when he put Risko to the mat with a right to the jaw for a count of 6 in the first round. Steele damaged both of Risko's eyes during the bout, which hampered the reigning champions ability to defend himself. The Associated Press gave Risko only 3 rounds of the well-attended bout. He died in his sleep at age 46 on March 7, 1957.[360]

357

358

359

360

Freddie Steele, 1936-1938

Steele was born on December 18, 1912, in Seattle, Washington, to Virgie and Charles E. Steele. As a youth, he played baseball, but in high school in Tacoma participated in basketball, soccer, football, golf, and swimming.[361]

He won the world middleweight championship from Eddie "Babe" Risko by unanimous decision on July 11, 1936, at Seattle's Civic Arena. Steele was a boxer-puncher who in his career beat top-notchers Joe Glick, Bucky Lawless, Baby Joe Gans, Vince Dundee, Babe Risko, Gus Lesnevich, Ken Overlin, and Solly Krieger.[362]

Steele made the first defense of his crown against perennial contender and one-time title claimant Gorilla Jones in Wisconsin. Steele had Jones down in round seven and won all but one round.[363]

He next defended in a fifteen-round rematch against Babe Risko. In a tedious decision in New York's Madison Square Garden, Steele won the unanimous decision to retain his crown before a Garden crowd of eleven thousand six hundred.[364]

Back home in Seattle, Steele won a third-round knockout over Frank Battaglia. He had Battaglia on the deck in all three rounds. A

361

362

363

364

stunning left hook in round three put the challenger down for the count.[365]

He lost the middleweight crown to Al Hostak in his next to last fight, in a first-round knockout of a scheduled fifteen-round contest at the Seattle Civic Arena on July 26, 1938. After two light taps from Steele in the first round, Hostak floored his opponent briefly for the first time, and again shortly after for a count of five. Celebrity referee Jack Dempsey stopped the fight after Steele arose after his third trip to the canvas before a record Seattle crowd of thirty-five thousand. After the third knockdown, Dempsey sent Hostak to a neutral corner and reached a count of seven before stopping the fight after Hostak tried to resume the fight.[366]

Steele's career had declined after the death of his manager, Dave Miller in 1938 after surgery. Steele lost his next and last fight to Jimmy Casino in 1941. His final record included one hundred twenty-five wins (sixty KOs), five losses, eleven draws, and one no contest.[367]

After his boxing career had ended, Freddie Steele worked in the film industry in Hollywood appearing in several motion pictures. Later on, he returned to Washington State, where he owned and operated Freddie Steele's Restaurant in Westport on the Washington Coast. He died in a nursing home in Aberdeen, Washington, on August 22, 1984. He was inducted in the IBHOF in 1996.[368]

Al Hostak, 1938–1940

Hostak was born in Minneapolis, Minnesota, to Slovak immigrants who eventually moved to Seattle, Washington, when Hostak was two, settling in South Seattle's Georgetown District. A stutterer in his youth, Hostak was drawn to boxing after fighting several of his tormentors. He would begin his boxing career as a sixteen-year-old in 1932, fighting many of his bouts in nearby White Center. Hostak

---

[365]

[366]

[367]

[368]

would go unbeaten for his first twenty-seven bouts in the Seattle area, all four and six-rounders, before losing a decision to Jimmy Best. He would continue to fight preliminary matches through the end of 1936, while he worked as a sparring partner for 1936 middleweight title holder Freddie Steele of Tacoma, Washington.[369]

Steele met his former sparring partner on July 26, 1938, at the Seattle Civic Center. Hostak dropped Steele three times in the first and became the new NBA Middleweight Champion.[370]

Hostak made his first title defense against Brooklyn's Solly Krieger on November 1, 1938, losing a fifteen-round decision before a crowd of ten thousand, in Seattle. Hostak broke both of his hands early in the bout. Krieger fought inside against Hostak, pounding his body. In the fourteenth round, Krieger sealed a majority decision victory, when he knocked down a tired Hostak for the first time in his career. With terrific body blows, and savage and effective infighting, Krieger wrested the championship from Hostak. Krieger employed a successful bob and weave strategy, which puzzled Hostak, and which he could not successfully defend, particularly in later rounds.[371] This man fought a world championship fight with two broken hands!

Fighting in Seattle again, before a crowd of twenty-two thousand Hostak KO'd Krieger in the fourth round on June 27, 1939. This win made Hostak the first to regain the middleweight title since Stanley Ketchel way back in 1908. [372]

Tony Zale was on the rise on July 19, 1940, when he defeated Hostak for the NBA and lineal crown. I should note here, that previous champions Vince Dundee, Teddy Yarosz, Eddie "Babe" Risko, Freddie Steele, and Al Hostak were all recognized by the National Boxing Association and the New York State Athletic Commission, the only two sanctioning bodies during that era. They were not, however, recognized by *The Ring* magazine and are excluded from some lineal lists. However, they were the generally recognized world champions by almost everyone who followed boxing during the nineteen

369
370
371
372

thirties. These excellent pugilists *were* the lineal link between Mickey Walker and Tony Zale.

Welterweights of the Thirties

As the decade of the nineteen thirties began, Tommy Freeman held the world welterweight championship. He didn't hold it for long after winning it from Jack Thompson in September of 1930.[373] On April 14, 1931, he lost it back to Jack Thompson. This established a pattern in the welterweight division for the next several years, and the title changed hands with regularity every few months. Thompson's second reign lasted just a little over six months when he was beaten on October 23, 1931, by Canadian Lou Brouillard in a decision after knocking Thompson down four times.[374] He lost the title a few months later to Jackie Fields who lost to Young Corbett III. Now, Fields wasn't exactly chopped liver. He beat Mickey Walker and Jimmy McLarnin, no small feat. Both are in the hall of fame.

Young Corbett III, 1933

Before a crowd of sixteen thousand on February 22, 1933, Corbett captured the welterweight championship of the world by decisioning Jackie Fields over ten rounds at San Francisco's Seals Stadium. He competed with a broken hand received from a sparring session three days before the fight and hurt his left thumb in the fifth round but continued to fight undaunted.[375] Young Corbett held the title only three months, before losing it to hall of famer and one of the greatest boxers of all time, Jimmy McLarnin, who knocked out Young Corbett III in only two minutes and thirty-seven seconds. He then went on to fight an epic three fight series with the great Jewish boxer and another hall of famer Barney Ross

373

374

375

between May 29, 1933 and May 28, 1938, with both men winning the title twice.[376]

Jimmy McLarnin, 1933–1934

Jimmy McLarnin could hang with any welterweight in history and beat almost all of them, including moderns like Pernell Whittaker, Floyd Mayweather Jr., and Manny Pacquiao. McLarnin was that good. Well, maybe. Whittaker, Mayweather Jr., and PacMan could hang with anyone in history too. But McLarnin was on the same level. In his day, McLarnin met and defeated luminaries such as Lou Ambers, Tony Canzoneri, Barney Ross, Benny Leonard, Billy Petrolle, Al Singer, Jack Thompson, Sammy Mandell, and Ruby Goldstein.

McLarnin was prodigious athlete. His main sports were football, baseball, and boxing and was considered a model of propriety by Rev. A. E. Roberts at the Methodist mission in Vancouver. He took up boxing at the age of ten after getting into a fight defending his newspaper-selling pitch. Former professional boxer Charles "Pop" Foster recognized McLarnin's talent at the age of thirteen. He constructed a makeshift gym for McLarnin to train in, sure that he would one day be the champion of the world. The two of them

---

376

would remain close, and when Foster died, he left everything he had to McLarnin.[377]

He lost and regained and lost again to another great, Barney Ross. What a great rivalry!

McLarnin retired in November 1936 still at the top of his game, having won his last two fights against all-time greats Tony Canzoneri and Lou Ambers. His record was 54 wins, 11 losses, and 3 draws in 68 contests. In 1996, *Ring* magazine voted McLarnin the fifth greatest welterweight of all time. On October 28, 2004, Jimmy "Baby Faced" McLarnin passed away in Richland, Washington.[378]

Barney Ross, 1934, 1935, 1938

Barney Ross (born December 23, 1909–January 17, 1967) became a world champion in three weight divisions and was a decorated veteran of World War II.[379]

Two years after Ross was born, his family moved to Chicago's Maxwell Street ghetto, where they opened a small grocery. Misfortune soon struck the family, however. By the time Ross was age fourteen, his father had been murdered by gangsters, his mother had suffered a nervous breakdown, and his younger siblings had been placed in

---

377

378

379

an orphanage. Ross dropped out of school and became a petty thief, an errand boy for mobster Al Capone, a street fighter, and eventually an amateur boxer. After winning a Golden Gloves amateur championship in 1929, Ross began his professional boxing career. He won a ten-round decision over American Tony Canzoneri on June 23, 1933, to gain simultaneously the world lightweight and junior welterweight (also known as super lightweight) titles. On September 18, 1933, Ross won a fifteen-round decision in a rematch with Canzoneri for both titles. Following three more successful defenses of his junior welterweight title, Ross moved up to the welterweight division and won the world championship by decision over Irish-born Canadian Jimmy McLarnin in fifteen rounds on May 28, 1934, but he lost the title back to McLarnin in a fifteen-round decision on September 17, 1934. Following three more successful defenses of his junior welterweight title, Ross relinquished it in order to fight McLarnin again for the welterweight title, which he won with a fifteen-round decision on May 28, 1935. This was an epic three bout series between two of the greatest welterweights in history. Ross defended it by winning fifteen-round decisions over American Izzy Jannazzo on November 27, 1936, and Filipino Ceferino Garcia on September 23, 1937. Ross lost the title in a fifteen-round decision to the reigning featherweight (one hundred twenty-six pounds) champion, Henry Armstrong of the United States, on May 31, 1938. It was the final fight in an eighty-one-bout professional career in which Ross compiled a record of 72 wins (22 by knockouts), 4 losses (all by decision), 3 draws, and 2 no decisions.[380]

Ross retired after losing to Armstrong and after the Japanese invasion Pearl Harbor he enlisted in the Marine Corp. Despite his celebrity, where he could have been an ambassador boxer, he chose to go into battle as an infantryman. He was awarded a Silver Star for "conspicuous gallantry and intrepidity in action" for his heroics at the Battle of Guadalcanal (August 1942–February 1943), where he was wounded. His autobiography, *No Man Stands Alone: The True Story of Barney Ross* (1957), includes a chapter on his struggles with

380

an addiction to morphine that began during his medical treatment on Guadalcanal. His life is depicted in the motion picture *Monkey on My Back* (1957).[381]

Ross was one of the greatest Jewish fighters of the 1930s, a period in which Jews were at the forefront of the boxing world. His battles with the Italian American Canzoneri and the Irish Canadian McLarnin revitalized public interest in the sport. Ross was inducted into the International Boxing Hall of Fame in 1990. I was thrilled when as a member of an army boxing team in 1965, Ross paid us a visit, posed for photos, visited with all of us, and showed films of some of his most memorable fights. Watching him in action against archrival Jimmy McLarnin, I have to say this guy could really fight!

Henry Armstrong, 1938–1941

When I really started learning about boxing history in the early Sixties, the fact of Henry Armstrong holding three undisputed world titles simultaneously made him seem kind of like a Superman.

He was born Henry Jackson Jr. on December 12, 1912, in Columbus, Mississippi. He was the son of Henry Jackson Sr., a share-cropper of African American, Irish, and Native American descent, and America Jackson, said to be a full-blooded Iroquois. By the twentieth century, many of their members also had European American heritage. As a child, Henry Jr. moved with his family to St. Louis, Missouri, during the early period of the Great Migration of African Americans from the rural South to industrial cities of the Midwest and North. There he became involved in boxing. He graduated as an honor student from Vashon High School in St. Louis. Later he took the surname Armstrong as his fighting name.[382]

Armstrong began his professional career on July 28, 1931, in a fight with Al Iovino, in which Armstrong was knocked out in three rounds. His first win came later that year, beating Sammy Burns by a decision in six. In 1932, Armstrong moved to Los Angeles, where

---

381

382

he lost two four-round decisions in a row to Eddie Trujillo and Al Greenfield. Following these two losses, however, he started a streak of eleven wins.[383]

In 1936, Armstrong split his time among Los Angeles, Mexico City, and St. Louis. A few notable opponents of that year include Ritchie Fontaine, Baby Arizmendi, former world champion Juan Zurita, and Mike Belloise. Early in his career, he fought some fights under the ring name Melody Jackson.[384]

In 1937, Armstrong won his first twenty-two bouts. He beat Casanova in three rounds, Belloise in four, Joe Rivers in three, former world champion Frankie Klick in four, and former world champion Benny Bass in four. Armstrong was given his first world title fight in the one-hundred-twenty-six-pound weight class against world featherweight champion Petey Sarron at Madison Square Garden. Armstrong knocked Sarron out in six rounds, becoming the World Featherweight Champion.[385]

Armstrong's two nicknames were Hurricane Henry and Homicide Hank.

In 1938, Armstrong started his season with seven more knock-outs in a row, including one over Chalky Wright, a future world champion. The streak finally ended when Arizmendi lasted ten rounds before losing a decision to Armstrong in their fourth fight. Armstrong's streak of twenty-seven knockout wins in a row qualifies as one of the longest knockout win streaks in the history of boxing, according to *The Ring* magazine.[386]

Being Henry Armstrong, a.k.a. Homicide Hank, he decided in 1938 to go up in weight and challenge for another title. The next weight up was the lightweight division. Well, Armstrong leap-frogged that division and challenged the great Barney Ross for the welterweight title. In other words, he went from the featherweight division, which tops out at 126 pounds, to the welterweight division, which tops out at 147 pounds. Quite an amazing challenge, really.

383

384

385

386

Armstrong, at 133 1/2 pounds, beat Ross, at 142 pounds, by unanimous decision, adding the World Welterweight Championship to his belt.[387] Barney Ross, like so many pugilists, went to the square jungle one too many times. Ross took tremendous punishment from Armstrong and somehow stayed on his feet for the entire fifteen rounds. It was a courageous performance by the Jewish champion. Armstrong lost weight in order to compete in the lower weight division, and beat World Lightweight Champion Lou Ambers by split decision. Each of these titles that Armstrong won were undisputed World Championships. He lost the welterweight title to Fritzie Zivic on October 4, 1940.

Armstrong's eighteen successful title defenses were the most in history in the welterweight division.

In 1945, Armstrong retired from boxing. His official record was 152 wins, 21 losses, and 9 draws, with 101 knockout wins.[388]

- In 1954, Armstrong was inducted into *The Ring* magazine Boxing Hall of Fame the year it was established.
- In 1987, he was among those inductees from the *Ring*'s list who were absorbed into the International Boxing Hall of Fame when it was established.[389]
- *The Ring magazine* ranked Armstrong as the second greatest fighter of the past eighty years.

387

388

389

CHAPTER VIII

Hard Times Part II

Lightweights of the Nineteen Thirties

Tony Canzoneri, 1930–1933

Turning our attention now to the smaller divisions, we begin with the lightweight division, which tops out at 135 pounds. Tony Canzoneri was the first lightweight champion of the decade of the Nineteen Thirties. As covered previously, he was already the World Featherweight Champion when he challenged Al Singer for the lightweight crown. On November 14, 1930, he knocked Singer out in one round at New York's Madison Square Garden.

On April 24, 1931, he knocked out Jack "Kid" Berg in three rounds to take the light welterweight title, making him a three division champion. On September 10, 1931, Canzoneri again defeated Berg in a rematch at the Polo Grounds in New York.[390] He successfully defended the lightweight title against Billy Petrolle, known as the Fargo Express, on November 4, 1932, in Madison Square Garden, reversing a previous loss to Petrolle two years earlier. Petrolle is considered by many experts to be one of the greatest boxers to never win a world title.[391]

390

391

Fighting against the great Jewish boxer Barney Ross in Ross's hometown at Chicago Stadium, Canzoneri, dropped a majority decision and the world lightweight championship. Three months later, in the Polo Grounds, Ross bested him again on a split decision. Upon a tournament to crown a new lightweight champ after Ross moved up to welterweight, Canzoneri got a second chance to be a champion.

On May 10, 1935, Tony Canzoneri beat Lou Ambers to regain the lightweight championship. He held the title for one successful defensed and then lost the rematch to Ambers on September 3, 1936.[392] He later lost to Ambers again and never again contended for a world title. He retired in 1939. Canzoneri had a record of 137 wins, 24 losses, 10 draws, and 3 no decisions (newspaper Decisions, 4-0-0). He is a member of the International Boxing Hall of Fame.[393]

Barney Ross, 1933, vacated

Ross was thoroughly covered in chapter six. He was a great lightweight before he became a welterweight and deserves more mention for his accomplishments in this chapter. I am talking about a truly great boxer here. Well, Barney Ross was a great lightweight champion. Soon after winning the title on June 23, 1933, by decision from Tony Canzoneri, he defended his title against a solid contender, Johnny Farr, and won by TKO in six. Next was a rematch with Canzoneri at the Polo Grounds in New York, and Ross won again by a close decision. Following this win, he moved up in weight to achieve his greatest fame as Welterweight Champion of the World.

Upon Ross's move up to welterweight, Canzoneri and Lou Ambers were matched for the vacant lightweight crown. On May 10, 1935, at a contest, Canzoneri won the world lightweight title by outpointing Ambers over fifteen rounds.[394] After successfully defending his lightweight title once, he lost it again in a rematch with Ambers by a fifteen-round decision. There was a rubber match between the

392

393

394

two and Ambers once again won a decision in fifteen rounds and claimed the lightweight championship of the world.[395]

Lou Ambers, 1936–1938

Managed by Al Weill and trained by Charley Goldman (the same team who later managed and trained Rocky Marciano) the Herkimer Hurricane, began his career losing only once in more than three years. He faced his greatest competitor, future hall of fame lightweight champion Tony Canzoneri, on May 10, 1935. Canzoneri defeated him over fifteen rounds on a decision in Madison Square Garden, robbing Ambers in his first shot at the title. Canzoneri had Ambers down twice in round 3. A faithful crowd of 17,433 cheered as Canzoneri easily retook the title, knocking Ambers down again shortly before the closing bell.[396]

World champion boxers do not discourage easily. They are not busboys or bellhops or schoolteachers or truck drivers. Those are all honorable professions. I am not disparaging any of them because I have been all of them except a schoolteacher. But they are not world champions. Lou Ambers did not give up. He won his next fifteen fights, including a very difficult win over Fritzie Zivic on July 1, 1935, in Pennsylvania, where Zivic broke his jaw in the ninth round.[397] Ambers stuck and took the decision. The guy had moxie.

Ambers got his due in a rematch with Canzoneri on September 3, 1936. He had been a sparring partner of Canzoneri, and he had learned how to fight him and potentially beat him. In a close, hard-fought battle, Ambers took the decision and was the new Lightweight Champion of the World.[398]

On August 17, 1938, Ambers met Henry Armstrong in an historic fight for the world lightweight title. Armstrong was attempting to become the first fighter in history to win and hold three world titles simultaneously. In a great fight, Ambers was knocked down

---

395

396

397

398

twice, in the fifth and sixth rounds, and appeared badly beaten. Ambers mounted a great comeback in the latter half of the match, but lost the controversial split decision. Armstrong was penalized three rounds in the close bout for fouls. Ambers lost the title for a year, until regaining it in a rematch one year later.[399]

Ambers's rematch with Henry Armstrong was as controversial as their first bout. Armstrong was penalized for low blows, which enabled Ambers to capture the fifteen-round decision on August 22, 1939, before a crowd estimated at thirty thousand. Penalized for low blows in the second, fifth, seventh, ninth, and eleventh rounds, Armstrong would have probably won the fight had it not been for his loss of points for fouls. James Dawson of the *New York Times* wrote, "*The title was not won on competition alone but on fighting rules and ethics… Armstrong was the victim of an injustice.*" Demonstrating the closeness of the fight before accounting for Armstrong's fouls, the *United Press* scored the fight seven rounds for Ambers, with six for Armstrong, and two even. Unlike their first meeting, Ambers remained on his feet throughout the bout, except for a single slip in one round. He used infighting consistently in the match, cutting and bruising Armstrong's face. Many boxing reporters considered the match Ambers's last great performance.[400]

On May 10, 1940, Ambers defended his title against the wild, free-swinging Lew Jenkins. Jenkins scored an upset when he knocked out the defending champion in the third round at Madison Square Garden. Ambers was down for a count of five in the first and briefly in the second. He had to arise from another fall to the canvas at least once prior to the referee stopping the bout 1:29 into the third. [401]

Ambers sought a rematch, and after a tune up win over Al "Bummy" Davis, he again faced Jenkins. This time he suffered a technical knockout from Jenkins in the seventh round before fifteen thousand on February 28, 1941, at Madison Square Garden. After a slow start, Ambers appeared game, taking tough blows from Jenkins

---

399

400

401

in the third through the sixth, while still using his left effectively at times. But in the seventh, Ambers was floored three times before the referee put an end to the fight, 2:26 into the seventh. [402]

After his retirement from boxing, Ambers served in the Coast Guard in WWII. He later operated a restaurant and worked in public relations. He died on April 25, 1995, in Phoenix, Arizona, and was interred at the Saint Francis Cemetery in Phoenix. He and his wife, Margaret Mary, had a daughter and two sons.[403]

Lew Jenkins, 1940–1941

Lew Jenkins (December 4, 1916–October 30, 1981) was an American boxer and Lightweight Champion of the World. He was born in Milburn, Texas, and was raised during the Great Depression. He began fighting in carnivals and later continued his boxing in the US Coast Guard. He was an exceptionally powerful puncher, and fifty-one of his seventy-three wins were by knockout. His managers included Benny Woodhall, Frank Bachman, Hymie Kaplan, and Willie Ketchum, and his trainer was Charley Rose.[404]

His punching power was legendary, and so were his drinking, carousing, and penchant for high-speed motorcycles. "The two toughest opponents I had were Jack Daniels and Harley Davidson," Lew Jenkins stated.[405]

Jenkins took the world lightweight championship on May 10, 1940, in a third-round TKO against Lou Ambers at New York's Madison Square Garden.[406]

Ambers was down for a count of five in the first, briefly down again from a left in the second, and was down in the third before the referee stopped the bout when Jenkins landed a final solid right to Ambers's jaw.[407]

402
403
404
405
406
407

The new champ defended his crown successfully against Tippy Larkin at Madison Square Garden in New York on March 8, 1940, knocking Larkin out in the first round. Next, again at the Garden, on November 2, 1940, he scored a second round knockout over Pete Lello.[408] Jenkins's career will be taken up again in the next chapter.

Featherweights of the Nineteen Thirties

Battling Battalino, 1929–1932

As the decade of the Nineteen Thirties rolled in, Bat Battalino was rolling over feather and lightweight opponents. He had taken the title on September 23, 1929, from Frenchman Andre Routis. In the meantime he had beaten Kid Chocolate, Bushy Graham, Fidel La Barba, and Freddie Miller. On September 15, 1931, Battalino defeated Al Singer by second round knockout in Madison Square Garden.

On January 27, 1932, Battalino once again defended the title against Freddie Miller, whom he had beaten on July 23, 1931, in Cincinnati, Ohio. The champion came in three pounds overweight and did not put up a good fight. Battalino went down in the third round from what the referee considered a harmless right to the

---

408

chin. When Battalino arose, Miller put him down again. The referee stopped the fight and declared Miller the winner. The National Boxing Association and the New York State Athletic Commission, however, overruled the referee and declared the bout a no contest. Having declared the bout a no contest, the title become vacant, as Battalino did not make the featherweight limit. To end any confusion about his championship status, Battalino voluntarily relinquished the title in March and moved up a weight class to fight at the lightweight limit.[409]

Freddie Miller, 1933–1936

Freddie Miller (April 3, 1911–May 8, 1962) was a prolific American boxer from Cincinnati, Ohio, who won over two hundred fights, and held the NBA world featherweight championship from 1933 to 1936. He was named in *Ring* magazine's list of the 80 Best Fighters of the Last 80 Years.[410]

On January 13, 1933, Miller fought Tommy Paul for the fourth time. Miller defeated Paul in a ten-round unanimous decision at Chicago Stadium, taking the National Boxing Association World featherweight title. In an exceptionally long reign as champion, Miller fought thirteen times in the next three years before finally losing the title to Petey Sarron on March 2, 1936. Miller successfully defended his title 12 times. He defeated Baby Arizmendi, Abie Israel in a rematch, Jackie Sharkey, Paul Dazzo, Nel Tarleton, Jose Girones, Nel Tarleton a second time, Vernon Cormier, Johnny Pena, Gene Espinosa, and Petey Sarron.[411]

On January 28, 1933, in Los Angeles, California, Miller successfully defended his NBA title against Baby Arizmendi and picked up world title recognition in California to add to his NBA title. He quickly followed that with another defense of his two titles with a win over Filipino Speedy Dado by decision. A fighting champion,

---

409

410

411

he next took on Abie Israel in Seattle, then Jackie Sharkey (not the heavyweight) in Cincinnati, winning by decision, and Paul Dazo, whom he knocked out in the fourth round.[412]

Following these defenses, he embarked on a European tour, boxing in England, Scotland, Wales, Spain, France, Belgium, and Ireland. In Paris, he decisioned reigning World Bantamweight Champion and future Hall of Fame Inductee, Panama Al Brown on Christmas Eve 1934.[413]

Upon returning to the United States, he defeated Johnny Pena and Petey Sarron. On May 11, 1936, he finally lost to Sarron for the NBA world featherweight title in a fifteen-round mixed decision at Griffith Stadium in Washington, DC. One judge ruled the bout a draw, but the other judge and referee ruled for Miller. It was Sarron's twelfth title fight since taking the partial title in January 1933 from Tommy Paul. He continued boxing until 1940, when he retired after losing eleven of his last fifteen fights. He died on May 8, 1962. He was inducted into the IBHOF in 1997.[414]

Petey Sarron, 1936–1937

Today, if anyone remembers Petey Sarron at all, they know that he was the guy whom Henry Armstrong beat for the world featherweight title. That may be a shame, but it is the destiny of many a pugilist who becomes an opponent to a legendary boxer. Well, Petey Sarron had a career of his own that is worth a few paragraphs of this book.

Pete Sarron was born in Birmingham, Alabama, on November 21, 1906. Sarron's parents immigrated to Alabama from Lebanon. Like many boxers of his era, he made early living selling newspapers, beginning at age six.[415] As a youth in life, he found Dave Evans at the Birmingham Boy's Club who mentored him in boxing, and helped manage his career. He would return the favor and support the club

---

412

413

414

415

after becoming a successful boxer. After high school, he had ambitions to study law and become an attorney.[416]

On May 11, 1936, Sarron first took the National Boxing Association World Featherweight championship from Freddie Miller in a fifteen round points decision at Griffith Stadium, an American League ball park, in Washington, D. C. Before an impressive crowd of twenty-three thousand, Sarron swarmed over Miller, came up with an early lead in points, and nearly scored knockouts in the thirteen and fifteenth rounds. Sarron had previously lost to Miller three times. The new champion bobbed and weaved expertly, sometimes ducking close to the floor to avoid the blows of Miller, who seemed to have an advantage in the first four rounds. In the ninth through fifteenth, Sarron showed his strongest advantage. Sarron collected the relatively modest sum of $10,000 for his win.[417]

He successfully defended the NBA featherweight title on two occasions. First he defeated Cuban boxer Baby Manuel in Texas on July 22, 1936, by a unanimous decision. Following that win, he defended and beat Freddie Miller a second time on a split decision on September 4, 1937, in Johannesburg, South Africa.[418]

On October 29, 1937, fate and Henry Armstrong came knocking on his door. In a fight at Madison Square Garden, Sarron fought courageously, but was knocked out from a left hook by Armstrong in round 6.

Peter Sarron retired on July 17, 1939. He died in Miami on July 3, 1994, and was posthumously inducted in the IBHOF in 2016. [419]

Henry Armstrong, 1937–1938

Homicide Hank went on a tear between winning the feather title from Sarron and the welter title from Barney Ross. According to my best source, boxrec.com, he fought fourteen times, scoring thirteen knockouts. Presumably many or all of these were championship

416

417

418

419

fights. The only boxer who took him to the limit during this stretch was Baby Arizmendi, the tough Mexican NYAC world titlist who went ten rounds in a losing effort against Armstrong at Wrigley Field in Los Angeles in a unification bout for the World Featherweight Championship. This important bout, which ended Armstrong's streak of twenty-seven straight knockouts, took place on August 4, 1936.[420] Henry Armstrong was one baaaad man!

Joey Archibald, 1939–1940

Archibald was born on February 20, 1914, in Providence, Rhode Island. He attended Providence College before his boxing career took off and once studied for the priesthood.

Archibald won the NYSAC version of the then vacant world featherweight championship when he defeated Mike Belloise, former NYSE featherweight champion, in a fifteen-round points decision at New York's lost boxing shrine, St. Nicholas Arena, on October 17, 1938.[421]

He gained universal recognition and the NBA world featherweight championship when he defeated Leo Rodak before a crowd of 5,500 on April 18, 1939, in a fifteen-round points decision at Rhode Island Auditorium in Providence. Rodak was considered the top contender for the NYSAC world featherweight title. Archibald was the aggressor throughout his bout with Rodak and landed the most punches in the opinion of the referee who scored for him. The Associated Press gave seven rounds to Archibald, with six for Rodak, and two even. Both fighters committed fouls in the eleventh, a round declared even by the referee as was the closely fought seventh. In the thirteenth and fourteenth, with the bout close but Archibald leading by a shade, Rodak broke loose and gained the advantage with long and wary rights. The fifteenth clearly went to Archibald. After

420
421

the fight, Rodak's manager complained of frequent low blows by Archibald.[422]

In April of 1939, the NBA withdrew recognition of the title he had fought hard to win because he did not choose to fight their chosen contender Petey Scalzo. This action has been a continuing problem in boxing that has been the primary cause of the diminished importance of boxing in the contemporary world.

Archibald lost the NYSAC and Baltimore version of the world featherweight title to Harry Jeffra on May 20, 1940, in a fifteen-round unanimous decision at the Coliseum in Baltimore. Jeffra was knocked to the canvas three times in the second round, twice for a count of nine. Archibald landed his blows in earnest in the eighth and ninth rounds with lefts to the body but was far too behind on points to pull ahead. The Associated Press gave Jeffra seven rounds; Archibald, three; with five even.[423]

Bantamweights of the Nineteen Thirties

Panama Al Brown, 1929–1935

Panama Al Brown, Bantamweight Champion of the World from June 18, 1929, until he was unjustly stripped of his crown by the NBA on April 16, 1934, was a freak of nature.

Standing just under 6 feet and weighing in at 118 pounds, Brown possessed both a height and reach advantage over most of his opponents. But he was much more than that and is today regarded as one of the greatest bantamweights in boxing history.

Brown won the NYSAC and lineal bantamweight titles in 1929 after defeating Gregorio Vidal. In 1930, he won both the NBA and IBU bantamweight titles, after defeating Johnny Erickson.[424], [425]

422

423

424

425

As an Afro-Panamanian in the US, Brown faced racial barriers throughout his boxing career, and had been stripped of the NYSAC and NBA titles by 1934. He held the IBU title until 1935, when he lost it to Baltasar Sangchili.[426]

On June 1, 1935, Brown lost the title to Baltasar Sangchili by a fifteen-round decision, at the Plaza de Toros, in Valencia, Spain.[427] After the loss, he chose to retire from boxing, instead performing in a cabaret. Suffering from the prolonged effects of drug use, he was persuaded by Jean Cocteau to detox, receiving treatment at the Sainte-Anne Asylum, and begin training for a comeback to boxing. His first fight was against former French bantamweight champion Andre Regis, at the Salle Wagram, Paris, on September 21, 1937, with Brown achieving a first-round knockout.[428] He had a rematch with Sangchili on March 4, 1938, avenging his earlier loss with a fifteen-round decision to win the vacant IBU bantamweight title, but by this time the International Boxing Union was no longer recognized in the United States. His rematch win over Sangchili is believed to be his last great night, and bowing to manager Cocteau's wishes, Brown vowed to retire after one more fight. That came in 1939 against Valentin Angelmann in Paris. Brown stopped him in eight rounds.

426

427

428

With the advent of the Second World War, Brown moved to the United States, settled in Harlem, and tried to find work of the cabaret sort he performed in Paris 39 when not fighting. There was none, and before long he was fighting again, but not well.

Brown went on fighting until 1942, challenging unsuccessfully for the Panamanian featherweight title on September 30, 1942, when he drew with Leocadio Torres, but retiring as a winner, defeating Kid Fortune by a decision in ten rounds on December 4 of the same year.

Not long after, he was arrested for using cocaine and deported for a year. He went back to New York afterward and, in his late forties, took a lot of beatings while serving as a sparring partner for up-and-comers at a gym in Harlem, making a dollar a round.

Brown died penniless of tuberculosis in New York City in 1951. He had fainted on Forty-Second Street. The police thought he was drunk and took him to the station. Eventually he was transferred to Sea View Hospital. He died there on April 11 unaware that not long before, one of the newspapers in Paris had begun talks about organizing a fund drive to pay for his trip home.

During five years of investigation, Spanish painter Eduardo Arroyo wrote a biography of Panama Al Brown, titled *Panama Al Brown, 1902–1951*, first published by Edition Jean-Claude Lattès, Paris, in 1982.[429]

Panama Al Brown's final record is believed to have been 123 wins, 18 defeats, and 10 draws, with 55 knockouts, placing him in the exclusive list of boxers who have won 50 or more wins by knockout. He was the recognized bantamweight world champion for six years and over that time made 10 title defenses against 8 different contenders, the best bantamweights and featherweights of his era.[430]

Brown quickly fell in love with Paris and as a result spent much of his life there. He was noted for dressing elegantly and enjoyed the nightlife of the city, frequenting bars and jazz clubs. Brown was gay and was involved in a long-term romantic relationship with Jean Cocteau. He owned a number of cars, including a 1929 Packard 645

---

[429]

[430]

Sport and several Bugattis. He joined Josephine Baker's *La Revue Nègre* as a tap dancer and made his cabaret debut as a song-and-dance man at the Caprice Viennoise.[431]

Following Panama Al Brown, the bantamweight division fell into a political squabble governed by men who would never step into the danger zone of a boxing ring. Thus, the 1930s played out with two men trading the National Boxing Association title back and forth, each winning and losing the title twice. This does not diminish the talents of both these men.

Baltasar Sangchili, 1935–1936

No, he wasn't from Thailand. Baltasar was Baltasar Belenguer Hervas October 10, 1911, in Valencia, Spain. On March 18, 1935, Sangchili got his chance to fight reigning World Bantamweight Champion Panama Al Brown, which ended in a draw, but Sangchili won their rematch in a points decision. He held the world title until June 29, 1936, where in a bout in Madison Square Garden, he was knocked out by Tony Marino in the fourteenth round. Sangchili was the first Spaniard to win a world title.[432]

Sixto Escobar, 1936–1937

Sixto Escobar was an excellent Puerto Rican bantamweight who won the NBA title. On August 7, 1935, Escobar defeated Pete Sanstol—who once held, in 1931, the Canadian Boxing Federation and Montreal Athletic Commission (MAC) world bantamweight titles—by unanimous decision in twelve rounds. However, Escobar still wasn't considered the division's undisputed champion because Balthazar Sangchili had defeated Panama Al Brown and was recognized by the IBU. Due to this, Sanstol sent a letter to the NYSAC noting that the fight was of eliminatory nature, even though it was recognized as a titular contest by the NBA and MAC. Wanting to be

---

431

432

recognized as such, Escobar pursued a title unification fight against Tony Marino, who had defeated Sangchili by knockout in his previous fight. He won the fight by knockout in the tenth round, receiving the "undisputed world champion" distinction. On November 13, 1935, Escobar became the first Puerto Rican to win a title fight in the first round, defeating Indian Quintana by knockout.[433] Confused? Yeah, me too.

On August 26, 1935, he lost the NBA title to Lou Salica, a boxer whom he had defeated earlier. The decision was hotly disputed. Many people felt the Escobar had won. Salica subsequently lost the world bantamweight championship to Escobar just two months later on November 15, 1935, in a fifteen-round unanimous decision at New York's Madison Square Garden. Escobar floored Salica for a nine count in the third round after a series of right crosses and staggered him several times during the bout. Having regained the title, he held on to it until meeting Harry Jeffra, a bantamweight out of Baltimore, Maryland.[434]

Jeffra, however, lost the title to Escobar in his home country in San Juan, Puerto, Rico, on February 20, 1938, in another classic fifteen-round points decision before a crowd of around thirteen thousand. Winning by a large margin, and probably inspired by the home crowd, Escobar floored Jeffra twice in the eleventh and once in the fourteenth. After the bout, Jeffra announced through his trainer that he would never again try to make the strict bantamweight limit. At least one source considered the restrictive dieting and heavy workouts required by Jeffra to make the one-eighteen bantamweight limit, and the resulting lack of stamina, to be one of the causes of his loss to Escobar.[435]

On October 4, 1939, Escobar vacated his title, the Bantamweight Championship of the World. Throughout his career, Escobar avoided being knocked down or out in any fight, all his losses being by decision. In April 1941, he was drafted by the Army and participated in

---

433

434

435

World War II. Sixto Escobar was inducted into the IBHOF on June 9, 1992.[436]

Lou Salica, 1940

On September 24, 1940, Lou Salica reclaimed the NBA bantamweight title against Georgie Pace closer to home in a fifteen round unanimous decision at the New York Coliseum in the Bronx. *The Arizona Republic* wrote, "*It was a dead close fight for nine rounds, but Pace tired in the stretch, and Salica came on to win. At the finish with a partisan crowd of 4,183 cheering him on, he* [Salica] *was barely breathing heavily.*"[437] The crowd of 4,183 was small for a title fight, perhaps due to fans being less interested in the bantamweight division than lightweight and above, as well as the frequency with which the title had changed hands. Sixto Escobar had vacated his claim to the NBA world bantamweight title the previous year. Pace was recognized as the NBA world Bantamweight title holder at the time of the fight, and Salica was still considered by the New York State Athletic Commission to hold their version of the world title, largely as a result of his win over Tony Olivera the previous year.[438]

Thus ends the wild and confusing saga of the bantamweight division in the decade of the thirties.

Flyweights of the Nineteen Thirties

1930–1935 confusion reigns

Since the retirement of Fidel La Barba in 1927, the flyweights were a very confusing lot of title claimants for the next few years. The NBA changed hands five times, between Frankie Genaro, June 1928–March 1929; Emile Pladner, March 1929–April 1929; Frankie Genaro again, April 1929–October 1931; Victor "Young"

436
437
438

Perez, October 1931–October 1932; and Jackie Brown, October 1932–September 1935.[439]

The lineal flyweight title remained in dispute until Scottish flyweight champion Benny Lynch's victory over NBA and British flyweight champion Jackie Brown on September 8, 1935, and American flyweight champion Small Montana on January 19, 1937, which unified the world titles.[440] That ended eight years of partial title claimants.

Benny Lynch, 1937–1938

Benjamin Lynch (April 2, 1913–August 6, 1946) was a Scottish professional boxer who fought in the flyweight division. He is considered by some to be one of the finest boxers below the lightweight division in his era and has been described as the greatest fighter Scotland ever produced. *The Ring* magazine founder Nat Fleischer rated Lynch as the number 5 flyweight of all time while his publication placed him sixty-third in its 2002 list of the Best Fighters of the Last 80 Years.[441] Like Fleischer, both statistical boxing website BoxRec and the International Boxing Research Organization also rank Lynch as the fifth greatest flyweight ever. He was elected to *The Ring* magazine Hall of Fame in 1986 and the International Boxing Hall of Fame in 1998.

Lynch won the British, European, and world flyweight titles from Jackie Brown in an historic bout held in Manchester on September 9, 1935, the two having fought a draw six months earlier. The fight attracted enormous support from Glaswegians who traveled en masse to watch Lynch floor his opponent eight times before the bout was stopped in the second round.[442]

There was dispute, on at least on one side of the Atlantic, as to who was the genuine world flyweight champion. Lynch, recognized as champion in Britain, settled the matter when he outpointed

---

439

440

441

442

American-recognized champion Filipino Small Montana in London in January 1937 to establish himself as the undisputed world fly-weight boxing champion.[443]

He was arrested in March 1938 and charged with driving offences after crashing his car while drunk and hitting a telegraph pole and a pram containing a twelve-week old baby and failing to stop after the accident.[444] His trial was delayed until after his world title fight with American Jackie Jurich.[445] He forfeited his world fly-weight title against Jurich, when he weighed in at 118.5 pounds, half a pound over the bantamweight limit. Lynch stopped Jurich in the 12th round, but lost the title. At his trial in July, he was fined and disqualified from driving for a year.[446]

The title was vacated when Lynch failed the weight require-ment to qualify for the flyweight division and surrendered the title. Peter Kane defeated Jackie Jurich on September 22, 1938, to win the championship. Benny Lynch died in 1946 at the age of 33. [447]

Peter Kane, 1938–1939, Vacated

Jurich and Kane were regarded as the chief contenders for the vacant world flyweight title, and a fight was arranged between them in September 1938, in Liverpool. Kane won on points after putting Jurich down five times during the fight.[448]

By 1939, Kane had outgrown the flyweight class and began boxing as a bantamweight. At the end of that year, the National Boxing Association of America stripped him of his title. Although he lost his title in America, he was still recognized in Europe as World Flyweight Champion.[449]

443

444

445

446

447

448

449

Kane continued to fight recording a string of victories with only the occasional defeat, but most of his fights were at bantamweight. Although he was the world flyweight champion, the British and Commonwealth titles were held by the Scotsman Jackie Paterson. In June 1943, a fight was arranged at Hampden Park, Glasgow, with all three titles at stake. Kane managed to make the flyweight limit for the fight but was knocked out in the first round. The fight lasted sixty-one seconds.[450]

After Kane abandoned his title, the NBA proclaimed Little Dado as champion in 1939. After one defense Dado could no longer make weight and the NBA reinstated Kane as champion in 1942.

Thus ends the saga of professional boxing in the Great Depression. While boxing mattered much more than it does today, crowd sizes were smaller than those of the twenties, due to the fact that most people had a very hard time putting food on the table, let alone paying money to watch a prize fight. Still, there were great fighters, many of whose names are still known these many years later. I would mention luminaries Joe Louis, Max Schmeling, Henry Armstrong, and Barney Ross.

---

[450]

CHAPTER IX

The War Years

On December 7, 1941, President Franklin Delano Roosevelt went
on the radio airwaves and declared that day, "A day that will live in
infamy." On that terrible day, Japanese forces attacked and destroyed
the United States Naval Base at Pearl Harbor in Hawaii. The attack
commenced at 7:48 a.m. The base was attacked by 353 Imperial
Japanese aircraft (including fighters, level and dive bombers, and
torpedo bombers) in two waves launched from six aircraft carriers.
All eight US Navy battleships were damaged, with four sunk. All
but USS *Arizona* were later raised, and six were returned to service
and went on to fight in the war. The Japanese also sank or damaged
three cruisers, three destroyers, an anti-aircraft training ship, and one
minelayer. One hundred eighty-eight US aircraft were destroyed,
2,403 Americans were killed, and 1,178 others were wounded.
Important base installations such as the power station, dry dock,
shipyard, maintenance, and fuel and torpedo storage facilities, as well
as the submarine piers and headquarters building (also home of the
intelligence section), were not attacked. Japanese losses were light:
29 aircraft and 5 midget submarines lost, and 64 servicemen killed.
Kazuo Sakamaki, the commanding officer of one of the submarines,
was captured.[451]

Following the attack on Pearl Harbor, the United States declared
war on Japan and the Axis Powers of Germany and Italy. World War

---

451

II was the deadliest conflict in human history, marked by 70 to 85 million fatalities, most of whom were civilians in the Soviet Union and China.[452] This tragic global conflict included massacres, genocides, including the Holocaust, strategic bombing, death from starvation and disease, and the only use of nuclear weapons in war.[453] Almost everyone's, including actors, musicians, athletes, industrialists, and your neighbors and my neighbors, lives were changed. For the next four years, it was the time of the Defense Production Act, Rosie the Riveter, the Boeing B-17 Flying Fortress, D-Day, the Battle of the Bulge, Hiroshima and Nagasaki, GI Joe, Gen. Douglas MacArthur, Gen. Dwight Eisenhower, Ernie Pyle, the horror of Dachau, the bombing of London, Schweinfurt and Berlin, Adolf Hitler, Mussolini, and Hirohito. It was a time when brave young men bravely stormed the beaches at Normandy into machine gun fire and kept advancing until a beachhead was established. Greatest Generation indeed. It was a time of heroes.

Heavyweights of the Nineteen Forties

Joe Louis, 1941–1949

One of those heroes, though not of D-Day, was Joe Louis. The Brown Bomber was the Heavyweight Champion of the World and the perfect figure to represent America in this terrible time. His famous quote, "We'll do our part and we'll win because we're on God's side," said it all. America needed a major athlete to step up the plate, and Joe Louis Barrow, the Brown Bomber, was the perfect man to step up. He was a great fighter and a great heavyweight champion. His bum-of-the-month string of lightly regarded competition ended with his bout against Billy Conn, the light heavyweight champion and a highly regarded contender. The fighters met on June 18, 1941, in front of a crowd of 54,487 fans at the Polo Grounds in New York City.[454] The fight turned out to be one of the greatest heavyweight boxing fights of all time.

Conn would not gain weight for the challenge against Louis, saying instead that he would rely on a hit-and-run strategy. Louis's famous response was, "He can run, but he can't hide."[455] However, Louis had clearly underestimated Conn's threat. In his autobiography, Joe Louis said, "*I made a mistake going into that fight. I knew Conn was kinda small, and I didn't want them to say in the papers that I beat up on some little guy, so the day before the fight, I did a little roadwork to break a sweat and drank as little water as possible so I could weigh in under 200 pounds. Chappie was as mad as hell. But Conn was a clever fighter, he was like a mosquito, he'd sting and move.*"[456]

Conn had the better of the fight through twelve rounds, although Louis was able to stun Conn with a left hook in the fifth, cutting his eye and nose. By the eighth round, Louis began suffering from dehydration. By the twelfth round, Louis was exhausted, with Conn ahead on two of three boxing scorecards. But against the advice of his corner, Conn continued to closely engage Louis in the later stages of the fight. Louis made the most of the opportunity, knocking Conn out with two seconds left in the thirteenth round.[457] The way I always heard it was that Conn, gaining confidence as the fight progressed, decided to try for a knockout. Big mistake.

454

455

456

457

The contest created an instant rivalry that Louis's career had lacked since the Schmeling era, and a rematch with Conn was planned for late 1942. The rematch had to be abruptly canceled, however, after Conn broke his hand in a much-publicized fight with his father-in-law, Major League ballplayer Jimmy "Greenfield" Smith. By the time Conn was ready for the rematch, the Japanese attack on Pearl Harbor had taken place. On January 9, Louis boxed former opponent Buddy Baer, the brother of former champion Max Baer, in a benefit for the United States Navy Relief Fund, donating his entire purse of $47,000. The next day, January 10, 1942, Joe Louis enlisted as a private in the United States Army. He was sent to Fort Riley, Kansas, for basic training. He boxed a second benefit against another former opponent, Abe Simon, on March 27, 1942. The proceeds amounted to over $36,000.[458] His thanks for these two donations, which totaled over $83,000, the great champion was getting slapped with an IRS bill for $100,000 with an interest rate of 90 percent that made it impossible for the champ to pay back. As a result, he had to continue fighting after his championship days were over.

Louis was eventually promoted to the rank of technical sergeant on April 9, 1945. On September 23 of the same year, he was awarded the Legion of Merit (a military decoration rarely awarded to enlisted soldiers) for "incalculable contribution to the general morale." Receipt of the honor qualified him for immediate release from military service on October 1, 1945.[459]

On June 19, 1946, Joe Louis met Billy Conn for the second time, before a disappointedly small crowd of 40,000 at Yankee Stadium. It was now apparent that the war years had taken the skills of both men. Louis stopped Conn in the eighth round of a lackluster fight.

By 1947, the Brown Bomber had been world heavyweight champion for ten years. He had served in the military for three years. He was still champion, and he next chose a battle-worn, old fighter

458
459

named Arnold Cream, better known as Jersey Joe Walcott, as his next opponent.

At age 33, Walcott was considered a has-been with a 44-11-2 record. Louis was installed as a 10 to 1 favorite. The two met December 5, 1947, at Madison Square Garden. Walcott proved to be more than a handful for Joe Louis at this stage of Louis's career. He had the champ down twice in the early rounds, and when Louis was announced as the winner by a split decision, boos erupted.

Louis was under no delusion about the state of his boxing skills, yet he was too embarrassed to quit after the Walcott fight. Determined to win and retire with his title intact, Louis signed on for a rematch. On June 25, 1948, about 42,000 people came to Yankee Stadium to see the aging champion, who weighed 213 1/2, the heaviest of his career to date. Walcott knocked Louis down in the third round, but Louis survived to knock out Walcott in the eleventh.[460]

This would prove to be the champion's last title defense. He retired, still world heavyweight champion, on March 1, 1949. He had been champion for over 11 years and had defended the title an astonishing 26 times! An entire generation had come of age with Joe Louis as their champion. The retirement was short-lived. At the time of Louis's initial retirement, the IRS was still completing its investigation of his prior tax returns, which had always been handled by Mike Jacobs's personal accountant.[461] In May 1950, the IRS finished a full audit of Louis's past returns and announced that, with interest and penalties, he owed the government more than $500,000.[462] Louis had no choice but to return to the ring.

The Louis camp negotiated a deal with the IRS under which Louis would come out of retirement, with all Louis's net proceeds going to the IRS. A match with Ezzard Charles, who had acquired the vacant heavyweight title in June 1949 by outpointing Walcott, was set for September 27, 1950. By then, Louis was 36 years old and had been away from competitive boxing for two years. Weighing in

---

460

461

462

at 218, Louis was still strong, but his reflexes were gone. Charles repeatedly beat him to the punch. By the end of the fight, Louis was cut above both eyes, one of which was shut tight by swelling. He knew he had lost even before Charles was declared the winner. The result was not the only disappointing aspect of the fight for Louis—only 22,357 spectators paid to witness the event at Yankee Stadium, and his share of the purse was a mere $100,458. Louis had to continue fighting.[463]

After facing several club-level opponents and scoring an early knockout victory over EBU champion Lee Savold (also defeating top contender Jimmy Bivins by unanimous decision), the International Boxing Club guaranteed Louis $300,000 to face undefeated heavyweight contender Rocky Marciano on October 26, 1951.[464] Despite his being a 6-to-5 favorite, few boxing insiders believed Louis had a chance.[465] Marciano himself was reluctant to participate in the bout, but was understanding of Louis's position: "This is the last guy on earth I want to fight."[466] It was feared, particularly among those who had witnessed Marciano's punching power firsthand, that Louis's unwillingness to quit would result in serious injury. Fighting back tears, Ferdie Pacheco said in the *SportsCentury* documentary about his bout with Marciano, "He [Louis] wasn't just going to lose. He was going to take a vicious, savage beating. Before the eyes of the nation, Joe Louis, an American hero if ever there was one, was going to get beaten up."[467] Louis was dropped in the eighth round by a Marciano left and knocked through the ropes and out of the ring less than thirty seconds later. It was, to this writer's eyes at least, one of the very saddest sights in boxing history.

In the dressing room after the fight, Louis's Army touring companion, Sugar Ray Robinson, wept. Marciano also attempted to console Louis, saying, "I'm sorry, Joe." "What's the use of crying?"

463

464

465

466

467

Louis said. "The better man won. I guess everything happens for the best."[468]

After facing Marciano, with the prospect of another significant payday all but gone, Louis retired for good from professional boxing. He would, as before, continue to tour on the exhibition circuit, with his last contest taking place on December 16, 1951, in Taipei, Taiwan. [469]

Starting in the 1960s, Louis was frequently mocked by segments of the African American community (including Muhammad Ali) for being an Uncle Tom. Drugs took a toll on Louis in his later years. In 1969, he was hospitalized after collapsing on a New York City street. While the incident was at first credited to "physical breakdown," underlying problems would soon surface. In 1970, he spent five months at the Colorado Psychiatric Hospital and the Veterans Administration Hospital in Denver, hospitalized by his wife, Martha, and his son, Joe Louis Barrow Jr., for paranoia.[470] In a 1971 book, *Brown Bomber*, by Barney Nagler, Louis disclosed the truth about these incidents, stating that his collapse in 1969 had been caused by cocaine, and that his subsequent hospitalization had been prompted by his fear of a plot to destroy him. Strokes and heart ailments caused Louis's condition to deteriorate further later in the decade. He had surgery to correct an aortic aneurysm in 1977 and thereafter used a POV/scooter for a mobility aid. [471]

Louis died of cardiac arrest in Desert Springs Hospital near Las Vegas on April 12, 1981, just hours after his last public appearance viewing the Larry Holmes-Trevor Berbick heavyweight championship. Ronald Reagan waived the eligibility rules for burial at Arlington National Cemetery, and Louis was buried there with full military honors on April 21, 1981.[472] His funeral was paid for in part by former competitor and friend, Max Schmeling, who also acted as a pallbearer.

468

469

470

471

472

Ezzard Charles, 1949–1951

Ezzard Mack Charles, known as the Cincinnati Cobra (July 7, 1921–May 28, 1975), was the world heavyweight champion from 1949 to 1951. Known for his slick defense and precision, he is considered one of the greatest fighters of all time by boxing critics. Charles defeated numerous hall of fame fighters in three different weight classes. Charles won more fights than any other heavyweight champion in boxing history, having retired with a record of 95 wins, 15 losses, and 1 draw.[473]

Charles started his career as a featherweight in the amateurs, where he had a record of 42–0. In 1938, he won the Diamond Belt Middleweight Championship. He followed this up in 1939 by winning the Chicago Golden Gloves tournament of champions. He won the national AAU Middleweight Championship in 1939. He turned professional in 1940, knocking out Melody Johnson in the fourth round. Charles won all his first 17 fights before being defeated by veteran Ken Overlin. Victories over future hall of famers Teddy Yarosz and the much-avoided Charley Burley had started to solidify Charles as a top contender in the middleweight division. However, he served in the US military during World War II and was unable to fight professionally in 1945.[474]

He returned to boxing after the war as a light heavyweight, picking up many notable wins over leading light heavyweights, as well as heavyweight contenders Archie Moore, Jimmy Bivins, Lloyd Marshall, and Elmer Ray. Shortly after his knockout of Moore in their third and final meeting, tragedy struck. Charles fought a young contender named Sam Baroudi, knocking him out in round 10. Baroudi died of the injuries he sustained in this bout. Charles was so devastated he almost gave up fighting. Charles was unable to secure a title shot at light heavyweight and moved up to heavyweight. After knocking out Joe Baksi and Johnny Haynes, Charles won the vacant National Boxing Association heavyweight title when he outpointed

---

473

474

Jersey Joe Walcott over 15 rounds on June 22, 1949. The following year, he outpointed his idol and former world heavyweight champion Joe Louis to become the official recognized lineal champion. Successful defenses against Walcott, Lee Oma, and Joey Maxim followed.[475] Those fights and others will be covered in the next chapter.

Light Heavyweights of the Forties

Billy Conn, 1939–1941

Billy Conn was a great Irish American boxer who held the light heavyweight title at the beginning of the decade of the 1940s. He is certainly most famous for his 1941 world heavyweight challenge against the great Joe Louis. After making several defenses of his title in May 1941, Conn attempted to become the first World Light Heavyweight Champion in boxing history to win the World Heavyweight Championship when he and Louis met on June 18, 1941, and incredibly, to do so without going up in weight. The fight became part of boxing's lore because Conn held a secure lead on the scorecards leading to round 13. According to many experts and fans who watched the fight, Conn was outmaneuvering Louis up to that point. In a move that Conn would regret for the rest of his life, he tried to go for the knockout in round 13, and instead wound up losing the fight by knockout in that same round himself. Ten minutes after the fight, Conn told reporters, "I lost my head and a million bucks." When asked by a reporter why he went for the knockout, Conn replied famously, "What's the use of being Irish if you can't be thick [i.e., stupid]?"[476] Later he would joke with Louis, "Why couldn't you let me hold the title for a year or so?" to which the Brown Bomber responded, "You had the title for twelve rounds and you couldn't hold on to it."[477] Of course there was an immediate outcry for a rematch.

475

476

477

On December 7, 1941, with the onset of World War II, a lot of boxing careers were interrupted. Conn and Louis were called to serve in the Army. Conn went to war and was away from the ring until 1946.

By then, the public was clamoring for a rematch between him and the still-world heavyweight champion Louis. This happened, and on June 19, 1946, Conn returned into the ring, straight into a World Heavyweight Championship bout. Before that fight, it was suggested to Louis that Conn might outpoint him because of his hand and foot speed. In a line that would be long-remembered, Louis replied, "He can run, but he can't hide."[478] The fight, at Yankee Stadium, was the first televised world heavyweight championship bout ever, and 146,000 people watched it on TV, also setting a record for the most seen world heavyweight bout in history. Most people who saw it agreed that both Conn's and Louis's abilities had eroded with their time spent serving in the armed forces, but Louis was able to retain the crown by a knockout in round 8. Conn's career was basically over after this fight, but he still fought two more fights, winning both by knockout in round 9.[479]

On December 10, 1948, he and Louis met inside a ring for the last time, this time for a public exhibition in Chicago. Conn would never climb into a ring as a fighter again. Retiring from the ring as a boxer did not mean retiring as a public figure for Conn. Conn, who appeared in a 1941 movie called *The Pittsburgh Kid*, maintained his boxing skills into his later years. He stepped into the middle of a robbery at a Pittsburgh convenience store in 1990 after the robber punched the store manager. Conn took a swing at the robber and ended up on the floor of the store, scuffling with him. "You always go with your best punch—straight left," Conn told television station WTAE afterward. "I think I interrupted his plans." The robber managed to get away, but not before Conn pulled off his coat, which contained his name and address, making the arrest an easy one. His wife

478
479

said jumping into the fray was typical of her husband. "My instinct was to get help," she said at the time. "Billy's instinct was to fight."[480]

Anton Christoforidis, 1941

Christoforidis was born in Mersin, Ottoman Empire. In 1922, he came to Athens, Greece, as a refugee with his mother and his two sisters. His father and seven other relatives were killed in Asia Minor. His mother died two years after the family came to Athens. He had a very poor childhood and was working in a hotel when he realized that he was a very strong boy and didn't mind fighting. He started boxing lessons and soon became the Athens champion, although he was only sixteen years old. Then he decided to go to Paris, where he grew up very soon in the boxing arenas.[481]

He made his United States debut on January 5, 1940, in Madison Square Garden, defeating Willie Pavlovich by decision. At that point, Christoforidis settled in Geneva, Ohio. Anton next built up an eight fight winning streak, which was stopped when future hall of famer Jimmy Bivins bested him over ten rounds. Anton once said, "I won that fight. It was strictly a hometown decision." In a rematch the next month, Christoforidis returned the favor and won a ten-round decision, handing Bivins the first defeat of his career.[482]

The Bivins victory and successful results he had against other American opponents earned Christoforidis a bout with Melio Bettina for the vacant National Boxing Association world light heavyweight title. He won the light heavyweight crown on January 13, 1941, in Cleveland, Ohio, by defeating Melio Bettina in a unanimous decision of a fifteen-round bout. Bettina was winning slightly after twelve rounds, but Christoforidis finished strong in the final three to win a decision popular with the spectators. The world light heavyweight title was recently stripped from Billy Conn, who failed to defend the

---

480

481

482

belt in six months due to moving up in weight to challenge heavyweight champion Joe Louis.[483]

After knockout wins over Italo Colonello and Johnny "Bandit" Romero in nontitle bouts, Christoforidis lost to Gus Lesnevich by unanimous decision on May 22, 1941. Although this was not an NBA title fight, Lesnevich was later awarded the title by the NBA regardless on May 24, 1941.[484]

On January 12, 1942, Christoforidis suffered his first knockout loss at the hands of rising contender and future light heavyweight legend Ezzard Charles in Cincinnati, Ohio. Christoforidis was down for "Six" and "Nine" before the fight was stopped.

Christoforidis fought his last bout on February 18, 1947, against Anton Raadik. He retired with a record of 53 wins (13 by knockout), 15 losses and 8 draws.

Gus Lesnevich, 1941–1948

Gus Lesnevich was born and raised in Cliffside Park, New Jersey. Lesnevich turned pro in 1934 and in 1939 took on World Light Heavyweight champion Billy Conn, but lost a decision. In 1941, he took on Anton Christoforidis, winning the NBA light heavyweight title by decision. Later that year he defended the title twice against Tami Mauriello, winning both decisions to become the undisputed light heavyweight champion. In 1948, he lost a decision to Freddie Mills along with his title recognition.[485]

Freddie Mills, 1948-1950

Freddie Mills, born June 26, 1919, was a British boxer who became the Light Heavyweight Champion of the World. He beat the highly regarded Jock McAvoy, and this win put him in line to challenge Len Harvey for the British and Empire light heavyweight title,

---

483

484

485

which he won by second round knockout.[486] This fight took place before a crowd of thirty thousand British boxing fans.

On May 14, 1946, he made a challenge to light heavyweight champion Gus Lesnevich but was beaten back and stopped by the champion after being knocked down twice in the tenth round after putting up a gallant effort.[487] He got his second shot at Lesnevich on July 26, 1948, and won a hard fought unanimous decision to become light heavyweight champion of the world.[488]

He lost the championship to an American, Joey Maxim, on January 24, 1950, by TKO in the tenth round of a bout at the Earls Court in London. He died on July 24, 1965, from a gunshot wound in his car, probably self-inflicted.[489]

Middleweights of the Forties

Between the years 1941 to 1950, there was no single unified champion of the world. Each of the several men who claimed the title were partial champions, either of the National Boxing Association (NBA) or the New York State Athletic Commission (NYSAC). They are as follows:

- Al Hostak, 1939–1940, NBA
- Ceferino Garcia, 1939–1940, NYSAC
- Ken Overlin, 1940–1941, NYSAC
- Tony Zale, 1940–1947, NBA
- Billy Soose, 1941, NYSAC
- Rocky Graziano, 1947–1948
- Marcel Cerdan, 1948–1949
- Jake LaMotta, 1950–1951[490]

486
487
488
489
490

Far and away, the biggest names on the list would be Tony Zale, Rocky Graziano, and Jake LaMotta. Al Hostak was covered in the last chapter. Some will remember Marcel Cerdan, the ill-fated French boxer and lover of French chanteuse Edith Piaf.

Ceferino Garcia, 1939–1940

On October 2, 1939, Garcia fought Fred Apostoli for the Middleweight title in the United States and won it by TKO in the seventh round. The title he won was only recognized in New York by the NYSAC. He defended that title three times until he lost to Ken Overlin on points. He was managed, during the final years of his career, by George Parnassus.[491]

Ken Overlin, 1940–1941

Ken Overlin (August 15, 1910–July 24, 1969) was an American-born middleweight boxer who fought professionally from 1931 to 1944, compiling a record of 131 wins (23 by knockout), 18 losses, and 9 draws. He took the world middleweight championship as recognized by the New York State Athletic Commission in a win against Ceferino Garcia in New York on May 23, 1940, and held it until May 9, 1941. Overlin was inducted into the international boxing hall of fame as part of the 2015 class.[492]

Tony Zale, 1941–1947

Probably the greatest fighter on this list and maybe the most famous is Tony Zale, the Man of Steel. Tony Zale, born Anthony Florian Zaleski (May 29, 1913–March 20, 1997), was an American boxer. Zale was born and raised in Gary, Indiana, a steel town, which gave him his nickname Man of Steel. In addition, he had the reputation of being able to take fearsome punishment and still rally to win,

---

491

492

reinforcing that nickname. Zale was known as a crafty boxer and strong body puncher who punished his opponents and steadily wore them down before knocking them out.[493]

Tony Zale is best remembered for his epic three fight series with Rocky Graziano. He made Rocky famous and Rocky made Tony famous. I will now go to Wikipedia to get the lowdown on the trilogy:

Zale was a 2-time world middleweight champion and made The Ring magazine's list of 100 greatest punchers of all time. Zale is best remembered for his three bouts over a 21-month period with Rocky Graziano for the middleweight crown. These three bouts were among the most brutal and exciting middleweight championship matches of all time. The first match took place in Yankee Stadium, New York City. Zale had served in World War II, was thirty-three years old, and had been inactive for about four years. Graziano was on a winning knockout streak and seemed to be in his prime. In their first match (September 27, 1946), after flooring Graziano in the first round, Zale took a savage beating from Graziano, and was on the verge of losing the fight by TKO. However, he rallied and knocked out Graziano in the sixth round to retain his title. The rematch, a year later in Chicago (July 16, 1947), was a mirror image of their first fight. Graziano was battered around the ring, suffered a closed eye and appeared ready to lose by a knockout, then rallied and knocked Zale out in the sixth round, becoming middleweight champion of the world.

Their last fight was held in New Jersey the following year (June 10, 1948). Zale regained his crown, winning the match by a knockout in the

493

third round. The knockout blows consisted of a perfect combination of a right to Graziano's body, then a left hook to Graziano's jaw. Graziano was knocked unconscious. This fight was Zale's last hurrah. His age and the many ring wars he fought seemed to catch up with him in his next fight against European Champion Marcel Cerdan later that year, who stopped him in the eleventh round to win the middleweight championship of the world (September 21, 1948).[494]

Because of the unique politics of boxing, even a great champion like Tony Zale had to be content with the NBA championship and for a time the NYSAC title.

Rocky Graziano, 1947–1948

Rocky Graziano. What a life. I read his life story and saw the movie *Somebody Up There Likes Me*. Well, as the cliché goes, truth can be stranger than fiction. Born in Brooklyn, New York, and raised in Manhattan's East Village, in and out of reform schools, a petty thief, street fighter, and New York tough guy, he seemed destined to go no place except the penitentiary. Forced by his father to fight his brother, older than him by three years, Rocky had to put on the gloves

---

494

almost every night. As a teenager, still in and out of reform schools, he became an amateur boxing champ in New York as a welterweight. Charged with parole violation, he was sent to Rikers Island. Upon his release, he was drafted into the Army, where he punched out a captain and went AWOL. He was caught and sentenced to nine months at Leavenworth Federal Penitentiary. He was then dishonorably discharged.[495]

In March 1945, at Madison Square Garden, Graziano scored a major upset over Billy Arnold, whose style was similar to that of Sugar Ray Robinson. He was a slick boxer with lightning-fast combinations and a knockout punch. *The Ring* magazine and various newspapers across the United States touted Arnold as the next Joe Louis or Sugar Ray Robinson. Arnold was a heavy favorite to defeat Graziano and then to go on to fight for the world title, but Graziano absorbed a beating in the early going, before going on to batter and knock Arnold out in the third round of the scheduled eight-round bout. Following his loss to Graziano, Arnold was never the same.[496]

Career-defining three fights with Tony Zale

On July 7, 1946, middleweight champion Tony Zale and Rocky Graziano met at Chicago Stadium in what would become the first fight of an all-out war for the trilogy. In this first fight, Zale knocked Rocky down in the first round, but then absorbed a horrendous beating from his New York challenger. On the verge of suffering a TKO loss, Zale rebounded and knocked Graziano out in the sixth round. It was unbelievable slugfest that is viewable on YouTube.com. Following the knockout loss in the third fight with Tony Zale, Rocky continued fighting and put together a win streak of twenty-straight fights with only one draw during this time. He got one last chance at the undisputed middleweight championship when he took on the peerless Sugar Ray Robinson and was knocked out in the third round in Chicago on April 16, 1952. He fought one last time on

---

495

496

September 17, 1952, when he lost a decision to Chuck Davey, who outboxed him over ten rounds. After the loss, Graziano announced his retirement.[497]

After his retirement from boxing, Graziano cohosted a short-lived series, *The Henny and Rocky Show* (1955), with famous comedian Henny Youngman. He was a semiregular on *The Martha Raye Show* as Raye's boyfriend. He appeared as a regular on the United Artists TV series *Miami Undercover* for its entire run and appeared in several series and shows, including *The Pat Boone Chevy Showroom, Car 54, Where Are You?*, and *The Naked City*. He portrayed Packy, an ex-boxer, in the 1967 film *Tony Rome*.[498]

Rocky Graziano, the bad boy who made good, died on May 22, 1990. He was inducted into the IBHOF in the same year.[499]

Marcel Cerdan, 1948–1949

Tony Zale's second reign as champion didn't last long. After Marcel Cerdan had won both the French and European middleweight titles, he traveled to America and met Tony Zale for the Middleweight Championship of the World. On September 21, 1948, the battle worn Zale lost to Cerdan by a twelve-round knockout. [500]

During his short period as a world champion, Cerdan became a popular figure of the Paris scene. Although married with three children, he had an affair with the famous singer Édith Piaf. The affair lasted from summer 1948 until his death in autumn 1949. They were very devoted to each other and Piaf dedicated one of her most famous songs, "*Hymne à l'amour*," to Cerdan.[501]

In his first defense, he was matched with Jake LaMotta, known as the Raging Bull. In the fight, held at Briggs Stadium in Detroit on June 16, 1949, Cerdan was knocked down in the first and dislocated his shoulder. Severely handicapped, he fought on bravely until he

---

497
498
499
500
501

finally gave up after the tenth round.[502] This would be the last fight of Cerdan's life.

A contract was signed for a rematch, and Cerdan went to training camp for it, but before camp began, he boarded an Air France flight to visit Piaf in New York, where she was singing. The *Lockheed L-749 Constellation* crashed into Monte Redondo (São Miguel Island, Azores), killing all eleven crew members and thirty-seven passengers on board, including Cerdan and the famous French violinist Ginette Neveu, while approaching the intermediate stop airport at Santa Maria.[503] Days later, LaMotta lauded Cerdan as a great sportsman. Cerdan was interred in the Cimetière du Sud, Perpignan, Pyrénées-Orientales, France. I will cover Jake LaMotta in the next chapter.

Welterweights of the Nineteen Forties

Fritzie Zivic, 1940–1941

In only his third year as a professional Zivic notably defeated Sammy Angott, reigning NBA lightweight champion, in a nontitle bout on August 29, 1940, in a ten-round unanimous decision at Forbes Field in Pittsburgh. The bout was part of an elimination match to determine who would face Henry Armstrong for his world welterweight title. Zivic took the last six of the ten rounds. According

502

503

to Zivic later, his purse of $3,200 for the win was the largest he had yet received.[504]

In the most significant win of his career, Zivic upset Henry "Hammering Hank" Armstrong on October 4, 1940, in a fifteen-round decision before 12,081 at Madison Square Garden, taking the world welterweight title despite being a 4-1 underdog. He started by scoring with short right uppercuts in the early rounds. By the ninth, Armstrong's left eye was a slit, and his right nearly as swollen, allowing Zivic to easily dance away when Armstrong attempted to mount a desperate clumsy attempt at a knockout in the final round. Zivic mounted a slow effective attack, but held no wide margin, as the referee and both judges awarded him eight of the fifteen rounds in the close bout. The Associated Press gave Zivic nine rounds with Armstrong six. Zivic did not take a points lead until the sixth and seventh when he banged away with short, accurate, right uppercuts.[505]

According to Zivic's account, the first bout with Armstrong included questionable tactics and fouls. Zivic claimed Armstrong started out fighting that way, noting, "Henry's givin' me the elbows and the shoulders and the top of the head, and I can give that stuff back pretty good, but I don't dare to or maybe they'll throw me out of the ring."[506]

After winning Armstrong's welterweight title on October 4, 1940, he faced the great boxer again in a rematch. In his most memorable victory, he won the world welterweight title rematch with Henry Armstrong in a twelfth-round technical knockout, at Madison Square Garden, on January 17, 1941. It was the first knockout ever registered against Armstrong in his stellar career as a multiple weight class champion. The impressive crowd of 23,190 fans, considered the largest indoor crowd ever to see a professional boxing match, witnessed Armstrong, the former welterweight champion, nearly helpless when the referee called the match 52 seconds into the twelfth round. Zivic lost his world welterweight title in a fifteen-round decision

---

504

505

506

against Red Cochran before 10,000 fans on July 29, 1941, at Rupert Stadium in Newark, NJ. Cochrane effectively threw left hooks to the belly against the straight rights of Zivic. He butted Zivic with his head, when Zivic attempted to illegally put an arm around his neck to hammer him with his left. In a back-alley-brawl type of fighting, Cochrane threw a left hook into Zivic's groin after he claimed to have been continuously thumbed in the eye by Zivic, though the resulting penalty call gave the round to Zivic. Zivic's late comeback attempt in the final five rounds was not overlooked by the press, as many considered him obtaining more points in each of the last five rounds. The referee gave Cochran seven rounds, four to Zivic, and four even, with the single judge scoring the same. The *United Press*, however, gave six rounds to each boxer, with three as draws. Most believed Cochrane's ability to force the fighting throughout and land more telling blows made him deserve the close decision.[507]

Freddie "Red" Cochrane, 1941–1946

Freddie Cochrane was born in Elizabeth, New Jersey, of May 6, 1915. He held the World Welterweight Championship from 1941 until 1946. He won the title by beating Hall of Fame champion Fritzie Zivic twice. His reign was interrupted by World War II, and after losing to Rocky Graziano, the future middleweight champion, he lost his title to Marty Servo. Servo then relinquished his claim to the crown, and Sugar Ray Robinson, the original Sugar Ray, who by beating top ranked Tommy Bell, claimed the welterweight championship of the world.[508]

Sugar Ray Robinson, 1946–1950, Vacated

The *MAN*, Sugar Ray Robinson (born Walker Smith Jr., May 3, 1921–April 12, 1989), was an American professional boxer who competed from 1940 to 1965. This is the one boxer of all boxers for

---

507

508

which the phrase pound for pound was created. He was inducted into the International Boxing Hall of Fame in 1990. He is widely regarded as the greatest boxer of all time, and in 2002, Robinson was ranked number one on *The Ring* magazine's list of 80 Best Fighters of the Last 80 Years.[509]

Robinson had a brilliant amateur career. He was 85–0 as an amateur with 69 of those victories coming by way of knockout, 40 in the first round. He turned professional in 1940 at the age of 19 and by 1951 had a professional record of 128-1-2 with 84 knockouts. I emphasize here: at one point in his career, Sugar Ray Robinson had a record of 128 wins, 1 loss, and two draws! The one loss was to Jake LaMotta.[510] Robinson subsequently beat LaMotta five times. From 1943 to 1951, Robinson went on a 91-fight unbeaten streak, the third-longest in professional boxing history. Robinson held the world welterweight title from 1946 to 1951 and won the world middleweight title in the latter year. He retired in 1952, only to come back two and a half years later and regain the middleweight title in 1955. He then became the first boxer in history to win a divisional world championship five times (a feat he accomplished by defeating Carmen Basilio in 1958 to regain the middleweight championship). Robinson was named fighter of the year twice: first for his performances in 1942, then nine years and over 90 fights later, for the second time.[511]

Okay, Sugar Ray was a great middleweight, but he was an even greater welterweight. By 1946, Robinson had fought 75 fights to a 73-1-1 record, and beaten every top contender in the welterweight division. However, he refused to cooperate with the Mafia, which controlled much of boxing at the time, and was denied a chance to fight for the welterweight championship. Robinson was finally given a chance to win a title against Tommy Bell on December 20, 1946. Robinson had already beaten Bell once by decision in 1945. The two fought for the title vacated by Marty Servo, who had himself lost twice to Robinson in nontitle bouts. In the fight, Robinson, who

509

510

511

only a month before had been involved in a 10-round brawl with Artie Levine, was knocked down by Bell. The fight was called a war, but Robinson was able to pull out a close 15-round decision, winning the vacant world welterweight title.[512]

On February 27, 1943, Robinson was inducted into the United States Army, where he was again referred to as Walker Smith. His military career was less stellar than his boxing career, and he was frequently in trouble.

Two of Robinson's most memorable contests were his two bouts with Cuban great, Kid Gavilan. Their first meeting, on September 23, 1948, in Yankee Stadium was a nontitle bout won by Robinson on a ten-round decision. They fought for the World Welterweight Title on June 11, 1949, and Robinson again won by decision over the bolo punching Cuban, this time in fifteen rounds. The fight was held at Philadelphia Municipal Stadium in Philly.[513]

On August 9, 1950, Robinson made the last of his Welterweight title defenses decisioning Italian American challenger Charley Fusari in a one-sided unanimous decision in Jersey City, New Jersey.[514]

512

513

514

CHAPTER X

The War Years Part II

Lightweights of the Nineteen Forties

Sammy Angott 1941-1942 (vacated crown)

Sammy Angott was one of those guys who fought anybody and everybody. He was born outside of Pittsburg, Pennsylvania, on January 17, 1915. He was known as a clever boxer who liked to follow up a clean punch by grabbing his opponent, causing him to be known as the Clutch. In his career, Angott met the best fighters in the welterweight and lightweight divisions. These included Sugar Ray Robinson, Bob Montgomery, Beau Jack, Fritzie Zivic, Henry Armstrong, Redtop Davis, Sonny Boy West, and Ike Williams. His manager was Charlie Jones.[515]

Angott retired with a record of 94 wins (23 KOs), 29 losses, and 8 draws. He was knocked out just once in his career, by Beau Jack in 1946. Statistical boxing website BoxRec lists Angott as the number 6 ranked lightweight of all time.[516]

Angott first faced the great Sugar Ray Robinson on July 21, 1941, at Shibe Park in Philadelphia, losing in a 10-round decision. He lost twice more to Robinson on July 31, 1942, in a 10-round decision at Madison Square Garden and on March 4, 1946, in a

---

515

516

10-round decision in Pittsburgh.[517] He should have left Sugar Ray alone!

He gained the NBA recognition as champion on May 3, 1940, beating Davey Day in Louisville on the eve of the Kentucky Derby. (The winning horse was Gallahadion.) On December 19, 1941, Angott took the New York State Athletic Commission (NYSAC) world lightweight title from Lew Jenkins before a crowd of 11,343 at New York's Madison Square Garden.[518] Angott became undisputed champion as he held both the NYSAC and NBA world lightweight championship. He dominated the fighting outpointing Jenkins over 15 rounds.[519]

Angott vacated his crown on November 14, 1942, throwing the lightweight championship of the world into a chaotic spin of partial champions, among them, Beau Jack, Bob Montgomery, Juan Zurita, and Ike Williams. Some were recognized by the NBA, others by the NYSAC. It wasn't until Ike Williams defeated Bob Montgomery August 4, 1947, for the undisputed title that there was a legitimate world champion again. Williams's defeats over Zurita and Montgomery, in 1945 and 1947, respectively, would become recognized as the universal lightweight champion. Williams held the title until May 25, 1951.[520]

Ike Williams, 1947–1951

517
518
519
520

Ike Williams won the NBA lightweight title from Juan Zurita in Mexico City on April 18, 1945, by a second round knockout and defeated Bob Montgomery in Philadelphia two years later on August 4, 1947, claiming both the NYSAC and undisputed crown.[521]

On September 23, 1948, Williams successfully defended his lightweight title against Jesse Flores, winning in a tenth-round technical knockout at Yankee Stadium in New York's Bronx. Flores had been on the canvas five times during the fight, down twice in the fifth, and twice in the eighth. The final blows were a left hook and then a right that sent Flores to the shower at 2:07 into the tenth round.[522]

He made another successful title defense at Wrigley Field, stopping challenger Enrique Bolanos in four rounds in 1948. Next, he took on Freddy Dawson at the Philadelphia Convention Center and won by a fifteen-round decision on December 5, 1949. He lost a ten-round nontitle bout to Johnny Bratton in the Philadelphia Arena on January 17, 1949. He bounced back with an eighth round KO over Bratton in a title fight on January 20, 1950, in Chicago. Bratton suffered a broken jaw in the third, but hung in there until the eighth.

He held on to the crown until May 25, 1951, when he was stopped by Jimmy Carter in a fourteenth-round technical knockout at New York's Madison Square Garden. Williams had been sent to the canvas four times before the fight was called. Williams was down for a count of five and eight in the fifth. He was down for a count of four and then six in the fourteenth before the referee ended the fight. Williams believed that his trouble making weight had weakened him for the fight.[523]

Williams, for part of his career, was managed by Frank "Blinky" Palermo, who later was suspected of having ties to organized crime. According to Williams, he was blackballed by the boxing manager's guild when he sought to manage himself. Palermo informed him he could resolve his problems with the guild, and Williams agreed

---

521

522

523

to let Palermo manage him. Williams testified before the Kefauver Commission that Palermo did not arrange for him to throw any fights, but that he shorted him his share of his purses. Nevertheless, Williams did claim to have taken a dive against Chuck Davey, a much-hyped contender for the welterweight crown.[524]

Featherweights of the Nineteen Forties

Willie Pep, 1942–1948

Willie Pep, "the Will of the Wisp," along with archrival Sandy Saddler, dominated professional boxing's featherweight division throughout the nineteen forties. Born in Connecticut in 1922, describing Pep as a great fighter is kind of like calling fire hot or calling water wet. They just are and so was Pep, the greatest of all featherweight champions. After a little more than two years, he had already run his professional record up to 52–0.[525] During this time, he twice beat title claimant Joey Archibald. Pep won the Undisputed World Featherweight Title, beating Chalky Wright by a fifteen-round unanimous decision in New York City's Madison Square Garden on November 20, 1942. He held the title until October 29, 1948, when he was stopped in four

---

524

525

rounds by Sandy Saddler at Madison Square Garden.[526] At the time of his stoppage, his record stood at 134 wins, 2 losses, and a draw.[527] He had held the featherweight title a week less than 8 years.

Pep regained the title in a brilliant performance on February 11, 1949, at Madison Square Garden. In a remarkable display of boxing skill, Pep battled the taller and stronger Saddler to win a hard fought unanimous decision. Unlike Pep's first championship reign, this one was short-lived. Seven months later, on September 8, 1950, at Yankee Stadium, Pep was unable to come out for the eighth round. He had dislocated his shoulder in the seventh.[528] Saddler was champion again.

He retired in 1960 at age thirty-eight and made a comeback in 1964. He fought forty-three times, winning all but five. All his opponents were club fighters with the lone exception being Hogan "Kid" Bassey, who would himself win the feather title in the late fifties. Willie Pep died on November 23, 2006. He was inducted into the IBHOF in its inaugural year of 1990. His final record was 229 wins, 11 losses, and 1 draw.[529] That's what greatness looks like.

Sandy Saddler, 1948–1949

526
527
528
529

Sandy Saddler had Pep's number. True, Pep outboxed him to regain the crown, but every other time they fought, Saddler won. Not only could Saddler fight like hell, his nephew was rapper Grandmaster Flash! Saddler is best known for his four-bout series with Willie Pep. However, he had ninety-three fights prior to facing Pep. In his long career, he faced such notables as Phil Terranova, Joe Brown, Jimmy Carter, Humberto Sierra, Harold Dade, Paddy Demarco, Orlando Zulueta, Lauro Salas, and Flash Elorde.[530]

Facing the great Willie Pep for the first time on October 29, 1948, Saddler scored a fourth-round stoppage after knocking Pep down four times. In their second meeting, Pep put together the fight of his life and regained the title by unanimous decision on February 11, 1949, at Madison Square Garden. The two met for a third time, this time at Yankee Stadium, and Saddler won the title back when Pep dislocated his shoulder in the seventh round and did not answer the bell for the eighth. Saddler was champion again. Once again the pair met on September 26, 1951, in what has been called one of the dirtiest fights in championship history. The fight was filled with head butts, thumbing, low blows, rabbit punches, and wrestling. The referee stopped the fight at the start of the fifteenth, and Saddler was declared winner and still Featherweight Champion of the World.[531]

Sandy Saddler continued to box as featherweight champion until 1956, when he lost to Larry Boardman in the Boston Garden that year. After suffering a serious eye injury in a taxi accident, he was forced to retire, vacating his title. He stayed in boxing years later and was once again in the spotlight as the trainer of heavyweight champion George Foreman in Foreman's first term as champ. Saddler is a 1990 Hall of Fame inductee. He died on September 18, 2001, at age 75.[532]

530

531

532

Bantamweights of the Nineteen Forties

Lou Salica

Louis "Lou" Salica (November 16, 1912–January 30, 2002) was an American boxer who captured the National Boxing Association world bantamweight title twice in his career, in 1935 and 1940. His managers were Hymie Kaplan and Willie Ketchum. Some sources list a different birth date for Salica, July 26, 1913.[533]

As a youth, Salica won the flyweight bronze medal as an amateur at the 1932 Summer Olympics in Los Angeles.[534] He turned professional in 1932 and won the NBA bantamweight title from Sixto Escobar on August 26, 1935, in a questionable, controversial decision. Many at ringside felt Escobar had done enough to win the decision. Escobar then regained the NBA title just two months later.

Salica took back the the NBA and lineal featherweight championship on September 24, 1940, beating NBA champion Georgie Pace by a unanimous decision at the New York Coliseum in the Bronx. Salica was recognized in New York as world champion, and the win gave both titles and lineal claim to the featherweight crown.

On August 7, 1942, he lost his second NBA world bantamweight title against Manuel Ortiz at Legion Stadium in Hollywood, California, in a twelve-round unanimous decision before a crowd of 6,000. Ortiz fought for only $250, and for the opportunity to take Salica's NBA world bantamweight title. The fight benefited the USO and helped to buy athletic equipment and stage athletic shows for servicemen.[535]

On February 1, 1946, Salica was sentenced to an eighteen-month prison term for obtaining kickbacks from civilian workers while working as a civilian carpentry foreman at an Army

---

533

534

535

base in his hometown of Brooklyn. Salica was working at the New York Port of Embarkation installation. He was officially sentenced with conspiracy to bribe. A jury of the federal court had found him guilty in mid-January.[536] During the initial arrests made on December 20, 1945, the FBI suspected mob activity as gangster methods consisting of physical violence were used to silence complaints. Several gangs were using muscle to compete for the lucrative kickbacks.[537]

Living a long life for a championship boxer, he died on January 30, 2002, in his hometown of Brooklyn at the age of 89.[538]

Manuel Ortiz, 1947–1950

Hall of fame inductee Manuel Ortiz was born in Corona, California, on July 2, 1916. He is regarded as one of the best boxers of the 1940s and one of the greatest bantamweight champions in history. Ortiz turned pro in 1938 and in 1942 won the world bantamweight title by beating Lou Salica. He defended the title 15 times against 12 boxers before losing to Harold Dade in 1947. He regained the title in a rematch later in the year and defended the title 5 more times before losing the belt to Vic Toweel in 1950. He retired 5 years later in 1955 with a professional record of 131 fights, 100 wins, 28 losses, and 3 draws. He won 64 fights by knockout.[539]

Ortiz served in the United States Army. In retirement, he owned a farm, a ranch, and a nightclub, but apparently, none were successful. He died in 1970 after a long illness.[540]

Unfortunately, there is surprisingly little information available about the life of this great pugilist.

536

537

538

539

540

The Flyweights of the Nineteen Forties

Jackie Paterson, 1943–1948

Jackie Paterson (September 5, 1920–November 19, 1966) was a Scottish boxer who was world flyweight boxing champion. He was also British champion at flyweight and bantamweight.[541]

Born in Springside, Ayrshire, Paterson emigrated with his family from Scotland when he was eight years old, to Scranton, Pennsylvania. He returned to Scotland in his early teens to work at John Brown & Co, shipbuilders on the Clyde. He later worked as a butcher. When he was thirteen, he joined the Anderson Club in Glasgow and began to box as an amateur. He turned professional when he was seventeen.[542]

In June 1943, Paterson fought former flyweight champion Peter Kane from Golborne in Lancashire for the vacant world flyweight championship.[543] The world title fight, held at Hampden Park in Glasgow, lasted only sixty-one seconds, as Paterson caught Kane early in the first round putting him down twice, before he was counted out the second time.[544] Paterson was the first southpaw to be world flyweight champion. By successfully defending his British flyweight title twice, he had also won a Lonsdale Belt outright.

Paterson was finding it more and more difficult to make the 112-pound flyweight limit. In July 1947, he was due to defend his world flyweight title against Dado Marino, but collapsed at the weigh-in after making overstrenuous efforts to lose weight. The result was that the National Boxing Association of America and the British Boxing Board of Control strip him of his British, Empire, and world titles. Rinty Monaghan of Northern Ireland fought and beat Marino to take the world title, but Paterson took out an injunction against the BBBC to prevent it from recognizing Monaghan as champion.[545]

541

542

543

544

545

After appealing to the board, his titles were reinstated in November 1947, and he was ordered to defend against Monaghan.[546]

Eventually, in March 1948, Paterson and Monaghan met in Belfast to decide the matter. Paterson had to lose four pounds, twelve ounces in a week to meet the eight-stone limit. As a result, he was dehydrated and weakened. Monaghan knocked him down in the second round, and Paterson retired at the end the seventh with a cut over his eye, Monaghan taking the world, British, and Empire titles.

Paterson had a sad ending. In 1966, Paterson was stabbed in the throat during a fight after a drinking session, and died at the age of forty-six.[547]

Rinty Monaghan, 1948–1950, Retired

John Joseph "Rinty" Monaghan (August 21, 1918–March 3, 1984) was a world flyweight boxing champion from Belfast. He became famous in the postwar period, eventually rising to become undisputed world champion and a hero to many people in his home city.[548]

In October 1947, the National Boxing Association world crown became his after outpointing the American Dado Marino at Harringay Stadium for the vacant title. The mantle of undisputed champion of the world rested on his shoulders after his defeat of the tough Scottish fighter Jackie Paterson on March 23, 1948.[549]

Monaghan endeared himself to his Irish fans singing "When Irish Eyes Are Smiling" from the boxing ring after his wins at Kings Hall, where he frequently fought. He was forced to retire in 1950 from a chronic chest ailment. He left as flyweight champion of the world with a record of 51 wins, 9 losses, and 6 draws.[550]

546
547
548
549
550

Terry Allen, 1950

Terry Allen was born on June 18, 1924, in Islington, London, England. He became world flyweight champion in 1950 defeating Honore Pratesi of France to claim the title after Monahan's retirement. In the first defense of his crown, he fought American Dado Marino in Honolulu and lost the title to Marino by unanimous decision in August 1950. His reign was less than four months from April 25 to August 1, 1950. He retired in 1954 with a record of 61 wins, 13 losses and 1 draw. He died April 8, 1987, at the age of sixty-two.[551]

---

[551]

CHAPTER XI

The Fifties Part I

It was a time of peace and prosperity for many Americans, but the beginnings of unrest were beginning to show. The baby boom had begun in 1946, and there were a lot of little tots running around as the decade came in. White America had jobs, security, two good Presidents, a Democrat and a Republican, and more spending money than at any previous time in history. Black America, on the other hand, still under Jim Crow law in part of the Country, had a very different story of unemployment, degradation, blatant racism, and poverty. Hispanic American culture was largely ignored. It was a white bread world. Everyone, *everyone, on* TV news or sitcoms was white.

Before the decade was out, there would be a War in Korea, a Cold War between the United States and the Soviet Union, the beginnings of a counter culture, television, mutually assured destruction from nuclear arsenals, the dominance of the New York Yankees with players like Mickey Mantle, Yogi Berra, and Whitey Ford, and of course, rock and roll music.

Boxing still mattered, especially since televisions were in most peoples' home now with the *Wednesday Night Fights* and the *Friday Night Fights*. Because of this, many boxers in the smaller weights became household names and, in some cases, as well-known as the heavyweights.

World Boxing Champions as of January 1, 1951

- Heavyweight, Ezzard Charles
- Light heavyweight, Joey Maxim
- Middleweight, Jake LaMotta
- Welterweight, Kid Gavilan
- Lightweight, Ike Williams
- Featherweight, Sandy Saddler
- Bantamweight, Vic Toweel
- Flyweight, Dado Marino

So that was the state of boxing as the fifties began. Let's start with Ezzard Charles and the heavyweights.

Heavyweights of the Nineteen Fifties

Ezzard Charles, 1949–1951

I really don't know why Ezzard Charles is not as well-remembered in this time as some other boxers from his Era. I have already covered him in Chapter IX and given him his due accolades. Just a refresher: he is generally considered the greatest light heavyweight in history even though he never held that title. As a heavyweight, he was almost as good, scoring victories over Jimmy Bivins, Jersey Joe Walcott, Freddie Beshore, Lee Oma, and some guy named Joe Louis.

On June 22, 1949, Charles outpointed Jersey Joe Walcott to win the NBA title and the following year he decisioned his idol, Joe Louis to gain the lineal Heavyweight Championship of the the World.

On July 18, 1951, he again fought Jersey Joe Walcott for the third time. He had beaten Walcott twice before. This time, Jersey Joe axed him in seven rounds with a stunning left hook at their champion battle in Forbes Field in Pittsburg. At the time, Walcott, at age thirty-seven, was the oldest person to ever win the heavyweight title. That record stood until George Foreman regained the heavyweight title twenty years after he lost it Muhammad Ali in 1974, when he knocked out Michael Moorer in 1994. Foreman was a youngster of forty-five.

Jersey Joe Walcott, 1951–1952

I would like to establish this one little fact before I talk about Jersey Joe. The fact is this: Jersey Joe Walcott had been boxing professionally for twenty-two years when he won the heavyweight championship of the world, knocking out Ezzard Charles. Walcott had turned professional in 1930, really a whole different era. He had his share of wins and he had his share of losses. With his weird shifting style, he could be a difficult opponent to figure out. But he was good; not great, but very good.

He was born as Arnold Raymond Cream, not a very intimidating name for a prize fighter, on January 31, 1914, in Pennsauken, New Jersey. His father was an immigrant from St. Thomas, Danish West Indies. His mother was from Jordantown (Pennsauken Township), New Jersey. Walcott was only fifteen years old when his father died. He quit school and worked in a soup factory to support his mother and elven younger brothers and sisters. He also began training as a boxer. He took the name of his boxing idol, Joe Walcott, the great welterweight champion from Barbados at the turn of the twentieth century. He added "Jersey" to distinguish himself and show where he was from.[552]

552

He debuted as a professional boxer on September 9, 1930, fighting Cowboy Wallace and winning by a knockout in round 1. After five straight knockout wins, in 1933, he lost for the first time, beaten on points by Henry Wilson in Philadelphia.[553]

He built a record of 45 wins, 11 losses, and 1 draw before challenging for the world title for the first time. Walcott lost early bouts against world-class competition. He lost a pair of fights to Tiger Jack Fox and was knocked out by contender Abe Simon. But that would change in 1945 when Walcott beat top heavyweights such as Joe Baksi, Lee Q. Murray, Curtis Sheppard, and Jimmy Bivins. He closed out 1946 with a pair of losses to future light heavyweight champ Joey Maxim and heavyweight contender Elmer Ray, but promptly avenged those defeats in 1947.[554]

On December 5, 1947, he fought Joe Louis, at thirty-three years of age, breaking the record as the oldest man to fight for the world heavyweight title. Despite dropping Louis in round one, and again in round four, he lost a fifteen-round split decision. Most ringside observers and boxing writers felt Walcott deserved the win. A debate ensued, and sportswriters carried the topic throughout America. The lone official to vote for Walcott, referee Ruby Goldstein was cast as a hero. Letters and telegrams poured in to the Goldstein household, praising his judgment. There was talk of an investigation being assembled for rule revisions in judging. Louis went into seclusion for a couple of days, then quieted dissent with the following, "I know Ruby. He calls them as he sees them and that should be good enough for anybody."[555] What controversy remained was the kind that builds the gate, and Jersey Joe was rightfully granted a rematch on June 25, 1948. Though dropped again, this time in the third, Louis prevailed by a knockout in round 11. The bout was the first closed-circuit telecast (CCTV) sports broadcast, distributed as theater-television.

On July 18, 1951, after losing twice previously to Ezzard Charles, lightning finally struck with a powerful left hook, and the thirty-

---

553

554

555

seven-year-old ring-worn veteran was now the new Heavyweight Champion of the World. On June 5, 1952, he defended against Charles in their fourth meeting and defeated him in a fifteen-round decision.[556]

For his second title defense, he took on the challenge of undefeated twenty-nine-year-old slugger from Brockton, Massachusetts, named Rocky Marciano, the "Brockton Blockbuster." The two met in Philadelphia at the Municipal Stadium on September 23, 1952. For the better part of thirteen rounds, Jersey Joe out boxed Marciano. In the thirteenth round, Marciano stalked the champion back against the ropes. Both boxers fired right hands, but Marciano landed first and the power of his punch left Walcott on the canvas with one hand draped over the bottom rope. Because of the fight the old champ had put up, a rematch was called for, and this time Rocky knocked out Jersey Joe in the first round.[557] The knockouts can be seen on YouTube.

Walcott retired after the second Marciano fight. He was in the news a dozen or so years later. In 1965, Walcott refereed the controversial world heavyweight championship rematch between Muhammad Ali and Sonny Liston. Walcott lost the count as Ali circled around a floored Liston, wildly yelling at Liston to "get up and fight," and Walcott tried to get him back to a neutral corner. Walcott then looked outside of the ring (presumably to the ringside count keeper) as Ali and Liston went at each other, before Walcott instructed them to keep on fighting. Walcott then approached the fighters and abruptly stopped the fight. Walcott was never again appointed as a referee after this bout.

In 1971, he ran for the second time for Camden County sheriff. He defeated Republican William Strang in the general election. He was the first African American to serve as Sheriff in Camden County. He died on February 25, 1994, leaving a record of 71 total bouts, with 51 wins and 32 by knockout, 18 losses, and 2 draws.[558]

556

557

558

Rocky Marciano, 1952–1955

Rocco Francis Marchegiano (September 1, 1923–August 31, 1969, best known as Rocky Marciano, was an American professional boxer who competed from 1947 to 1955 and held the world heavyweight title from 1952 to 1956. He is the only heavyweight champion to have finished his career undefeated.[559] His six title defenses were against Jersey Joe Walcott, Roland La Starza, Ezzard Charles (twice), Don Cockell, and Archie Moore.

Known for his relentless fighting style, formidable punching power, stamina, and exceptionally durable chin, Marciano is included by boxing historians in lists of the greatest boxers of all time and is currently ranked by BoxRec as the fifth greatest heavyweight boxer in history.[560] His knockout-to-win percentage of 87.76 percent remains one of the highest in heavyweight boxing history.[561]

As a baby, young Rocco almost died from pneumonia. As a boy, he worked out on homemade weightlifting gadgets and made a heavy bag out of a mail bag and hung it on tree. Later, he studied a Charles Atlas course.

In March 1943, Marciano was drafted into the United States Army for a term of two years. Stationed in Swansea, Wales, he helped ferry supplies across the English Channel to Normandy. After the

559
560
561

war ended, he completed his service in March 1946 at Fort Lewis, Washington. While there, he won the 1946 All Army and Interservice boxing championships.[562]

In late March 1947, Marciano and several friends traveled to Fayetteville, North Carolina, to try out for the Fayetteville Cubs, a farm team for the Chicago Cubs baseball team. Marciano lasted three weeks before being cut.[563] After failing to find a spot on another team, he returned to Brockton and began boxing training with long-time friend Allie Colombo. Al Weill and Chick Wergeles served as his managers and Charley Goldman as his trainer and teacher.[564] Marciano turned professional on June 12, 1948, with a win over one Harry Bilazarian. His ring record shows an earlier win over Lee Epperson, whom he knocked out in three rounds, before returning to the amateur ranks. Now a professional, he won his first sixteen bouts, all before the fifth round and nine in the first round.[565]

Early in his career, he changed the spelling of his last name, Marchegiano. The ring announcer in Providence, Rhode Island, could not pronounce it, so Marciano's handler, Al Weill, suggested they create a pseudonym. The first suggestion was Rocky Mack, which Marciano rejected, deciding to go with the more Italian-sounding Marciano.

Versus Jersey Joe

Marciano, 29, faced the World Heavyweight Champion, 38-year-old Jersey Joe Walcott, in Philadelphia, on September 23, 1952. Walcott dropped Marciano in the first round and steadily built a points lead. In the thirteenth, Walcott used his trademark feint to set up his right hand, but Marciano's Suzie Q landed first, a powerful right hook, causing Walcott to slump to his knees with his arm draped over the ropes. He lay motionless long after he had been counted out and Marciano became the new World Heavyweight

---

562

563

564

565

Champion. At the time of the stoppage, Walcott was leading on all scorecards, 8–4, 7–5, and 7–4.[566]

One year later, he faced the now 39-year-old Walcott again, and this time, he starched him in the first round.

Roland LaStarza

Marciano had met Roland LaStarza the previous year and had beaten him by a razor-thin split decision. The second time around, Marciano was leading on the scorecards when he stopped the game LaStarza in the eleventh round at the Polo Grounds in New York on September 24, 1953.[567]

Versus Ezzard Charles

The following year, Rocky took on former heavyweight champion and light heavyweight legend, Ezzard Charles. The first fight which took place on June 17, 1954, was an exciting affair that saw Charles make a gallant effort against the undefeated champion only to lose a unanimous decision after fifteen hard-fought rounds. Exactly three months later, on September 17, 1954, both men fought again, and true to Marciano's rematch record of improving over a first fight, this time he stopped Charles in eight. Both fights were held at Yankee Stadium.[568]

Versus Don Cockell

On May 16, 1955, at Kezar Stadium in San Francisco, Rocky Marciano took on British and European champion Don Cockell and knocked him cold in the ninth round for his forty-eighth consecutive win against no defeats.

566

567

568

Versus Archie Moore

For his next and final fight, he took on light heavyweight champion and sometime heavyweight contender Archie Moore on September 21, 1955, at Yankee Stadium.[569] It was in this fight Archie came closest to wearing the belt. A Moore surprise right hand in the second round sent Marciano down for the second and final time in his career, setting the stage for a legendary battle, but also creating controversy as far as shared memory. In subsequent years Moore made much of Referee Harry Kessler's handling of the pivotal moment. A half decade on, in Archie's autobiography, he describes in detail the referee, though Rocky arose at "Two," continuing a superfluous mandatory eight-count, *"Kessler went on, three, four. The mandatory count does not apply in championship bouts (1955)... My seconds were screaming for me to finish him and I moved to do so, but Kessler...carefully wiped off Rocky's gloves, giving him another few seconds...he gave him a sort of stiff jerk, which may have helped Rocky clear his head."* Moore admits to being angry enough at what he saw as interference, he went recklessly, "blind and stupid with rage," going for the knockout toe to toe.[570]

At any rate, Marciano recovered and went on to knock Moore down five times, and Moore got up four times, but not the fifth time and final time in the ninth round. There will be more to the story of Archie Moore. Marciano announced his retirement on April 27, 1956. His record forever stands at 49 wins, 43 by knockout, and 0 losses.[571]

On August 31, 1969 (the day before his 46th birthday), Marciano was a passenger in a small private plane, a Cessna 172 heading to Des Moines, Iowa. It was night time and bad weather had set in. The pilot, Glenn Belz, had 231 total hours of flying time, 35 of them at night, and had no instrument rating. Belz tried to land the plane at a small airfield outside Newton, Iowa, but the aircraft

---

569
570
571

hit a tree two miles short of the runway. Flying with Marciano in the back seat was Frankie Farrell, 28, the oldest son of Lew Farrell, a former boxer who had known Marciano since his childhood. Marciano, Belz, and Farrell were killed on impact. When rescuers reached the crashed aircraft, they saw Marciano's body still strapped in a seat. Upon hearing what had happened, people in boxing remembered what was said about Stanley Ketchel after Ketchel had been shot dead, "Start counting ten over him. He'll get up."[572]

Marciano holds the record with heavyweights John L. Sullivan and Brian Nielsen for the longest undefeated streak by a heavyweight. He also holds the record for being the only world heavyweight champion to go undefeated throughout his career. He is a 1990 inductee in the IBHOF.[573]

Floyd Patterson, 1956–1959

Floyd Patterson (January 4, 1935–May 11, 2006) was the first heavyweight champion to regain his title after losing it against Ingemar Johanson. At the age of twenty-one, he became the youngest boxer in history to win the title, and was also the first heavyweight to regain the title after losing it. As an amateur, he won a gold medal in the middleweight division at the 1952 Summer Olympics.

572

573

In 1956 and 1960, Patterson was voted Fighter of the Year by *The Ring* magazine and the Boxing Writers Association of America. He was inducted into the International Boxing Hall of Fame in 1991.[574]

After winning gold at the Olympic Games, Floyd Patterson turned professional beating Eddie Godbold by fourth round knock-out at St. Nicholas Arena in Brooklyn, which was Floyd's hometown. He then won seven of his next ten fights by knockout, beating mostly journeymen.[575]

His first loss came on June 7, 1954, at the Eastern Parkway Arena. Joey Maxim, the former light heavyweight champ, beat the nineteen-year-old Patterson on an eight-round unanimous decision. Following the loss, a string of fourteen consecutive wins put him in line to participate in a tournament to determine a successor to recently retired champion Rocky Marciano. On June 8, 1956, he won a close split decision over Tommy "Hurricane" Jackson to face number one ranked contender Archie Moore for the undisputed heavyweight title.[576]

Patterson and Moore met on November 30, 1956, at Chicago Stadium. Patterson had grown in weight and muscle. He was incredibly fast with his hands and combinations, too much for ancient Archie. He knocked him down twice in the fifth, the first time with a left hook that caught the light heavyweight champion square and, on rising, was met with another quick combination from Floyd that knocked him down for the count.[577] Floyd Patterson was now the youngest Heavyweight Champion of the World in history and the first Olympic gold medalist to win the heavyweight crown.

Managed by the ultracautious Cus D'Amato (who later managed Mike Tyson), Patterson defended against three fringe contenders in the next three years. In a rematch with Hurricane Jackson, whom he had fought the year before when he won a close decision, this time he stopped Jackson in ten rounds on July, 29, 1957, at the Polo Grounds.

574

575

576

577

Next was a questionable defense against 1956 Olympic heavyweight gold medalist Pete Rademacher of Washington State. The fight, held in Seattle at Sick's Stadium, was Rademacher's first professional fight. As an amateur, he had never gone beyond three rounds. Now he was scheduled for fifteen and the professional championship of the world. Patterson was too much for the Olympian's debut and stopped him in the sixth round of an action filled fight after being dropped himself earlier on in the second.[578] For the record, Floyd Patterson was knocked down more times than any other heavyweight champion. (He also got back up more than any other champion.)

Patterson next defended against a colorful contender from the colorfully named Texas town of Cut and Shoot. His name was Roy Harris, and Patterson stopped him in the twelfth round after knocking Harris down four times. At the time, Patterson was having difficulty getting title fights even though he was champion. His manager, Cus D'Amato, didn't trust or get along with any of the governing bodies of boxing.[579]

Following Roy Harris, Patterson next fought British and Empire heavyweight champion Brian London in a forgettable fight and knocked him out in the eleventh round in Indianapolis on May 1, 1959.

Patterson lost his title on June 26, 1959, at Yankee Stadium when hard punching Swedish challenger Ingemar Johanson knocked him down seven times in the third round and won the title by a technical knockout.[580]

One year later, Floyd found his inner tiger and knocked the Swede cold with a stunning left hook in round five on June 20, 1960, leaving him unconscious on the canvas with his left foot twitching. He then defended against Johanson in 1961 and also against Tom McNeeley that same year. Defending against dreadnaught Charles "Sonny" Liston in Chicago on September 26, 1962, he lost by a one round knockout. One year later in their second meeting, Sonny once again KO'd Floyd in the first.[581]

578

579

580

581

A very sensitive individual, Patterson then went into seclusion, sometimes wearing a disguise so as not to be recognized. He continued boxing well into the 1970s, fighting and beating several marquee names such as Eddie Machen, Jimmy Ellis, George Chuvalo, and Oscar Bonavena. He twice challenged Muhammad Ali but was beaten both times. Following his retirement, he became the New York State Athletic Commissioner and served two terms.

In retirement, he and Ingemar Johansson became good friends who flew across the Atlantic to visit each other every year, and he served two terms as chairman of the New York State Athletic Commission. He was also inducted into the International Boxing Hall of Fame in 1991. In 1983, he and his friend Ingemar Johanson ran the Stockholm Marathon together.

Floyd Patterson died on May 11, 2006. He was known as the Gentleman of Boxing.[582]

Ingemar Johanson, 1959–1960

America had barely heard of Ingemar Johanson when he challenged Floyd Patterson for the heavyweight championship until about a week before the fight, when my city's local newspaper, the *Seattle Post Intelligencer*, began the ballyhoo buildup for the fight. Yes, they did that in my era when boxing mattered. I knew he had knocked

---

582

out a pretty good American heavyweight named Eddie Machen in the first round in a 1958 fight because I had most likely read about it in *The Ring* magazine. I may have seen his name in *The Ring*'s ratings, but I would barely have noted it, because he wasn't as familiar to me as the American boxers. I soon learned his fighting name was Ingo he traveled with his pretty secretary Birgit Lundgren, and he referred to his right hand in mystical terms, calling it either toonder and lightning or the Hammer of Thor. He was quite colorful.

He was a 5–1 underdog when he entered the ring to face champion Floyd Patterson on June 26, 1959, at Yankee Stadium. There, in round three, the Hammer of Thor struck. For the first two rounds, Johanson had thrown a sort of flimsy jab which Floyd easily avoided. In round three, he threw a left hook, drawing Patterson's hands apart to block it and then fired a hard right that sent Patterson down for the first of seven knockdowns, before referee Ruby Goldstein stopped the fight making Sweden's Ingemar Johanson the new Heavyweight Champion of the World.[583]

Ingemar Johanson knew how to be the champion. Training for the rematch, he was cocky but likeable. He trained at Grossinger's Resort in the Catskills, and his ever-present secretary, Birgit, was always by his side. Whereas Patterson had been private and humble, Johanson was friendly to the press and the press was friendly to Johanson.

Patterson, by contrast, went into seclusion and ran his training camp like a Trappist monastery. The odds of Patterson regaining the crown were very long. Throughout boxing's long history several men had tried and failed at regaining the heavyweight title, among them, James J. Corbett, Bob Fitzimmons, James J. Jeffries, Jack Dempsey, Max Schmeling, Joe Louis, Ezzard Charles, and Jersey Joe Walcott.

The second Johanson-Patterson fight was held at the Polo Grounds in New York on June 20, 1960. It was a different Floyd Patterson who showed up for the rematch. He was bigger looking and stronger looking. For the first fight he had weighed 184 pounds. Six pounds heavier now at 190, at the bell he came out more aggressively than the first

---

583

fight. Ingo landed one good right, and Patterson was momentarily stung, but he continued his aggressive tactic. In round five, he caught Ingemar with a right and left hook and Ingemar was down. He rose and Patterson was on him like a tiger going after prey. A tremendous left hook from Patterson landed flush and Johanson went down for the second and last time. He was out cold with his left foot quivering. The referee counted ten over him as Patterson gloated to the ringside press. Goldstein could have counted to one hundred. I actually thought Patterson might have killed the Swede. I remember feeling elated about Patterson's victory. He was my favorite boxer at the time.[584]

Finding his inner tiger, Patterson kayos
Ingemar Johansen in 1960

Floyd Patterson had done it. He had made history by being the first heavyweight champion to regain the title. He was once again Heavyweight Champion of the World!

Patterson and Johansson fought their final match on March 13, 1961. Johansson appeared to be in the worst physical condition of his three bouts with Patterson. A. J. Liebling, writing in *The New Yorker*, said the outcome seemed preordained and that Johansson was not dieting for the fight, eating creamed chicken, strawberry short-cake, and cherry cheesecake. Nonetheless the fight was competitive.

584

Johansson caught Patterson leaping at him in the very first round and knocked him down. He followed his advantage up by scoring another knockdown, but was caught going in wide open by that famous Patterson left hook, resulting in a knockdown. As the fight progressed, it became obvious that Johansson was spent. Patterson won when the referee swiftly stopped the contest in round six after Johansson had been knocked down once again.[585]

Ingemar Johanson retired in 1963 after winning four straight and re-annexing the European heavyweight title. He retired with a record of 26 wins and two losses. He won 17 of his 26 wins by knockout. He died on January 30, 2009. He was seventy-six years old.[586]

Although Johanson is not considered in the top tier of heavyweight champions, he was strong, athletic, a fair boxer, and a hard puncher. He enjoyed being the heavyweight champion of the world. In his brief time at the top, Ingemar Johanson lit up the boxing world. The sporting press lionized him.

Floyd Patterson Second Reign, 1960–1961

Patterson had begun his second reign as heavyweight champ in the third fight with Ingemar Johanson, which he won by sixth-round KO in a wild slugfest where both men were down. His next defense was against a journeyman contender, Tom McNeeley, of Arlington, Massachusetts. The crewcut Irishman was known as a hard puncher and a somewhat crude boxer. He had played football at Michigan State University. Patterson easily disposed of him in four rounds at the Toronto Maple Leaf Garden on December 4, 1961.[587]

Dark clouds were already forming even as Patterson dispatched McNeeley. The specter of Charles "Sonny" Liston was more evident with every victim Liston KO'd. The public felt that Patterson was avoiding Liston, the number one contender by fighting Tom McNeeley.

585

586

587

Light Heavyweights of the Nineteen Fifties

Joey Maxim, 1950–1952

Joey Maxim (Giuseppe Antonio Berardinelli), American boxer (born, March 28, 1922, Cleveland, Ohio; died June 2, 2001, West Palm Beach, Florida), was the world light heavyweight champion from 1950 to 1952. On January 24, 1950, Maxim knocked out heavily favored Englishman Freddie Mills in London to win the world light heavyweight title. In one of the most memorable boxing matches in history, Maxim defended his title against Sugar Ray Robinson on June 25, 1952, at Yankee Stadium in New York City. The fight took place before a crowd of 48,000 spectators and with the temperature above 38°C (100°F). Late in the bout Robinson, who was ahead on the scorecards, began to suffer from fatigue and dehydration and failed to answer the bell for the 14th round. Maxim was awarded the victory by technical knockout. He lost the light heavyweight crown to Archie Moore later that year. Maxim was inducted into the International Boxing Hall of Fame in 1994.[588]

Archie Moore, 1952–1960

Archibald Lee Wright, a.k.a. Archie Moore, born in 1916, turned professional in 1935 and fought until 1963. He was known

---

[588]

as the Mongoose and later as the Old Mongoose. Now think about this. This man fought from the time of Franklin Delano Roosevelt to John Fitzgerald Kennedy, through Roosevelt, Truman, Ike, and Kennedy. He went through six light heavyweight champions, from Bob Olin in 1935 until he won the title from Joey Maxim in 1952. He had a total of 219 fights, scoring 131 knockouts! That is the most knockouts any boxer has ever scored. Sam Langford is second with 129 knockouts. Moore was denied a shot at the world title for over ten years and spent many of those years fighting on the road with little to show for it. He fought everybody and anybody during these years. Some of the names that show up on his record include future champion Harold Johnson, Jimmy Bivins, Alabama Kid, Bob Satterfield, Ted Lowry, Ezzard Charles, Curtis Shepherd, Holman Williams, and many other standouts of two generations of boxers.[589]

It took Archie Moore seventeen long years before he finally got a title shot against slick boxing champion Joey Maxim. He had Maxim's number, beating him by unanimous decision. Finally, at age thirty-six, Archie Moore had achieved his dream of being a champion boxer. He went on to defeat Maxim four times. Like the man said, he had Maxim's number.

One of his standout title defenses was against future lightheavy champion and IBHOF inductee Harold Johnson on August 11, 1954. Johnson, a very good boxer, gave Moore all he could handle for thirteen rounds, before Moore knocked him down and TKO'd him in the fourteenth round to retain his title. He defended against middleweight champion Bobo Olson early in 1955, knocking him out in three. Following the knockout over Olson, Moore made his first challenge for the heavyweight championship against Rocky Marciano.[590]

Despite dropping the Rock in the second round and a courageous effort, Archie Moore was counted out in the ninth round after being dropped five times at Yankee Stadium on September 21, 1955.

589

590

He then made a light heavyweight title defense, beating Yolande Pompey by a tenth-round TKO. He made his second try at the heavyweight crown on November 30, 1956, against Floyd Patterson and the younger faster Patterson proved too much for him as he was knocked out in five rounds.[591]

He made four more defenses of the light heavyweight crown. He knocked out top contender Tony Anthony in seven rounds in 1957 and then defended in a most memorable fight against Canadian slugger Yvonne Durelle in Montreal, Quebec, Canada, on December 10, 1958. It was a war. Durelle dropped champion Moore, three times in round 1, and had Archie on the verge of a knockout. Somehow, he made it to the bell and was dropped for a fourth time in round 5! Finding the inner reserve of what makes a champion a champion, he came back from the dead and knocked Durelle out in the ninth round in one of the greatest fights of all time. The two met again, and this time, Moore dispatched Durelle in round 3, again in Montreal.[592] In 1960, he took a little time off to make a movie where he played the part of Jim the runaway slave in the movie *The Adventures of Huckleberry Finn*. He got favorable reviews for his characterization.[593] He then dropped a nontitle ten-round decision to Italian Giuliano Rinaldi but decisioned Rinaldi in 1961 for his final defense. In 1961, the National Boxing Association stripped probably the greatest light heavyweight champion of the title he had held for nine years. By 1962, even the NYAC and *The Ring* magazine had left him to recognize NBA champion Harold Johnson, victor over Doug Jones.[594]

That year he fought a young heavyweight out of Louisville, Kentucky, named Cassius Clay. Clay, who often mocked opponents, went after Moore with rhyme saying, "Moore must fall in four!" Archie responded saying, "I have invented a new punch for Clay. It's called the Lip Buttoner punch." Clay knocked out the forty-eight-year-old Moore in four as predicted.

591

592

593

594

Archie Moore fought for the last time in 1963, scoring a TKO win over wrestler Mike DiBiase in Phoenix, Arizona.

An important figure in the American black community, he became involved in African American causes once his days as a fighter were over. He also established himself as a successful character actor in television and film. Moore died in his adopted home of San Diego, California. He was eighty-one years old.[595]

Middleweights of the Nineteen Fifties

Jake LaMotta, 1949–1951

Thanks to the movie *Raging Bull*, the name Jake LaMotta is known to the public at large. He has always been known to boxing fans, however, especially from his six fights against the great Sugar Ray Robinson. Even though he lost five of them, he did win one, becoming the first man to beat Robinson, who was considered unbeatable at the time. He also had Robinson down on a few occasions in the course of these bouts.

Born Giacobbe LaMotta in either 1921 or 1922 in New York's Lower East Side and raised in the Bronx, he was the undisputed Middleweight Champion of the World from June 16, 1949, when he won the crown from Marcel Cerdan until February 14, 1951,

---

595

when he lost the crown in the St. Valentine's Day Massacre to Sugar Ray Robinson.

LaMotta was known as an aggressive, swarming brawler who was willing to take a punch or two in order to land one. In his title winning fight against Marcel Cerdan, he knocked the Frenchman down in the first round, and Cerdan dislocated his shoulder. Cerdan could not continue and his corner stopped the fight between the eighth and ninth round. Jake LaMotta was now the middleweight champion of the world. The scheduled rematch between LaMotta and Cerdan never happened. Cerdan was killed in a plane crash before the bout was to take place.

LaMotta defended his title successfully a couple of times, and then on February 14, 1951 in his final bout against Sugar Ray Robinson, he was TKO'd in the thirteenth round and lost the title. The fight was represented in the movie by actor Robert De Nero taking incredible punishment from Robinson while refusing to go down. That was factual. LaMotta could absorb beatings in an almost superhuman way and come back and win. There was no coming back against Sugar Ray, however, and Robinson won the first of his five world middleweight championships.

After retiring from the ring, LaMotta owned and managed a bar at 1120 Collins Avenue in Miami Beach. He also became a stage actor and stand-up comedian. In 1958, he was arrested and charged with introducing men to an underage girl at a club he owned in Miami. He was convicted and served six months on a chain gang, although he maintained his innocence.[596]

Jake LaMotta lived an extraordinary and colorful life. On November 14, 1947, LaMotta was knocked out in the fourth round by Billy Fox. Suspecting the fight was fixed, the New York State Athletic Commission withheld purses for the fight and suspended LaMotta. The fight with Fox would come back to haunt him later in life, during a case with the Federal Bureau of Investigation.[597]

---

[596]

[597]

In his testimony and in his later book, LaMotta admitted to throwing the fight to gain favor with the Mafia. All involved agreed the fix was obvious and their staging inept.

LaMotta wrote as follows:

> *The first round, a couple of belts to his head, and I see a glassy look coming over his eyes. Jesus Christ, a couple of jabs and he's going to fall down? I began to panic a little. I was supposed to be throwing a fight to this guy, and it looked like I was going to end up holding him on his feet... By [the fourth round], if there was anybody in the Garden who didn't know what was happening, he must have been dead drunk.*

The thrown fight and a payment of $20,000 to the Mafia got LaMotta his title bout against World Middleweight Champion Marcel Cerdan.[598]

Jake LaMotta went to his final reward on September 19, 2017. He was ninety-six years old. He was one tough old pug.

Sugar Ray Robinson, 1951

Sugar Ray Robinson might well have been the greatest welter-weight in history, with the possible exception of Henry Armstrong Jimmy McLarnin or another Sugar, this one named Leonard. All four stand above the rest, even Barney Ross, Jose Napoles, and Joe Walcott. He was also a great middleweight who won the middle-weight title five times and lost it four times, the last being to Paul Pender when he was forty years old. Yes, Sugar Ray Robinson is probably the greatest pound-for-pound boxer of all time. The first loss as middleweight champion was to Randy Turpin. Turpin was certainly no pushover and he was very tough.

598

Turpin won sixty-six fights in his career against only eight losses, but he was fighting a guy with a record of one hundred twenty-nine wins against 1 loss and a lot of recognizable names on his résumé. Who had Turpin beat? A lot of European boxers nobody knows. Now I don't mean to disparage Randy Turpin. He won the undisputed middleweight championship of the world from the man considered the greatest pound-for-pound fighter in the world. I can tell you how he did it. Robinson was on the last leg of his whirlwind European tour, and when he got to England, he was treated like one of the Beatles. He got the full rock star treatment, with Bobbies always around him to protect him. He was the great Sugar Ray, with one hundred twenty-one wins against only one loss that he had reversed not once but five times. He played golf more than he trained. Did success spoil Sugar Ray? He met a young, hungry fighter with nothing to lose and everything to gain. Turpin had an awkwardness that Ray just could not fathom and when the fight was over, Randy Turpin was the winner by fifteen-round decision in London on July 10, 1951, and the Undisputed Middleweight Champion of the World. Sugar Ray had lost his second fight.

Randy Turpin, 1951

Randolph Turpin was born June 7, 1928, in Leamington Spa, Warwickshire, England, the son of a black father and a white mother. He grew up in a completely, or nearly completely, Anglo-Saxon neighborhood. He had brothers who were also boxers. They experienced prejudice from the neighbor kids, probably from day one, as children tend to pick on and mock anyone different from themselves. Randy and his brothers were different. They all had darker skin than the others. Adversity is the primary ingredient in making a young person fight. So Randy, like his brothers, became a boxer. Soon, he eclipsed the talent of them and developed his talent in the boxing booths at the regional fairs.

He became a professional boxer on September 17, 1946, stopping one Gordon Griffiths by TKO in Harringay, North London.[599]

He soon embarked on a weight-training regime designed by a man called Arthur Batty and built up his physical strength. Weight training was frowned upon in boxing circles because it was thought that it made fighters muscle bound and inflexible in their movements. Turpin proved to be the exception to this rule and many of his future opponents, including Sugar Ray Robinson, would comment on his immense physical strength. Turpin developed a knockout punch with either hand and became a formidable force for any fighter to deal with.[600]

Following a string of victories and the acquisition of British and European titles he was matched with Sugar Ray Robinson. Few people gave Turpin a chance of winning against Robinson, and in fact, many people thought that it was a mismatch and that Turpin could be badly hurt. Robinson had been unbeaten as an amateur and had only lost one fight out of a total of 132 as a professional, and that was to Jake LaMotta. He had subsequently avenged the loss to LaMotta, beating him 5 times.[601]

Stepping into the ring with Robinson, Turpin no doubt thought, "This guy is only human. He isn't Superman. He has two arms and two legs, just like me. I can beat him and I will."

He did. He took the fight to Robinson in the first round and never let up. After fifteen rounds, he had soundly beaten the unbeatable Robinson and became a national hero in Great Britain.

His glory didn't last too long. They fought a rematch at the Polo Grounds on September 12, 1951, before a crowd of over 61,000 people. The fight was very close, but Robinson might have been slightly ahead in the scoring. Robinson had gotten a bad cut over one of his eyes, and in the tenth round he went for a desperation knockout. A hard right knocked Turpin down and on arising, Sugar Ray swarmed

---

599

600

601

him with punches until referee Ruby Goldstein waved Robinson off, Turpin's reign as champion lasted only 64 days.[602]

Randy Turpin continued boxing long past his prime until 1964. His ending was tragic. He had lived the life as a boxer and spent all his earnings. To support himself, he became a wrestler and soon went through all his earning. He died by apparent suicide at age 37 on May 17, 1966. He was found with a bullet in his head that had missed his brain and another in his heart. His daughter had also been shot but was rushed to the hospital and made a full recovery.

Randy Turpin was inducted in the IBHOF in 2001. His record was 66 wins, 8 losses, and 1 draw.[603]

> So we leave this game which was hard and cruel.
> And down at the show on a ringside stool.
> We'll watch the next man, just one more fool."
> (Written by Randy Turpin)

Sugar Ray Robinson, 1951–1952

In 1952, he fought a rematch with Bobo Olson, whom he had already beaten, winning by a decision. He next defeated former champion Rocky Graziano by a third-round knockout, then challenged world light heavyweight champion Joey Maxim. In the Yankee Stadium bout with Maxim, Robinson built a lead on all three judges' scorecards, but the 103°F temperature in the ring took its toll. The referee, Ruby Goldstein, was the first victim of the heat and had to be replaced by referee Ray Miller. The fast-moving Robinson was the heat's next victim. At the end of round 13, he collapsed and failed to answer the bell for the next round, suffering the only knockout of his career.[604]

On June 25, 1952, after the Maxim bout, Robinson gave up his title and retired with a record of 131-3-1-1. He began a career in

---

602

603

604

show business, singing and tap-dancing. After about three years, the decline of his businesses and the lack of success in his performing career made him decide to return to boxing. He resumed training in 1954.[605]

Carl Bobo Olson, 1953–1955

Carl Olson was born in Honolulu, then territory of Hawaii on July 11, 1928. (Hawaii did not achieve statehood until 1959.) He got the nickname Bobo from his younger sister, who mispronounced *brother*.[606]

Using a fake identity card, Olson obtained a boxing license at the age of sixteen. His earliest fights were in his native Kalihi, Hawaii. He had won his first three contests, two by knockout, before his true age was discovered. During 1945, Olson ran off to San Francisco in order to continue his boxing career. By the time he was 18, he had amassed a record of 13 successive wins (10 by KO).[607]

The first real test of Olson's career came on March 20, 1950, against the Australian Dave Sands. Olson's record at this point was forty wins and two losses. Olson lost to a close points decision in Sydney. Seven months after this Olson had his first fight against Sugar Ray Robinson, for the lowly regarded Pennsylvania State world middleweight title. Olson, who was widely seen as a slow starter, failed to get into the fight, even though Robinson was not having one of his best fights. Olson managed to hold on for eleven rounds before being knocked out. Despite his great record, it was clear that Olson was still too inexperienced to be fighting at that level.[608] He fought Robinson again, going fifteen rounds, on March 13, 1952, losing a decision in fifteen rounds against the great Sugar Ray.[609]

605
606
607
608
609

Following the loss to Robinson, he put together a ten-fight winning streak. Meanwhile, Robinson had retired from boxing to go into show business, leaving the middleweight crown vacant.

Olson's winning streak paid off. In a title elimination bout against Randy Turpin, Bobo Olson captured the World Middleweight Championship in Madison Square Garden on October 21, 1953. Olson, always a slow starter, lost the first few rounds, but gathered steam as the fight progressed. He knocked the Brit down in the tenth and eleventh rounds en route to winning a unanimous decision.[610]

The year 1954 was a very good one for Bobo Olson. In addition to three successful title defenses, he also packed in four nontitle bouts, all wins. On April 2, 1954, the great Cuban welterweight Kid Gavilan challenged Olson for the middleweight championship, only to be beaten back. The fight was close, and Olson was the winner by majority decision. The fight was held at Chicago Stadium. Then, on August 20, in San Francisco's Cow Palace, he turned back the challenge of Rocky Castellani in a unanimous decision. French boxer Pierre Langlois was next. Olson stopped him in round 11 for a TKO win.[611]

Just as 1954 had been a good year for Bobo Olson, 1955 was a very bad year for the champ. After nontitle wins over TV stalwart Ralph Tiger Jones and former light heavyweight champion Joey Maxim, and probably pumped up by the latter win, he challenged light heavyweight champion Archie Moore on June 22 at New York City's Polo Grounds for the title. Moore knocked him down for the count with a hard left hook in third round.[612]

Following the knockout loss to Archie Moore, Olson elected to go back down the middleweight to defend his crown. Sugar Ray Robinson, who had retired in 1955 for a career in show business, soon found out he was a better boxer than song-and-dance man. He made a comeback in 1955 and, despite a loss to Ralph Tiger Jones, soon found himself the number one ranked middleweight contender.

610

611

612

Already a two-time middleweight champion he took on Bobo Olson on December 9, 1955, in Chicago Stadium and knocked Olson out in the second round after a fairly competitive round 1. Champion again, Robinson gave Olson a rematch on May 18, 1956, at Wrigley Field in Los Angeles, this time stopping Olson in four rounds.[613]

Olson never again fought for a world title, but he stayed busy, beating some pretty decent middleweights and light heavyweights, among them contenders Jesse Bowdry, Hank Casey, Wayne Thornton, and Piero del Papa. He retired after losing to Don Fullmer in 1966, ten years after losing the world middleweight title. Carl Bobo Olson died on January 16, 2002, in Honolulu. He was inducted in the IBHOF in 2000. His record forever stands at 97 wins, 16 losses, and 2 draws.[614]

Sugar Ray Robinson, 1955–1957

In 1955, Sugar Ray Robinson stepped into a competitive boxing ring for the first time since the Maxim fight three years before. In his biography, he claimed that his dancing had kept him fit to fight. Well, dancing is dancing and fighting is fighting. On January 5, he beat Joe Rindone [615] in Detroit, and then just two weeks later in Chicago, he lost to popular Ralph "Tiger" Jones, a regular television boxing personality. Jones lost almost as many fights as he won, but he won this night.

Undaunted, he soldiered on. He won seven straight, including two more wins, both by knockout over Bobo Olson to win the middleweight championship for the third time. Now a three-time middleweight champion, he lost his middleweight title to the rugged and awkward Mormon from Utah, Gene Fullmer. The fight took place on January 2, 1957, and Fullmer beat Robby by decision at Madison Square Garden. It could be hard watching Fullmer, certainly not the most aesthetically graceful boxer to ever lace 'em up, but he would

613

614

615

probably be the last person I would want to meet in a back alley without a shotgun. The fight was technically for the NBA version of the title, but along with it came lineal and *Ring* magazine recognition as champion.[616]

Gene Fullmer, 1957

Lawrence Gene Fullmer was born July 21, 1931, in West Jordan, Utah. He lived most of his life in West Jordan, Utah, and that is where he died on April 27, 2015. He was one tough cookie. He won the World Middleweight Championship from Sugar Ray Robinson by a unanimous decision on January 2, 1957. He held the title for only four months when Robinson knocked him out with the perfect punch on May 1 of that year.[617]

Carmen Basilio, 1957–1958

Shortly after the second Fullmer fight, Robinson took on the standing welterweight champion, Carmen Basilio of Syracuse, New York. Robinson was now thirty-six years old, and his skills and timing were no longer that of a younger man. On September 23, 1957,

616

617

after fifteen hard-fought rounds in Yankee Stadium, Carmen Basilio had triumphed and was now the World Middleweight Champion.[618] By the rules of boxing at the time, Basilio had to abandon his welterweight crown. The fight was very close and ended in a split decision. There was an immediate rematch.

That bout took place on March 25, 1958, at Chicago Stadium. The talk was mainly around Sugar Ray. He had already won the title over Jake LaMotta, Randy Turpin, Bobo Olson, and Gene Fullmer. He had been a professional boxer for almost twenty years. At his age, could he possibly win back his title for a fifth time? The fight was very close, just as the first one had been. Basilio's left eye was totally swelled shut and looked like a discolored grapefruit. But he fought on although Robinson won and was now a five-time middleweight champion, many in the crowd felt Basilio had won. There will be more to the Basilio story in the welterweight section of this chapter.[619]

Meanwhile, the NBA had stripped Sugar Ray of his crown for failure to defend and matched Gene Fullmer against Carmen Basilio to be their champion. Fullmer won the NBA title, and once again, a world championship was split. Fullmer was a fighting champion. On December 4, 1959, he took on Oklahoman Spider Webb and defeated him by decision of fifteen rounds in Logan, Utah. That defense was followed by a wild brawl in Bozeman, Montana, between Fullmer and perennial contender Joey Giardello of Philadelphia. There was almost as much headbutting as punching and during one round, Giardello blatantly headbutted Fullmer in retaliation for Fullmer's constant use of his head as a weapon. The fight was called a draw, and Fullmer retained his title.[620]

He fought Carmen Basilio again, this time in Salt Lake City, and stopped him again by a twelfth-round TKO. In what might have been the most memorable defense, he took on Sugar Ray Robinson for the third time on December 3, 1960. Robinson fought a magnificent fight and won either ten or eleven rounds. The crowd erupted

---

618

619

620

with boos when the draw decision was announced, allowing champion Fullmer to keep his crown. I watched this fight on television with my father, and both of us were dumfounded at the decision. Watching it now sixty years later, Robinson still wins. Boo!

In the meantime, Sugar Ray had taken on Brookline, Massachusetts, boxer Paul Pender on June 22, 1960, at the Boston Garden, and Pender triumphed behind a good jab and a hard right cross. The fight was viewed as a tremendous upset since Pender was unknown outside of his home state of Massachusetts. It proved to be a sound decision as Pender then beat Robinson for a second time for the lineal and world crown. Both fights were close. Robinson would challenge one more time, this time against Fullmer, and the Mormon won a unanimous decision. Robinson would never again challenge for a world title. He fought on until 1965 in a series of ten round bouts but retired after losing to light hitting Joey Archer. His final record stands at 200 fights, 173 wins, 19 losses, 6 draws, and 2 no contests. Almost all the 19 losses came after the age of forty.[621]

Paul Pender, 1960–1961, 1962–1963

Pender was born in the Boston suburb of Brookline, Massachusetts, the son of William and Anna (Leicester) Pender. A 1949 graduate of Brookline High School, Pender was recruited as an all-American football player at Michigan State University and Penn

621

State but instead chose to enter professional boxing, while attending Staley College. Although a champion, he regarded boxing as his second job and being a Brookline firefighter his first. As an amateur, he won the New England welterweight championship.[622]

Paul Pender turned professional on January 28, 1949, beating Paul Williams by knockout in Boston. He then proceeded to run up a record of nineteen wins and one draw. By 1950, his hands began bothering him. Pender had several broken hands during his career. In 1954, he underwent surgery to remove a piece of floating bone in his hand.[623] But any hopes that the problem had been solved evaporated when he broke his hand again outpointing Ted Olla.

Satchel Sam Silverman, the Boston promoter who had staged virtually all of Pender's fights, persuaded Robinson that the apparently nonthreatening and brittle-handed Pender would not pose much of a problem and would give the champion an easy defense. His persuasiveness paid off. [624] Pender beat Sugar Ray not once, but twice.

Welterweights of the Nineteen Fifties

Kid Gavilan, 1951–1954

Gerardo González (January 6, 1926–February 13, 2003), known in the boxing world as Kid Gavilan, was a World Welterweight Champion from Camagüey, Cuba.[625] Boxing Writers Association of America named him Fighter of the Year in 1953. Gavilán was voted by *The Ring* magazine as the twenty-sixth greatest fighter of the last eighty years. He turned professional on June 5, 1943, when he beat Antonio Diaz by a decision in four rounds in Havana.[626]

Gavilan moved to the United States from Cuba in 1948 and soon established himself as a contender with wins over Tommy Bell

---

622

623

624

625

626

and Tony Pellone and losses to Ike Williams and Sugar Ray Robinson. No shame there! On June 11, 1949, he challenged a peak Sugar Ray Robinson for the welterweight championship of the world, but he was outpointed by Robinson over fifteen rounds. Finally, on May 18, 1951, Kid Gavilan became the Welterweight Champion of the World in a fifteen-round decision over Johnny Bratton in Madison Square Garden. He made the first defense of his crown against the highly skilled Billy Graham (not the Evangelist). It was a very close fight with Gavilan winning a split decision on August 29, 1951, in Madison Square Garden.[627]

Now champion, Gavilan fought four nontitle bouts and then defended the crown against Bobby Dykes in Miami on February 24, 1952. Gavilan won by split decision after fifteen. In July of that year, he defeated Gil Turner at the Municipal Stadium in Philly and won by an eleventh-round TKO. He defeated Billy Graham again and then stopped Chuck Davey in another successful defense.[628]

On September 18, 1953, he eked out a close win over ruff n' tuff Carmen Basilio. He then fought Bobo Olson over the weight and lost to the middleweight champion in fifteen rounds. He then dropped back down to welterweight and lost the title to Johnny Saxton.[629]

From that point until 1958, when he retired, he had a career of ups and downs. He lost to Dykes, Jones, Eduardo Lausse, former world champion Tony DeMarco, Vince Martinez, and Gaspar Ortega, but he also beat Ortega, Jones, and Chico Vejar, among others. After losing to Yama Bahama by decision in ten on June 18, 1958, he never fought again, announcing his retirement on September 11 of that year. Gavilan was one of the few boxers never knocked out in their professional careers. Gavilán was a 1966 inductee to *The Ring* magazine's Boxing Hall of Fame (disbanded in 1987) and was an inaugural 1990 inductee to the International Boxing Hall of Fame. He had a record of 107 wins, 30 losses, and 6 draws, with 1 no con-

---

[627]

[628]

[629]

test and 27 wins by knockout in a career that spanned 143 professional fights.[630]

Johnny Saxton, 1954–1955

Saxton turned professional in 1949 and ran up forty wins without a defeat before losing to Gil Turner in 1953. His win over Joey Giardello and Johnny Bratton helped propel him to fight with Kid Gavilán (or Gavilan) in 1954 for the world welterweight championship. He beat Gavilan via a fifteen-round decision to take the title. He lost the title the following year via technical knockout against Tony DeMarco. In 1956, he won the title again with an upset win over Carmen Basilio, but lost the title in a rematch with Basilio later in the year. He retired in 1958.[631]

Saxton, brother of Richard Eugene Kyle, who boxed for the US Army, was managed by Frank "Blinky" Palermo, a member of the Philadelphia crime family. Palermo was imprisoned in 1961 for conspiracy and extortion for the covert ownership of prizefighters. Saxton's career was often marred by rumors of shady dealings. His two biggest wins, against Gavilan and Basilio, were both controversial and unpopular with many in the boxing world.[632]

His career record: Won, 55 (KOs, 21); Lost, 9; Draw, 2.[633]

Tony DeMarco, 1955

DeMarco was born Leonardo Liotta in 1932 in Boston. When Leonardo was ready to turn pro, he was only sixteen years old, so he borrowed a friend's, Tony DeMarco's, birth certificate to show he was eighteen.[634] On October 21, 1948, he knocked out Mester Jones in one round, and voila! His name was now Tony DeMarco. While he only held the welterweight title a little over two months, he fought

---

630
631
632
633
634

a number of top men in the division. Among those he fought were Paddy DeMarco, Teddy "Red Top" Davis, Chico Vejar, Don Jordan, and in winning the welterweight championship of the world, he beat Johnny Saxton by a TKO in the fourteenth round of their bout at the Boston Garden on April 1, 1955.[635]

Poor Tony. Despite impressive wins on his way to the title, he is best remembered for his two exciting fights against future hall of fame boxer Carmen Basilio. Both fights were toe-to-toe slugfests with several ebbs and flows that kept the fans at the edges of their seats. Both fights ended in the twelfth round, with DeMarco suffering a TKO. [636] In their first bout, DeMarco was the defending champion. He risked his title by taking on Basilio, who was the top-ranked contender. Although Basilio prevailed, the fight was so exciting that the pair were rematched. The second fight was almost a carbon copy of the first, with Basilio wearing down DeMarco, but not before a wicked DeMarco left hook had Basilio out on his feet. DeMarco was unable to capitalize on this advantage and lost the match on a twelfth-round TKO. [637]

Carmen Basilio, 1955–1956

Carmen Basilio (Born Carmine Basilio, April 2, 1927, in Syracuse, New York—November 7, 2012) was an American professional boxer who was the world champion in both the welterweight and middleweight divisions, beating Sugar Ray Robinson for the latter title. An iron-chinned pressure fighter, Basilio was a combination puncher who had great stamina and eventually wore many of his opponents down with vicious attacks to the head and body.[638]

He won the world welterweight championship on June 10, 1955, on a twelfth-round TKO over defending champion Tony DeMarco. Their second fight took place on November 30 of that same year, and again, Basilio stopped Tony in twelve. He then lost the

635

636

637

638

title briefly to Johnny Saxton on March 14, 1956, and then regained it from Saxton on September 12, 1956. He won the rubber match on February 22, 1957, and then abandoned the crown to move up to middleweight where he challenged Sugar Ray Robinson, winning and losing. He continued his career as a middleweight, losing twice to Gene Fullmer and fought on until 1961, losing his last fight in a challenge to lineal champion Paul Pender. He died in 2012. He was eighty-five.[639]

Virgil Akins, 1958

Virgil Akins was born in St. Louis, Missouri, in 1928. He turned professional in 1948 and won the World Welterweight Championship in a six-man tournament to replace Carmen Basilio, who had moved up to middleweight. En route to the title, he posted wins over Tony DeMarco (twice), Isaac Logart, and favored Vince Martinez in the finals, whom he knocked out in the fourth round on June 6, 1958, after knocking Martinez down nine times.

For his first defense, he took on Los Angeles-based welterweight Don Jordan on December 5, 1958, and lost by fifteen-round decision. Akins died on January 22, 2011. He was eighty-two.[640]

Don Jordan 1958–1960

Don Jordan was born on June 22, 1934, in Los Angeles, California. He had a brief amateur career consisting of just fifteen fights of which he lost just one. Jordan turned professional in April 1953 and made steady progress through the welterweight ranks. After twice beating Mexican contender Gaspar Ortega, he was matched against Virgil Akins for the World Welterweight Championship. On December 5, 1958, he outboxed Akins to become champion.[641]

639

640

641

Akins contested the decision, and in the rematch, Jordan again won, this time convincingly. Next, he successfully defended against Portland, Oregon, contender Denny Moyer and then took on Cuban welter Benny Kid Paret on May 27, 1960, at the Las Vegas Convention Center.[642] Boxing was beginning to move west, and over the next several years, the professional boxing epicenter would no longer be New York City, but Las Vegas, Nevada.[643]

642

643

CHAPTER XII

The Fifties Part II

By the middle of the decade in the middle of the twentieth century, many people were familiar with a lot of the boxing champions. The reason? Boxing had become one of the most popular pastimes on television, and by now, almost everyone owned a TV set. Most, if not all the boxers I have written about in the last chapter were on television, and America watched them. It was both a blessing and a curse. Television ate away at the live crowds, and gone were the days when ninety-one thousand fans packed Boyles Thirty Acres to watch Jack Dempsey knock out Georges Carpentier. Now Americans by the millions could watch Ralph Tiger Jones, Gaspar Ortega, Sugar Ray Robinson, Kid Gavilan, Gene Fullmer, Joe Brown, Carmen Basilio, and others absolutely free while sipping a cold beer in their favorite chair. If the picture was a little fuzzy, no problem. Just get up and adjust the rabbit ears. Here are more of the standout champions and contenders of the Fifties.

Lightweights of the Nineteen Fifties

Ike Williams, 1947–1951

Both a skilled boxer and a hard puncher, Ike Williams had won the lineal world lightweight championship in 1947. Already the NBA champion, he took on NYSAC champion Bob Montgomery on August 4, 1947, and knocked him out in six rounds in Philadelphia.

The win unified the title and Ike Williams was now Undisputed World Lightweight Champion.[644]

Williams made successful defenses of his title in Wrigley Field, Madison Square Garden, Yankee Stadium, and Chicago Stadium. Imagine one of the lightweight champions today fighting in outdoor stadiums. Boxing mattered.

Ike Williams held his title until he was stopped in the fourteenth round by Jimmy Carter (not the President) in Madison Square Garden on May 21, 1951.[645] He continued boxing until 1955.[646]

Williams was managed for part of his career by mobster Frank "Blinky" Palermo. He was called to testify in 1961 before the Kefauver Commission investigating criminal activity in professional boxing. In 1961, in his testimony, Williams stated that all boxers are asked to take bribes and that he was boycotted as a result of trying to manage himself. He explained that he could not get a fight because he did not use a manager and that he could not book a fight until he found a manager from the managers' guild. He explained that he did not receive his share of his purse in two fights, which included Jesse Flores in Yankee Stadium, for the lightweight title on September 23, 1948, and Beau Jack at Shibe Park in Philadelphia, on July 12, 1948, and September 23, 1948. In those fights, the money owed him was $32,500 and $32,400. He testified he told the boxing association to temporarily hold on to the money for these two fights for tax purposes. Later when he asked for his money, he discovered that his shares of the profits had been taken by his manager, who claimed to have fallen on hard times and spent it. Williams still had to pay the taxes on his share of the profits, though he never received them.[647]

He further testified that his manager was offered $30,000 for him to throw a championship fight against Freddy Dawson in Philadelphia on December 5, 1949, though he declined. He testified that ten minutes before the fight, he heard the judges being told if he

---

644

645

646

647

did not win by a knockout, the fight would go to Dawson. Williams won the fight and told the media afterward that he had heard a rumor that the fight would be fixed to go to Dawson by decision of the judges if he did not win by a knockout. Williams believed that the judges, upon hearing that he called the media, decided to not fix the fight by giving an unfair decision to Dawson. Nonetheless, Williams was fined $500 for his comments to the media.[648]

He also recalled a fight against Kid Gavilan on January 28, 1949, at Madison Square Garden, in which he was offered $100,000 to throw the fight. Again, Ike Williams did not take the money, an action he regretted because he lost the fight even though a plurality of reporters in subsequent news stories that cover the fight believed he had won. This made Williams conclude that the judges may have also been influenced in this fight to vote for his opponent in the case of a point's decision.[649]

Williams also believed he lost his lightweight title in a bout with the boxer Jimmy Carter on May 25, 1951, in a bout where the judges were also influenced. He testified he was again offered to throw the fight for a sum of $50,000. Again, Williams said he regretted not taking the money as he lost the fight in a similar fashion as before.[650]

Williams testified he never took the money offered to him to fix fights because too many people were counting on him and that too many of his friends had bet their hard earned money on him.

He died at his home of natural causes on September 5, 1994. He was seventy-one.

648

649

650

Jimmy Carter, 1951–1952

Jimmy Carter, born December 15, 1923, in South Carolina and raised fighting in the streets of Harlem, began boxing as an amateur at the age of fourteen at a Catholic Boys Club. He turned professional on February 24, 1947,[651] winning a decision at St. Nicholas Arena in New York City. He won twenty-two of his first twenty-six fights, notable opponents during this phase of his career included future lightweight champion Joe Brown and future featherweight champion Sandy Saddler.[652]

Carter won the World Lightweight Championship by a fourteenth round TKO at Madison Square Garden on May 25, 1951, over Ike Williams. Williams was heavily favored and the Carter win was considered an upset. Carter scored four knockdowns in the win before the referee stopped the contest.[653] He successfully defended against Art Aragon at the Olympic Stadium in Los Angeles to whom he had lost earlier in a fight that may have been a fix; his manager was thought by some to be Mafia kingpin Frankie Carbo.[654]

Carter lost the title on May 18, 1952, to Lauro Salas in a controversial split decision at the Olympic Auditorium in Los Angeles.[655]

651

652

653

654

655

Lauro Salas, 1952

Salas was known as a tireless puncher, who often would wear his opponents out in the late rounds with a volume of punches. Boxing as a featherweight for much of his early career, he was given a title shot against lightweight champion Jimmy Carter on April 1, 1952, at the Olympic Auditorium in Los Angeles. Appearing to be well behind for the first ten rounds, Salas staged a late rally in the championship rounds, which he capped off with a two-count knockdown of the champion in the fifteenth round. Carter would win the unanimous decision, even as Salas won a lot of respect for his valiant effort.[656]

Six weeks later as a 4-to-1 underdog he faced Carter again for the title at the Olympic in a rematch. This time around, he got off to a much better start, cut the champion, and once again overwhelmed Carter with his pressure in the late rounds. This time around, he was awarded a split decision over Carter, to win the world lightweight title.[657]

On October 15, 1952, Salas fought a rubber match with Carter at Chicago Stadium. In the rematch, Carter established control inside, dictating the pace, and cutting Salas over both of the eyes. With his vision hampered by cuts, along with the punishment he had taken from Carter, he was unable to sustain a late rally. Carter was awarded a wide unanimous decision to regain the Lightweight title for the second time.[658]

Jimmy Carter, Second Reign, 1952–1954

On March 5, 1954, Carter lost his second World Lightweight Championship against Paddy DeMarco in a fifteen-round unanimous decision at New York's Madison Square Garden.[659] DeMarco, a 4–1, underdog, won the decision with ease rocking the crowd of 5,730 with a remarkable upset. Carter tried for a knockout through-

---

656
657
658
659

out the bout, but DeMarco scored continuously with fleet footwork and a punishing left.[660]

Carter lost his title for the second time to Brooklyn scrapper Paddy DeMarco on March 5, 1954, at Madison Square Garden. DeMarco, a 4-1, underdog won the decision with ease rocking the crowd of 5,730 with a remarkable upset. Carter tried for a knock-out throughout the bout, but DeMarco scored continuously with fleet footwork and a punishing left. Both judges gave DeMarco nine rounds, with the referee giving him 7.[661]

Paddy DeMarco, 1954

In 1954, DeMarco twice challenged reigning World Lightweight Champion Jimmy Carter for the Lightweight Championship of the World. He won the first meeting on March 5, 1954, in a fifteen-round unanimous decision at Madison Square Garden. In a major upset, that saw him as a 4-1 underdog in the early betting, DeMarco won the bout decisively on points and took the world title. In the first two rounds, DeMarco gained a lead on points with close range jabs, hooks, and body punching. Though losing the fourteenth round, DeMarco dominated on points particularly from the sixth and subsequent rounds where he clearly looked the winner.[662]

In DeMarco's first defense, he clearly did not look the winner, losing the title on November 17, 1954 to…guess who? If you answered Jimmy Carter, you win! Carter won the title Lightweight Championship of the World for the third time in a little over three years. In the brutal and savage bout, the referee stopped the fighting in the final round, with DeMarco virtually out on his feet, his left eye nearly swollen shut, and his cheek rapidly turning a dark blue. Carter had him down twice, once for a four count from a left hook to the chin in the ninth and once in the fourteenth.[663]

660

661

662

663

Jimmy Carter, Third Reign, 1954–1956

Carter lost the title for the last time to Wallace "Bud" Smith at Boston Garden in a fifteen-round split decision on June 29, 1955.[664] Though the bout was close, Carter took one of the worst beatings of his career from Smith requiring fifteen stitches over his eyes. Smith himself needed three stitches to fix a cut over his own eye. The crowd of only 1,983 saw a razor close, hotly contested title match. Two of the officials gave a margin of only one point between the two boxers.

Jimmy Carter, three-time Lightweight Champion of the World, died of a heart attack on September 21, 1994, at the age of seventy. He was inducted in the IBHOF in 2000.[665]

Wallace "Bud" Smith, 1955–1956

Wallace "Bud" Smith (April 2, 1924–July 10, 1973) was a world lightweight boxing champion in 1955, who also competed in the 1948 Olympic Games. His trainer was John Joiner of Cincinnati, and his manager was Vic Marsillo.[666]

Born in Cincinnati, Ohio, Smith was the 1947 AAU featherweight champion. He won Chicago's 1948 lightweight Golden Gloves inter-city tournament with a furious attack against Luis Ortiz, achieving a knockout in 2:45 of the second round. He represented the United States at the 1948 Olympic Games in the lightweight division. Smith defeated Chuck Davey of Michigan State University to earn a spot on the team.[667]

Smith turned pro on November 29, 1948, with a first-round knockout of Torpedo Tinsley at the Music Hall in Cincinnati. Over the next seven years, Smith established himself as one of the

---

664

665

666

667

world's top lightweights with victories over top-rated Red Top Davis, Orlando Zulueta, and Arthur Persley.[668]

On June 29, 1955, Smith beat the 4-1 odds against him and defeated 3-time world lightweight champion Jimmy Carter in a 15-round split decision at Boston Garden to take the title. The fight was fierce and bloody, and only 1,983 fans turned out for the contest between the black contestants who were not especially well-known. Carter needed fifteen stitches over his eyes to mend from the rough bout, in which he likely took the worst damage of his career. Even Smith needed three stitches to recover from the bout.[669]

He made one successful defense, again beating Jimmy Carter. On August 24, 1956, Smith lost his title in an upset to Joe Brown in a 15-round split decision in New Orleans. Smith was down twice in the fourteenth round. The Associated Press had Smith ahead 8 rounds to 7, though the officials gave him a greater lead, and Smith might have won the bout if not for suffering a broken right hand in the second round. In a rematch with Brown on February 13, 1957, Smith lost to Brown in an 11th-round TKO in Miami. Smith went on to fight one more year, ending his career after losing 11 straight fights, half by knockout.[670]

Smith retired in 1959. On July 10, 1973, Smith saw a man beating up a woman in Cincinnati and stepped in. After a struggle, the man pulled a gun and shot Smith in the head, killing him.[671] A sad ending to a very likeable man.

668
669
670
671

Joe Brown, 1956–1962

At around age twelve, I fell in love with boxing. Because of my great passion for the sport, the televised *Wednesday Night Fights* and later the *Friday Night Fights* were always on in our living room. My older brother was a musician, and sometimes even the members of his band would come by and watch the fights with me. My favorite boxer at the time was Joe "Old Bones" Brown, a savvy, smart light-weight who also had a good punch. I don't really know what makes a person like one boxer he or she has never met, but there was some-thing about Old Bones that resonated with me.

Brown was born May 18, 1926. So he would have been around thirty-three years old the first time I saw him. The last time I saw him, against Carlos Ortiz, I probably went into mourning. Bones had his share of defeats, mostly early in his career and late in his career (he fought into his forties), but while he was champion from 1956, when he defeated Wallace "Bud" Smith by a split decision to win the lightweight crown until he lost it in 1962 to Carlos Ortiz, he was a marvelous champion.

Once champion, Brown hoped that his newly acquired status would confer the riches and popular recognition denied to him for so long. Yet as George Gainford (manager of Sugar Ray Robinson) noted, the name Joe Brown was hardly inspirational. Realizing this, Brown attempted to solve his problems by billing himself as Joe "Old Bones" Brown. The gimmick worked and he became something of a draw for the remainder of his championship career.[672] I had never heard this story about how he came to known as Old Bones, and I

672

couldn't find a footnote about it. So I will just credit it to Wikipedia, who has been so helpful to me in the writing of this book.

Over the next six years, Joe Brown defended the lightweight title eleven times. In that time, all the boxers he fought were top contenders. In his reign, he beat Smith again, this time by knockout in eleven rounds. After demolishing Smith, Brown beat Orlando Zulueta, Joey Lopes, Ralph Dupas, Kenny Lane, Johnny Busso, Paolo Rosi, Cisco Andrade, Bert Somodio, and Dave Charnley (twice).[673]

Brown fought on for another eight years, before retiring in 1970, at the age of 44, with a record of 104 wins, 44 losses, and 13 draws with 47 KOs. Joe "Old Bones" Brown died on December 4, 1997, in New Orleans, the city that he loved.[674] Brown was inducted in the IBHOF in 1996. He was a great fighter and a great champion. Could he have beaten Roberto Durán or Floyd Mayweather Jr.? Probably not, but he would have fought them both and given them both a heck of a fight.

Featherweights of the Nineteen Fifties

Sandy Saddler, 1951–1956

Sandy Saddler ruled the featherweight division from the time he beat the great Willie Pep in 1950 until he retired on January 1, 1957. After winning back the world featherweight championship, he defended against Willie Pep and beat him again on September 26, 1951, in Madison Square Garden. This fight goes down in infamy as the dirtiest fight of all time. He stayed busy fighting ten round nontitle fights and did not defend his title again until February 25, 1955, when he won a fifteen-round unanimous decision over Teddy Davis in Madison Square Garden. During that rather lengthy spell, he fought fifteen nontitle fights. On January 18, 1956, he took on the great Filipino boxer Flash Elorde. Saddler reversed an earlier loss to Elorde in a nontitle affair, and now with the title on the line, Saddler scored a thirteenth round TKO to successfully defend his title in Oakland, California.

673

674

Saddler retired from boxing in 1956, aged 30, after an eye injury sustained in a traffic accident.

His record stands at 162 total fights, of which he won 144, scoring 103 knockouts. He is one of a handful of professional prize fighters to have scored over 100 knockouts. He had just 16 losses and 2 draws. He was a 1990 inductee into the IBHOF. He died on September 18, 2001.[675]

Hogan Kid Bassey, 1957–1959

Hogan Kid Bassey was born in Nigeria, West Africa, as Okon Asuquo Bassey on June 3, 1932. He was the first world champion of Nigerian descent. He relocated to Liverpool, UK, after his early fights in Nigeria.[676]

Upon the retirement of Sandy Saddler, Bassey was matched with French Algerian boxer Cherif Hamia for the vacant World Featherweight Championship. He won the world crown by defeating Hamia in Paris in 1957.[677]

Bassey successfully defended his world title against Mexican challenger Ricardo Moreno in Los Angeles, California, on April 1, 1958, by stopping Moreno via third-round KO. He beat a faded Willie Pep by ninth-round TKO, and then he met star-crossed boxer Davey Moore of Springfield, Ohio, and was TKO'd when Bassey's manager threw in the towel in the thirteenth round, and the title passed to the Ohioan.[678]

Davey Moore, 1959–1963

Davey Moore was born on November 1, 1933, in Lexington, Kentucky. Moore first gained wide attention from his performance on the 1952 US Olympic boxing team, as a bantamweight amateur.[679]

675
676
677
678
679

Moore made his professional debut on May 11, 1953, aged 19, beating Willie Reece by a decision in six rounds. He boxed 8 times in 1953, with a total record that year of 6 wins, 1 loss and 1 no contest.

From the beginning of his career through 1956, Moore fought a total of 29 bouts, with a total record of 22-5-1, and 1 no contest. Beginning with his April 10, 1957, fight against Gil Cadilli, Moore had an 18-bout winning streak, ending when he lost to Carlos Morocho Hernández on March 17, 1960, with a TKO. On March 14, 1960, he won a match against Bob Gassey in the first round. As a result of the knockout, Gassey lost all but two teeth. It was during this period, on March 18, 1959, that Moore won the world featherweight title from Hogan "Kid" Bassey. Moore retained the title through the remainder of his career, defending it successfully 5 times, and losing it to Sugar Ramos on March 21, 1963.[680]

On March 21, 1963, Moore took on Cuban challenger Sugar Ramos in Los Angeles in a nationally televised fight. It was on this night that Davy Moore met his Waterloo. In the tenth round of the championship fight, Ramos knocked Moore down. Moore was clearly hurt, but he got to his feet at "nine" and lasted out the tenth round, but the referee stopped the contest before the eleventh round. He gave an apparent clear-headed interview before he left the ring, but once in his dressing room he lapsed into a coma and died seventy-five hours later on March 25, 1963.[681]

Davey Moore died with a record of 59 wins, 7 losses, and 1 draw with 30 knockouts. His death created quite a stir among the "ban boxing" crowd, coming only a year after another nationally televised championship fight between Emile Griffith and Benny Kid Paret ended in tragedy. As he lie in state, over ten thousand people stopped to pay respects.[682] I am surprised he is not in the IBHOF. This is a glaring omission.

680

681

682

Bantamweights of the Nineteen Fifties

The lighter weight classes of boxing have never captured the imagination of American boxing fans the way heavyweights, light heavyweights, middleweights, and welterweights have. Maybe it is because so many of the smaller men come from foreign countries such as Korea, Japan, Thailand, Mexico, Panama, and Nicaragua. Even during the golden era of televised boxing in the Fifties and Sixties, it would have been extremely rare to see a bantam or fly-weight fight on American network TV. As a result, the pugilists I will be covering are not generally well-known. Let's see if I can change that. The first undisputed World Bantamweight Champion in fact came from South Africa. His name was Vic Toweel.

Vic Toweel, 1950–1952

Vic Toweel was born January 12, 1928, in South Africa. He was the first South African to hold a world title.[683]

Toweel's father, better known as Pappa Mike, taught his sons Jimmy, Victor, Fraser, Willie, and Allan the basic rudiments of box-ing and forged a family legacy in a makeshift corrugated iron gymna-sium in the backyard of his home in Benoni. All the Toweel brothers achieved success in the boxing world: Willie won an Olympic bronze medal and fought for a world title, Allan was a top trainer, Maurice was an outstanding matchmaker, and Jimmy was a South African champion.

Vic Toweel was an instinctive boxer who, at his best, flaunted incredible stamina, perfect balance and a blazing work ethic. His greatest asset as a fighter was his ability to throw nonstop batteries of punches without tiring.[684]

On May 31, 1950, in his 14th fight, at the age of 21, he won the world bantamweight championship.

683

684

Fighting using nicknames including Dynamite, Benoni's Mighty Mouse, the Benoni Buzzaw, and the white Henry Armstrong for his constant attack fighting style, Toweel beat world bantamweight champion Manuel Ortiz, who was recognized as one of the greatest bantamweight champions of all time. At that stage, Manuel Ortiz was a veteran of 110 fights, whereas Vic had had only fought 13 contests as a professional.[685]

During his reign as a world champion, Toweel had 13 bouts consisting of 3 successful title defenses and 10 successful nontitle fights against world rated contenders.

He successfully defended his world title against Danny O'Sullivan (KO 10th round), whom he dropped 14 times, winning him a place in the *Guinness World Records* for the most knockdowns in a world title fight.[686] His second and third title defenses were against Luis Romero (won in 15 rounds) and Peter Keenan (won in 15 rounds). A drastically weight-weakened Vic was dethroned by Australian Jimmy Carruthers in his fourth title defense.[687]

Carruthers gave Toweel a return match on March 21, 1953, and a crowd of 35,000 saw him holding his own until the sixth round, when he began to fade. He was counted out in the tenth.

On November 6, 1953, Vic had his last fight, in the welterweight division, when he stopped Harry Walker in the 8th.

After years of battling with his weight and only two months short of his 27th birthday, he decided to hang up his gloves with a professional record was 28-3-1 (14).[688]

685

686

687

688

Jimmy Carruthers, 1952–1954, Retired

James William Carruthers (July 5, 1929–August 15, 1990) was an Australian boxer who became world champion in the bantamweight division. He stopped Vic Toweel on November 11, 1952, and repeated with another stoppage over Toweel on March 21, 1953. Both contests took place at Rand Stadium in Johannesburg.

On May 2, 1954, Carruthers went all the way to Bangkok, Thailand, to successfully defend against Thai boxer Chamroen Sonhgkitrat. Chamroen took him the distance, and Carruthers won by a unanimous fifteen-round decision.[689]

Jimmy Carruthers retired on May 16, 1954, as undefeated world bantamweight champion. His record reads 21 wins and four losses with 13 knockouts. He died August 9, 1990. He was inducted into the IBHOF in 1995.[690]

Robert Cohen, 1954–1956

Robert Cohen was a French Jewish boxer who was born November 15, 1930, in French Algeria. After turning professional, he won the French bantamweight title and the European title. On September 19, 1954, he won the vacant world title in a fifteen-round split decision in Bangkok, Thailand, against Chamroem Songkitrat. An enormous crowd

---

689

690

of sixty thousand that included the king and queen of Thailand watched the bloody contest. Cohen was left with a badly sprained or broken wrist in the fifth and his opponent with a broken nose. Cohen was formerly the European Bantamweight Champion.[691]

Two days before Christmas, on December 23, 1954, the NBA stripped Cohen of the title he fought for because he didn't defend within ninety days of their preferred opponent, Raton Macias.[692] Cohen lost a title bout to deaf-mute Mario D'Agata on June 29, 1956, before a crowd of thirty-eight thousand, in a seventh-round technical knockout in Rome. D'Agata dropped Cohen to the canvas for a nine-count near the end of the sixth. After the sixth ended, the referee stopped the fight due to a serious gash over the left brow of Cohen. D'Agata appeared superior in the in-fighting, and many of Cohen's blows were wide of his mark. America's National Boxing Association (NBA) did not recognize the match as a title bout, though nearly every other world boxing organization did. Only a year and a half earlier, D'Agata had been injured by a shotgun blast.[693]

Mario D'Agata, 1956–1957

D'Agata was born on May 29, 1926, in Arezzo, Italy. He had a tough childhood as a consequence of his disabilities, the victim of taunting from fellow schoolchildren. Feeling the need to prove himself equal, he resorted to street fighting as a way to demonstrate his equality. D'Agata was one of three children (out of seven) to be born deaf in his family. His parents moved him from Tuscany to Rome at an early age, hoping to find doctors who would cure him.[694]

One afternoon he noticed a poster of a boxer adorning the door to a boxing gym. Upon entering, he was enamored with how the boxers practiced their fighting in a polished, stylized way. D'Agata was drawn into boxing from that moment on. Due to the outbreak of the Second World War, however, D'Agata had to wait until he was 20 years old to fight as an amateur. In 1946, he began an amateur career that saw him win 90 out of 110 bouts.

691
692
693
694

D'Agata fought his way up through the professional ranks beginning on October 14, 1950, and ran his record up to 10 wins, before suffering his first defeat. In 1953, he won the Italian bantamweight championship, and then he traveled to Tunisia and lost a ten round decision to Robert Cohen. After two more wins, he embarked on what would have been a long tour of Australia, a trip cut short after three wins when he was shot by his associate.[695]

On June 29, 1956, D'Agata finally received his world title opportunity, when former conqueror Cohen gave him a chance to win the world bantamweight title in Rome. D'Agata made his dream come true by knocking Cohen out in six rounds in front of 38,000 fans, many of whom rushed to the ring the moment the fight was over, carrying D'Agata out of the ring on their arms. With that win, D'Agata made history as the first deaf world champion of boxing.[696]

On April Fool's Day 1957 in Paris, France, he took on local boxer Alphonse Halimi and lost the title in a fifteen-round unanimous decision. His reign had lasted ten months.

Alphonse Halimi, 1957–1959

He was born in Constantine, Algeria, to an Orthodox Jewish family. He was the last of 13 children, only seven of whom reached

695
696

adulthood. His father was a postal inspector. At the age of 10, he ran away from home for the first time, living for long periods of time on the streets of a nation torn by war. A tailor named Dianoux, of Algiers, took Halimi under his wing and trained him to work as a tailor by the age of 12.[697]

After Dianoux caught him in a street fight, he encouraged Halimi to take up boxing. He became an amateur boxer at age 16 and ultimately had more than 100 fights, winning amateur and military titles. Turning professional in 1955 Halimi ran up a record of 18-0 with 11 knockouts.[698]

On April 1, 1957, at the Vélodrome d'hiver in Paris, Halimi became world bantamweight champion by defeating the Italian deaf-mute boxer Mario d'Agata in a fifteen-round decision. The partisan Parisian crowd of 17,000 watched Halimi take 11 of the 15 rounds, while D'Agata managed to win only two.[699]

Halimi made his first title defense on November 6, 1957, against NBA recognized Raul Macias in Los Angeles' Wrigley Field. Halimi unified the split title by a narrow split decision. The now unified Bantamweight Champion of the World took on Mexican challenger Jose Becerra on July 8, 1959, before 15,000 rabid pro-Becerra fans. Becerra dropped Halimi with a left hook to the jaw and when Halimi arose Becerra went after him until the flurry of punches that followed dropped Halimi for the ten count. With that, Jose Becerra became the new bantamweight champion.[700]

In retirement, Halimi opened café in Vincennes, outside of Paris. An avid swimmer, Halimi also worked as a swimming instructor. He died November 12, 2006.

Jose Becerra, 1959–1960

Becerra was born in Guadalajara, Jalisco, Mexico, and the youngest of the five children. His parents were Maria Covarrubias

697

698

699

700

and Jesus Becerra. At age twelve, in the fifth grade, Becerra quit school to work in a carriage repair shop.[701]

Becerra turned professional on August 30, 1953, in Guadalajara, knocking out Ray Lopez. By the time he got his title shot against Alphonse Halimi, he had close to fifty fights. After two successful title defenses, Becerra lost a stunning upset, being knocked out by club-fighter Eloy Sanchez in a nontitle fight. Becerra was so dejected by the defeat that he announced his retirement at age twenty-four.

Jose Becerra left this Earth on August 6, 2016. He was eighty years old. He had a professional record of 75-5-3 with forty-two knockouts.[702]

Flyweights of the Nineteen Fifties

Dado Marino, 1950–1952

The new decade began with American Dado Marino atop the flyweight division. In August 1950, Terry Allen, the English holder of the world flyweight title, came to Honolulu to defend his title against Marino. Marino became world champion when he won a unanimous points decision.[703]

In November 1951, Allen returned for a rematch in Honolulu, but Marino retained the title with another unanimous decision.[704]

In his next fight, a nontitle fight, Marino was stopped in seven rounds, in Honolulu, by Yoshio Shirai, of Japan. Marino was down six times before his manager leapt through the ropes to halt the fight.

Despite this defeat, Marino agreed to defend his title against Shirai in May 1952. The title fight was in Tokyo, Japan, in front of forty thousand spectators. Shirai took Marino's title with a unanimous point decision.[705]

701

702

703

704

705

In November 1952, Marino tried to regain the title in a rematch with Shirai, again in Tokyo, but the Japanese won another unanimous decision. This was Marino's last fight.

Yoshio Shirai, 1952–1954

Yoshio Shirai was the first Japanese boxer to win a professional world title when he won the Flyweight Championship of the World from Dado Marino.[706]

He fought flyweight world champion Dado Marino on May 21, 1951, in a nontitle match. Shirai lost by split decision but fought Marino again in December 1951, to mark a seventh-round KO win. On May 19, 1952, he met Marino for the third time for the world flyweight title. Shirai won by fifteen-round decision, becoming the new world champion, and first ever Japanese boxer to win a world title.[707]

Shirai made four defenses of the world title before losing his title to Pascual Perez in November 1954 by unanimous decision. He fought Perez again in May 1955, but lost decisively by KO in the fifth round. He announced his retirement after this loss. His professional record was 48-8-2 (20 KOs).[708]

---

[706]

[707]

[708]

Pascual Perez, 1954–1960

Pascual was an Argentinian flyweight boxer who held the fly-weight title for six years. He was considered by some to be one of the four greatest flyweight champions along with Jimmy Wilde, Miguel Canto, and Roman "Chocolito" Gonzalez. He was born on May 4, 1926, in Argentina. His first notable boxing achievement was win-ning a Gold Medal at the 1948 Summer Olympics in the United Kingdom.

According to my Wikipedia source, he began boxing in gram-mar school, reputedly boxing against a kangaroo! Returning to Argentina after winning the gold, he found a lot of doors suddenly open to him. He had won virtually every amateur title in Argentina before the Olympics, but this was the impetus he needed to start his professional career.[709] On December 5, 1952, Pérez beat José Ciorino by knockout in round four at the small Argentine city of Gerly to begin his professional boxing career. After winning his first six fights by knockout, he challenged Marcelo Quiroga, November 11, 1953, for the Argentine flyweight title, winning the fight by a fourth-round knockout at Buenos Aires.[710]

709

710

Pascual won his first eighteen fights by knockout. When he fought Yoshio Shirai for the world title, he brought a record of 23 wins with 22 by knockout.[711]

On November 26 of 1954, Pérez fought what was both his first fight abroad outside the Olympics and his first world title fight. The Argentine knocked down the champion in the 2nd round and again in the 12th, in which the champion returned to his corner almost knocked out. From rounds 13 to 15, Perez nearly knocked out Shirai several times. After the fight, the score reflected a wide difference unanimously in favor of the Argentine. Referee Jack Sullivan had it 146–139, Judge Bill Pacheco, 143–139, and Judge Kuniharu Hayashi, 146–143, all in Perez's favor. He made history by beating Shirai by a fifteen-round decision, becoming Argentina's first world champion boxer, in Tokyo.[712] Pascualito became the smallest flyweight boxer to win a title.[713] Due in part to the highly international flavor of flyweight boxing, Perez became a globetrotting champion. Over the course of Pérez's next fights, he would defend his title nine times, lose for the first time, and fight in Brazil, the Dominican Republic, Curaçao, Japan, Paraguay, the Philippines, Thailand, Uruguay, and Venezuela.

Pérez would lose his title to another first time world champion, Thailand's Pone Kingpetch, who made history for his country by beating Pérez by a fifteen-round decision at Bangkok on April 16, 1960. A rematch between Pérez and Kingpetch was fought on September 22 of the same year, at Los Angeles, but Pérez's first fight in the United States was also his first knockout defeat, as he was beaten in eight rounds by Kingpetch.[714]

Perez soldiered on, winning twenty-eight nondescript fights in a row, before meeting flyweight contender Bernardo Caraballo, who beat him on a decision. After losing four of his last six fights, Pascual Perez retired in 1964.[715]

711

712

713

714

715

CHAPTER XIII

Muhammad Ali and the Sixties

The Nineteen Sixties, the most important era of social change since the Roaring Twenties. President John F. Kennedy promised us a New Frontier. Dynamic, smart, charismatic, and relatively youthful, Kennedy was as much of a pop star as any President since Teddy Roosevelt, sixty years before. America bought into it enthusiastically, and a wild ride of a decade began. The changes were dramatic. The baby boomers, the kids born in the aftermath of World War II, were now adolescents chafing at the bit for change from the old order. The new decade really started on November 22, 1963, two years into President Kennedy's first term. That day, a President was shot and died. The second Lee Harvey Oswald pulled the trigger, the 1950s ended, and the sixties began. On February 8, 1964, a British rock band called the Beatles performed on the *Ed Sullivan* variety television show and was seen by an estimated 73,000,000 people, and the Beatles took over music and culture forever. The Sixties had arrived. The decade saw the rise of the counterculture that both shocked and angered the parents of the boomers. Sex, drugs, and rock and roll became the rallying cry of hippies that embraced the counter culture lifestyle. It was also the era of Cassius Marcellus Clay, who later, as Muhammad Ali, was the perfect boxer for this time of radical change in America. It could be said that he, as much as anyone else, personified the Sixties. And of course there was the little matter of the Vietnam War.

These were the lineal World Champion on January 1, 1961.

- Heavyweight, Floyd Patterson
- Light heavyweight, Archie Moore
- Middleweight, Paul Pender
- Welterweight, Benny Kid Paret
- Lightweight, Joe Brown
- Featherweight, Davey Moore
- Bantamweight, vacant
- Flyweight, Pone Kingpetch

(Courtesy of Boxing Wiki)

Heavyweights of the Nineteen Sixties

Floyd Patterson, 1960–1962

Coming off being the first man to ever regain the heavyweight championship of the world, Patterson had defended against a journeyman, Tom McNeeley, and beaten Ingemar Johanson again in a wild rubber match. In the public mind, he could only be considered champion if he beat one man: Charles "Sonny" Liston.

Sonny Liston, 1962–1964

Charles "Sonny" Liston, born either in 1930 or 1932, was what is sometimes referred to as a bad apple. He was born dirt poor in Arkansas, but grew up in trouble in St. Louis. Liston tried going to school, but he soon left after being mocked and jeered because of his illiteracy. So he turned to crime. He soon led a gang of thugs who committed muggings and armed robberies. Because of the shirt he wore during robberies, the St. Louis police called Liston the Yellow-Shirt Bandit. When caught in January 1950, Liston gave his age as twenty, while the *St. Louis Globe-Democrat* reported that he was twenty-two. Convicted and sentenced to five years in Missouri State Penitentiary, Liston started his prison time on June 1, 1950.[716]

He was released from prison on October 31, 1952, and embarked on a brief but successful amateur career winning several amateur titles. He turned professional in 1953. The only backers willing to put up the necessary money for him to turn professional were close to underworld figures, and Liston supplemented his income by working for racketeers as an intimidator-enforcer. These connections to organized crime were an advantage early in his career, but were later used against him.[717]

Liston's criminal record, compounded by a personal association with a notorious labor racketeer, led to the police's stopping him on sight, and he began to avoid main streets. On May 5, 1956, a policeman confronted Liston and a friend about a cab parked near Liston's home. Liston assaulted the officer, breaking his knee and gashing his face. He also took his gun. He claimed the officer used racial slurs. A widely publicized account of Liston resisting arrest, even after nightsticks were allegedly broken over his skull, added to the public perception of him as a nightmarish monster impervious to physical punishment.[718] He was paroled after serving six months of a nine-month sentence, but prohibited from boxing during 1957. After repeated overnight detention by the St. Louis police and a thinly veiled threat to his life, Liston left for Philadelphia, Pennsylvania.[719]

By 1961 Liston had become the number one ranked heavyweight contender. By now, the pressure was on Floyd Patterson from two sides, those who thought Patterson was ducking Liston and

---

716

717

718

719

should give him a title shot and those, among them the NAACP, who felt that Liston would hurt the Civil Rights Movement and set a bad example for youth. Now President Trump is accused of the same thing. How times have changed! Even President John Kennedy got into the debate stating that he did not want Patterson to fight Liston. When Patterson met with the President in January 1962, Kennedy suggested that Patterson avoid Liston, citing Justice Department concerns over Liston's ties to organized crime.[720]

Sonny Liston was tough. Very tough. *The Ring* magazine ranks Liston as the tenth greatest heavyweight of all time, while boxing writer Herb Goldman ranked him second and Richard O'Brien, senior editor of *Sports Illustrated*, placed him third.[721] Alfie Potts Harmer in the *Sportster* also ranked him the third greatest heavyweight and the 6th greatest boxer at any weight. Liston was inducted into the International Boxing Hall of Fame in 1991.[722]

Enroute to earning his inevitable title shot, Liston plowed through notable heavyweight contenders Mike DeJohn (TKO, 6), Cleveland Williams (TKO, 3, and TKO, 2), Cuban heavyweight Nino Valdez (KO, 3), Roy Harris who had gone 12 rounds with Floyd Patterson (TKO, 1), Zora Folley (KO, 3), and Eddie Machen (UD, 12) according to BoxRec.com.[723]

When Sonny Liston finally met Floyd Patterson in Chicago on September 25, 1962, and the two men came into the ring, it looked for the entire world like Liston, wearing a bathrobe with towels wrapped around his neck and shoulders, which made him look even bigger would kill Patterson. Liston was arguably the greatest intimidator in boxing history. The fight was over in two minutes and six seconds. Patterson chose to take the fight to Sonny, and it was like taking peashooter to a bazooka fight. Liston knocked Patterson out with ease to become Heavyweight Champion of the World.

I have never been sure why Liston and Patterson had a rematch, but they did. The fight that took place on July 22, 1963, in Las Vegas

---

720

721

722

723

lasted four seconds longer than the first. Liston disposed of Patterson, again with ease. I don't remember who said it, but someone said, "If they fought fifty times, Liston would knock out Patterson fifty times."

After Liston lost the title to Muhammad Ali in 1964, he fought on until 1970, when he was found dead by his wife, Geraldine, in their Las Vegas home. Like his life, his death was controversial and full of theories about how/why he died. His death date was January 5, 1971. The police report claimed it was a heroin overdose. But Liston apparently had a fear of needles, and there was no evidence of a tourniquet or even a spoon to cook the drug. Officially, Liston died of lung congestion and coronary heart failure.[724] The Sonny Liston story is a very sad story.

Cassius Clay, 1960–1963

In the summer of 1960, a Louisville, Kentucky teenager named Cassius Marcellus Clay captivated the world at the 1960 Summer Olympic Games in Rome, Italy. Already, he was funny, cocky, showy, and man, could he fight! He was the star of the whole Olympic Games, in which he won a Gold Medal in the light heavyweight division and was constantly getting attention for himself interviewing with the media in the Olympic Village. The sometimes-brash eighteen-year-old even outshone such standouts as Wilma Rudolph, Rafer Johnson, Oscar Robertson, and Jerry West.

The Clay-Ali story is now legend. Many times the story has been told of how the twelve-year-old Clay, reporting his bicycle stolen, told Police Officer Joe Martin that he was going "to whup" whoever stole it. And as the legend goes, Martin told the fuming Clay that he should learn to box first.

He did, winning six Kentucky Golden Gloves titles, two National Golden Gloves titles, an AAU National title, and an Olympic Gold Medal in 1960. He turned professional later that year amid much hype and ballyhoo and defeated a veteran journeyman named Tunney Hunsaker in his first professional fight on October 29, 1960.[725] From there on, he was off on a tear. Because of his celebrity, most of his fights from 1962 on were on national television and became breakfast table conversation in millions of homes. Spoiler Billy Daniels, Argentinian Alejandro Lavorante, ancient, but still active Archie Moore, NFL football player Charlie Powell, and British champion Henry Cooper all televised matches which Clay won, and usually wrote poetry about, were as widely covered as baseball or football or basketball. Not yet even a World Champion, Cassius Clay became the most famous boxer in the world.

I want to make a case here for Doug Jones, a New York City heavyweight contender who fought Cassius Clay on March 13, 1963, at Madison Square Garden. Clay had hyped up the fight by calling Jones "an ugly little man" and saying, "He's too ugly to whup me. I'm too pretty," or something to that order. Truth be known, Doug Jones gave Clay his hardest fight up to that point. He staggered Clay in the first round and was competitive with Clay throughout the contest. Most people at ringside felt that Jones deserved the decision for Clay, which was met with boos.[726] I watched that fight on television, and I honestly believe Doug Jones beat Cassius Clay that night.

After Jones, it was Henry Cooper, a very cut-prone boxer who Clay tangled with on June 18, 1963, at London's Wembley Stadium. Cut and bleeding by the fourth round, Cooper landed his signature punch, a left hook to the jaw of Clay, and kaboom, Clay was down. He got up just as the bell rang, and then something that could only happen in boxing, as his trainer, the wily old pro Angelo Dundee, who for some mysterious reason just happened to have a razor blade, sliced the stiches between the thumb and body of one of Clay's boxing gloves. He started waving frantically to the referee saying the glove had come apart during the fight. The referee called for a new set of gloves, and Clay's corner had bought enough time for him to recover. He stopped Cooper in the next round.[727]

725

726

727

By late 1963, Clay had become the top contender for Sonny Liston's title. The fight was set for February 25, 1964, in Miami Beach.[728] Liston was an intimidating personality, a dominating fighter with a criminal past and ties to the mob. Based on Clay's uninspired performance against Jones and Cooper in his previous two fights, and Liston's destruction of former heavyweight champion Floyd Patterson in two first-round knockouts, Clay was a 7–1 underdog. Despite this, Clay taunted Liston during the prefight buildup, dubbing him the big ugly bear, stating, "Liston even smells like a bear," and claiming, "After I beat him, I'm going to donate him to the zoo."[729] Clay turned the prefight weigh-in into a circus, shouting at Liston that "someone is going to die at ringside tonight." Clay's pulse rate was measured at 120, more than double his normal 54.[730] Many of those in attendance thought Clay's behavior stemmed from fear, and some commentators wondered if he would show up for the bout.

Well, Cassius showed up and put a whuppin' on Sonny. The fearsome intimidator that had destroyed Patterson not once but twice was made to look slow and awkward against the dancing master, Clay.

I have seen this fight many times on YouTube. As early as round 1, Clay buckled Liston's knees and was stinging him like a bee with his jab, which soon opened a cut under Sonny Liston's eye. By the third round, Clay was landing combinations at blinding speed that Liston could not stop. Clay's round. In round 4, Clay appeared to be bothered by something in his eye. Liston took the round because Clay was not really fighting, just dancing away and concerned about his eyes. At the bell, he told Angelo Dundee to cut off his gloves because he could not see. Dundee refused and, washing out Clay's eyes, told him to go out there and fight. In round 5, he still appeared bothered for the first part of the round, and Liston was chasing after him trying to knock him out. Even in this blind state, Clay managed to avoid most of Liston's desperate punches. Toward the end of the

---

728

729

730

round, Clay was now fighting back, and the crowd was now on his side. In round 6, Clay was dominating Liston, hitting with three- and four-punch combinations. Again, he buckled Liston's knees and appeared to hurt Sonny. The crowd was stunned. Liston was supposed to knock this brash, young upstart out in a round or two.

Sonny Liston did not answer the bell for round 7, and pandemonium erupted. Clay, realizing Liston had quit in his corner, began a shuffling dance, and as the ring filled with officials and announcers, Clay was jumping around and shouting, "I told you! I told you I would beat the bum! I talk to God every day! I must be the greatest!" And with that, Cassius Marcellus Clay was the new Heavyweight Champion of the World.

The reaction in the crowd was mixed. Some thought the fight was a fix and started booing. Some were mad because Liston quit in his corner. Others were caught up in Clay's incredible upset victory and were standing up cheering.

Aftermath: Liston claimed he quit because he had dislocated his shoulder. The film of the fight doesn't appear to validate this claim as Sonny is still fighting hard, just getting whupped. This writer has been around boxing a long time. My belief is that as the fight progressed and it became aware that Clay was winning, Liston simply decided that rather than getting knocked out and humiliated by someone who was a seven-to-one underdog, he would claim he was injured and couldn't continue. Very few people bought into his argument, including the man writing this book. When told by Joe Louis that Liston had thrown his arm out of the socket, Clay replied, "Yeah, swinging at nothing, who wouldn't?"[731]

In the days following the fight, Clay announced to the press that his name was now Cassius X. The last name Clay was a "slave name" and that he had now joined the Nation of Islam, also known as the Black Muslims, and he would soon be given a new name by founder Elijah Muhammad. He was given the name, and from that time on, he was known as Muhammad Ali.

---

[731]

Muhammad Ali, 1964–1970, retired

His popularity took a nosedive. To most people, both white and black, the Nation of Islam was too far out of the mainstream and was viewed with hostility and suspicion. Clay, now Ali, was often seen with members of the Nation of Islam and was photographed with the controversial Malcolm X. At the time, in 1964, most Americans probably thought of Islam as something from the Middle Ages that had been a part of the Crusades. If they even gave them a serious thought, they were just people in faraway places like Africa and the Middle East. To some, they were even regarded as the enemy of Christianity, and Muhammad Ali, now the heavyweight champion of the world, symbolized that fear and threatened their security.

Second Liston Fight

Ali then faced a rematch with Liston scheduled for May 1965. It had been scheduled for Boston the previous November but was postponed for six months due to Ali's emergency surgery for a hernia three days before.[732] Due to Ali's unpopularity at the time, and the controversial ending of their first fight, ticket sales were low. Just 2,400 people attended the fight in a facility that seated only 5,000. It was a hard sell. The second Ali-Liston fight was held in a high

---

732

school gymnasium in Lewiston, Maine, and again, the fight was controversial. Midway through the first round, Liston was knocked down by a difficult-to-see blow the press dubbed a phantom punch. Referee Jersey Joe Walcott did not begin the count immediately after the knockdown, as Ali refused to retreat to a neutral corner. Liston rose after he had been down for about twenty seconds, and the fight momentarily continued. However a few seconds later Walcott, looking like a deer in the headlights and having been informed by the timekeepers that Liston had been down for a count of ten, stopped the match and declared Ali the winner by knockout. The entire fight lasted less than two minutes.[733]

Of course there was speculation and doubt. Some swore the so-called anchor punch Ali claimed to have learned studying Jack Johnson had not even landed. Others thought it landed but certainly was not a hard enough punch to knock out someone as powerful as Sonny Liston. Rumors flew about. Some thought Liston took a dive because he had been threatened by the Black Muslims. Others suspected he had bet against himself.

Did Liston take a dive? Based upon his character as a man, it is entirely possible. As he is lying there looking up at his tormenter, Ali is shouting, "Get up, sucker! Get up and fight!" There is an iconic photograph on that moment. If one looks closely enough, some in the audience are looking very much like they paid hard-earned money and Liston took a dive and they are angry. Watching it in slow motion very carefully, you will see Liston throwing a left lead, and as it comes back, Ali's right lands on Liston's head. It does not look like an especially hard right, but Liston goes down. He does not appear to be out, and he does appear to be aware of Ali, Walcott, and the latest price index from Wall Street, Einstein's theory of relativity, and perhaps the play *Hamlet*, by Shakespeare. I believe Sonny Liston took a dive in Lewiston, Maine, in 1965.

733

First Ali versus Patterson

Floyd Patterson infuriated Ali by insisting on calling him Cassius Clay. The fight took place on November 22, 1965, at the Las Vegas Convention Center.[734] Patterson made a heroic effort, but he was never really into the fight. He was stopped in the twelfth round. Again, the audience was largely pro-Patterson and against the brash but colorful champion. Patterson fought several rounds in pain as a result of throwing his back out, and Ali could have taken him out earlier but chose instead to carry him into the twelfth.

The following year, 1966 was a busy year for Muhammad Ali. In succession, he successfully defended against Canadian George Chuvalo (W, UD), Henry Cooper (TKO on cuts again), an easy defense against Brian London (KO, 3), then to Germany for a defense against southpaw Karl Mildenberger (TKO, 12), and to the Houston Astrodome for his last defense of 1966 against a somewhat faded Cleveland Williams (TKO, 3).[735]

The year 1967 was a difficult year for Muhammad. The National Boxing Association had stripped Ali of his crown for his refusal to be drafted. They named a tall Chicago heavyweight named Ernie Terrell as champion. Virtually no one took this seriously. Ali, controversially or not, was the real heavyweight champion of the world. On February 6, 1967, Ali took Terrell on in the Houston Astrodome.[736] Terrell could fight, but he was no match for a prime Muhammad Ali. Like Floyd Patterson two years earlier, he insisted on calling Ali Cassius Clay. Ali dominated Terrell and showed a rather mean streak, hitting him and saying, "What's my name, Uncle Tom?" Pop, pop. Again, "What's my name?" pop, bam. Again and again. Ali was clearly out to humiliate the NBA pretender, and he did. At the end it was a unanimous decision for Ali. In 1967, Muhammad Ali was virtually untouchable. He had said for years that he was the greatest, and by now, it looked like he might have been right.

734

735

736

Draft Evasion

In March 1966, Ali refused to be inducted into the armed forces. He was systematically denied a boxing license in every state and stripped of his passport. As a result, he did not fight from March 1967 to October 1970, from ages twenty-five to almost twenty-nine, as his case worked its way through the appeals process before his conviction was overturned in 1971.[737] These were his prime championship years. What if he had been allowed to fight? Would he have beaten Joe Louis's record of twenty-five title defenses? During this time of inactivity, as opposition to the Vietnam War began to grow and Ali's stance gained sympathy, he spoke at colleges across the nation, criticizing the Vietnam War and advocating African American pride and racial justice. There was, of course, tremendous backlash, particularly from boxing fans old enough to remember Joe Louis serving his country during World War II. He was called unpatriotic, draft dodger, and a lot of other names I will not print here.

He stayed in the public eye not only through his controversies but simply by being Muhammad Ali. He was outspoken in his opposition to the Vietnam War he claimed because he was a minister of the Nation of Islam. The late Sixties were a time of intense cultural change. Huge antiwar protests erupted across the country and radicalism on college campuses and cities with groups like the Students for Democratic Society (SDS), the Black Panther Party, and the Weathermen. All these groups were sparked by the counterculture movement, and Muhammad Ali was lionized as a martyr by the New Left.

With Ali stripped of his legitimate title, a tournament was set up by the NBA to determine a new champion. Typically, the NYAC disagreed. The winner of the NBA Tournament was Louisville heavyweight and former Ali sparring partner Jimmy Ellis, a slick boxer with fair power. On his way to the NBA title, Ellis beat top contenders Leotis Martin, Oscar Bonevena, and Jerry Quarry. In the finals, Ellis defeated Quarry by decision. The NYAC matched unbeaten Joe

737

Frazier of Philadelphia against oversized heavyweight Buster Mathis, who regularly came in at over three hundred pounds. Surprisingly, he was a good boxer and had good hand speed.

Ellis defended the NBA title against old warhorse Floyd Patterson in Stockholm, Sweden, and received a gift decision. Most people felt Patterson had done enough to win. But Jimmy Ellis retained his crown.

Meanwhile, Frazier had knocked out Buster Mathis for the right to be called NYAC champion. The stage was set for the shootout at the OK Corral between Smokin' Joe Frazier and Jimmy Ellis. Then surprisingly Muhammad Ali announced his retirement. This gave legitimacy to Frazier versus Ellis. The fight to determine the undisputed champion took place on February 16, 1970, at New York's Madison Square Garden. Ellis did his very best, but he was simply overpowered by Smokin' Joe.[738]

Ellis's trainer, Angelo Dundee, threw in the towel, and Joe Frazier was now the Heavyweight Champion of the World. Meanwhile Muhammad Ali had now changed his mind and embarked on a comeback that would culminate in a showdown with Joe Frazier.

Light Heavyweights of the Nineteen Sixties

Archie Moore, 1952–1962

Archie Moore had begun his ten year reign as light heavyweight champion way back in 1952. He had made nine successful defenses on his crown. Not that he was inactive. He twice challenged for the heavyweight title but was beaten back both times, first by Rocky Marciano and second by Floyd Patterson. He also stayed busy fighting ten-round nontitle fights. After beating Buddy Turman in 1961, he defended his title for the last time against Italian Giulio Rinaldi in New York on October 6, 1961. Rinaldi had won a ten-round decision from him the previous year in Rome, Italy. On October 23, 1961, he stopped former Olympic Gold Medalist and heavyweight

---

738

fringe contender Pete Rademacher by a technical knockout in the sixth round.

Stripped by all sanctioning bodies of his titles, he fought on through 1962 defeating Alejandro Lavorante (who was carried from the ring on a stretcher), perennial heavyweight contender Howard King, and drew with future champion Willie Pastrano. Six months later, on November 15, 1962, at the age of forty-six, he took on rising heavyweight contender then known as Cassius Clay. The fight was heavily ballyhooed, and the press made much of the now-forty-six-year-old Moore taking on the brash, young Louisville Olympic champion and undefeated professional in Los Angeles. Twenty-six years separated Moore and the twenty-year-old Clay, who predicted "Moore will fall in four!" And he did. Clay, less than two years away from winning the heavyweight championship of the world, simply was too much for the old champion, who had been fighting since the 1930s. Dancing flicking jabs and rights and then dancing away before Moore could retaliate, he knocked Moore down three times in round 4 and backed up his prediction. Moore fought for the very last time on March 15, 1963, knocking out professional wrestler Mike DiBiase. It was Moore's one hundred and thirty first knockout, an all-time record. Sam Langford is second with one hundred twenty-nine.

Archie Moore, possibly the greatest light heavyweight boxer in history, died on December 9, 1998. He was eighty-one. He was inducted into the IBHOF with the vanguard class of 1990.

Harold Johnson, 1962–1963

Harold Johnson, born in 1928, was a dominant light heavyweight for many years. He ruled the division in the early sixties beating Jesse Bowdry to claim the NBA title in 1961 after the NBA had stripped Archie Moore of his title the same year for failure to defend. He cemented his claim winning the lineal title with a win over Eddie Cotton by split decision in Seattle on August 29, 1961. The following year, he gained *The Ring* magazine recognition after beating Doug Jones. An interesting footnote to the Harold Johnson story was that his father, Phil Johnson, was also a professional fighter, and both of them fought future heavyweight champion Jersey Joe Walcott. Dad lost to Walcott in 1936 by third-round TKO, and son lost to Walcott in 1950 also by third-round TKO.

Johnson met Archie Moore a total of five times, with Moore winning all but one. Nonetheless, Johnson was considered a master boxer and a decent puncher. And it is no disgrace to lose to Archie Moore. In his career, he held wins over Nino Valdez, Ezzard Charles, Eddie Cotton, Doug Jones, Bert Whitehurst, Von Clay, and Gustav Schultz. He defended successfully one time, beating Gustave Schultz by unanimous decision in Berlin, Germany, on June 23, 1962.[739] In his next defense, he lost the light heavyweight title to slick New Orleans light heavy Willie Pastrano in the Las Vegas Convention Center on June 1, 1963. At the time, Johnson was thirty-five years old. He fought on until 1971, winning seven of nine fights.

He retired in 1971, leaving a stellar record of 76 wins, with 32 knockouts, and 11 losses.[740] Johnson was inducted into the World Boxing Hall of Fame in 1992 and the International Boxing Hall of Fame in 1993.[741]

Johnson was named the 7th greatest light heavyweight of the 20th century by the Associated Press in 1999.[742] Three years later, *The Ring* magazine ranked Johnson 7th on the list the 20 Greatest Light Heavyweight of All Time and 80th on the list "the 80 Best Fighters of the past 80 Years." The writer ranks him 7th. Johnson died at the age of 86 on February 19, 2015.[743]

Willie Pastrano, 1963–1965

Wilfred Raleigh Pastrano was born in New Orleans on November 27, 1935. Pastrano's best friend, Ralph Dupas, started training in boxing at a local gym. Pastrano, who weighed over 250

739

740

741

742

743

pounds, decided to start working out with his friend. As Willie lost weight, he realized two things. First, he loved boxing. Second, he hated getting hit. So Pastrano developed a style of boxing in which he hardly got hit and, in return, tried not to hurt his opponent as well.[744]

The talented Pastrano won the World Light Heavyweight Championship when he outpointed the great Harold Johnson on a close fifteen-round decision. He successfully defended his crown by stopping Gregorio Peralta of Argentina on a TKO and by coming back from a certain defeat on points to KO English challenger Terry Downes in eleven rounds in Manchester, England. Pastrano lost his crown when he was TKO'd by José Torres in ten rounds (the same fight where the ringside doctor asked if he knew where he was, leading to Pastrano's legendary line of, "You're damn right I know where I am! I'm in Madison Square Garden getting the shit kicked out of me!").[745] In the Torres fight, Pastrano was knocked down for the only time in his career by a powerful left hook to the liver. Pastrano retired after that match and never fought again.

Managed by the legendary Angelo Dundee, Pastrano was a smooth, quick boxer with a great left hand. He was a stablemate of Muhammad Ali and often sparred with the future champion early in Ali's career. His talent was dissipated by his aversion to training and a fondness for partying and carousing. His success was also limited by his lack of punching power, hence his record of only 14 knockout wins in his 84 fights. Nevertheless, he defeated most of the light heavyweight challengers of his generation. He also outpointed former light heavyweight champion Joey Maxim, and boxed a draw with the legendary Archie Moore. He retired with a record of 63 wins (14 by KO), 13 losses, and 8 draws.[746]

744
745
746

Jose "Chegui' Torres, 1965–1966

Born in the city of Ponce, Puerto Rico on May 3, 1936, Torres began boxing when he joined the United States Army as a teenager (he was seventeen years old). His only amateur titles had come in Army and interservice championships, several of which he had won. Torres was still in the Army when he won the silver medal in the light middleweight division at the 1956 Melbourne Olympic Games, where he lost to László Papp of Hungary in the final.[747]

After his military service, Torres trained at the Empire Sporting Club in New York City with trainer Cus D'Amato.[748] Like Floyd Patterson and Mike Tyson, Torres fought out of the peekaboo stance with both gloves up by his face. That was the mark of a D'Amato boxer. He turned professional in New York in 1958. He ran up a string of twelve straight victories with ten by knockout before fighting a ten-round draw against future welterweight champion Benny "Kid" Paret. Aside from that draw, Torres stayed undefeated until May 5, 1963, when he was TKO'd in the fifth round by Cuban KO artist Florentino Fernandez in San Juan, Puerto Rico. He bounced back with wins over Don Fullmer, Wilbur "Skeeter" McClure, Gomeo Brennan, and a one-round knockout of former middleweight champion Carl "Bobo" Olson.[749]

747

748

749

Torres got his shot at the light heavy title on March 30, 1965, and he made the most of it, punishing and then stopping champion Willie Pastrano in round 9, when the referee stopped the fight after the round. Jose Chegui Torres was the new Light Heavyweight Champion of the World.[750]

In 1966, Torres made three successful title defenses beating Wayne Thornton by unanimous decision in New York City, forty-year-old Eddie Cotton by a very controversial decision in Las Vegas, and Scottish challenger Chic Calderwood by second round knockout in San Juan, Puerto Rico. On December 16, 1966, in Madison Square Garden, Nigerian boxer Dick Tiger outfought Torres and won by unanimous decision. There was a rematch, and Tiger got the decision again, but many people felt that Torres had deserved the decision. Dick Tiger was now the Light Heavyweight Champion of the World.[751]

In his years after retiring from boxing, he became a representative of the Puerto Rican community in New York, meeting political leaders, giving lectures, and becoming the New York State Athletic Commission's commissioner from 1984 to 1988. In 1986, he was chosen to sing the United States National Anthem before the world lightweight championship bout between Jimmy Paul and Irleis Perez in Atlantic City, New Jersey. In 1990, he became president of the WBO, and he was president until 1995. He is also a member of the International Boxing Hall of Fame.[752]

Dick Tiger, 1966–1968

Coming out of Nigeria in West Africa, Dick Tiger, born Richard Ihetu in Amaigbo Colony, Nigeria, in 1929 became a two-time Middleweight Champion and Light Heavyweight Champion of the World. Known as Dick Tiger, he fought his first seventeen professional fights in Nigeria beating exotic named boxers like Koko Kid,

---

750
751
752

Easy Dynamite, Lion Ring, Blackie Power, Mighty Joe, and Super Human Power.[753] Relocating to England in 1955, he lost his first four fights before more skill and new management turned his career around.

Tiger was inducted into the International Boxing Hall of Fame in 1991. *The Ring* magazine named him Fighter of the Year in 1962 and 1965, while the Boxing Writers Association of America (BWAA) named him Fighter of the Year in 1962 and 1966. In 2002, Tiger was voted by *The Ring* magazine as the 31st greatest fighter of the last 80 years.[754]

He first gained attention with a cut-eye TKO-5 victory over Brit Terry Downes, in a battle of future champions on May 14, 1955. He was now managed by Jersey Jones, a former fighter, manager, trainer, and sports writer. Jones was a regular contributor to *The Ring* magazine until his death in 1973. Tiger had a spotty record after coming to America but caught fire in 1961 beating Gene "Ace" Armstrong, Hank Casey, Spider Webb, and Florentino Fernandez, all top-ranking middleweights.[755] After these important wins, Tiger finally got his title shot against NBA middleweight champion Gene Fullmer in San Francisco's Candlestick Park on October 23, 1962, outboxing and outfighting the rugged Fullmer, who had been champion of the NBA since 1959. Dick Tiger was now the Middleweight Champion of the World.[756]

After losing the Middleweight Title to Emile Griffith, Tiger challenged Light Heavyweight Champion Jose Torres at Madison Square Garden on December 16, 1966 and won the World Light Heavyweight

753

754

755

756

Championship by a unanimous decision. Tiger won the rematch, this time on a split decision, again in Madison Square Garden.

Next, he traveled to Las Vegas, Nevada, to take on challenger Roger Rouse of Anaconda, Montana. The two fought a close battle, Rouse, the taller of the two with a reach advantage, and Tiger constantly stalking his prey. Rouse took the early rounds, but Tiger, a notoriously slow starter, began to pick up the pace in the middle round, and the fight was even by round 12, when Tiger threw a hard right hand that knocked Rouse down. He arose, but the referee after questioning him determined the fight over and Dick Tiger was the winner by a round-12 TKO.[757]

On May 24, 1968, Dick Tiger met his match when he took on six-foot-three-inch Albuquerque, New Mexico, light heavyweight contender Bob Foster. The left hook that knocked Tiger cold in the fourth round was rated among the 10 Deadliest Punches of the Last 25 Years in 1975.[758] That is saying something. Tiger continued fighting until 1970, winning three of his last four fights. Dick Tiger died of liver cancer on December 14, 1971. He was forty-one years old.

Bob Foster, 1968–1974

Bob Foster, truly a great light heavyweight, had one flaw in his mental makeup. He was *not* a heavyweight. I want to clear this up

---

[757]

[758]

before I go any further. As early as 1962, he went up against Doug Jones who stopped him in eight rounds, Ernie Terrell, who TKO'd Foster in seven in 1964; Zora Folley, who beat him in ten in 1965; Joe Frazier, who knocked Foster senseless in the second round in 1970; and at the end of his career to Muhammad Ali, who KO'd him in eight.

Okay, Bob Foster was not destined to be a heavyweight. That established, he was one heck of a light heavyweight. After his title winning knockout of Dick Tiger, he successfully defended the crown fourteen times. And these were not exactly bums he was fighting; he consistently fought and beat the best light heavyweights in the world. You may not recognize all these names, but if you are of a certain age, you will remember some of them—Roger Rouse, Frankie DePaula, Andy Kendall, Mark Tessman, and Mike Quarry among them. All good, all top-ten-rated light heavyweights.

Middleweights of the Nineteen Sixties

Paul Pender, 1960–1961

A ring-worn Sugar Ray Robinson took on Boston challenger Paul Pender. In 1959, the National Boxing Association withdrew its recognition of Sugar Ray Robinson as middleweight champion. Gene Fullmer and Carmen Basilio fought for the vacant NBA title, and Fullmer won. Pender beat Robinson, one of the greatest fighters of all time, for the disputed middleweight championship title and won by split decision in fifteen rounds. Pender fought Robinson once again to defend his title and went on to beat him by split decision.

In 1961, Pender took on British middleweight champion Terry Downes in Boston and successfully defended his crown stopping Downes by TKO on January 14, 1961. The two fought a rematch in Wembley Pool, London, and Downes returned the favor, stopping Pender on cuts in the ninth round. In the rubber match, held in Boston on April 7, 1962, Pender regained the title by a fifteen-round unanimous decision. He won the first and the third bout, but the last would prove to be the only fight of that year for Pender and the last of his career. The New York Boxing Commission stripped Pender of his title for not defending it against Dick Tiger. Pender sued and won on appeal.[759]

Paul Pender retired May 7, 1963, from brittle hands that hampered his entire career. His career record was 40 wins (20 by KO), 6 losses, and 2 draws. He died January 12, 2003.[760]

Terry Downes, 1961–1962

Terry Downes was born in Paddington, London, England on May 9, 1936. He moved with his family to the United States in 1952, while still a teenager, to live with his trapeze artist sister Sylvia, who had lost an arm in a traffic accident, and went on to serve in the US Marine Corps from 1954–56, being recruited after boxing against them for the YMCA. In the marines, he won several amateur trophies, including the all-services championship and the Amateur Golden Gloves. He missed out on selection for the US Olympic team, being ruled ineligible on residence grounds, and after his term of service, he returned to London and turned professional.[761]

Managed by Sam Burns, Downes won his first two pro fights before a defeat to future world champion Dick Tiger.[762] Downes made his climb up through the world middleweight ranks, first winning the British middleweight championship in 1958. After losing his first world title challenge to Paul Pender, Downes won the middleweight championship of the world on July 7, 1961, in a fight in London's Wembley Stadium, when the fight was stopped due to cuts over both of Pender's eyes. His reign was short. On April 7, 1962, in the Boston Garden, the Paddington Express lost the championship back to Paul Pender.[763]

759

760

761

762

763

He then moved up to the light heavyweight division and challenged Willie Pastrano for that crown, but was beaten back and stopped in round 11 on November 30, 1964.[764]

Like many former boxers, Terry Downes worked as an actor and had roles in a number of films after retiring from the ring. He also had a reputation for memorable quips. After a particularly brutal fight early in his career against Dick Tiger, Downes was asked who he wanted to fight next. He replied, "The bastard who made this match," in reference to Mickey Duff.[765]

Downes fought six world champions and beat three: Robinson, Pender, and Joey Giardello. His record was 44 fights, 35 wins (28 KOs), 9 losses. He died in London on October 6, 2017. He was eighty-one.[766]

Dick Tiger, 1963

After winning the WBA middleweight title from Gene Fullmer in 1962, he gave the Utah Mormon a rematch on February 23, 1963, at the Las Vegas Convention Center and the two fought a fifteen-round draw. In the rubber match between the two on August 10, 1963, in Ibadan, Nigeria, he stopped the seemingly indestructible Fullmer when the referee stopped the contest in the seventh round. This was especially significant because for the first time since the NBA had stripped Sugar Ray Robinson of his title for "failure to defend," the title became unified. With the victory, Dick Tiger was now the WBA, inaugural WBC title, the lineal title, and the *Ring* recognition as World Middleweight Champion.[767]

On December 7, 1963, he lost the middleweight championship of the world to seasoned Philadelphia pugilist Joey Giardello by close decision at the Atlantic City Convention Center. Then a win over Don Fullmer, a split decision loss to Joey Archer, and ten-round decision of hard punching Ruben "Hurricane" Carter, he faced

764

765

766

767

Giardello again on October 21, 1965, in Madison Square Garden and regained the title with a unanimous decision to once again rule the middleweights.[768]

Joey Giardello, 1963–1965

Joey Giardello, born July 16, 1930, as Carmine Tilelli in Brooklyn, New York, was raised in Philadelphia, where as a teenager he took up boxing.

On December 7, 1963, he won the Middleweight Championship of the World at age thirty-three from Nigerian Dick Tiger.[769]

He reigned as world champion for nearly two years, winning four fights during that time. The most notable was a December 14, 1964, title defense against Rubin Carter. He won the fight handily, using a slick jab to keep Carter at bay, despite taking a few solid rights to the head in the early rounds, though Carter was not able to follow them up. By the fifth round, Giardello had taken control of the fight and was awarded a unanimous decision. However, the fight's depiction in the 1999 film *The Hurricane* has led many nonboxing fans to believe the decision was in some way corrupt or even racist. However, the decision was agreed upon by boxing experts present at the fight, to the tune of a Giardello victory by a 3–1 margin. A subsequent informal poll of sportswriters present agreed that Giardello had won. Carter himself agreed with the decision.[770] As detailed further down this page, after the release of *The Hurricane* in 1999, Giardello was awarded damages relating to the inaccurate depiction of him and manner of his win.

On October 21, 1965, he squared up against Dick Tiger again, and this time the Nigerian won a unanimous decision to regain the middleweight crown. Giardello fought just four more times over the next two years before retiring.

768

769

770

Joey Giardello died on September 4, 2008, in Cherry Hill, New Jersey. He was seventy-eight years old.[771]

Dick Tiger, 1965–1966

Dick Tiger's second reign at the top of the middleweights was brief. On February 18, 1966, he traveled to Dortmund in what was then West Germany and beat Peter Mueller by a third-round knockout in a ten-round nontitle fight. Then on April 25 in Madison Square Garden, he took on standing welterweight champion Emile Griffith. Griffith won a unanimous decision and became World Middleweight Champion. Due to the rules of boxing at the time, he had to surrender the welterweight title. Tiger then campaigned as a light heavyweight for the remainder of his career.

Emile Griffith, 1966–1967

Now middleweight king, Griffith set about defending his new title. He had two successful defenses again light hitting but clever boxing contender Joey Archer. Both fights were held in Madison Square Garden, and Griffith won both by decision.[772]

On April 17, 1967, he faced off against Italian challenger Nino Benvenuti and lost the fight. Benvenuti become the new champion. On September 29, 1967, Griffith regained the title in Shea Stadium.

771
772

He then defended it once and lost it again to Benvenuti. Griffith will be covered in more detail in the Welterweight section of this chapter.

Nino Benvenuti, 1967, 1968–1970

Giovanni "Nino" Benvenuti (born April 26, 1938) is a retired Italian boxer and actor. As an amateur welterweight boxer, he won the Italian title in 1956–60, the European title in 1957 and 1959, and an Olympic gold medal in 1960, receiving the Val Barker trophy for boxing style. In 1961, having an amateur record of 120-0, he turned professional and won world titles in the light-middleweight division and twice in the middleweight division.[773]

On January 20 1961, Benvenuti made his professional boxing debut, beating Ben Ali Allala by decision in six rounds. He then won twenty-nine fights in a row before challenging for the Italian middleweight title, on March 1, 1963, in Rome against Tommaso Truppi. His winning streak extended to thirty when he knocked out Truppi in round 11. His winning streak reached forty-six wins in a row when he met former world junior middleweight champion Denny Moyer on September 18, 1964, beating Moyer on points in ten rounds.[774]

On March 4, 1968, Benvenuti and Griffith completed their trilogy, once again at Madison Square Garden, with Benvenuti knocking Griffith down in round 9 and winning a fifteen-round decision to regain the world middleweight title. On December 14, 1968, in San Remo, he and Don Fullmer met once again. They had met the first time in 1966, with Benvenuti winning both times. Benvenuti retained the world middleweight title with a fifteen-round decision. After Fullmer, the champion defended against Fraser Scott, Luis Rodriguez, Tom Bethea, and then he met his match against a young Carlos Monzon in a title fight in Rome, Italy, on November 7, 1970. Nobody expected Monzón to beat Benvenuti in their title match (very few knew of him). Yet Monzón applied pressure from the start, and in the twelfth, a right hand landed perfectly on Benvenuti's chin, and

773

774

the title changed hands. Monzón also beat Benvenuti in a rematch, this time in only three rounds in Monte Carlo when Benvenuti's seconds threw in the towel.[775]

Following the loss, Benvenuti retired on a third-round TKO, Benvenuti retired. After boxing, Benvenuti became a successful businessman, show host, and city counselor in Trieste. He opened a high-class restaurant and forged friendships with Monzon and Griffith. In 1980, he asked Griffith to become the godfather of one of his sons and later helped him financially.[776] Monzon was a guest of honor at Benvenuti's television show several times.

Welterweights of the Nineteen Sixties

Emile Griffith, 1961

Emile Alphonse Griffith (February 3, 1938–July 23, 2013) was a professional boxer from the US Virgin Islands who became a world champion in the welterweight, junior welterweight, junior middleweight, and middleweight divisions. Coming to New York City and growing up there, he won the New York Golden Gloves Open Championship in 1958 and turned professional the same year.[777]

He won the World Welterweight Championship for the first time, knocking out Cuban boxer Benny "Kid" Paret on April 1, 1961, at the Miami Beach Convention Center. He took a 23 win 2 loss record into the fight. The two losses were to Randy Sandy in 1959 and highly ranked Portland, Oregon, welterweight Denny Moyer in 1960. He would later defeat Moyer in a title bout. Paret was a very tough champion, and their first fight was close and competitive. In the thirteenth round, Griffith landed a left jab followed by a point-blank right cross that knocked Paret out. He took the full count glassy eyed propped on his elbows. Emile Griffith, just

---

775

776

777

three years into his professional career, was now the Welterweight Champion of the World.[778]

They fought a rematch for the welterweight title on September 30, 1961, in New York City's Madison Square Garden. Again, the fight was close and competitive, but this time the edge went to Benny "Kid" Paret, who became the Welterweight Champion of the World for the second time.[779]

A little over two months later, on December 9, 1961, Paret challenged NBA middleweight champion Gene Fullmer and suffered a savage beating before Fullmer stopped him in ten, knocking the brave Paret down three times in that round. I watched this fight, and believe me, it was hard to watch.

Griffith and Paret met for a third and fateful time on March 24, 1962, three months after that frightful beating at the hands of Fullmer. Still, Paret was competitive. In the sixth round, Paret came close to stopping Griffith with a multipunch combination, but Griffith was saved by the bell. In round 12, an infuriated Griffith trapped Paret in a corner and unleashed several blows to Paret's head. At one point he even appeared to be holding Paret up with one hand while he continued clubbing away with the other. The referee, highly respected Ruby Goldstein, seemed to stare transfixed as Paret slowly sagged to the canvas. Griffith was welterweight champion again, but at what a cost. The television audience of millions watched as Paret was carried from the ring on a stretcher. He never regained consciousness and died ten days later in the hospital. Griffith understandably took the death of Paret very hard. What had infuriated Griffith, a known bisexual man, was what happened earlier at the weigh-in. Paret had taunted Griffith, calling him the Spanish word for *faggot* and touching his buttocks. Griffith was unsuccessful in his attempts to visit Paret in the hospital, and it was said he was troubled by nightmares for forty years.[780] This was a fight I watched on television with my father, and it is still visible in my memory. I can

___

778

779

780

still visibly see Goldstein pulling Griffith back as Paret slowly sinks to the canvas.

Emile Griffith, 1962–1963

Four weeks later, on July 13, 1962, Griffith defended his title at the Las Vegas Convention center against perennial contender Ralph Dupas and won a fifteen-round unanimous decision. A ninth-round stoppage of Jorge Fernandez in Las Vegas followed. He then defeated Ted Wright in a fifteen-round decision in Vienna, Austria, and followed that with a ninth round TKO win over Christian Christiansen in Copenhagen, Denmark.[781]

On March 21, 1963, at Dodger stadium in Los Angeles, Griffith lost the title to another tough Cuban Luis Rodriguez. Three months later, on June 8, he regained the title in Madison Square Garden by a narrow split decision.[782]

Luis Manuel Rodriguez, 1963

Luis Manuel Rodríguez (June 17, 1937–July 8, 1996) was a Cuban professional boxer. Known as El Feo, he began his career in pre-Castro Havana. In Cuba, he twice defeated the ill-fated and future welterweight champion Benny Kid Paret. He held the WBA, WBC, and lineal welterweight titles in 1963 and challenged once for the WBA and WBC middleweight titles in 1969.[783]

After the Cuban Revolution, Rodríguez campaigned in the United States. Fighting out of Miami, Rodriguez decisioned top welterweights such as Virgil Akins and Rudell Stitch.[784] He quickly ran off an unbeaten streak of 35-0, beating such notables of the era including Charley Scott, Gomeo Brennan, Benny Paret, Isaac Logart, Chico Vejar, and Yama Bahama before losing for the first time to the great Emile Griffith by a split decision on December 17, 1960, in

781
782
783
784

Madison Square Garden. Rodriguez then won his next four before losing to future champion Curtis Cokes in Dallas; a decision he later reversed in a rematch.[785]

After defeating highly ranked Joey Giambra by decision on January 19, 1963, he was given a title shot against against Emile Griffith, who had beaten him in 1960. This time he beat Griffith on March 21, 1963, in Dodger Stadium, Los Angeles, and Luis Manuel Rodriguez became the Welterweight Champion of the World. Three months later, back in Madison Square Garden, Griffith regained the title on a split decision.[786]

He soldiered on through 1963 and 1964 beating standouts Denny Moyer, Olympian Wilbur McClure, and Holly Mims.[787]

Facing Emile Griffith for the third time on June 12, 1964, in Miami Beach, he gave his all and came up short as Griffith took a split decision. He continued on running up a record of 96-7 to face world middleweight champion Nino Benvenuti in Rome, Italy, on November 22, 1969, and was TKO'd by the champion in round 11. Rodriguez fought on until 1971 when he retired. He passed away on July 8, 1996, leaving a stellar record of 121 fights with 107 wins and 13 losses. He was inducted into the IBHOF in 1997. *The Ring* magazine ranked Luis Rodriguez as the third greatest Cuban boxer, behind Kid Gavilan and Kid Chocolate.[788]

Emile Griffith, 1963–1965

In June of 1964, he beat Rodriguez in their rubber match, again on a razor's edge split decision. Emile Griffith then was shocked by middleweight contender Ruben "Hurricane" Carter, who knocked him out in one round of a nontitle bout.[789] In 1964, he bounced right back with two successful title defenses in London, England, the first against Brian Curvis, winning by unanimous decision, and against

785

786

787

788

789

Dave Charnley, whom he stopped in nine rounds. Both bouts took place in Wembley Stadium in London. In 1965, Griffith made the final defense of the Welterweight crown, defeating Manual Gonzales at Madison Square Garden. He took a unanimous decision.[790]

On March 25, 1966, Emile Griffith became the Middleweight Champion of the World, beating titleholder Dick Tiger in Madison Square Garden.[791] He would go on to lose and regain that title as well, thus becoming a three-time Welterweight Champion and two-time Middleweight Champion. Griffith retired in 1977 after losing his last three fights in a row. His record stands at 112 fights with 85 wins, 24 losses (most in the latter years of his career), 2 draws, and 23 knockouts. It has been speculated that Griffith went light on some of his opponents after the Paret tragedy. The great champion died on July 23, 2013, and was inducted into the IBHOF with its inaugural class of 1990.[792]

Curtis Cokes, 1966–1969

Curtis Cokes was born June 15, 1937, in the great city of Dallas, Texas, where he has been a lifelong resident.

On March 24, 1958, he began to box professionally, defeating a boxer who would later fight for the world title, Manuel Gonzalez, by a six-round decision. He won eleven fights in a row, including a second match with Gonzalez, before losing to Gonzalez in their third fight, on April 27, 1959. His next fight, against Garland "Rip" Randall, on June 18 of the same year, ended in a three-round no contest. He and Randall had an immediate rematch, and on August 27, he knocked out Randall in the first round. He had an additional fourteen fights, going 11-2-1 in that span (his one draw was against Kenny Lane, a boxer who twice challenged Carlos Ortiz for world championships), before facing Luis Rodriguez, another world welterweight champion, on September 3, 1961. He beat Rodriguez by

---

790

791

792

a ten-round decision, outpointed Gonzalez in their fourth fight, and lost to Rodriguez in their second fight, also by points.[793]

After winning three fights in a row, he and Gonzalez were matched for a fifth time, on August 24, 1966, this time for the vacant WBA/WBC welterweight title in New Orleans. Cokes outpointed Gonzales to become undisputed champion of the division after the title was vacated by Emile Griffith. On November 28 of 1966, he retained the crown against Jean Josselin of France by a fifteen-round decision. Over the next three year between 1966 and 1969, Cokes defended his crown successfully five times. He also fought numerous nontitle fights in that span with just one loss, to Gypsy Joe Harris.

He lost the title to the great Jose Napoles on April 4, 1969. With both eyes nearly swollen shut, Cokes's manager told the referee to stop the fight before the start of the thirteenth round. The rematch, two months later, ended similarly with Cokes unable to continue beyond the tenth round. Curtis fought for three more years before hanging up his gloves. He compiled a 62-14-4 record, including 30 knockouts.[794]

Curtis Cokes was inducted into the IBHOF in 2003.

Jose Napoles, 1969–1970

Jose Napoles was one helluva welterweight. In fact he was one of the very greatest in the division's history.

José Ángel Nápoles was nicknamed *Mantequilla* (Butter), referring to his smooth boxing style. He was born in Santiago de Cuba, Cuba, on April 13, 1940. Napoles turned professional on August 7, 1958, at age eighteen. He won his debut by a first-round knockout. He fought his first twenty one bouts in Cuba, winning all but one.[795]

In 1961, after the communist revolution in Cuba, President Fidel Castro outlawed professional boxing in the country, forcing Napoles, like other professional boxers, to leave Cuba. He found ref-

---

793

794

795

uge in Mexico, where he took residence in Mexico City. He became a citizen of Mexico and lived there for the remainder of his life.

On April 18, 1969, he successfully challenged World Welterweight Champion Curtis Cokes at the forum in Inglewood, California. Napoles had become a very popular boxer there, and he stopped Cokes in the thirteenth round by a TKO.[796] Cokes's corner would not let their man come out to receive more punishment. He defeated Cokes again, this time stopping him in ten, when the referee stopped the match. Four title defenses later, including a unanimous decision win over former champion Emile Griffith, he loaned out his title to young Billy Backus of Syracuse on December 3, 1970. A hard right by Backus opened a cut over Napoles's eye in the first round, and the fight was called in the fourth round as a TKO win for Backus.[797] He was now the Welterweight Champion of the World.

[796]

[797]

CHAPTER XIV

The Sixties Part II

Lightweights of the Nineteen Sixties

When the new decade rolled in on January 1, 1961, professional boxing was in a pretty good state in the lighter divisions. Joe Brown had been the lightweight champion since 1956 and would continue for another year. Another great lightweight boxer was waiting in the wings, Puerto Rican Carlos Ortiz. In Panama, a young featherweight named Ismael Laguna was beginning his career that would ultimately lead him to the lightweight division and the world title, while in Sao Paolo, Brazil, a young bantamweight named Edre Jofre was beginning his hall of fame career. Let us begin with Joe Brown and the lightweights.

Joe "Old Bones" Brown, 1956–1962

He would turn thirty-five years old in 1961. On April 18, 1961, he traveled to England to take on the challenge of British lightweight challenger Dave Charnley. In the famed Earl's Court Arena in Kensington, Brown retained the title with a unanimous fifteen round decision. On April 21, 1962, Carlos Ortiz came knocking on his door. After fifteen rounds of a cautious fight, Ortiz won the unanimous decision to become the new Lightweight Champion of the World.[798]

798

Carlos Ortiz 1962–1965

Carlos Ortiz (born September 9, 1936) is a two-time light-weight champion. Along with Félix Trinidad, Miguel Cotto, Wilfredo Gómez, Héctor Camacho, and Wilfred Benítez, Ortiz is considered among the best Puerto Rican boxers of all time by sports journalists and analysts.[799] As of January 2018, Ortiz holds the record for the most wins in unified lightweight title bouts in boxing history at 10.[800]

Turning pro in 1955, Ortiz won his first twenty-seven fights, before dropping a split decision to Johnny Busso in Madison Square Garden on June 27, 1958. Less than three months later, he reversed the decision, again in the Garden against Busso winning a unanimous ten round decision on September 19, 1958. Two fights with southpaw Kenny Lane in the junior. welterweight division, a loss and then a win made Ortiz a serious contender for Joe Brown's lightweight crown.[801]

After taking the championship, Ortiz traveled to Tokyo, Japan, and successfully defended his lightweight crown against Teruo Kosaka, stopping the Japanese challenger by a thirteenth-round TKO on December 3, 1962. Then on April 7, 1963, he made his San Juan debut, stopping Doug Valliant in thirteen by TKO.[802]

Following successful defenses against Filipino great Flash Elorde and Kenny Lane, he traveled to Panama City to defend against Panamanian challenger Ismael Laguna. Laguna won a close majority decision and the Lightweight Championship of the World. Ortiz soon regained the title back in Puerto Rico, this time stopping Laguna in round 4.[803] He fought Laguna for a third time in 1967, this time defeating the smooth boxing Panamanian by unanimous decision.

799

800

801

802

803

Ismael Laguna, 1965

Ismael Laguna was born in Colon, Panama, June 28, 1943. He turned professional in 1960 and by 1962 won the Panamanian featherweight title. He eventually moved up to the lightweight class, and on April 10, 1965 he decisioned Carlos Ortiz to become the Lightweight Champion of the World. In the rematch in San Juan, Ortiz bested Laguna at Shea Stadium in Queens, New York, on August 16, 1967, to regain the crown. During his short reign, he took on Carlos Hernandez (TKO, 8) and dropped a nontitle decision to Flash Elorde. In 1967, he lost the rubber match to Ortiz, but he was not done yet!

Carlos Ortiz, 1965–1968

Champion for the second time, Carlos Ortiz defeated Johnny Bizarro, Cuban great Sugar Ramos, and Flash Elorde again. These fights took place in 1966. Then, on June 28, 1968, he took on Dominican challenger Carlos Teo Cruz and lost the crown for the final time on a split decision in Santo Domingo, Dominican Republic. He retired after losing at Madison Square Garden by a knockout in six rounds to Ken Buchanan. It was the only time he was stopped in his career. His final record was of 68 wins, 7 losses, and 1 draw, with one bout declared a no-contest and 30 knockout wins. Ortiz is a member of the International Boxing Hall of Fame.

Carlos Teo Cruz, 1968–1969

Carlos Teo Cruz was born in the Dominican Republic on November 4, 1937. He was the Lightweight Champion of the World, having won the title from the great Carlos Ortiz in Santo Domingo on June 28, 1968. He defended his crown against Californian Mando Ramos, winning a fifteen round unanimous decision. Ramos won the rematch, and sadly, Carlos Teo Cruz lost his life, along with his wife and children when on February 15, 1970, when he was flying to a fight in San Juan when the *Dominicana de Aviacion* DC-9 crashed, killing all on board. His record stands at 43 wins, 14 losses, and 2 draws with 14 wins coming by knockout. RIP, Carlos.

Mando Ramos, 1969–1970

Ortiz was upset by Teo Cruz and so Mondo Ramos took the fight to the new champ, narrowly losing in a decision. Ramos won the rematch via stoppage. The fight was held at the Memorial Coliseum in Los Angeles, and this time, Mando Ramos TKO'd Cruz and became the youngest Lightweight Champion of the World in history.[804]

804

Mando was the first fighter (Perhaps since Georges Carpentier) to draw hordes of women to the fights. When a Mando Ramos fight was held in Los Angeles, movie stars such as John Wayne, Bill Cosby, Kirk Douglas, Liz Taylor, and Connie Stevens attended. Women from all walks of life caught Mandomania, and Hollywood loved the Wonder Boy.[805]

In 1970, he faced former champion Ismael Laguna and this time came up short. Laguna stopped him by TKO in nine rounds. Mando was cut and bleeding and outboxed and outpunched by the great Panamanian. Like another fighter I know well, he was a party animal and used drugs and alcohol, a bad combination for a professional fighter. His final record was 37 wins and 11 losses. He was finished as a fighter at age twenty-six.[806]

Ismael Laguna, 1970

Upon regaining the lightweight championship five years after losing it, Laguna defended successfully against Japanese challenger Guts Ishimatsu on June 6, 1970, stopping him in the thirteenth round. Next, he took the (relatively) unknown Scot Ken Buchanan. In San Juan, Puerto Rico on September 26, 1970, and lost the title by split decision to Buchanan. He would make one last attempt to win the lightweight crown in a second fight with the now-champion Ken Buchanan. In Madison Square Garden, Buchanan outfought him and won a unanimous decision.[807] This was the Panamanian's last fight. Laguna was a complete fighter, both an excellent boxer with good speed and combinations and a hard puncher who knocked out near half of his opponents. His standing record is 65 wins with 37 KO's, 9 losses and 1 draw in seventy-five professional fights. He is a 2001 inductee into the IBHOF.[808]

805

806

807

808

Featherweights of the Nineteen Sixties

Davey Moore, 1961–1963

Featherweight Champion Davey Moore had a busy year in 1961. That year he made a European tour, taking on Graceiux Lamperi in Paris, France, on January 9, 1961. From there he went to Madrid, Spain where he TKO'd Fred Galiana on January 27, 1961. It was then off to Rome, Italy, where he won a ten-round decision over Ray Noble on February 10 of that same year. All these were nontitle bouts. Then, back to the United States, he defended his title with a first-round knockout over Danny Valdez in Los Angeles on April 8, 1961.[809]

Davey Moore made the most of being the "World" Featherweight Champion. After two fights in Mexico, a ten-round decision win, and a TKO, he next traveled to the other side of the world to Tokyo, Japan, to defend against Kazuo Takayama, winning a unanimous decision in fifteen rounds on November 13, 1961.[810] It was his ninth fight in six countries in one year!

Starting off 1962, he fought twice in Los Angeles, beating Cisco Andrade by TKO in seven and knocking out Mario Diaz in the second round on July 9, 1962. Then he was off once again, this time to Helsinki, Finland, where he stopped Olli Maki in two rounds.

Back home in 1963, Moore had two nontitle fights in in Texas and California and then defended against Sugar Ramos, on March 21, 1963, in Los Angeles. It was a fateful night for Moore, who was knocked out by Ramos and died from hitting his neck on the bottom rope.

Davy Moore was a great fighter. He was a member of the 1952 Olympic Team, a world featherweight champion and a globe-trotting champion. His record stands at 59 wins, 7 losses and 1 draw.[811] He

809

810

811

was memorialized in a 1963 song by Bob Dylan called *Who Killed Davey Moore.*

Sugar Ramos

Ultiminio Ramos Zaqueira (December 2, 1941–September 3, 2017) was a Cuban-born Mexican boxer who was better known as Sugar Ramos.

Ramos fought out of Mexico where he was adopted as a national hero. He was a world featherweight champion and member of the International Boxing Hall of Fame.[812]

Sugar Ramos was the Cuban featherweight champion before fleeing to Mexico after the Castro Regime outlawed professional sports. He fought most of his first twenty-eight fights in Cuba before resettling in Mexico City. Ramos was a great boxer. Sadly, he is forever linked to the tragic Davey Moore.

Ramos lost his titles in 1964 to Vicente Saldivar after the fight was stopped in the twelfth round due to cuts. Ramos then moved up to lightweight, eventually earning a shot at then champion Carlos Ortiz in 1966. Ramos would lose the fight via fifth round TKO, and then an immediate rematch by TKO in the fourth round. He continued boxing until 1972. Sugar Ramos died at the age of 75 on September 3, 2017 in his adopted home of Mexico City due to complications from cancer. He was survived by his 4 children. His professional record forever stands at 55 wins, 7 losses (five toward the end of his career) and 4 draws. He scored 40 knockouts.

Vicente Saldivar 1964–1967

Vicente Samuel Saldívar García (May 3, 1943–July 18, 1985) was a Mexican boxer. He was a former undisputed featherweight champion. Saldivar has frequently been ranked among the greatest in the history of that division by many noted boxing historians and critics. He currently holds the record for the most wins in unified

---

812

featherweight title bouts and the longest unified featherweight championship reign in boxing history at eight title bouts and seven title defenses respectively. Saldívar fought in front of the fourth largest crowd ever, ninety thousand in Estadio Azteca, and has also regularly been cited as one of the finest left-handed fighters of all time.[813]

Yes, he was. Little known in the US except to boxing fans, Saldivar turned professional in 1961, and three years later in February 1964 he won a decision from future lightweight champion Ismael Laguna. On September 26, 1964, Saldívar won the WBA and WBC featherweight titles by upsetting fellow Mexican fighter and future hall of famer Sugar Ramos with an eleventh-round knockout in an extremely bloody battle.[814] His first reign as champion would last three years, in which Saldívar made eight successful title defenses. At the time, Saldivar was my favorite boxer. I followed all his fights very closely through *The Ring* magazine since I was overseas in the military at the time and could not see the fights televised or live.

In the first defense of his title, he defeated tough Raul Rojas by TKO in the fifteenth round on May 7, 1965, in Los Angeles. Next Saldivar traveled to London, where he decision rugged Welshman Howard Winstone in fifteen hard-fought rounds. Back home in Mexico City, he knocked out Ghanaian contender Floyd Robertson in two rounds.

On August 7, 1966, he faced the skilled Japanese contender Mitsunori Seki, winning a unanimous fifteen-round decision. In the rematch six months later also in Mexico City, he halted Seki in the seventh round. He then went to Cardiff, Wales, to face Howard Winstone a second time on June 15, 1967, and won a unanimous decision after fifteen rounds. The two met a third time October 14, 1967, this time in Mexico City and Saldivar stopped the gallant Welshman in the twelfth round. [815]

813

814

815

After three straight wins over Howard Winstone and a nontitle win over Jose Legra and a successful defense against Aussie Johnny Famechon, Saldivar retired.

Johnny Famechon, 1969–1970

Johnny Famechon was born in Paris, France, on March 28, 1945. He immigrated to Australia with his family when he was five years old.[816]

Over his twenty-year career, he developed a reputation for being a beautifully skilled boxer whose strength was his defense. His career record is 56 wins (20 by KO), 6 draws, and 5 losses.[817]

His first major win was over Les Dunn to become Victorian featherweight champion in 1964, then he was Commonwealth featherweight champion in 1967 after defeating the Scot John O'Brien. He became lineal and WBC featherweight champion on January 21, 1969, after he defeated the Cuban Jose Legra on points at the Albert Hall in London.

He defended his WBC featherweight title against Fighting Harada of Japan and won in a controversial points decision. In the rematch for the world title, against Harada in Japan six months later, Famechon decisively won by knocking Harada out in the fourteenth round.

He defended his WBC title on May 9, 1970, in Rome to Mexican Vicente Saldivar, and after losing the fight in a close points decision, he retired soon afterward.[818]

Vincente Saldivar, 1970

The great Mexican champion made a comeback in 1970 and defeated Johnny Famechon and regained the title he had abandoned three years previous. He didn't hold it for long. In his first defense,

---

816

817

818

he dropped a decision to Kuniaki Shibata of Japan on December 11, 1970, to lose his title. After losing to Shibata, he retired, but seven months later he was back and beat Frankie Crawford at the venerable Olympic Auditorium in Los Angeles in 1971. He then announced his retirement.[819]

He returned at the age of thirty after two years and three months of inactivity for another title attempt on October 21, 1973. His opponent was fellow hall of famer and former bantamweight champion Éder Jofre. Jofre, who was thirty-seven, had won the featherweight crown after coming out of his own retirement (albeit a brief seven-month one). Saldívar's skills had greatly diminished and Jofre won the contest with a fourth-round knockout in Brazil. After the fight, Saldívar retired for good. His standing record is 47 wins, and 3 losses.[820] He is a 1999 IBHOF inductee. Vicente Saldivar was a great fighter.

Kuniaki Shibata, 1970–1972

Born March 29, 1947, in Hitachi, Japan, Kuniaki Shibata is a little-known boxer in North America who nonetheless won fifty-six professional fights and a world championship. Shibata won his debut match in 1965 with a first-round knockout and fought for the Oriental and Pacific Boxing Federation featherweight title in 1969, but lost by sixth-round knockout. In April 1970, he challenged the vacant Japanese featherweight title and won by tenth-round knockout. He retained the title to challenge WBC featherweight champion Vicente Saldivar for the lineal title and won the title when Saldivar gave up after the twelfth round.[821]

He made his first defense by first-round knockout and retained his title in his second defense with a draw, but lost to Clemente Sanchez in May 1972.[822]

819

820

821

822

Bantamweights of the Nineteen Sixties

Éder Jofre, 1962–1965

Upon the retirement of Jose Becerra in 1960, the bantamweight division was without a lineal champion for the next two years. Rising up through the rankings between 1959 and 1962 was a young Brazilian bantamweight named Éder Jofre. Jofre was born in Sao Paulo on March 26, 1936. In time, he would go on to become one of the greatest boxers in history. He is ranked number 85 on *Ring* magazine's 100 Greatest Punchers of All Time list. He was named the nineteenth greatest fighters of the past 80 years by *The Ring* magazine.

By 1959, Éder was on fire. A win over Leo Espinosa, two knockout victories over Angel Bustos, and a decision win over Filipino Danny Kid put him in contention for the South American bantamweight title. On February 19, 1960, he beat highly rated contender Ernesto Miranda of Argentina by unanimous decision to take that title. He fought Miranda a second time and knocked him out in three.[823] These wins boosted Jofre up the world rankings in the bantamweight division.

On August 18, 1960, Jofre made his US debut in Los Angeles, beating top contender Jose Medel by a tenth-round knockout. On November 18, again in Los Angeles, Jofre was matched with Eloy Sanchez of Mexico for the vacant NBA title. At Los Angeles's fabled Olympic Auditorium, he dominated and knocked the Mexican out in the sixth round. He proved to be a busy champion. From 1960 to 1965, he retained his title against Piero Rollo, Ramon Arias (in Caracas, Venezuela), Johnny Caldwell, Herman Marques, Jose Medel, Katsuyoshi Aoki (in Tokyo), Johnny Jamito (in Manila), and Bernardo Caraballo (in Bogotá, Colombia).[824]

In addition, he defeated such fighters as Billy Peacock, Sadao Yaoita, and Fernando Soto in nontitle bouts. After the fight with

---

823

824

Aoki, Jofre was also recognized as World Bantamweight Champion by the WBC, therefore, becoming the Undisputed World Champion. [825]

On May 17, 1965, his streak as an undefeated fighter was broken when he lost to Fighting Harada by a controversial fifteen-round split decision in Nagoya, Japan, to lose the world bantamweight title. Harada was the only fighter ever to defeat Jofre as a professional.

After losing to Harada by unanimous decision at a rematch held in Tokyo on June 1, 1966, Jofre retired. He will be covered more in chapter 16.

Masahiko "Fighting" Harada, 1965–1968

How good was Fighting Harada? He beat Éder Jofre not once, but twice 'Nuff said. Harada was arguably one of Japan's most popular boxers. His fame reached international status, and Puerto Rico's Wilfredo Gómez declared that Harada was his idol as a child. Harada was inducted into the International Boxing Hall of Fame in 1995. In 2002, he was ranked as the thirty-second greatest boxer of the past eighty years by *Ring* magazine.

Harada was already the standing World Flyweight Champion when he moved up to challenge Jofre. The two clashed on May 18, 1965, in Nagoya, Japan. In a close, hard-fought fifteen-rounder, Harada shocked the boxing world by handing Jofre his first defeat in fifty fights to become the Bantamweight Champion of the World.[826] In case anybody doubted, he beat Éder Jofre again on June 1, 1966, in Tokyo. He is the only boxer to ever beat Jofre.

After two successful defenses, on February 27, 1968, Harada lost the bantamweight title to Lionel Rose, the first indigenous Australian to ever win a world boxing championship.[827] Later, he twice fought Johnny Famechon for the featherweight title, only to be turned back both times.

825

826

827

Harada led a rather quiet life after retirement. In 1996, he was elected into the International Boxing Hall of Fame in Canastota, New York. Éder Jofre, one of the boxers Harada beat to win world titles, is also enshrined at the IBHOF.

Masahiko Harada became president of the Japanese Boxing Commission in 2002.[828]

Lionel Rose, 1968–1969

Lionel Rose was the first indigenous Australian to win a world boxing title. He was probably the first indigenous Australian to become a top-tier world class professional boxer, period.

On February 27, 1968 he won the World Bantamweight Championship in Japan by unanimous decision over Fighting Harada, at Budokan, which is famous as a venue for rock acts such as the Beatles, Cheap Trick, Eric Clapton, Tina Turner, ABBA, Judas Priest, and Deep Purple. On this night, however, it was a boxing venue, and Lionel Rose outfought Fighting Harada for fifteen rounds to become the Bantamweight Champion of the World.[829]

Rose defended against Japanese Takao Sakurai, again in Budokan on June 2, 1968, and won by majority decision. Perhaps Rose's biggest wins, to Western fans at least, were his split decision win over Chuco Castillo on December 6, 1968, which caused a near riot from Castillo fans[830] and another win over British bantamweight Alan Rudkin, a Beatle-moptop-wearing pugilist whom he beat in another split decision win on March 8, 1969, in Melbourne.[831]

Rose was presumably at the top of his game when he faced Ruben Oliveres, on August 22, 1969, at the Inglewood Forum in Los Angeles. Well, so was Oliveres, one of the hardest-punching bantamweights in history. Oliveres knocked Rose out in the fifth round and became the new Bantamweight Champion of the World.[832] Like

---

828

829

830

831

832

many champion boxers, Lionel Rose fought on long after his championship tenure. He retired after getting knocked out in the second round in 1976.

Lionel Rose became a successful businessman after his retirement. He enjoyed the monetary benefits his fame and career afforded him. His standing record as a professional pugilist is 42 wins in 53 fights with 12 wins by knockout and 11 losses. Lionel Rose the first indigenous Australian to win a world boxing title died on May 8, 2011.[833]

Ruben Olivares, 1969–1970

Rubén Olivares Avila (born January 14, 1947) is a former Mexican boxer and a member of the Boxing Hall of Fame. A native of Mexico City, Olivares was twice an undisputed world champion considered by many as the greatest bantamweight champion of all time. He was very popular among Mexicans, many of whom considered him to be Mexico's greatest fighter for a long period. He currently holds the record for the most wins in unified title bouts in bantamweight history, at 6. Olivares also had cameo appearances on Mexican movies, and he participated in more than 100 professional bouts.[834] For a guy who fought at 118 pounds, Ruben Olivares was one tough little cookie.

Like Zale and Graziano, Ali and Frazier, Saldivar and Winstone, Rubin Oliveres's three fights with fellow Mexican Chuco Castillo were epic. In their first fight, April 18, 1970, Castillo scored a knockdown but Oliveres came back to win a 15-round decision at the Forum in Inglewood. The much anticipated rematch took place on October 16, 1970, again at the Forum. This time, Oliveres suffered a cut in the first round and was finally TKO'd in the fourteenth. It was Oliveres's first defeat after an astonishing record of 60 wins and no defeats with only 1 draw. The rubber match of the trilogy was fought on April 2, 1971. This time, Oliveres prevailed.[835] The rest of the story will be told in chapter 16.

Flyweights of the Nineteen Sixties

Pone Kingpetch, 1960–1962

He became Thailand's first world boxing champion on April 16, 1960, when he defeated Argentine Flyweight Champ Pascual Perez at Lumphini Boxing Stadium in Bangkok for the World Flyweight Championship. In his second title defense he lost the title to Fighting Harada of Japan on October 10, 1962, via eleventh-round knockout. Pone Kingpetch regained the world championship after outpointing Harada in a rematch on January 12, 1963. However it again proved to be short reign as Hiroyuki Ebihara knocked Pone out in the first round to become the new flyweight champion of the world. In his final title win, he defeated Ebihara in a rematch on January 23, 1964, to become a three-time flyweight champion. After the win in Japan, he traveled to Italy to defend his title against Salvatore Burruni and lost a fifteen-round decision to the Italian in his final world title fight. He retired from the sport altogether in 1966 at the age of thir-

834
835

331

ty-one. Kingpetch died on March 31, 1982, from pneumonia and heart failure. He was forty-seven years old.[836]

Fighting Harada, 1962–1963

Fighting Harada, already covered under the Bantamweights, was the Flyweight Champion of the World from 1962–1963. He won his first twenty-fights scoring nine stoppages along the way. His first loss came against Edmundo Esparza, a Mexican flyweight on June 14, 1962, in Tokyo by split decision in ten rounds. Harada bounced back on October 10, 1962, against Thailand's Pone Kingpetch to win the world championship by tenth-round knockout in Tokyo. Three months later, in the rematch, Kingpetch bested the Japanese to regain the crown in Bangkok, Thailand.[837] Fighting Harada went on the campaign as a bantamweight and, as covered, won the bantam-weight championship, beating the great Éder Jofre.

Pone Kingpetch, 1963

Inspired by his home crowd, no doubt, Kingpetch outboxed Fighting Harada to regain the crown in Bangkok on January 12, 1963.[838]

The Thai didn't reign for long. On September 18, 1963, he was shocked in Tokyo by another Japanese boxer, Hiroyuki Ebihara, getting knocked out in the first round. True to form, he improved the next time around and beat Ebihara by a split decision on Bangkok.

Hiroyuki Ebihara, 1963–1964

Hiroyuki Ebihara was born on March 26, 1940. He died on April 20, 1991.

836

837

838

He won the Flyweight Championship of the World on September 18, 1963 when he knocked out Pone Kingpetch of Thailand in the first round at Tokyo, Japan. He held the title about four months, losing the rematch to Kingpetch on January 23, 1964, in Bangkok.

Ebihara has a standing record of 68 fights, 62 wins, 5 losses, and 1 draw, with 33 wins by knockout.[839]

Pone Kingpetch, 1964–1965

On April 23, 1965, three-time world champion Pone Kingpetch traveled to the Palazzetto dello Sport in Rome, Italy, to face Italian challenger Salvatore Barunni for the flyweight title. After fifteen rounds of fast and furious flyweight action, the Italian won the Flyweight Championship of the World. Kingpetch would never again contend for a world title. He had two more fights, a loss and a win, and retired in 1966. His record stands at 35 fights, with 28 wins and 7 losses.

Salvatore Barunni 1965–1966

Salvatore Barunni was an Italian professional boxer who briefly held the world flyweight championship in the mid-1960s. He fought most of his contests in his native Italy compiling a 67 win, 2 loss record. On April 23, 1965, he fought Pone Kingpetch for the fly-

---

839

weight championship of the world at Palazzo dello Sport in Milan, Italy, and won the undisputed Flyweight Championship.

However, on November 1965, WBA and WBC stripped him of the title following his refusal to meet the mandatory challenger, Hiroyuki Ebihara. Justifiably, Barunni defied the sanctioning bodies and defended the lineal title on December 2, 1965, knocking out Australian challenger Rocky Gattellari in thirteen rounds. On June 14, 1966, he lost the flyweight title to Walter McGowan of Scotland, whom he had defeated previously.[840]

Walter McGowan, 1966

Walter McGowan was born in Hamilton, North Lanarkshire, in Scotland on October 13, 1942. He was a very quick boxer who used the whole ring with excellent footwork, a good left jab, and a good right cross. He was also very cut prone and lost fights he could have otherwise won. That has been the fate of more than one fighter from the United Kingdom.

Wee Walter, as he was often called, challenged Salvatore Barunni on June 14, 1966, at the Empire Pool, Wembley, London, England. He outboxed Barunni and despite a bad cut over his left eye that kept his corner busy between rounds, won a unanimous decision, and became the Flyweight Champion of the World.[841] He next took on British bantam Alan Rudkin and decisioned him in fifteen to claim the British bantamweight crown. Stepping back down to flyweight. In December 1966, he defended his world title against Chartchai Chionoi in Bangkok, Thailand. The Thai fighter won and took the title when McGowan suffered a badly cut nose in the ninth round and the referee was forced to stop the fight.[842]

The two boxers had a rematch at the Empire Pool in September 1967, but again the Thai boxer won and kept his title, when cuts to both McGowan's eyes and his forehead caused the referee to stop

840

841

842

the fight in the seventh. Maybe Wee Walter should have considered another line of work.

In 1968, he fought Rudkin again and this time lost his British bantamweight crown by a fifteen-round unanimous decision. He fought six more times, all wins, before retiring in 1969. Along with Benny Lynch and Ken Buchanan, Walter McGowan is one of the greatest Bravehearts to come from Scotland. His record stands at 32-7-1. Most of the seven losses were on cuts.[843]

Wee Walter McGowan, flyweight world champion, died in Lanarkshire, the same place he was born, on September 15, 2016.[844]

Chartchai Chionoi, 1966–1969

Chartchai Chionoi was born near Bangkok, Thailand, on October 10, 1942, and passed away on January 21, 2018. He was twice the lineal Flyweight Champion of the World. Chionoi turned professional on March 27, 1959, winning a second round knockout.[845]

On December 30, 1966, Chionoi challenged the flyweight champion Walter McGowan (lineal champion, recognized by EBU, BBB of C, and *The Ring*). He stopped McGowan in the nineth round to capture his first world title. Chionoi made four successful title defenses during this first reign as champion, including victories over McGowan in their rematch, and Efren Torres.

On February 23, 1969, Chionoi lost his title to Efren Torres in a rematch. The fight was stopped in the eighth round because Chionoi's left eye had swollen shut. He won two out of three fights to earn a rematch with Torres.

843

844

845

Efren Torres, 1969–1970

Efren Torres was born on November 29, 1943, in La Palma, Michaocaon, Mexico, and briefly held the world flyweight title.

Known as El Alacrán (the Scorpion), Torres turned pro in 1961, and in 1969 after two unsuccessful bids at a major title, he defeated WBC and lineal champion Chartchai Chionoi of Thailand by decision to become the flyweight world champion. He lost the title in his second defense to Chartchai Chionoi by decision in 1970. He retired in 1972.[846]

Chartchai Chionoi, 1970

In March 1970, in front of over forty thousand of his countrymen, Chionoi won a fifteen-round unanimous decision over Torres in their rubber match, to once again claim the WBC flyweight championship.[847] His second title reign was short-lived.

In his first title defense, Chionoi was knocked out by Erbito Salavarria in the second round. Salavarria made several successful title defenses before losing the WBC Flyweight Championship. He later reigned as WBA flyweight champion as well.

Chionoi lived a comfortable life in retirement with his wife of over forty-five years, spending as much time as possible with their four children. Despite some lasting ill effects from his years as a boxer, he had fond memories of his career and no regrets.

He died on the evening of January 21, 2018, at seventy-five years old.[848]

846

847

848

Erbito Salavarria, 1970–1973

Salavarria was a Filipino flyweight boxer who December 17, 1970, to claim the lineal world flyweight championship, beating Chartchai Chionoi of Thailand. He will be covered in chapter 16.

So that is the story of professional boxing in the nineteen sixties. There were so many great boxers in that decade! Think Muhammad Ali, Archie Moore, Dick Tiger, Gene Fullmer, Emile Griffith, Luis Rodriguez, Éder Jofre, Vicente Saldivar, Fighting Harada, and many, many more. It was time of great fights and controversy: Ali-Liston I and II and terrible tragedy, Griffith-Paret III, and Davey Moore-Sugar Ramos. Whatever else it was, it led to the next decade, the Nineteen Seventies, and Ali-Frazier, Ali-Foreman, Carlos Monzon, Bob Foster, the rise of Sugar Ray Leonard, and the reign of the great Roberto Durán.

CHAPTER XV

The Big Guys Ali, Frazier, and Foreman

The Seventies

Looking back, the Seventies were not especially great years. They decade came in with student protests, riots, Richard Nixon, and Watergate. There was a wide cultural divide with white suburbanites, blue-collar workers, rednecks, and cops against urban blacks, liberals, the college educated, hippies, pacifists, and radicals, a scene that would play out again nearly fifty years later.

Football and basketball had supplanted baseball and boxing as the biggest sports attractions. But boxing still mattered, and three of the biggest fights of all time, all involving Muhammad Ali, took place in the first half of the decade.

Standing world boxing Champions on January 1, 1971:

- Heavyweight, Muhammad Ali and Joe Frazier (both had legitimate claims)
- Light heavyweight, Bob Foster
- Middleweight, Carlos Monzon
- Welterweight, Billy Backus
- Lightweight, Ken Buchanan
- Featherweight, Kuniaki Shibata
- Bantamweight, Chucho Castillo
- Flyweight, Erbito Salavarrio

Heavyweights of the Seventies

Muhammad Ali, 1970–1971

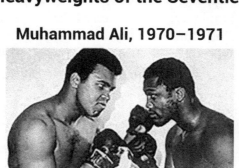

As 1971 began, Muhammad Ali was still the standing lineal champion and still undefeated. His draft conviction had been over-turned and he could once again earn his living as a professional pugilist, but in the meantime, he had lost nearly four years; the prime years of a boxer's life. The draft evasion, if anything only served to make Muhammad even more famous and controversial than as a prize fighter, and of course there was the matter of his being a Black Muslim.

Joe Frazier of Philadelphia had recently gained the title of world champion by defeating Buster Mathis for the NYAC title and Jimmy Ellis for the WBA title. Frazier was a sensitive man who felt like he had to beat Muhammad Ali to gain the peoples recognition as champion. You can have a lot of alphabet titles, but you still gotta beat the man who beat the man who beat the man. In this case the man was Muhammad Ali, still the most famous pugilist on Earth. Naturally, there was already talk of a super fight between the unde-feated Smokin' Joe Frazier and the still-undefeated Muhammad Ali.

After missing the past few years, Ali had not fought since 1967, when he had knocked out Zora Folley, his management decided that he would need a couple of tune-up fights before taking on Frazier. His return naturally befitted a glorious king returning to take back his kingdom. The City of Atlanta Georgia was the first to grant Ali a boxing license, and he was matched with a high-ranking white heavyweight from California named Irish Jerry Quarry. On October 26, 1970, the two stepped into the ring in Atlanta. The racial issue was not lost on anyone with half a brain. Muhammad Ali was the persecuted African American, and Jerry Quarry was the White Irish American opposing him.

The fight proved to be a disappointment as Ali cut the cut-prone Quarry early in the fight, and it was called after the third round. Muhammad was back.

Next he took on Argentinian heavyweight Oscar Bonavena. Bonavena, like Ali, was a colorful character. The free-swinging Bonavena soon ran into trouble outside the ring. He called Muhammad Ali a black kangaroo and even a chicken for draft dodging. Ali was furious. Oscar was one of the few people to upstage Ali in prefight press conferences.

Perhaps the needling threw Ali off his game, or perhaps it was a classic case of ring rust, but in the December 7, 1970, fight at Madison Square Garden, the great Ali looked very ordinary until a sudden dramatic last round knockout ended the fight with another comeback victory for Ali. To Muhammad's credit, Bonavena was a very awkward spoiler who could make anyone look less than great. Joe Frazier must have been licking his chops, thinking how he could beat what looked like a past his prime Ali.

Immediately, the buildup began for Ali-Frazier now being ballyhooed as the fight of the century between two undefeated heavyweights, both with a legitimate claim to the title of Heavyweight Champion of the World.

This fight, scheduled for March 8, 1971, in New York City's Madison Square Garden now took the complete attention of not only the boxing world, but the sports world in general. Not only the rich and famous, but a lot of outrageously dressed fans came out that night for "The Fight." Celebrities in attendance included Frank Sinatra, who was taking pictures for *Life* magazine, Burt Lancaster, Archie Moore, Woody Allen and many, many more.

The fight itself exceeded even its promotional hype and went the full fifteen-round championship distance. Ali dominated the first two rounds, peppering the shorter Frazier with rapier-like jabs that raised welts on the champion's face. In the closing seconds of round three, Frazier connected with a tremendous hook to Ali's jaw, snapping his head back. Frazier began to dominate in the fourth round, catching Ali with several of his famed left hooks and pinning him against the ropes to deliver powerful body blows.

Ali was visibly tired after the sixth round, and though he put together some flurries of punches after that round, he was unable to keep the pace he had set in the first third of the fight. At one minute and fifty-nine seconds into round eight, following his clean left hook to Ali's right jaw, Frazier grabbed Ali's wrists and swung Ali into the center of the ring; however, Ali immediately grabbed Frazier again until they were once again separated by Mercante.

Frazier caught Ali with a left hook at nine seconds into round 11. A fraction of a second later, slipping on water in Frazier's corner, Ali fell with both gloves and his right knee to the canvas. Mercante stepped between Ali and Frazier, separating them as Ali rose. Mercante wiped Ali's gloves and waved no knockdown. At eighteen seconds into round 11, Mercante signaled the fighters to engage once again. Round 11 wound down with Frazier staggering Ali with a left hook. Ali stumbled and grabbed at Frazier to keep his balance and finally stumbled back first to the ropes before bouncing forward again to Frazier and grabbing on to Frazier until the fighters were separated by Mercante at 2:55 into the round.

Heading into round 15, all three judges had Frazier in the lead (7-6-1, 10-4-0, and 8-6-0), and Frazier closed convincingly. Early in the round, Frazier landed a left hook that put Ali on the canvas. Ali, his jaw swollen noticeably, got up at the count of four and managed to stay on his feet for the rest of the round despite several terrific blows from Frazier. A few minutes later the judges made it official: Frazier had retained the title with a unanimous decision, dealing Ali his first professional loss.

Joe Frazier, 1970–1973

The boxer that the world would come to know as Smokin' Joe Frazier was born into a family of twelve children in Beaufort, South Carolina, January 12, 1944. The Frazier's were sharecroppers. Joe came to New York to live with a brother of his in 1958 when he was about fourteen years old. He finally settled in Philadelphia. "I was fifteen years old, and I was on my own."[849]

As an amateur he won a gold medal at the 1964 Summer Olympics. His amateur record was 38-2. Frazier was known for his strength, durability, formidable punching power, and relentless pressure fighting style. He was also the first boxer to beat Muhammad Ali. I watched him rise through the ranks in the Sixties, beating Jerry Quarry, Oscar Bonavena, Buster Mathis, Doug Jones, George Chuvalo, and Jimmy Ellis on his way to becoming the undisputed heavyweight champion. It was a time when a premium boxer's fights were still shown on network television.

After beating Muhammad Ali in the fight of the century, he made two successful defenses of the title in 1972 against fringe contenders Terry Daniels on January 15, stopping him in four rounds

---

849

and against Ron Stander whom he also stopped in four. In both fights, it was apparent that the Ali fight had taken something away from Joe. Before Ali, he probably would have blown both of these guys out in a hurry.

Just how much he had slipped was proven when he took on 1968 Olympic heavyweight Gold Medalist and undefeated professional George Foreman in Kingston, Jamaica on January 22, 1973. He quickly showed how *not* to fight Foreman who dropped him six times on the way to a second round TKO.

He fought one more time in 1973, winning by decision over British heavyweight Joe Bugner. He and Ali fought a second time, January 28, 1974, and this time Ali defeated Joe on a unanimous decision after twelve rounds. Ali staggered Joe in round 1, but the bell rang early, saving him.

Frazier next took on previous opponents Jerry Quarry and Jimmy Ellis, both of whom he had previously beat and stopped both of them, Quarry in five and Ellis in nine rounds.

On October 1, 1975, in Quezon City, Philippines, he met his nemesis for a third time. Each had owned a victory over the other in their two previous encounters. The rubber match was built up by both men, especially Ali, who had mocked and demeaned Frazier calling him the Gorilla. Frazier, a proud African American, was deeply hurt by this insult, and the two had a brief tussle in the television studio before it was broken up.

Ali continued badgering Frazier and threw in one of his little rhymes:

It'll be a thrilla and a chilla
When I beat the gorilla in Manilla.

The fight was a war, and one of the very greatest prize fights ever. Frazier came out smokin', and Ali, as promised, was "a-peckin and a-pokin and pouring water on Frazier's smokin'." Ali was scoring with his jab and an occasional combination while Joe, when he could get inside was ripping Ali's body with paralyzing body blows. The two great warriors, both probably a little past their primes fought their hearts out and the battle swayed back and forth. In round 14, Ali, going to his superhuman reserve, hurt Frazier and had him on the verge of a knockout. Back in his corner, his trainer Yank Durham, seeing his fighter puffed, cut, and beaten, refused to let him come out for the fifteenth round. Ali, realizing he had won, collapsed in his corner. Later, he famously said, "It was the closest thing to dying."[850]

Joe Frazier fought two more times. He again was stopped by George Foreman, himself now an ex-champ after losing to Ali, and finally on December 3, 1981, ten years after the Fight of the Century, he fought a ten-round draw with Floyd "Jumbo" Cummings and retired.

Frazier was diagnosed with liver cancer in late September 2011. By November 2011, he was under hospice care, where he died on November 7, 2011, at the age of sixty-seven.

His final record stands at 32 wins, 4 losses, and 1 draw. He scored 27 knockout victories. He is enshrined in the IBHOF. In 1999, *The Ring* magazine ranked him the eighth greatest heavyweight. BoxRec ranks him as the eighteenth greatest heavyweight of all time.

George Foreman, 1973–1974

George Edward Foreman (born January 10, 1949) in Marshall, Texas, is an American former professional boxer who competed between 1969 and 1997. Nicknamed Big George, he is a two-time world heavyweight champion and an Olympic gold medalist. Outside of boxing, he is also an author and entrepreneur.

There have been two George Foreman's in public life. George I: sullen, withdrawn, dark and intimidating. George II: happy, smiling, spirit-filled, and likeable. A millionaire several times over, he should be happy!

Foreman has been inducted into the World Boxing Hall of Fame and International Boxing Hall of Fame. The International Boxing Research Organization rates Foreman as the eighth greatest heavyweight of all time. In 2002, he was named one of the twenty-five

---

850

greatest fighters of the past eighty years by *The Ring* magazine. The *Ring* ranked him as the ninth greatest puncher of all time. He was a ringside analyst for HBO's boxing coverage for twelve years until 2004. Outside boxing, he is a successful entrepreneur and known for his promotion of the George Foreman Grill, which has sold more than 100 million units worldwide. In 1999, he sold the naming rights to the grill for $138 million.

George grew up in the Fifth Ward community of Houston, Texas. By his own admission in his autobiography, George was a troubled youth. He dropped out of school at the age of fifteen and spent time as a mugger. At age sixteen, Foreman had a change of heart and convinced his mother to sign him up for the Job Corps after seeing an ad for the Corps on TV. As part of the Job Corps, Foreman earned his GED and trained to become a carpenter and bricklayer. After moving to Pleasanton, California, with the help of a supervisor he began to train in boxing.

The world became aware of George Foreman during the 1968 Olympic Games following the raised black gloved fists of Tommie Smith and John Carlos during the playing of the United States National Anthem. Upon winning the gold medal in the heavyweight boxing competition, Foreman produced a miniature American Flag and was seen waving it proudly. This might or might not have been in reaction to the black power salute of Smith and Carlos. At any rate, it made George Foreman an American hero to White as well as Black Americans.

Big George turned professional on June 23, 1969, at Madison Square Garden, winning a third-round TKO over Don Waldhelm. One week later in Houston, he knocked out Fred Askew in the first round. Over the next thirty-five fights, he was undefeated, scoring wins over the likes of Chuck Wepner, Roberto Davila, Levi Forte, Jack O'Halloran, Gregorio Peralta, George Johnson, George Chuvalo, Boone Kirkman, and other fringe contenders.

His 37-0 record with 34 knockouts brought him to a position of a top contender and a shot at Heavyweight Champion Joe Frazier. The fight between two great punchers took place on January 22, 1973, in Kingston, Jamaica, with Foreman dominating the fight to win the championship by technical knockout. In ABC's rebroadcast, Howard Cosell made the memorable call, "Down goes Frazier! Down goes Frazier! Down goes Frazier!" Before the fight, Frazier was 29-0 (25 KO) and Foreman was 37-0 (34 KO). Frazier was knocked down six times by Foreman within two rounds (the three-knockdown rule was not in effect for this bout). After the second knockdown, Frazier's balance and mobility were impaired to the extent that he was unable to evade Foreman's combinations. Frazier managed to get to his feet for all six knockdowns, but referee Arthur Mercante eventually called an end to the one-sided bout. Big George Foreman was now the undisputed lineal Heavyweight Champion of the World.

On September 1, 1973, in his first title defense, Foreman knocked out Jose Roman in one round in Tokyo. Roman was never even in the fight. Next he took on a much tougher opponent, Ken Norton. Norton who had fought Muhammad Ali twice and broken his jaw in the first fight was an awkward fighter who figured to give champion Foreman all he could handle. Foreman handled just fine, knocking Norton out in the second round after stalking him through-out the first. Norton was demolished by Foreman. Muhammad Ali was at ringside doing commentary and had picked Norton to win the fight in Caracas, Venezuela.

He was next. The epochal fight known as the *Rumble in the Jungle* took place in Kinshasa, Zaire, on October 29, 1974. Foreman, based on his destruction of both Ken Norton and Joe Frazier and at his peak at age twenty-five, was favored to beat the thirty-two-year-old ex-champ Ali. Many, this writer among them, thought Ali was past his prime. The ex-champ had hyped up the fight with his usual ballyhoo calling Foreman the Mummy and mimicking his stiff style in comic fashion. In addition, Ali had endeared himself to the local fans, who began to regard him as a black savior. Ali was funny, cocky, and quick-witted, while Foreman was sullen and intimidating. Some people likened him to Sonny Liston. By the time the fight began, George Foreman was perceived by the African fans as the enemy. This fight was listened to all over the world. It could safely be said that on October 29, 1974, the world stopped turning for the Foreman-Ali fight. On this night in the far-off land of Zaire in Central Africa, boxing still mattered.

When the bell rang for round 1, Ali surprised George by coming out aggressively and landing a couple of quick punches. At first he was the old Ali, dancing and using the whole ring as Foreman malevolently stalked him. Soon, he had Ali on the ropes and looked like it might even be a rerun of his Ken Norton knockout. Ali soon got himself back in center ring and landed a few more punches in round 1. In round 2, Foreman backed Ali against the ropes, and there he stayed, covering, leaning back, and punching back as Foreman threw punches that could knock down a cement wall. How could anyone withstand this assault from Foreman? Someone could and that someone was George's tormenter as the rounds wore on, and Ali, in his rope-a-dope, watched as George got more and more tired and arm weary. Every time Ali landed, the African crowed yelled out "Ali! *Bomaye!*" (Ali, kill him!) Round 3 passed, and more of the same, Ali against the ropes and George throwing haymakers while Ali taunted Foreman. "Is that all you got, George? Are you getting tired, George?" Round 4 passed, then round 5, 6, and 7. Now George's arms must have felt like lead. He could barely throw a hard punch. He was so tired. Then in round 8 with Ali in a corner, he suddenly exploded with a combination that staggered

Foreman and a hard right to Foreman's head, and he was down…
for the count![851] History had been made. From the time he won the
Olympic Gold medal to this great moment, Ali had proclaimed he
was the greatest.

In the wake of this bout, know generally referred to as the
Rumble in the Jungle, Muhammad Ali, victor over George Foreman
by a huge upset went from being the most famous boxer in the
world to become the world's most famous man. Across the Americas,
throughout Europe, Africa, the Middle East, Russia, China, every-
where people knew the name Muhammad Ali. It has been said that
there were grass huts in the Sudan where people had his picture on a
wall. They might not have known exactly what he did, but they knew
he was a very, very important Black man.

Muhammad Ali, 1974–1978

Muhammad may have been the most famous man on Earth,
but he was still a prize fighter and he had to fight. Now, once again
he had a championship to defend. His first fight after Foreman
was against a rough-and-tumble club fighter from Bayonne, New
Jersey, named Chuck Wepner. Wepner was a former Marine who had
worked as a bouncer. Due to the number of cuts he had received as a
professional boxer, he was known as the Bayonne Bleeder.[852] He was
not expected to last long with the champion who in his last fight had
knocked out George Foreman. Surprisingly, Wepner put up a good if
not great fight against Ali, even knocking him down in round nine.
He went back to his corner, as the story goes, and told his manager,
"Drive us to the bank. We're millionaires," thinking he would stop
Ali. His manager replied, "You better turn around. He's getting up,
and he looks pissed off." Following the knockdown, Ali stepped up
the pace and outboxed Wepner, cutting him over both of his eyes
and breaking his nose. Ali was far ahead on the scorecards when the

---

851

852

referee stopped the fight with nineteen seconds left in the fifteenth and final round.

After Wepner's fight, Sylvester Stallone wrote the script for *Rocky*, which was released in theaters in 1976. Like Wepner, Rocky Balboa lasts fifteen rounds, but unlike Wepner, he actually goes the distance. For years after *Rocky* was released, Stallone denied that Wepner provided inspiration for the movie. Hmm...[853]

On May 16, 1975, Ron Lyle, an ex-con out of Denver, was given an opportunity to face heavyweight champion Muhammad Ali during Ali's second title defense in his second reign as champion. Lyle had Bobby Lewis and Chico Ferrara in his corner. Lyle was the more aggressive fighter in the early rounds, with Ali conserving his energy and covering up in the center of the ring allowing Lyle to score. Lyle also showed restraint and did not respond to Ali's attempts at the rope-a-dope ploy. Though in danger of falling too far behind on points, Ali appeared to be in control of the pace of the fight and picked his moments to score. The fight was close going into the eleventh round, with Lyle winning on all three of the judges' score cards. Ali then hit Lyle with a strong right hand and followed with several flurrying punches, scoring. The referee stopped the fight, seeing that Lyle was unable to defend himself and Ali was punching him in the head at will. Lyle's corner was not happy with the referee's decision.

On June 30, 1975, Ali traveled across the globe to Kuala Lumpur, Malaysia, where he defeated British champion Joe Bugner by unanimous fifteen-round decision.

Then, in the already described *Thrilla in Manila*, he met former champion Joe Frazier for the third time on October 1, 1975, in what many consider his last great fight. The fight ended when Frazier's corner stopped it and Ali was declared the winner by TKO. Neither fighter was ever the same after this epic encounter.

Now, a faded Ali carried on. On February 20, 1976, in San Juan Puerto Rico, he knocked out Belgium heavyweight Jean Pierre Coopman in five rounds. The matchup between the champ and a

---

[853]

decidedly unthreatening challenger was not up to championship standards, and Ali easily dispatched him.

Then on April 30, in Landover, Maryland, he encountered a lot more than he expected when spoiler Jimmy Young of Philadelphia, an awkward, defense-minded counter puncher, gave Ali fits over fifteen rounds. Young had come up through the Philly gyms and had learned his craft in a city of several good professional boxers. Although Ali won a unanimous decision, the fight was very close. It was becoming clear: Muhammad was not the formidable boxer he had been a few years earlier.

Although on May 24, 1976, he knocked out British heavy-weight Richard Dunn in Munich, Germany, it was hardly a challenge. Dunn was knocked out in round 5. This would be the last knockdown that Ali would ever score. Following the Dunn fight, which hardly anyone paid attention to, feeling he had to take on a serious challenger, he met Ken Norton, a boxer he had fought twice before, losing and suffering a broken jaw the first time and winning a decision the second time.

The rubber match between Ali and Norton took place in New York's Yankee Stadium on September 28, 1976. Although Ali won the decision, it looked for all the world like a fix. The decision was loudly booed by almost everyone at ringside. He could still beat the Coopmans and Dunns, but against any world-class opponent, he would struggle. Nonetheless, the bout is forever on Ali's record as W15.

On May 16, 1977, Ali stepped into the ring in Landover, Maryland, the same place he had gone fifteen rounds with Jimmy Young, to face Uruguayan challenger Alfredo Evangelista. Again, Ali struggled going fifteen rounds against a boxer who would not have lasted five rounds against Ali a few years before.

Ali struggled in his next fight against Earnie Shavers that September, getting rocked a few times by punches to the head. Ali won the fight by another unanimous decision, but the bout caused his longtime-doctor Ferdie Pacheco to quit after he was rebuffed for telling Ali he should retire. Pacheco was quoted as saying, "The New York State Athletic Commission gave me a report that showed Ali's kidneys were falling apart. I wrote to Angelo Dundee, Ali's trainer, his wife, and Ali himself. I got nothing back in response. That's when I decided enough is enough."[854]

Not only were his kidneys failing, his speech was getting noticeably affected as well. His voice had become much quieter, and he sometimes slurred his speech. The hard punches he had taken over the years from Joe Frazier, George Foreman, Sonny Liston, Ken Norton, Earnie Shaves, and others were now taking their toll.

It had to happen sooner or later. On February 16, 1978, in Las Vegas he faced 1976 Olympic light heavyweight champion Leon Spinks. An out-of-shape, poorly trained Ali was almost certainly overconfident facing his challenger, whose record was 7 wins, 0 losses, and 1 draw. Ali looked listless, and the relatively inexperienced Spinks outboxed him over fifteen rounds. Spinks was now the Heavyweight Champion of the World.

Leon Spinks, 1978

Leon Spinks (born July 11, 1953) competed from 1977 to 1995. In only his ninth professional fight, he won the undisputed heavyweight championship in 1978 after defeating Muhammad Ali in a split decision, in what was considered one of the biggest upsets in boxing history. Spinks was later stripped of the WBC title for facing Ali in an unapproved rematch seven months later, which he lost by unanimous decision.

854

Besides being heavyweight champion and his characteristic gap-toothed grin (due to losing two and later all four of his front teeth), Spinks gained notoriety for the disaster which befell his career following the loss to Ali. However, he did challenge once more for the WBC heavyweight title in 1981 (losing to Larry Holmes by TKO in the third round) and the WBA cruiserweight title in 1986 (losing to Dwight Muhammad Qawi by TKO in the sixth round).

As an amateur, Spinks won numerous medals in the light heavyweight division. The first was bronze at the inaugural 1974 world championships, followed by silver at the 1975 Pan American Games, and gold at the 1976 Summer Olympics, the latter alongside his brother Michael Spinks, who won middleweight gold. Leon served in the United States Marine Corps from 1973 to 1976.

Spinks also had a brief career as a professional wrestler in the 1990s, working for Frontier Martial-Arts Wrestling (FMW) and holding the FMW Brass Knuckles Heavyweight Championship in 1992.

Muhammad Ali 1978–1979

Seven months later, in the Superdome in New Orleans in front of seventy thousand fans, an in-shape Muhammad Ali beat Spinks to regain the lineal heavyweight championship of the world for the third time. Again, the fight went fifteen rounds, but this time, Ali outboxed his younger rival winning 10 or 11 of the fifteen rounds.

On July 7, 1979, Ali announced his retirement, vacating the lineal title. His retirement didn't last for long, however, and shortly after he announced his comeback to fight the WBA champion, Larry Holmes. The fight was largely motivated by Ali's need for money. Boxing writer Richie Giachetti said, "Larry didn't want to fight Ali. He knew Ali had nothing left. He knew it would be a horror."[855]

It was. The fight took place on October 2, 1980, in Las Vegas Valley, with Holmes easily dominating Ali, who was weakened from thyroid medication he had taken to lose weight. Giachetti called the fight, "Awful…the worst sports event I ever had to cover." Actor

---

855

Sylvester Stallone was at ringside and said that it was like watching an autopsy on a man who was still alive. In the eleventh round, Angelo Dundee told the referee to stop the fight, making it the only time that Ali ever lost by stoppage. The Holmes fight is said to have contributed to Ali's Parkinson's syndrome. Despite pleas to retire, Ali fought one last time on December 11, 1981, in Nassau, Bahamas, against Trevor Berbick, losing a ten-round decision.

This was the end of the line for Muhammad Ali, considered by many to be the greatest heavyweight champion in history. He transcended the sport in a way few, if any others have. Even giants like Babe Ruth and Michael Jordan never quite reached the ceiling that Muhammad had reached. Everyone alive has heard of Muhammad Ali. His final record stands at 61 fights, 56 wins, 37 knockouts, and 5 losses. He died on June 3, 2016, at age seventy-four.

Larry Holmes, 1980–1985

Larry Holmes was born in Georgia November 3, 1949. He was raised in Easton, Pennsylvania, and earned the moniker Easton Assassin. Like James J. Corbett, Gene Tunney, and Ezzard Charles, who had misfortune to win the championship from John L. Sullivan, Jack Dempsey, and Joe Louis, Larry Holmes had the misfortune to win the title from Muhammad Ali.

Early in his career he worked as a sparring partner for Muhammad Ali, Joe Frazier, Earnie Shavers, and Jimmy Young. He was paid well and learned a lot. "I was young, and I didn't know much. But I was holding my own sparring those guys," Holmes said. "I thought, 'Hey, these guys are the best, the champs. If I can hold my own now, what about later?'"[856]

Holmes got his first big break when in a nationally televised fight he fought an epic battle with WBC champ Ken Norton on June 9, 1978. Like the gods of Valhalla, the two pugilists went at each other in a tough, competitive fight. After fourteen rounds, the fight was dead even. Holmes rallied in the fifteenth; really he outtoughed

---

856

Norton and won the decision. Anyone who attended that fight got a lot more than their monies worth. He was now the WBC Champion. It was one of the greatest fights this writer ever saw.

He defended the Alphabet title easily knocking out Alfredo Evangelista, who had given Ali a fight, lasting the distance against Ali. He then beat Ossie Ocasio, March 23, 1979, and then on June 22 he took on lightly regarded Mike Weaver who came into the fight with a 20-win, 8-loss record compared to Holmes' 30-0. Weaver performed like *he* was 30-0 and gave the WBC champion a very tough fight. In the eleventh round, Holmes dropped Weaver with a right uppercut and finished him by a TKO with Weaver still on his feet in round 12. Weaver would go on to become WBA heavyweight champion.

On October 2, 1980, at Caesars Palace in Las Vegas, Holmes, defended his title against Muhammad Ali. The fight, already covered, was a disaster and painful to watch. It was Ali's only loss without going the distance for a judges' decision. After the win, Holmes received recognition as world heavyweight champion by *The Ring* magazine. More important, it gave him respect and recognition as the universal lineal Heavyweight Champion of the World, a title he surely deserved. This was the last heavyweight title fight of the 1970s.

Light Heavyweights of the Nineteen Seventies

Bob Foster, 1968–1974

Bob Foster of Albuquerque, New Mexico, might or might not have been the greatest light heavyweight in history up to his time, but if he wasn't, he was a damn good light heavyweight champion. He won the title way back in 1968 with a spectacular knockout over the highly respected Nigerian Dick Tiger. Before he was done by retirement in 1974, he had defended the light heavyweight title fourteen times.

Foster began the new decade by stopping Hal Carroll in four rounds at Scranton, Pennsylvania, on March 2, 1971. This was followed by a decision win over Ray Anderson in Tampa, Florida on March 24. Next on Mr. Foster's agenda was Brian Kelly, whom he beat in Oklahoma City. Then, for some Mickey Mouse reason, the WBA decided to take away recognition of a truly great light heavyweight and decide to make Vincente Rondon of Venezuela *their* champion. Foster quickly settled the score knocking out Rondon in two rounds on April 7, 1972, at the Miami Beach Convention Center.

On June 27, 1972, he fought on a card underneath Muhammad Ali advertised as the Soul brothers versus the Quarry brothers. Ali took on Jerry Quarry for the second time, stopping the Bellflower Bomber in the seventh round. Foster, throwing a left hook out of hades knocked Mike Quarry, Jerry's younger brother out cold. It was flashback time evoking his knockout of Dick Tiger a few years before.

Following a fourteenth-round stoppage of Chris Finnegan in London, champ Foster took on Muhammad Ali in Stateline, Nevada, on November 21, 1972. Foster cut Ali, who had never suffered a cut in his career, but then Ali took charge. After knocking Foster down seven times, referee Mills Lane stopped the contest in the eighth round.

In 1973, Foster defended his title twice against South African Pierre Fourie, once in Albuquerque and once in Johannesburg. He was heavily criticized for not addressing Apartheid while in Johannesburg.

He defended the title one last time, holding on to it by a draw in his hometown of Albuquerque in 1974. Following that scare, he announced his retirement. It was short-lived; he fought eight more losing his last two. He retired on June 2, 1978. His record stands at 56 wins with 46 knockouts, 8 losses, and 1 draw. Nearly all his losses were against heavyweights. He died November 21, 2015, in Albuquerque, New Mexico. He was inducted into the IBHOF in 1990.

Following Bob Foster's retirement in 1974, the light heavyweight title was divided up between various sanctioning bodies until Michael Spinks unified the lineal title in 1983.

Middleweights of the Seventies

Carlos Monzon, 1970–1977

Carlos Roque Monzón (Santa Fe, Argentina, August 7, 1942–Santa Fe, Argentina, January 8, 1995), nicknamed Escopeta (*shotgun* in Spanish), was an Argentine professional boxer who held the undisputed world middleweight championship for 7 years. He successfully defended his title 14 times against 11 different fighters and is widely regarded as not only one of the best middleweights in history but also one of the greatest boxers of all time pound for pound. Known for his speed, punching power and relentless work rate, Monzon ended his career with a record of 87-3-9 with 59 knockouts, each one of his losses were early in his career and were avenged. Inducted into the International Boxing Hall of Fame in 1990, he was chosen by *The Ring* magazine in 2002 as the 11th greatest fighter of the last 80 years and voted him as the best middleweight title holders of the last 50 years in 2011. As of January 2018, Monzón holds the 2nd longest unified championship reign in middleweight history at 9 consecutive defenses. To put it mildly, Carlos Monzon was one of the greatest middleweights in history. He might have even been the greatest. Fitzimmons, Ketchel, Greb? Greb gives him the toughest fight. Robinson, Hagler, Hopkins, Alvarez? Interesting, and hard to call. A prime Sugar Ray Robinson, possibly.

Argentinians adored Monzon throughout his career. His glamorous and violent life was avidly followed both by the media and Argentine people. He was, however, accused many times of domestic violence by his two wives and many mistresses and of beating paparazzi. Charged with killing his wife, Alicia Muñiz, in Mar del Plata in 1988, the former champion was sentenced to 11 years in jail. He died in a January 1995 car crash during a weekend furlough.

In his career, he beat the following: Jose Napoles, Emile Griffith, Bennie Briscoe, Fraser Scott, Denny Moyer, Tom Boggs, and Nino Benvenuti, plus several outstanding South American boxers who are not familiar to American fans. His final record stands at 100 fights, with 59 knockouts, 3 losses, and 9 draws with 1 no contest. He retired as champion.

Rodrigo Valdez, 1977–1978

Rodrigo Valdéz (December 22, 1946–March 14, 2017) was a Colombian boxer who was the undisputed world middleweight champion, whose rivalry with Carlos Monzón has long been considered among the most legendary boxing rivalries. Valdez was trained by International Boxing Hall of Fame coach Gil Clancy. Many people consider him, Antonio Cervantes, and Miguel "Happy" Lora to be the three greatest boxers ever to come from that country. He is twenty-ninth on *Ring* magazine's list of one hundred greatest punchers of all time.

Valdez had nineteen wins in a row when he met Philadelphia legend Bennie Briscoe for the NABF middleweight title, in Nouméa, New Caledonia, on September 1, 1973, beating Briscoe in a twelve-round decision to capture the regional championship and becoming a world-ranked middleweight contender. After this win, Valdez challenged for a world title shot at Monzon.

With 26 straight wins, a WBC title claim and a 57-4-2 record, he was ready to challenge the great Carlos Monzon for the undisputed world title. The two met on June 26, 1976, in Monaco to decide who the real champion was. After fifteen rounds, Monzon won a unanimous decision and was once again undisputed middleweight champion. One year later at the same location on July 30, 1977, they fought again and again Monzon won by unanimous decision.

Upon Monzon's retirement, Valdez was matched with Bad Bennie Briscoe, a tough Philadelphia middleweight for the WBC-WBA, *Ring* magazine lineal World Middleweight Championship. Rodrigo Valdez won, beating Briscoe by a unanimous decision on November 11, 1977, in Lombardy, Italy.

He didn't hold the title for long. On April 22, 1978, Hugo Corro, a middleweight from Argentina took the crown by unanimous decision. The two fought a rematch in Buenos Aires, November 11, 1978, and again Corro beat Valdez by decision.

Valdez fought 2 more times and retired. Valdez had a record of 63 wins, 8 losses and two draws as a professional boxer, with 42 wins by knockout.

Hugo Corro, 1978–1979

Hugo Corro was born on November 5, 1953, in San Carlos, Mendoza, Argentina. He turned professional on August 30, 1973, winning his debut by TKO in six. With only two losses in forty-six fights, he challenged Rodrigo Valdez for the world middleweight title, winning a unanimous decision on April 22, 1978.

He made two successful defenses of the championship, first beating American Ronnie Harris on August 5, 1978, in Buenos Aires by decision, followed by a second victory over Rodrigo Valdez on November 11 of that year.

The following year, Corro traveled to Monaco to defend against Vito Antuofermo of Italy. After a very close fight, Antuofermo took the title by a split decision on June 30, 1979.

Corro had a record of 50 wins, 7 losses and 2 draws as a professional boxer, with 29 wins by way of knockout. On June 15, 2007, he died after suffering from an acute liver disease.

Vito Antuofermo, 1979–1980

Vito Antuofermo was born February 9, 1953, in Italy. His family moved to New York City when he was seventeen. He grew up in a tough neighborhood and he had to learn out to fight. He won the New York Golden Gloves 147-pound title and turned professional soon after.

On June 30, 1979, Antuofermo became World Middleweight Champion by beating defending champion Hugo Corro by a decision in 15 rounds at Monte Carlo. According to an article in the *Ring*, Howard Cosell, who was working on that fight's live broadcast to the USA, was telling viewers that Corro was, in his opinion, way ahead on the judges' cards. When someone on the American television crew found out it was Antuofermo who was actually leading on the cards, Cosell then began to say he had Antuofermo ahead.

On the morning after winning the title, Antuofermo and his crew were driving to a small vacation in Italy, when he saw a car fly off a bridge under which they were passing. The car landed right in front of his, but luckily the accident did not injure any occupants in Antuofermo's car. He was so shocked that he kept driving and never found out what happened to the occupants of that car. He came back to his senses about 20 minutes later.

In Las Vegas, Nevada on November 30, 1979, Vito Antuofermo defended his title in Caesars Palace against the very tough southpaw, Marvelous Marvin Hagler. The fight resulted in a highly controversial draw after 15 rounds. In his next title defense, on March 16, 1980, at Caesars Palace in Las Vegas, Antuofermo lost the championship to British challenger Alan Minter on a split decision. In the rematch on June 28, this time in London, Minter lacerated Antuofermo's face and the bout was stopped in the eighth round with Minter the winner by TKO.

After retirement, Antuofermo began to pursue an acting career. In 1990, he landed a small role in *The Godfather Part III* as the chief bodyguard of gangster Joey Zasa. He has landed several small speaking roles in movies and television shows since, included the critically acclaimed television show *The Sopranos* as a mobster. He has also done many theater plays.

Antuofermo's record reads 50 wins, 7 losses, and 2 draws, with 21 wins by knockout.

Alan Minter, 1980

Alan Minter was born in London on August 17, 1951. He won the undisputed middleweight title from Vito Antuofermo in 1980, having previously held the British middleweight from 1975 to 1976, and the European middleweight title twice between 1977 and 1979. As an amateur, Minter won a bronze medal in the light-middleweight division at the 1972 Summer Olympics.

In 1975, he won four fights in a row. By the end of the year, he challenged Kevin Finnegan for the British Middleweight title, winning it by a fifteen-round decision.

Victories over Tony Licata, Sugar Ray Seales, Emile Griffith, as well as Finnegan put Minter in line for a shot at Antuofermo and the world middleweight crown. As stated earlier, Minter beat Antuofermo and beat him a second time as well. Marvelous Marvin Hagler would just have to wait.

Alan Minter was now the Middleweight Champion of the World. Minter then defended against Hagler, who dominated and then stopped the Brit in three rounds. In the run-up to the fight, Minter had caused controversy by stating that he "did not intend to lose his title to a black man." After the fight was stopped, Minter's supporters caused a riot, throwing beer cans and bottles into the ring, and both boxers had to be ushered away by the police. Minter fought three more times winning one and losing two. He retired after the second loss. His record stands at 49 fights with 39 wins, 23 by knockout and 9 defeats.

Welterweights of the Nineteen Seventies

Billy Backus, 1970–1971

Having won the title from the great Jose Napoles on a cut eye stoppage, Billy Backus became the Welterweight Champion of the World. After making two nontitle appearances and winning both, he faced Napoles again on June 4, 1971. The first fight was held in Backus's hometown of Syracuse. This time it was on more neutral ground at the Forum in Inglewood. Predictably, Napoles, won, this time stopping Backus by an eight-round TKO to regain the crown. Billy Backus fought on until 1978. In his final fight he was knocked out by WBA champion Pipino Cuevas in one round. He retired with a record of 74 fights of which he won 49, lost 20 and had 5 draws. Although he is not a hall of fame candidate, he got one shot at greatness and beat Jose Napoles, albeit on a cut eye, but he won nonetheless.

Jose "Mantequilla" Napoles, 1971–1975

After three nontitle wins, including one over Jean Josselin, Napoles faced Hedgemon Lewis on December 14, 1971, retaining the world title with a decision in fifteen rounds, but Nápoles' training habits were suffering; he was alleged to be coming into the gym stinking of alcohol with an attitude toward his seconds.

In 1972, he retained the title knocking out Ralph Charles in seven in England, and then Adolph Pruitt again, this time with the world welterweight title on the line. Nápoles retained his crown by knockout in round 2.

World traveler Nápoles began 1973 by retaining the title against Lopez again, by knockout in 7, then he visited Grenoble, France, where he retained the crown with a fifteen-round decision over Roger Menetrey, and Toronto, Ontario, Canada, where he beat Clyde Gray, once again retaining the world title with a fifteen-round decision.

On February 9, 1974, Jose Napoles moved up to the middleweight division and challenged fellow great Carlos Monzon for the middleweight championship of the world. The fight was fairly even for two rounds, but then the taller and rangier Monzon found his rhythm and repeatedly hurt Napoles, causing the welterweight champion's corner to signal to the referee to stop the fight after the sixth round.

Back down to the welterweight class, still-champion Jose Napoles beat Hedgemon Lewis for the second time on August 2, 1974, in Mexico City, stopping the American challenger by TKO in 9. Then after two successful defenses against Armando Muniz, the aging champion finally lost to British boxing teacher John H. Stracey after having defended his title fourteen times over two reigns. His record stands forever at 88 fights with 81 wins and 7 losses. He scored 54 knockouts. He is a member of the vanguard class of the IBHOF in 1990.

John H. Stracey, 1975–1976

John H. Stracey (born September 22, 1950) is a British former professional boxer who competed from 1969 to 1978. He is a former welterweight world champion, having held the WBC and lineal welterweight titles between 1975 and 1976. At regional level, he held the British and European welterweight titles between 1973 and 1975 and is ranked by BoxRec as the eighth best British welterweight of all time.

During the 1970s, it was a common practice to give world title shots to boxers that held continental titles. For example, the OPBF (Oriental Pacific Boxing Federation) champion would be given priority over other challengers for world title fights. Stracey was not the exception, and after winning five more fights in a row (including a win over Ernie Lopez), he received his first world title shot: challenging WBC welterweight champion José Nápoles, in Nápoles's hometown of Mexico City, Mexico, on December 6, 1975. Stracey was sent down in round 1, but he recuperated to close Nápoles's eye and have referee Octavio Meyran stop the fight in the sixth round, Stracey winning the world championship by a technical knockout. The new champion declared, "He [Nápoles] could have knocked me down in every round, but I'd have won it anyway." It was Nápoles's last fight.

Stracey made one successful defense of the title, beating perineal contender Hedgeman Lewis on March 20, 1976, at the Empire Pool in London. Shortly after, on June 22, again at the Empire Pool, he was beaten and TKO'd in the twelfth round by California based Mexican Carlos Palomino, who wore Stracey down with body blows and devastating punches to the liver.

After losing the title to Palomino he lost by tenth round TKO to future Sugar Ray Leonard opponent Dave Boy Green. He fought once more and retired to open a pub that bore his name. His record stands at 51 fights 45 wins and 37 knockouts, 5 losses, 1 draw.

Carlos Palomino, 1976–1979

For a time, Carlos Palomino, born on August 10, 1949, had it all. He was good-looking, smart, and talented and gained immense popularity in Southern California in the 1970s. While in the United States Army, he won the 1971 and 1972 All-Army Championship. Upon his discharge, he won the National AAU light welterweight championship in 1972.

Turning professional in 1972, he ran up ten straight wins with one draw before his first defeat at the hands of Andy Price on August 2, 1974, losing a split decision in San Diego. Back in the win column excluding a couple of draws, he was matched with World Champion John H. Stracey on June 22, 1976, at the Empire Pool in Wembley, London, England. There, before an internationally televised audience, Palomino beat down Stracey before stopping him in the twelfth round to become the Welterweight Champion of the World.

He waited six months for his next fight, against another very popular boxer of Mexican background: cross-town rival Armando Muñíz. This was a fight that had many fans guessing who'd win it for months before it happened, but it also made history in the boxing books: when Palomino and Muñíz met, on January 21, 1977, it was the first time in boxing history two college graduates met for a world title. Palomino earned a degree in recreation administration from Long Beach State, while Muniz had graduated from Cal State, Los Angeles, where he majored in Spanish and minored in math, and was working toward a graduate degree in administration. Palomino and Muniz (now a high school teacher in California) fought what the book *The Ring: Boxing in the 20th. Century* has described as one of the best fights of 1977. After fourteen rounds, all three judges had the fight tied on their scorecards, but Palomino scored two knockdowns in the fifteenth and final round, and he retained the world title by a knockout in that final round.

Palomino made six more defenses of the title, including one more over Muñíz, before traveling to San Juan, Puerto Rico, on January 14, 1979, to meet boxing *wunderkind*, twenty-one-year-old

Wilfred Benitez. Already a junior welterweight champion at age seventeen, the young man known as El Radar outpointed Palomino in a very close controversial decision.

Now an ex-champ, Palomino jumped from the frying pan into the fire, taking on the great soon-to-be-a-legend lightweight champion Roberto Durán, losing a unanimous ten round decision. He retired immediately after the fight. There was a brief comeback, as almost all ex-champions feel compelled to do and ran up a few wins, but sensibly quit after another loss. He was forty-eight years old.

In 1978, while still the WBC welterweight champion, Palomino appeared as Carlos Navarone in the ABC sitcom *Taxi*. Appearing in the second episode of the opening season ("One-Punch Banta"), he spars with Tony Banta (Tony Danza himself a former professional boxer with a 9-3 record) and takes a dive. Palomino appears as himself in an episode of "The White Shadow" in 1979.

In 1980, Miller Lite beer signed Palomino as a spokesman as part of a television commercial campaign that also included Walt Frazier and other noted athletes. As a consequence of the enjoyable experience and the media exposure that followed, he decided to launch a career as an actor.

Carlos Palomino became a member of the IBHOF (International Boxing Hall of Fame) in 2004.

Wilfred Benitez, 1979

For starters, Wilfred Benitez was a professional boxing world champion when most boys his age were still hoping the cute redhead would go to the prom with them. In fact, his first world champion contest as a junior welterweight was against thirty-year-old Antonio Cervantes, a veteran of eighty-six professional fights who had defended his title ten times. With his high school classmates in attendance, Benitez won a fifteen-round split decision over the future hall ff Famer. The date was March 6, 1976. He was seventeen years old.

After winning his first title, his record now stood at 17-0. He defended his title successfully three times, before moving up to the welterweight division, defeating Columbian Emiliano Villa,

American Tony Petronelli, and another Columbian, Ray Chavez Guerrero.

On January 14, 1979, now a welterweight, he challenged Carlos Palomino for the world title. The fight took place in San Juan, Puerto Rico, where Benitez was now a national hero. On a split decision, Benitez won the fight and was now the Welterweight Champion of the World. He was twenty years old.

After outpointing Harold Weston Jr. in his first defense (avenging an earlier draw), Benítez fought Sugar Ray Leonard in Las Vegas, Nevada on November 30, 1979. It was a scientific fight by both fighters, who demonstrated their defensive skills throughout the bout. Benítez suffered a third-round knockdown and a cut on his forehead, which was opened by an accidental head butt in round six. Leonard put Benítez down again in the fifteenth round and the referee stopped the fight with six seconds left in round fifteen. Wilfred Benitez would go on to greater glory.

Sugar Ray Leonard, 1979–1980

Born Ray Charles Leonard (after *the* Ray Charles) in Wilmington, North Carolina on May 17, 1956, Sugar Ray Leonard became one of the greatest boxers at any weight in history. The family moved to Washington, DC, when Ray was three and then settled in Palmer Park, Maryland when he was ten.

Leonard was a shy child, and aside from the time he nearly drowned in a creek during a flood in Seat Pleasant, Maryland, his childhood was uneventful. He stayed home a lot, reading comic books and playing with his dog. His mother said, "He never did talk too much. We never could tell what he was thinking. But I never had any problems with him. I never had to go to school once because of him."[857]

In 1976, Leonard made the US Olympic Team as the light welterweight representative. The team also included Leon and Michael Spinks, Howard Davis Jr., Leo Randolph, Charles Mooney, and

---

[857]

John Tate. Many consider the 1976 US team to be the greatest boxing team in the history of the Olympics. Leonard won his first four Olympic bouts by 5–0 decisions. He faced Kazimierz Szczerba in the semifinals and won by a 5–0 decision, avenging his last amateur loss. Like Muhammad Ali, then known as Cassius Clay before him, who was the star of the 1960 games, Leonard became a star of the 1976 Olympics.

Initially, Leonard had no plans to turn professional. He claimed to have already achieved what he had set out to do: win an Olympic gold medal. He planned to go to college and in fact was given a scholarship to the University of Maryland in appreciation by the citizens of Glenarden, Maryland.

Leonard had hoped to get lucrative endorsements following his gold medal win, but the negative publicity from a paternity suit chased off any big commercial possibilities. To make matters worse, his father was hospitalized with meningitis, and his mother suffered a heart attack. With neither parent able to work, with his child and the mother of his child to support, and without any endorsement opportunities, Leonard decided to become a professional boxer.

It's an old story, but with a new twist. Sugar Ray Leonard was no Cinderella Man. For his professional debut, he got over $40,000 for his first pro fight. Even after he paid off his manager, he still wound up with 27 grand. I got paid $175 for my first and last pro fight.

At any rate, Sugar Ray Leonard was off and rolling. Scanning his record, it is not until his fourteenth fight that a name opponent is recognized. That would be Dickey Eklund, known to those of us who follow boxing closely, even if he is not known to the general public or casual boxing fan. From there the names become more familiar: Floyd Mayweather Sr., Randy Shields, Armando Muniz, Adolpho Viruet, Pete Ranzany, and Andy Price all led up to his appointment on November 30, 1979, with Mr. Wilfred Benitez, Welterweight Champion of the World. As the boxers stood in center ring, Benitez looking for all the world like the great boxer he was, stood looking down his nose at his challenger as if to say, "How dare you think you can be in the same ring with me?"

The fight was a tactical battle. In the third round, Leonard dropped Benitez with a stiff left jab. Benitez jumped right up, more embarrassed than hurt. It was a wakeup call. He began finding his range on Leonard and began landing his right. In the sixth there was an accidental clash of heads, which opened up an ugly gash on Benitez's forehead. Blood dripped down his face but did not get into his eyes. By now, Leonard was leading on the scorecards. The fight stayed competitive until the final round. In the fifteenth, Leonard once again dropped Benitez with a hard left. Benitez got up but was met with a flurry of Sugar Ray Leonard punches. The referee, seeing Benitez hurt and unable to defend himself, stepped in with six seconds remaining in the fight and stopped it. The time was 2:54 of round fifteen. Sugar Ray Leonard had TKO'd Wilfred Benitez and was now the Welterweight Champion of the World.

Roberto Durán, 1980

Panamanian boxer Roberto Durán, who held the welterweight boxing championship for a time in 1980, was born on June 16, 1951, in the slums of El Chorrillo. He is the greatest lightweight champion of all time. He won the Lightweight Championship of the World on June 26, 1972, in Madison Square Garden, knocking out lightweight champion Ken Buchanan of Scotland.

Vacating the Lightweight title was a buildup for an attempt at the welterweight title. Durán earned wins against former WBC welterweight champion Carlos Palomino and Zeferino Gonzales, among others, setting the stage for a title bout against then-undefeated welterweight champion Sugar Ray Leonard. The venue chosen was the Olympic Stadium in Montreal (the same location where Leonard won an Olympic gold medal during the 1976 Summer Olympics). Durán resented the fact that he was getting only one-fifth of the money that Leonard was getting, despite the fact that Durán was entering the bout with an incredible 71-1 record and seen by many as the best boxer of the 1970s decade that had just ended. To the surprise of Leonard and his camp, who had expected a warm homecoming from the place where Leonard had won Olympic gold, Leonard only got a mixed reception in Montreal, while Durán was incredibly popular with the crowd, with Leonard later admitting that Durán's popularity in Canada "threw me for a loop."[858] On June 20, 1980, Durán captured the lineal welterweight title by defeating Leonard via a 15-round unanimous decision (145–144, 148–147, 146–144), although it was incorrectly announced as a majority decision in the ring with the 148–147 scorecard being incorrectly announced as 147–147. The fight became known as *The Brawl in Montreal*.

It was an incredible fight. Durán hurt Leonard in the first round, but Sugar Ray stood his ground and fired back. One thing you should know about Roberto Durán. If you try to stand your ground and slug it out with him, you are probably going to lose. Sugar Ray Leonard lost. Now, Roberto Durán was the Welterweight Champion of the World. At the conclusion of the fight, Leonard reached his hand out to Durán in sportsmanship. Durán, ever the tough guy, brushed it away.

Sugar Ray Leonard, 1980–1982

There was a rematch. On November 25, 1980, Leonard, now the challenger and Durán, now the champion fought before 25,038 fans in the New Orleans Superdome. The fight, now known to boxing fans as the *"no mas"* fight was very different from their first encounter. This time, Sugar Ray refused to stand and slug it out. He moved, he danced. He seemed to be mocking Durán, always moving, sometimes even sticking his chin out as if defying Durán to hit him. Durán seemed stymied by Leonard's actions. In the seventh round, Leonard suddenly stopped and started winding his right hand around as if to throw a bolo punch, ala Kid Gavilan. As Durán, puzzled watching him Leonard hit him in the face with a left jab, causing his eyes to water. He continued to taunt Durán, mercilessly. Shortly after, Durán turned to the referee and said, *"No mas."* This came as a tremendous shock to the boxing public. The great Roberto Durán, known as stone hands, had quit? The man who had outrum-

858

bled Sugar Ray in Montreal had quit? He had. That was it. *No mas.* No more.

Apparently Durán had gone on a partying binge following his win over Leonard in their first fight. He had abused his body with alcohol and drugs and gained about fifty pounds. Now he had to lose that weight to get back down to the welterweight limit of 147 pounds. His lack of fire put into this context was understandable. Also, Roberto Durán was a proud man. After being mocked and humiliated, I think he thought to himself, "This guy is making a fool of me. I don't have to take this shit." It is a common malady for boxers who win a big fight, to celebrate on and on and on. Think Leon Spinks, Andy Ruiz Jr., and going back nearly a century, Battling Siki. After beating Leonard in Montreal, Durán was feted in his home country. His legend had reached icon status. Now he had tumbled and fallen. He would, of course, redeem himself in the next decade.

Sugar Ray Leonard was once again the welterweight champion of the world.

CHAPTER XVI

Ya Gotta Love the Little Guys

Lightweights of the Nineteen Seventies

Ken Buchanan, 1970–1972

When the decade of the Seventies opened, a Scottish boxer, Ken Buchanan held the world lightweight title. He was born in Edinburg on June 28, 1945. Turning professional in 1965, he steadily climbed the ratings until on September 26, 1970, he traveled to San Juan, Puerto Rico and challenged Panamanian world lightweight champion Ismael Laguna for the WBA championship. He upset Laguna to win the title in fifteen rounds by unanimous decision. There was some dispute among the sanctioning bodies as to who was the champion, but Buchanan kept plugging away, and on February 12, 1971, he beat Ruben Navarro for the vacant WBC title to become the undisputed lineal champion.

On September 13, 1971, in a rematch with Laguna, he won again over his now challenger to successfully defend the lightweight title. In his next defense on June 26, 1972, at Madison Square Garden, he faced a young undefeated Panamanian named Roberto Durán. Fighting Durán, Buchanan discovered was like fighting the lightweight champion of hell. Durán won that night by a controversial technical knockout at the end of the thirteenth round. Both fighters, apparently not hearing the bell, continued punching and Durán apparently landed a low blow that sent the soon to be ex-champion to the canvas in pain. The referee then awarded the fight to Durán, who was ahead on all the scorecards. Ken Buchanan was now an ex-champion. As I watched the televised fight, I couldn't help but think "Wow" at seeing Durán. Ken Buchanan continued fighting until 1982 as well as battling alcoholism. His boxing record shows 61 wins with 37 knockouts and 8 losses. He is an inductee into the IBHOF.

Roberto Durán, 1972–1979

Junior Middleweight Champion

I will tell you how good Roberto Durán was. He is the greatest lightweight champion of all time, even better than Joe Gans and Benny Leonard. He was voted the outstanding boxer of the Seventies (over such luminaries as Muhammad Ali and Joe Frazier), and to some, including this writer, he may be the greatest fighter of all time at any weight. That is really saying a lot.

Overall, Durán made twelve successful defenses of his title (eleven coming by knockout) and amassed a record of 62–1, his last defense coming in 1978 when Durán fought a third bout with De Jesus in unification match wherein Durán once again knocked out De Jesus and captured his WBC lightweight championship. Durán gave up the undisputed lightweight championship in February 1979. Following Durán, the lineal line of lightweight champions was vacant until consolidated by another great, Alexis Arguello, in 1981.

Roberto Durán held world championships in four different weight classes: lightweight, welterweight, light middleweight, and middleweight, as well as reigns as the undisputed and lineal lightweight champion and the lineal welterweight champion. He is also the second boxer to have competed over a span of five decades, the first being Jack Johnson. Durán was known as a versatile, technical brawler and pressure fighter, which earned him the nickname of *Manos de Piedra* (Hands of Stone) for his formidable punching power and excellent defense.

In 2002, Durán was voted by *The Ring* magazine as the fifth greatest fighter of the last 80 years, 7 while boxing historian Bert Sugar rated him as the eighth greatest fighter of all time. The Associated Press voted him as the best lightweight of the 20th century, with many considering him the greatest lightweight of all time. Durán retired for good in January 2002 at age 50, following a car crash in Argentina in October 2001, after which he had required lifesaving surgery. He had previously retired in November 1980, June 1984, and August 1998, only to change his mind. Durán ended his career with a professional record of 119 fights, 103 wins, and 70 knockouts. From May 1971 up until his second fight against Sugar Ray Leonard in November 1980, as well as in his fight against Wilfred Benítez in January 1982, Durán was trained by legendary boxing trainer Ray Arcel.

Featherweights of the Nineteen Seventies

Kuniaki Shibata, 1970–1972

Japanese featherweight boxer Kuniaki Shibata was born March 29, 1947, in Hitachi, Japan.

Shibata made won his debut match in 1965 with a first-round knockout, and fought for the Oriental and Pacific Boxing Federation featherweight title in 1969, but lost by sixth-round knockout. In April 1970, he challenged the vacant Japanese featherweight title and won by tenth-round knockout. He returned the title to challenge

WBC featherweight champion Vicente Saldivar and won the title when Saldivar gave up after the twelfth round.

He made his first defense by first-round knockout and retained his title in his second defense with a draw, but lost to Clemente Sanchez in May 1972.

Clemente Sanchez, 1972

Sánchez turned pro in 1963 and captured the lineal and WBC featherweight title with a third round KO over Kuniaki Shibata in 1972. He lost the title in his first defense by TKO to Jose Legra, but Sanchez had been stripped of his WBC belt after failing to make weight prior to the fight. He retired in 1975. He was shot and killed by police after a traffic dispute in 1978.

Jose Legra, 1972–1973

José Legrá was born in Baracoa, Cuba on April 19, 1943. Legra turned professional in 1960. He began fighting in Cuba and had 34 fights in Mexico and Cuba before moving to Spain in 1963. Nicknamed Pocket Cassius Clay, he won the vacant European featherweight title in December 1967 with a third-round knockout win over France's Yves Desmarets.

On December 16, 1972, Legrá fought Clemente Sanchez for the vacant featherweight title, Sanchez was stripped of the title before the fight, but the title was still on the line for Legrá. Legrá would TKO Sanchez in the tenth round to win.

Legrá lost the title in his very next fight to Brazilian Éder Jofre by majority decision. He would fight 3 matches after that, beating Jimmy Bell by points, losing to Alexis Arguello by KO and beating Daniel Valdez by points. Legra retired in 1973 soon after losing to Arguello. His complete record stands at 144 fights, 129 wins with 49 KOs, 11 losses, and 4 draws.[859]

859

Éder Jofre, 1973–1974

As previously noted, Éder Jofre might have been the greatest bantamweight champion in history. A decade later, he might have slipped slightly, but he was still good enough to win the lineal featherweight championship from Jose Legra on May 5, 1973.

If that wasn't enough, he beat Mexican great Vicente Saldivar in what was billed as the super fight by fourth-round knockout on October 21, 1973. The World Boxing Council, WBC, showing no class whatsoever, then stripped Jofre, one of the greatest boxers in history, for failure to defend against "their" contender. Jofre fought 7 more times, winning all before retiring on October 8, 1976, with a record of 72 wins with 50 knockouts, 2 defeats, and 4 draws.

Alexis Arguello, 1975–1977

Alexis Arguello was a Nicaraguan boxer who achieved his greatest fame as a lightweight in the 1980s. He achieved his first fame as a World Featherweight Champion in the seventies. Arguello turned professional in 1968 and ran up a streak of 31-3 before losing to Ernesto Marcel for the WBA featherweight title. Marcel took a unanimous verdict over Arguello on February 16, 1974.[860]

Following the abdication of Éder Jofre, Argüello put together another streak of wins and found himself contending for the WBA featherweight title, this time against Ruben Olivares in the latter's first defense. The fight took place at the Forum in Inglewood on November 23, 1974. After Olivares had built a small lead on the judges' scorecards, Argüello and Olivares landed simultaneous left hooks in round thirteen. Olivares's left hand caused a visible expression of pain on Argüello's face, but Argüello's left hand caused Olivares to crash hard against the canvas and put Olivares out cold. Ten seconds later, Argüello was the new WBA featherweight champion.[861] Three fights later, on May 31, 1975, he added the lineal title

---

860

861

winning over Rigoberto Riasco, stopping the Panamanian in the second round. He was now the featherweight champion of the world. Arguello was a popular television attraction and became well-known in households across America, especially in the Eighties, fighting people like Ray "Boom Boom" Mancini, Cornelius Boza Edwards, and the great Aaron Pryor.

Sadly, Alexis Argüello, a truly gifted and great boxer, committed suicide shooting himself in the heart on July 12, 2009. His final record stands at 88 fights, with 77 wins, 62 KOs, and 8 losses.[862]

Danny "Little Red" Lopez, 1979–1980

Known for his tremendous punching power, *The Ring* magazine rated Lopez at number 26 on their list of 100 Greatest Punchers. In 2010, Lopez was inducted into the International Boxing Hall of Fame.

He made his professional debut on May 27, 1971, knocking out Steve Flajole in one round in Los Angeles. He was a very popular boxer in the Los Angeles area and fought most of his fights in that city. He was also a popular television personality with many of his fights televised. He won the WBC Featherweight Championship November 6, 1976, beating Ghanaian David Kotey (Kotei) by unanimous decision in Accra, Ghana.

Between then and when he won the World lineal Title he defended the WBC title five times. On March 10, 1979, at Salt Palace, Salt Lake City, he knocked out Roberto Castañón of Spain and became the undisputed Featherweight Champion of the World. He made two successful defenses, first against Mike Ayala in 1979 *Ring* magazine's Fight of the Year and followed that up by stopping Jose Caba of the Dominican Republic in three rounds by TKO.[863]

Lopez's reign as world champion came to an end on February 2, 1980, at the Arizona Veterans Memorial Coliseum in Phoenix. He met Salvador Sánchez that day, and he lost by knockout in round 13

862

863

in a one-sided affair. A rematch was fought on June 21, in Las Vegas, and that time around, Lopez was knocked out in the fourteenth round, in a replay of the first fight. He announced his retirement after that fight.[864]

Salvador Sánchez, 1980–1982

He (January 26, 1959–August 12, 1982) was a Mexican boxer born in the town of Santiago Tianguistenco, Estado de México. Sanchez was the WBC and lineal featherweight champion from 1980 to 1982. Many of his contemporaries as well as boxing writers believe that, had it not been for his premature death, Sánchez could have gone on to become the greatest featherweight boxer of all time. Sánchez died on August 12, 1982, in a car accident from Querétaro to San Luis Potosi.[865]

In 1991, Sánchez was inducted into the International Boxing Hall of Fame. *The Ring* magazine named both him and Sugar Ray Leonard as Fighter of the Year in 1981. In 2002, he was named the 24th greatest fighter of the past 80 years by *The Ring* magazine. In 2003, the *Ring* rated Sánchez number 88 on the list of 100 greatest punchers of all time. Sánchez was voted as the number 3 feather-weight of the Twentieth Century by the Associated Press.

Bantamweights of the Nineteen Seventies

Chuco Castillo, 1970–1971

Jesús Castillo Aguilera (June 17, 1944–January 15, 2013) better known as Chuco Castillo was the World Bantamweight Champion for a brief time in the Nineteen Seventies. He was born in Mexico on June 17, 1944.

Castillo made his first world title attempt against Australia's Lionel Rose, the first Aborigine ever to win a world title. The fight

---

864

865

was held on 6 December 1968 at the Forum in Inglewood, where Rose won a very unpopular fifteen-round decision in front of a decidedly pro-Castillo crowd, causing a riot.[866]

Castillo got his second shot at the Bantamweight Title on April 18, 1970. This fight was the first in a memorable trio of fights between Castillo and Ruben Oliveres. There, at the Forum in Inglewood, Oliveres turned back the challenge of Castillo, winning a fifteen round unanimous decision.

A rematch between the two fighters took place on 16 October. Castillo cut Olivares in round one, and when it was determined that Olivares could not continue in Round 14, Castillo was declared winner by a technical knockout, winning the World Bantamweight Championship. After one nontitle win, Castillo met Olivares for a third time on 3 April 1971, when Olivares recovered the crown by outpointing Castillo despite suffering an early knockdown.

Chucho Castillo fought on until 1975 with a record of 47 wins with 23 knockouts, 17 losses and 2 draws.[867]

Ruben Oliveres 1971–1972

After regaining the Bantamweight Championship from Chucho Castillo, Oliveres scored six knockouts including two in title defenses. On March 19, 1972 he lost the championship to Rafael Herrera, another Mexican who beat him by knockout in the eighth round of their fight in Mexico City.[868]

Oliveres fought on until he retired in 1988. He twice won and lost alphabet featherweight titles in the Seventies. His record stands at 88 wins with an unbelievable 78 KOs, 13 losses, and 3 draws. He is a 1991 inductee into the IBHOF.

866

867

868

Rafael Herrera 1972

Herrera turned pro in 1963 and in 1972 defeated Rubén Olivares by TKO to capture the Lineal, WBC and WBA bantamweight titles. He lost the titles in his first defense to Enrique Pinder. Herrera retired with a record of 61 fights, 48 wins, 20 KOs, 9 losses, and 4 draws.[869]

Enrique Pinder 1972–1973

In 1966, Pinder began his professional career successfully. In late July 1972, he boxed against Rafael Herrera for the lineal, WBC, and WBA Bantamweight championships and won by unanimous judges' decision. He lost his world titles in his first defense in January of the following year to Romeo Anaya of Mexico by knockout. After suffering back-to-back defeats in the same year, Pinder ended his career with a record of 35 wins with 13 knockouts, 7 defeats, and 2 draws.

Romeo Anaya 1973

Anaya became the world bantamweight champion when he defeated Lineal and WBA Bantamweight Champion Enrique Pinder of Panama on January 20, 1973. On November 3, 1973, Romeo Anaya and Arnold Taylor met in a match refereed by Stanley Christodoulou in Johannesburg in South Africa. The 14 round fight is considered by many to be one of boxing's classic fights. One South African sportswriter called it *"the bloodiest fight in South African boxing history."* Taylor suffered a cut and was knocked down once in round 5 and three times in round 8. Nevertheless, Taylor also cut the champion, and, in round fourteen, he connected with a right hand to Anaya's jaw, sending him to the floor. Feeling that this was his moment to become a world champion, Taylor screamed to his trainers "He's gone!" from a neutral corner. It took Anaya two minutes to get up, and Taylor won the lineal and WBA Bantamweight titles.

---

[869]

Anaya retired with a record of 72 fights, 50 wins, 42 knockouts, 21 losses, and 1 draw.

Arnold Taylor, 1973–1974

Arnold Taylor was born in Johannesburg, South Africa on July 15, 1943. Taylor was a white South African who lived during the Apartheid era. On 3 November 1973, Taylor met the Lineal and WBA World Bantamweight champion, Mexico's Romeo Anaya. He won the title by a fourteenth round TKO. He wasn't the champion for long. After a couple of nontitle wins, he defended against South Korean boxer Soo Hwan Hong on July 3, 1974, and after visiting the canvas several times, he came up the loser in a fifteen round unanimous decision.

Taylor died on November 22, 1981. While driving a motorcycle belonging to his eldest daughter Charmaine, he was involved in an accident in which he was knocked over and he died at the scene of the accident. His record forever stands at 50 fights, 40 wins, 17 KOs, 8 losses, 1 draw, and 1 no contest.

Soo Hwan Hong, 1974–1975

Soo Hwan Hong was born in Seoul, South Korean on May 26, 1950. He briefly held the world bantamweight title. Hong turned pro in 1969 and in 1974 captured the lineal and WBA bantamweight title with a decision win over Arnold Taylor in a fight in which Taylor was down in the first, fifth, and fourteenth rounds. He lost his title by fourth round knockout in his 2nd defense to Alfonso Zamora in 1975.[870]

Alfonso Zamora 1975–1977

He was born Alfonso Zamora Quiroz in a little town called Mexico City on February 9, 1954. Zamora was the Silver Medalist at

870

the 1972 Olympic Games in Munich, Germany. He won the Lineal and WBA Bantamweight championship on 14 March 1975 when he knocked out Soo-Hwan Hong in four rounds, two years after turning pro. Zamora defended his title twice that year via knockout, against Thanomchit Sukhothai and Socrates Batoto. On April 3, 1976, he knocked out future Hall-of-Famer Eusebio Pedroza in the second round. Later that year, he successfully defended his title via knockout against Gilberto Illueca and a rematch with Soo-Hwan Hong.

It was inevitable that a clash between the two Zs would take place. Carlos Zarate was recognized by the WBC as champion and Zamora was the WBA and lineal World Champion. Because of the silliness of the two sanctioning bodies, this incredible matchup of two premier knockout artists that should have been a unification bout was officially fought nontitle in Los Angeles, so no matter who won the bout, he would not be recognized as a unified champion.

There, at the Inglewood Forum on March 23, 1977, Carlos Zarate knocked out lineal champion Alfonso Zamora in round four of a ten round nontitle fight between two recognized champions in the same weight class. Because neither body would sanction it, Zarate never got recognition as the undisputed lineal champion.[871] Zamora never quite got over the loss, and his career went downhill after that. He lost his next fight and the lineal World Championship to Panamanian Jorge Luján on November 19, 1977, by tenth round knockout. He lost three of his next seven fights and finally retired in 1980.[872]

Jorge Luján, 1977–1980

Luján was born in Colon, Panama on March 18, 1955. He received a world title try in 1977, facing the hard-hitting and popular champion, Alfonso Zamora, 29-1, with all 29 wins by knockout coming in. Despite being recognized as lineal and WBA bantamweight world champion, Zamora had also lost his last fight, a

871

872

nontitle affair to WBC champion Carlos Zarate. On November 19, 1977, in what also constituted Luján's debut in the United States as a professional boxer at the Los Angeles Sports Arena in Los Angeles, California, Luján built a six-point lead in one judge's scorecard and four point leads in the other two scorecards before becoming world champion by knocking Zamora out in round ten.

Luján was a busy champion, defending his title with success five times in the next three years, including an eleventh-round knockout of Mexico's Roberto Rubaldino at the Freeman Coliseum in San Antonio, Texas, after Luján had been dropped in round one on Luján's birthday of March 18, 1978; a fifteen-round decision win over future world champion Alberto Davila at the Superdome, New Orleans, Louisiana as part of the second Muhammad Ali-Leon Spinks fight's undercard on September 15, 1978; his Caesar's Palace debut when he beat Cleo Garcia with a technical knockout at 2:29 of round fifteen on April 8, 1979; a rematch win against Roberto Rubaldino, this time stopped in round fifteen at the La Villa Real Convention Center in McAllen, Texas, on October 6, 1979; and a ninth-round knockout win over challenger Shuichi Isogami at the Kuramae Kokugikan, Tokyo, Japan, on April 2, 1980.[873]

On August 29, 1980, Luján faced Puerto Rican challenger, undefeated Julian Solís, 20-0 at the time of their bout. Luján and Solís had a closely contested bout at the Miami Beach Convention Center in Miami Beach, Florida, but Luján lost his world championship to the Puerto Rican by a split fifteen-round decision.

Jorge Luján retired in 1985. Unlike too many boxers who attempt comebacks after they retire, Luján wisely never fought again. His record stands at 27 wins and 9 losses with 16 wins by knockout.

Julian Solís, 1980

Julian Solís was born in Rio Piedras, Puerto Rico, January 7, 1957. A former lineal and WBA bantamweight champion, Solís is

873

the only world champion in a family that produced two other world-class boxers.

He began his professional boxing career in 1975, outpointing Ray Negron in four on November 11. He won his first five fights in Puerto Rico.

In 1979, he won four fights, including one over Julio C. Saba knocked out in eight rounds in Buenos Aires. Solís continued on his travels in 1980. He retained the Latin American title with a 12th-round knockout of future world title challenger Edgar Roman in Venezuela, won a fight in South Africa, and challenged the lineal and WBA bantamweight champion Jorge Luján in Miami on August 29, winning on points.

For his first defense, Solís returned to Miami, but he lost the belt and his undefeated record to Jeff Chandler on November 14 when he was knocked out in the fourteenth round. After beginning 1981 with a win, he met Chandler again on 25 July, at Atlantic City, New Jersey. This time Chandler did the job in half the time, knocking out Solís in the seventh round.

Solís retired with a record of 41 wins, 13 losses and 1 draw, with 22 knockouts.[874] He remains active as a public figure in Puerto Rico, occasionally participating in charity exhibitions.

Jeff Chandler, 1980–1984

Joltin Jeff Chandler, Philadelphia bantamweight, closes out the bantamweight division for this chapter. The five-foot-seven-inch-tall Philadelphian began his professional career with a four-round draw in 1976 after only two amateur bouts. Chandler then began a four-year string of victories culminating in a challenge for the world's lineal and WBA one-hundred-eighteen-pound championship held by Julian Solís.[875] On November 14, 1980 Chandler won the title by a fourteenth-round knockout in Miami, becoming the first American fighter to hold the bantamweight crown in over 30 years.

874

875

Chandler's first defense was against former champion Jorge Luján, winning on points in fifteen rounds. He then traveled to Japan to face Asian champion Eljiro Murata, and although he was almost floored in the early rounds, Chandler came back to hold his title with a draw. Many ringside observers felt Chandler deserved a clear point's victory. With his status in the boxing world rising, Chandler followed this up with a repeat victory over Solís, this time in seven rounds. Chandler finished 1981 against Murata, earning a thirteenth-round knockout rematch win.[876]

He finished his career in 1984 with a record of 33 wins, 2 losses and 2 draws. Jeff Chandler provided boxing fans with many memorable performances. In 2000, he was elected to the International Boxing Hall of Fame at Canastota, New York.[877]

Flyweights of the Nineteen Seventies

Erbito Salavarria, 1970–1973

Salavarria was born in Santa Cruz, Manila, Philippines, January 20, 1946. He won the lineal Flyweight Championship of the World by defeating Thailand's Chartchai Chionoi by a second round knockout on December 7, 1970. Following a draw verdict against Betulio Gonzales in 1971, Salavarria was stripped of the WBC title. He lost the lineal world title to on February 9, 1973. His record stands at 54 fights, with 40 wins, 11 knockouts, 11 losses, and 3 draws.[878]

Venice Borkhorsor, 1973

Venice Borkhorsor (born April 6, 1950, in Nakhon Phanom) is a boxer from Thailand. He obtained the WBC world flyweight title on September 29, 1972, by defeating Betulio González in Bangkok, Thailand in a tenth-round TKO and later defeating the Lineal

---

876

877

878

Flyweight Champion Erbito Salavarria. He vacated the title following his last fight against Julio Guerrero on July 10, 1973.

Miguel Canto, 1975–1979

Miguel Canto was born January 30, 1948, in Mexico. He began his professional boxing career on February 5, 1969. He became one of those rare cases in boxing, like Alexis Argüello, Henry Armstrong, Bernard Hopkins, Victor Luvi Callejas, and Wilfredo Vazquez, where a boxer loses his first fight and goes on to become a world champion.[879] He lost that day to Raul Hernandez, in Canto's hometown of Mérida, by a knockout in round 3.[880]

He lost his first try for the WBC flyweight title, getting outpointed by another great, Betulio Gonzales on August 4, 1973, in Maracaibo, Venezuela. He continued his reign as Mexican flyweight champion, a title he had won in January of 1972. He finally struck gold January 8, 1975 in Japan, outpointing Shoji Oguma to win the vacant WBC and lineal flyweight championship of the world. His winning record was 40-4-3. He would go on to defend the flyweight title fourteen times, twice more defeating Oguma as well as Betulio Gonzales, his former conqueror. He held the flyweight title until March 18, 1979, when he lost by unanimous decision to

---

879

880

South Korean challenger Chan-Hee Park in Busan, South Korea. On September 9 of the same year, they two fought a rematch in Seoul, and it was ruled a majority draw after fifteen.

Miguel Canto fought for another three years, but after losing four of his last five fights, he retired in 1982.[881] He was inducted in the IBHOF in 1998. His final record stands at 61 wins, 9 losses, and 4 draws. He scored 15 knockouts.[882]

Chan-Hee Park, 1979–1980

Or Park Chan-Hee, take your pick. He was born on March 23, 1957, in Pusan, South Korea. As a member of the 1976 South Korean Olympic team, he finished fifth in the flyweight division, won that year by USA flyweight Leo Randolph.

Park turned professional in 1976 and became the WBC and lineal flyweight champion with a decision win over Miguel Canto in 1979. He lost the titles to Shoji Oguma by KO in 1980.

Shoji Oguma 1980–1981

In 1980 Oguma landed a shot at WBC and Lineal Flyweight Champion Chan-Hee Park and KO'd Park in the ninth round to capture the titles. He defended the titles twice the same year, including a split decision over Park, and his annual performance was named *Ring* magazine Comeback of the Year for 1980. In 1981 Oguma defended the titles successfully again against Park, but lost the belts in his following bout by KO to Antonio Velar. He then moved up in weight and in 1982 took on WBA Super Flyweight Title holder Jiro Watanabe, but was TKO'd in the twelfth. Oguma retired after the bout.

881

882

CHAPTER XVII

A Dozen Great Boxers Who Were Never Champions

Okay, I have given you a book with over four hundred pages of ministories and profiles of lineal world boxing champions. But what a about the guys who were as good as and in some cases better than the world champions of their time? Some of these boxers achieved considerable recognition, despite either being ignored by the champion, refusing to cooperate with the mob during the years the mob ran boxing, losing a title bid, by racial prejudice, or simply being too good for their own good. Here they are. They are bulleted rather than numbered. They were all great.

- Peter Jackson
- George Godfrey
- Billy Petrolle
- Jack Blackburn
- Lew Tendler
- George Benton
- Harry Wills
- Charley Burley
- Packey McFarlane
- Billy Graham
- Newsboy Brown
- Sam Langford

Peter Jackson, Active 1888–1898

First on the list is the name Peter Jackson, a man that was just born too soon. Peter Jackson Jr. was born in Christiansted, Danish West Indies (today the American Virgin Islands), on July 3, 1861.[883] Jackson won the Australian heavyweight title in 1886 with a knockout of Tom Lees in the thirtieth round. He was at one stage a pupil of the Black Diamond Jack Dowridge, a Barbadian immigrant who pioneered boxing in Queensland, Australia. Among Dowridge's other pupils was Gentleman Jack John Reid McGowan, a fellow Australian National Boxing Hall of Fame Inductee. After establishing his boxing career, and like many of Australia's best boxers of this era, Jackson left for America. He arrived in San Francisco in May 12, 1888, and promptly beat Old Chocolate Godfrey to gain the world colored heavyweight championship. During his stay in America, Jackson frequently sparred with Lees. Jackson would become an instructor at the California Athletic Club in San Francisco. He was considered one of the most scientific boxers of his day due to his footwork and technical proficiency.[884]

Jackson repeatedly tried to secure a fight against world champion John L. Sullivan, to no avail. Sullivan cited the color bar as the reason for his refusal, claiming he would never fight a black man.[885]

On May 21, 1891, Peter Jackson fought his memorable bout against future heavyweight champion Jim Corbett.[886] Corbett was the boxing instructor at the rival Olympic Club in San Francisco. Both were upper-crust athletic clubs. When the two met, it was an early cross-town rivalry. The bout was widely publicized, and the ensuing battle was widely heralded. Now, one hundred and twenty-nine years later, it's fame has endured.

883

884

885

886

After sixty-one rounds, with both men exhausted, the fight was declared no contest, [887]probably frustrating both combatants. I mean, "We just fought sixty-one rounds for this?"

Jackson's next important contest was against Frank Slavin at the National Sporting Club in London, England, on May 30, 1892. At stake was the Commonwealth title, which was held by Jackson. Peter Jackson was a good-looking dude, and that probably led to jealousy between Slavin and Jackson over a woman known as Josie Leon. I don't know if Jackson pursued her or if she pursued the handsome boxing instructor. This was in the later Victorian era, but things still got a little hanky-panky. Jackson beat Slavin, stopping him in the tenth round. I wonder what ever happened to Josie?

After beating Slavin, Jackson boxed several exhibitions, but largely took time off between the 1892 Slavin fight and the 1899 James J. Jeffries fight, seven years had elapsed. Jeffries knocked out the ring rusty thirty-eight-year-old in the second round on March 22, 1899, in San Francisco.[888]

Despite his celebrity, Jackson would run into financial troubles following his retirement from the ring. Jackson's health rapidly decayed following his bout against Jeffries, making it impossible for him to box. Several benefits were held in order to send him back to

---

887

888

Australia. Peter Jackson, one of the very greatest early era pugilists, died of tuberculosis on July 13, 1901. He was forty years old. He is a 1990 inductee to the IBHOF.[889] Jackson won 42 of 52 fights, 30 by knockout, with 5 losses, 3 draws, and 2 no contests.

George Godfrey, Active, 1879–1896

A well-known contemporary of Peter Jackson, George Godfrey was born March 20, 1853, in Charlottetown, Prince Edward Island, Canadian Province.[890] He was small for a heavyweight, weighing only about 175 pounds, and he was 27 years old when he began his professional career, but he achieved great success as a heavyweight boxer, winning the "Colored" Heavyweight Championship and fighting many notable pugilists of the era.[891] Among those he fought were Jake Kilrain, Peter Jackson, Denver Ed Smith, Joe Choynski, Charles Hadley, and Peter Maher.[892] There is one glaring omission here. That would be John L. Sullivan, who once again pulled the color bar, claiming he would never fight a black man. Godfrey might or might not have had the skills to beat Sullivan; we will never know.

It was during the last stages of his career, as the years took their toll and his ring skills visibly faded that the unenlightened press of the day took to calling him by the deprecatory sobriquet of Old Chocolate.[893]

Godfrey died at his home in Revere, Massachusetts, on October 19, 1901. He had acquired considerable real estate by the time of his death.[894]

889
890
891
892
893
894

Billy Petrolle, Active, 1926–1934

Known famously as the Fargo Express, Billy Petrolle was born on January 10, 1905, in Berwick, Pennsylvania. He died in 1983.[895] He is one of the most respected nonchampion boxers of all time. BoxRec lists Petrolle as the number 18 ranked lightweight of all time. He is a member of four halls of fame including the IBHOF.[896]

His career highlight was on November 4, 1932, when he challenged a peak Tony Canzoneri for the World Lightweight Championship in New York's Madison Square Garden. He dropped a fifteen-round unanimous decision. Other notables he fought and beat include an earlier win over Canzoneri, Jimmy McLarnin, and Battling Battalino.[897]

Petrolle retired during the Great Depression with $200,000 and an iron foundry in Duluth, Minnesota. He later owned a religious goods and gift shop in Duluth and was the chairman of the board of directors of the Pioneer National Bank.[898]

Jack Blackburn, Active, 1900–1923

895
896
897
898

I had read a biography about Joe Louis in my teenage years, and that was where I first encountered the name Jack "Chappie" Blackburn, the famous trainer of Joe Louis. I knew he was an old-time fighter, although I didn't know what weight division he fought in and I had no idea what a great fighter he had been. I eventually learned that he had been a great lightweight and one heck of a fighter. He fought welterweights, middleweight and even heavyweights, although he never weighed more than 140 pounds.

Chappie was born in Versailles, Kentucky on the twentieth day of May in 1883.[899] He was said to have possessed a strong left jab, quick hands, good defense, and a good left hook. He claimed to have fought over 400 times in his career. That would be a little over 17 fights a year for 23 years. He fought 147 recorded fights. In his career, he fought the boxing hall of fame. He fought Harry Greb, who is arguably the greatest middleweight champion in history. He took on the great Sam Langford six times! He fought the great Joe Gans three times, and mixed punches with Philadelphia Jack O'Brian, Gunboat Smith, Kid Norfolk, Dave Holly, and Panama Joe Gans.[900] This was a racially charged time and African American boxers often had the door to a title shot closed to them. During Blackburn's career, Jimmy Britt, Battling Nelson, Ad Wolgast, Willie Ritchie, Freddy Welsh, and Benny Leonard were all Caucasian lightweight champions, none of whom gave Blackburn a title shot. So the black boxers did the next best thing and fought each other over and over and over.

Blackburn fought the extraordinary Sam Langford a noteworthy six times in his career. On December 23, 1903, perhaps in one of his most memorable fights, Blackburn met Langford for the first time in a twelve-round pre-arranged draw at the Central Athletic Club in Boston, Massachusetts. Three local Boston papers, including the *Boston Globe* and *Herald*, wrote that Blackburn likely had the better of the bout. On January 11, 1904, Blackburn and Langford fought a six-round draw at the Washington Sporting Club in Philadelphia, Pennsylvania. On September 9, 1904, Blackburn drew

---

899
900

with Langford at the Marlborough Opera House in Marlborough, Massachusetts in a fifteen-round points decision. The fight was sensational, and Blackburn may have been outweighed by Langford by well over thirty pounds.[901]

On September 20, 1905, in front of a substantial crowd of six hundred, at the Lyric Athletic Club in Allentown, Pennsylvania, Blackburn and Langford met in a ten-round draw. The boxing was fierce and drew blood and both boxers had the better of their opponent at times, with Langford finding a way to counter the keen left of Blackburn. In the third round, Blackburn was doubled over the ropes by Langford, and may have been out but for the bell.

Gans and Blackburn met earlier on August 18, 1905, in Leiperville, Pennsylvania, in what was considered a great bout, though Blackburn lost in a fifteen-round points decision. Langford would rightfully claim the World Colored Heavyweight Championship when Jack Johnson vacated it in July 1909, and defend it for several fights, though he would be denied a chance at Johnson's new world heavyweight title. Langford would take the world colored middleweight championship, defeating Young Peter Jackson in a twenty-round bout on November 12, 1907, at the Pacific Athletic Club in Los Angeles.[902]

On November 20, 1907, before around 3000 spectators, Blackburn impressively defeated 1908 World Welterweight Champion Harry Lewis, though the six-round, no-decision bout at the National Athletic Club in Philadelphia was decided by newspaper decision of the *Philadelphia Item* and *Philadelphia Record*. The bout was a carefully boxed defensive show with neither boxer landing knockout blows. Showing an effective defense against such an exceptional boxer as Lewis was a considerable achievement for Blackburn.[903] Blackburn appeared to land more blows than Lewis in the first two rounds, but was cautious in the third and fourth. He opened up in the fifth and sixth, being urged on by the crowd, and

901
902
903

connected with a few powerful rights, particularly one to the ribs of Lewis which caused him to cover up. Characteristic of Blackburn's style, he effectively used his left jab throughout the bout. Blackburn's three inch reach advantage was used to his benefit. The *Wilkes-Barre Evening News* wrote that "*the bout was so palpably one sided, even the most ardent admirers of Lewis were quieted before the third round was over.*" Each man collected around $1,000 from the well-attended bout.[904] The *New York Age* wrote that "*Blackburn was a marvel of science, and self-possession, outboxing his opponent at every angle, judging distance better and hitting a harder blow.*"[905]

Chappie was no angel. He served four years and eight months for manslaughter as the result of a tragic shooting spree he instigated that led to several deaths in Philadelphia in 1909.[906]

Years later, in 1935, he was in trouble again. He was the trainer of rising heavyweight Joe Louis when he was indicted for manslaughter on charges of two shootings. The charges were later dropped, but Blackburn spent time in jail again.[907]

In 1914, he lost a close decision to 6'2" heavyweight Gunboat Smith, giving up over forty pounds. Smith would go on to fight Jack Dempsey, before the Manassa Mauler became champion. On January 25, 1915, he lost a six-round decision to the great Harry Greb. Chappie fought on until 1923 meeting top men such as Kid Norfolk and Panama Joe Gans.[908]

With Louis, Chappie Blackburn had a successful second career as the trainer of Joe Louis. According to his bio on the IBHOF, Blackburn was at first skeptical about taking on Louis. Probably remembering his own career and the prejudice he endured as well as remembering Jack Johnson, the first heavyweight champion, he felt that there would not be many opportunities for an African American heavyweight in the nineteen thirties. Still, he took the Brown Bomber on, gradually teaching him better balance, combination punching

---

904

905

906

907

908

and hitting with accuracy. The two African American boxers had a close bond, Louis fondly calling him "chappie" and Blackburn calling Joe the same.[909]

He had problems with drinking and violence and his health deteriorated. In 1942, as Joe Louis was serving his country, Jack Chappie Blackburn died of a heart attack.[910]

Lew Tendler, Active, 1913–1928

The great city of Philadelphia, Pennsylvania, is possibly the very apex of boxing talent and has been for over a century. This is the city that spawned Meldrick Taylor, Sonny Liston (sort of), Philadelphia Jack O'Brian, George Benton, Joey Giardello, Matthew Saad Muhammad, Benny Bass, Battling Levinsky, Bennie Briscoe, Tommy Loughran, Joe Frazier, Bernard Hopkins, and Lew Tendler who just happens to be the subject of this section.

Well, Lew never won a world title. Not that he didn't come close; on July 27, 1922, Tendler fell to fellow Jewish boxer Benny Leonard in a twelve round newspaper decision in Jersey City in a lightweight world title match, that may have been the most remarkable bout of Tendler's career. Before a record audience of over 60,000 enthralled fans, Leonard won five rounds, Tendler four, with three even. Tendler

909

910

may have led in the first five rounds, as Leonard could not adjust to or penetrate his unique Southpaw stance, style, and defense. In the eighth, Tendler crashed a terrific left to the midsection which had followed a left to the head, and Leonard held on to Tendler as he sank to one knee. Then Leonard rose and distracted Tendler by mumbling a few words, then going to a clinch to rest for much of the remainder of the round. Tendler never delivered the follow up knockout blow, and Leonard, getting time to recover, dominated the next seven rounds.[911] The excitement of this meeting prompted a rematch. That fight held in Yankee Stadium on July 24, 1923. This time the great Leonard boxed his way to a clear unanimous decision.[912]

Tendler got another crack at a world title when he challenged welterweight champion Mickey Walker for his crown. Tendler fell to Walker in a ten round unanimous decision on June 2, 1924. The *Pittsburgh Daily Post* gave Walker five rounds with only the seventh and eighth to Tendler.[913] In a fast and exciting bout, Tendler drove Walker from rope to rope in the seventh with rights and lefts to the body and head, looking like he might take the decision. Walker had an edge in the final two rounds, however, as Tendler tired, and scored most frequently with blows to the body.[914]

The great southpaw retired in 1928 and opened a restaurant in Philly in 1932 that specialized in steaks. It was called Tendler's Tavern and was so successful he opened branches in Atlantic City and Miami Beach. The original stayed open for many years.

Lew Tendler died on November 7, 1970. His record shows 169 total bouts with 59 wins, 11 losses, 2 draws, 96 newspaper decisions, and 1 no contest. He fought during the era of newspaper decisions which account for the disparity in his record. He was inducted into the IBHOF in 1999.[915]

911

912

913

914

915

George Benton, Active, 1949–1970

George Benton was the quintessential Philadelphia professional boxer. He was born on May 15, 1933, in the City of Brotherly Love during the height of the Great Depression. Benton had his first amateur fight when he was thirteen. He turned professional when he was sixteen and spent the rest of his life in and around Philly boxing. Like Jack Blackburn, he became one of the very best trainers of boxers after his fighting days were over.

In 1962, Benton beat Joey Giardello and was expecting a title shot against champion Dick Tiger. Instead, Tiger opted to fight Giardello, who subsequently beat Tiger and never gave Benton the title shot he deserved. Benton continued fighting until 1970, losing some, but winning more. Benton's boxing career ended in 1970 after he was shot. The shooter had tried to pick up Benton's sister in a bar, and Benton's brother beat him up. Vowing to kill someone from the Benton family, the man shot Benton in the back. He was in and out of the hospital for two years. The bullet remained lodged near Benton's spine for the remainder of his life.[916]

His fighting days over, Benton, like many other ex-boxers became a trainer, in fact one of the best trainers ever. He had a great teacher, Mr. Eddie Futch. As the head trainer for Main Events, Benton trained greats Evander Holyfield, Oliver McCall, Mike McCallum,

Pernell Whitaker, and Meldrick Taylor. He was also in demand as a cornerman. He was in the corner of fellow Philadelphian Joe Frazier in his losing effort in the *Thrilla in Manila* against Muhammad Ali. He was in Leon Spinks corner when Neon Leon upset Ali.[917] In 1989 and 1990, he was named the trainer of the year by the Boxing Writers Association of America.[918], [919]

Benton was a member of the IBHOF class of 2001. He died of pneumonia on September 19, 2011. His ring record forever stands at 62 wins (37 by knockout), 13 losses, and 1 draw.[920]

Harry Wills, Active, 1911–1932

Harry Wills was born in New Orleans, May 15, 1889. He held the World "Colored" Heavyweight Championship three times. Many boxing historians consider Wills the most egregious victim of the color line drawn by white heavyweight champions. Wills fought for over twenty years (1911–1932) and was ranked as the number one challenger for the throne but was denied the opportunity to fight for the title. Of all the black contenders between the heavyweight championship reigns of Jack Johnson and Joe Louis, Wills came closest to

917

918

919

920

securing a title shot.[921] He fought many of the top contenders of his era, including Gunboat Smith, Willie Meehan, who had frustrated Dempsey and Luis Angel Firpo, the Wild Bull of the Pampas.[922]

The top black fighters of Wills's era were forced to continuously fight one another, as many white fighters also drew the color line. As a result, Wills fought the redoubtable Sam Langford 22 times. His record against Langford was 6 wins, 2 losses, and 14 no decisions, although the two losses were by knockout. He beat Langford three times for the colored heavyweight title, with Langford winning it back twice. (He was forced to vacate his third title when he fought Jack Sharkey in 1926 and was lost the bout due to a disqualification.) Wills also defeated colored heavyweight champ Sam McVey three times and fought two no decision bouts with Joe Jeanette.[923]

The Jack Johnson syndrome: Because Jack Johnson's reign as heavyweight champion had stirred so much controversy in the previous decade, life was very difficult for a leading African American heavyweight contender. Promoters envisioned race riots if Dempsey won and race riots if Wills won. The two actually signed an agreement to meet in a title bout, but it was banned by New York Governor Alfred E. Smith. Many people still recalled the riots surrounding the films of the Jack Johnson and James J. Jeffries in movie theaters. Dempsey stated that he was willing to meet Wills for the championship, but no promoter was willing to risk another Jack Johnson. And Dempsey had stated after winning the championship that he would not fight another black man.

He took on future heavyweight champion Jack Sharkey and lost by disqualification. Next he took on Basque heavyweight Paulino Uzcudun and was knocked out on July 13, 1927, at Ebbets Field in Brooklyn. He fought sporadically after that and retired in 1932. His record according to BoxRec.com is 70 wins (56 by KO), with 9 losses and 3 draws.[924]

921

922

923

924

After Wills's retirement, he ran a successful real estate business in Harlem. He died in 1958 and was enshrined in the IBHOF in 1992.[925]

Charley Burley, Active, 1936–1950

Charley Burley was one of the greatest boxers who never contended for a world title. He was born on September 6, 1917, in the steel mill town of Bessemer, Pennsylvania, to a black father and a white mother.[926]

He began boxing at age twelve in the local Boys Club. He won a number of amateur titles before turning professional on September 29, 1936. Less than two years later, he became the "Colored" Welterweight Champion of the World, beating Cocoa Kid over fifteen rounds. He twice lost to the great Ezzard Charles and won and lost the world colored middleweight title to the equally talented Holman Williams in 1942.[927]

Burley was never granted a world title shot by any of the world welterweight and world middleweight champions of his era and was avoided by many of the top white contenders. Among the fighters who "ducked" Burley were Hall of Famers Billy Conn (who fought Joe Louis for the heavyweight title), Frenchman Marcel Cerdan (who was supposed to face Burley in his American debut) and even Sugar Ray Robinson, considered by many boxing historians as the best pound-for-pound fighter of all time.[928]

Of course not everyone ducked Charley Burley. He twice decisioned Fritzie Zivic, beat the great Archie Moore by decision, and easily beat the future NYSAC middleweight champion Billy Soose.[929] Perhaps these wins made other contenders duck him?

Eddie Futch, the great trainer, called Burley "the finest all-around fighter I ever saw."

925
926
927
928
929

Burley was named to *The Ring* magazine's list of 100 greatest punchers of all time, elected to the Boxing Hall of Fame in 1983 and the International Boxing Hall of Fame in 1992. Burley was ranked 39th on *Ring* magazine's list of the 80 Best Fighters of the Last 80 Years. Charley Burley died on October 16, 1992. He was 75 years old. His boxing record according to BoxRec.com forever stands at 83 wins (50 by KO), 12 losses, and 2 draws.[930]

Packey McFarland, 1904–1915

The most amazing thing about Packey McFarland, the great turn of the Twentieth-Century lightweight is his boxing record. Between the years 1904 and 1915, eleven years in which time he packed in 70 wins (50 by knockout), 0 losses, and 5 draws.[931] That's a pretty good record. That is from the website BoxRec.com. Wikipedia differs. According to that source, McFarland had 105 wins (51 by KO), 1 loss, 6 draws, and 1 no contest.[932] That is also a pretty good record. Who to believe? Take your pick. McFarland fought over a century ago. He was good, and he won a lot of fights. That much

---

930

931

932

is sure. Packey McFarland was born in the Windy City of Chicago, Illinois, on November 1, 1888, a year before the epic Sullivan-Kilrain bare-knuckle championship fight in Mississippi that Sullivan won after 75 rounds.

Not much is known about McFarland's youth or amateur experience. He was a tough Irish kid who grew up in a tough city. He grew into arguably the greatest fighter, along with Barney Ross that Chicago ever produced. He turned professional in 1904. In 1905 he beat Jimmy Britt, who had a disputed claim to be the lightweight world champion, although this fight was not for a title. In 1908 he defeated future lightweight champion Freddie Welsh in one bout and drew with him in another. He also defeated old foe Britt in another bout that year. In 1910, he met Welsh again for the British version of the lightweight title. The bout ended in another draw, with Welsh retaining his title. McFarland never fought for another world title bout.[933]

He retired in 1915 after fighting to a draw with Mike Gibbons. He was a boxing instructor at Camp Zachary Taylor in 1918. On January 27, 1933, he was appointed to the Illinois Athletic Commission by Governor Henry Horner. McFarland also managed his sizable investments and was director of two banks.[934] He died at Joliet, Illinois on September 22, 1936. He was forty-seven years old. He was a 1992 IBHOF inductee.

Billy Graham, Active, 1941–1955

A hundred and two wins and fifteen losses and never won a world title? Well, he had his chance against the great Kid Gavilan, but he lost a split decision in their championship bout in Madison Square Garden on August 8, 1951, in a fight that might or might not have been fixed by underworld figures Frankie Carbo and Blinky Palermo. Graham was never knocked off his feet in over one hundred

933
934

pro fights and he is an inductee in the International Boxing Hall of Fame (IBHOF).

In a 2002 interview with the *Observer*, Budd Schulberg talked about mob involvement in boxing in the 1950s and how Gavilan both won and lost the welterweight championship due to mob interference.

> *Frankie Carbo, the mob's unofficial commissioner for boxing, controlled a lot of the welters and middles... Not every fight was fixed, of course, but from time to time Carbo and his lieutenants, like Blinky Palermo in Philadelphia, would put the fix in. When the Kid Gavilan-Johnny Saxton fight was won by Saxton on a decision in Philadelphia in 1954, I was covering it for Sports Illustrated and wrote a piece at that time saying boxing was a dirty business and must be cleaned up now. It was an open secret. All the press knew that one—and other fights—were fixed. Gavilan was a mob-controlled fighter, too, and when he fought Billy Graham it was clear Graham had been robbed of the title. The decision would be bought. If it was close, the judges would shade it the way they had been told.*[935]

Billy Graham was born on Manhattan's East Side on September 9, 1922. He beat Sugar Ray Robinson as an amateur. He turned professional on April 14, 1941, winning a technical knockout over one Connie Savoie at New York's famed St. Nicholas Arena. He then went on a tear, going undefeated, save six draws, in his next fifty fifty-seven fights. He rarely fought outside of New York or New Jersey until 1951 when he was a world ranked contender.[936] He fought Kid Gavilan three times, winning once, Carmen Basilio three times, win-

---

[935]

[936]

ning one, losing one, and drawing one.[937] Among the other notables Graham faced were Paddy DeMarco, Tony Pellone, Rocky Castellani, Joey Giardello, Art Aragon, and Chico Vejar. He retired following a couple of losses to Vejar in 1955.[938]

When his boxing days were over, he worked as a representative for liquor companies, including *Seagram's*. Graham died of cancer at his home in West Islip, Long Island, New York, on January 22, 1992.[939]

Newsboy Brown, Active, 1921–1933

It's an old story. Many years ago, say 1900 to 1960, in almost any American city, you could find a kid hawking newspapers on a street corner. The best corner, sold the most papers and the kid made the most money. I really don't know how often this happened but in the old story I am telling, you had to be tough to hold on to your territory, the best corner. Often one had to fight to defend it. This is the story of David Montrose, a.k.a. Newsboy Brown, who was born in the old Russian Empire in 1905.[940] He grew up in Sioux Falls, Iowa, like many young boys who were immigrants he learned to be tough at an early age.

He began his professional boxing career on April 21, 1921, stopping somebody named Kid Pitts by TKO. The story goes that the ring announcer could not remember his name and introduced him as Newsboy Brown. With that, he began his hall of fame career. Almost all his early fights, either victories or draws, were fought in or around Sioux Falls.[941]

In 1925, his fifth year as a pro, he moved to Los Angeles and fought the remainder of his career fighting such stellar names as Corporal Izzy Schwartz, W10, Speedy Dado, TKO 6, Midget Wolgast, W10, and the great Panama Al Brown, whom he decisioned in a ten round nontitle fight.[942]

937

938

939

940

941

942

Brown briefly claimed the California version of the flyweight title, and the NYSAC flyweight title, although neither was recognized as undisputed lineal title. He retired in 1933 after losing three straight. Newsboy Brown retired with a record of 58 wins, 13 losses, and 5 draws.[943]

After his boxing retirement, he broke into the motion picture business by coaching cowboy star Tom Mix in his fight scenes. As a result of his association with Mix, he landed a job in the properties department of one of the Hollywood studios, where he worked in his later years. He died on February 18, 1977, in his adopted city, Los Angeles, California.[944]

Sam Langford, Active, 1902–1926

Sam Langford was the toughest little
son of a bitch that ever lived.
—Jack Johnson

Sam Langford, the great African American boxer, called the greatest fighter nobody knows by ESPN, was born March 4, 1886, in Nova Scotia. It was said he was born with both of his little fists clenched.[945] He was known as the Boston Bonecrusher, the Boston Terror, and his most infamous nickname, the Boston Tar Baby. Langford stood 5 feet 7 1/2 inches and weighed 185 pounds in his prime. He fought from lightweight to heavyweight and defeated many world champions and legends of the time in each weight class. Considered a devastating puncher even at heavyweight, Langford was rated number 2 by the *Ring* on their list of 100 greatest punchers of all time.[946] Jack Dempsey claimed that as a young boxer in 1916, he refused a fight with Langford. According to Dempsey, "I think Sam Langford was the greatest fighter we ever had."[947]

943
944
945
946
947

Langford left home at an early age, to escape an abusive father. He became a wandering vagrant, taking work wherever he could find it and eventually winding up in a gym in Boston as a janitor and watching and later sparring with the boxers that trained there. When he was fifteen years old, he won a state amateur championship and promptly turned professional.[948]

Because of the dominant racism of the era, Langford, like nearly all his fellow African American boxers had to fight one another over and over and over and over. But those who fought him knew very well how good he was. Joe Jeanette and Harry Wills, both outstanding black contemporaries of Langford, rated him the best they ever fought. Old time fight manager Charley Rose rated Langford the best heavyweight of all time, and Dan Morgan, another old time manager, stated, "Sam would finish Joe Louis in about six or seven rounds."[949]

Sam fought the great lightweight champion Joe Gans on December 8, 1903, winning a fifteen-round decision, but the title was not on the line. He challenged another great, Joe Walcott, "the Barbados Demon," on September 5, 1904, for the world welterweight title and despite a majority of viewers claiming Langford won, the

948
949

fight was ruled a draw, thus allowing Walcott to retain the crown.[950] He fought Jack Blackburn, trainer of the legendary Joe Louis, six times. The first three fights were draws, the fourth a decision win for Langford, the fifth another draw, and the sixth a no contest.[951]

Langford fought heavyweight Joe Jeanette fourteen times, losing the first by eighth round retirement, winning second by decision, third and fourth were a draw via points, winning the fifth through eighth by decision, ninth was a draw via points, winning the tenth on decision, eleventh was a draw via points, lost the twelfth by decision and winning the thirteenth by seventh round knockout and fourteenth by decision.[952] He fought Sam McVea fifteen times, Battling Jim Johnson twelve times and Harry Wills seventeen times.[953] That is a total of sixty-four fights between just five opponents.

Toward the end of his career, he began to go blind. It was said that he was blind in his left eye and only saw shadows in his right eye. Nonetheless, he continued fighting and winning. His last fight was in 1926 when complete blindness forced him to retire at age forty-three.

Langford eventually went completely blind and ended up penniless, living in Harlem, New York City. In 1944, a newspaper column was published about his plight after which close to $10,000 was donated by fans to help Langford. The column was titled "A Dark Man Laughs," and it was written by Al Laney of the New York *Herald Tribune*. Eventually funding was obtained to pay for successful eye surgery. Langford was enshrined in the *Ring* Boxing Hall of Fame and Canada's Sports Hall of Fame in 1955. He died a year later in Cambridge, Massachusetts, where he had been living in a private nursing home.[954] His boxing record forever stands at 245 total bouts, 178 wins (with 126 knockouts, a record that stood for several years until Archie Moore topped it with 131 KOs) 29 losses, and 38 draws.[955]

950
951
952
953
954
955

CHAPTER XVIII

The State of the Sweet Science

There it is, one-hundred years of professional boxing history. And what a history! Think of all the great names who laced 'em up between 1880 and 1980—John L. Sullivan, Jack Dempsey, Joe Louis, Rocky Marciano, Muhammad Ali, Joe Frazier, and George Foreman, and those are just the heavyweights. There are stellar names across all the divisions from flyweight Jimmy Wilde to Miguel Canto. The great bantamweight Éder Jofre; the Saddler Pep series, legendary lightweights Joe Gans, Benny Leonard and Roberto Durán; peerless Sugar Ray Robinson; Jack Johnson; Sam Langford; and Carlos Monzon.

Then there were the great fights. Going all the way back to 1906 in Goldfield, Nevada, the epic forty-two-round fight for the ages between Joe Gans and Battling Nelson certainly fits that category. Then the classic Jack Johnson-James J. Jeffries first "Fight of the Century." Louis-Conn first fight, Dempsey-Tunney long count, the Ali-Frazier *Thrilla in Manila*, and Archie Moore-Yvonne Durelle in 1958, with Moore down three times in round one, coming back to knock Durelle out in the eleventh.

These were all world championship fights. Some of them were recognized by one sanctioning body or another, but the winners all wound up as champions of the world. So what happened? The first sanctioning body, the WBA, was founded in 1921 as the National Boxing Association or NBA. It became the World Boxing Association

(WBA) in August of 1962. To explain this malady, I go to Wikipedia, the article I am printing in its entirety.

> As has been the case with all major boxing sanctioning organizations, the WBA has been plagued with charges of corrupt practices. In a 1981 Sports Illustrated article, a boxing judge claimed he was influenced by WBA President Gilberto Mendoza to judge certain fighters competing for their titles more favorably. The same article also discussed a variety of bribes paid to WBA officials to obtain championship bout opportunities, or higher placement within the organization's rankings. In a 1982 interview, boxing promoter Bob Arum claimed that he had to pay off WBA officials to obtain rankings for his fighters. Further support for allegations of this nature came in the 1980s and 1990s as two other organizations would have similar corruption exposed, including the conviction and imprisonment of IBF President Bob Lee and Graciano Rocchigiani's successful civil prosecution of the WBC that resulted in the organization briefly filing for bankruptcy before reaching a settlement that saved it from collapse.
>
> The WBA presently can recognize up to four world champions in any given weight division, to a point of rendering it technically impossible under certain conditions for a WBA world champion to even hold sole recognition from the organization as its champion in a division.
>
> The most prominent designation is that of the WBA (Super) champion, formerly reserved for champions who are simultaneously recognized by the WBC, IBF or WBO. A WBA (Super) champion is afforded special consideration by the organization with respect to meeting mandatory defense

obligations to maintain championship recognition, but it also has opened the door for the organization to recognize a separate world champion, the WBA (Regular) champion; creating confusion among fans as to who holds the de facto championship title. Some world champions have been upgraded to WBA (Super) champion status without winning another organization's title, among them Floyd Mayweather Jr., Chris John, Anselmo Moreno and Manny Pacquiao; or upon defending their WBA (Regular) title five or more times. Upon awarding a WBA (Super) championship, the regular world champion status is deemed vacant, whereupon it is filled by the organization as a separate championship.

The WBA further complicates this from time to time by recognizing an interim champion, ostensibly in cases where a designated world champion is, for some reason, prohibited from making a timely defense of their title. Under such conditions, the interim title holder is to be the next person to compete for one of the full championship titles once the champion is in a position to compete. In practice, however, this actually occurs rarely if ever and in 2019 the organization began awarding the WBA Gold title, for which no provision exists even within the organization's own governing documents. As of December 2019 for example, they simultaneously recognized a WBA (Super) champion (Anthony Joshua), WBA (Regular) champion (Manuel Charr), WBA interim champion (Trevor Bryan) and WBA Gold champion (Robert Helenius).

There have even been instances where different WBA world champions have defended versions of the same title, in the same weight class, on the same date in different events.

And that is just the WBA. Reading the current edition of *The Ring* magazine ratings (July 2020), here is what they show.

Heavyweight: There are two champions, Tyson Fury (*Ring* and WBC) and Anthony Joshua (IBF, WBA, and WBO). If that is confusing, the cruiserweight division has three champions, none of which are recognized by the *Ring*. The light heavyweight division has two champions, and again the *Ring* has the title vacant. The super middleweights show four different champions, including Callum Smith, recognized by the *Ring*. Continuing on, the middleweight division ruled by champion Canelo Alvarez also sports four different boxers, including Alvarez calling themselves world champions. Okay, you get the picture. It is the same for the junior middleweights, welterweights, junior welterweights, lightweights, junior lightweights, featherweights, junior featherweights, bantamweights, junior bantamweights, flyweights, junior flyweights, and strawweights. I list all seventeen divisions, because each of these divisions average between three and four world champions. The sanctioning bodies have made a complete mess of boxing. Today, as this is being written, there are seventeen weight classes an unbelievable fifty-two boxers throughout those seventeen weight classes all claiming to be xchampions of the world. Well, poor old Joe Blow. Remember him? No wonder nobody knows his name.

With all that said, there are several outstanding boxers of the last forty years, who, by the subject matter of this book, are excluded. There are several, but I cannot list them all. Here are the best, by bivision:

- Heavyweight: Larry Holmes, Mike Tyson, Evander Holyfield, Lennox Lewis, Vladimir Klitchko, Anthony Joshua, and Tyson Fury, who is still active.
- Light heavyweight: Michael Spinks and Dariusz Michalczewski
- Middleweight: Marvelous Marvin Hagler, James Toney, Bernard Hopkins, Sergio Martinez, Gennady Golovkin, and Canelo Alvarez

- Welterweight: Sugar Ray Leonard, Donald Curry, Pernell Whitaker, Oscar De La Hoya, Errol Spence Jr., Sugar Shane Mosley, Terrance Crawford, Manny Pacquiao, and Floyd Mayweather Jr.
- Lightweight: Alexis Arguello, Julio Cesar Chavez, Pernell Whitaker, Floyd Mayweather Jr., Aaron Pryor, Juan Manuel Marquez, and Manny Pacquiao
- Featherweight, Salvador Sanchez, Eusebio Pedroza, Antonio Espararragoza, Marco Antonio Barrera, and again Manny Pacquiao
- Bantamweight: Jeff Chandler, Richie Sandoval, and Jose "Gaby" Canizales
- Flyweight: Shoji Oguma, Antonio Avelar, Sot Chitalada, Yuri Arbachakov and Roman Gonzales

Great fighters all, and several hall of famers.

Today, both professional and amateur boxing face competition from mixed martial arts with the popularity of self-defense methods such as kickboxing, muay thai, taekwondo, and karate. Television shows such as *Kung Fu* both romanticized and popularized martial arts to a generation removed from regularly televised boxing. All these are very effective forms of self-defense. But for pure drama there is something very special, something very basic and essential, about two well-conditioned professional boxers, facing each other in a twenty-foot ring, stripped to the waist putting their dukes up and giving their all. For many years boxing was regularly referred to as the manly art of self-defense.

Professional boxing has been around for three hundred years, since James Figg in 1720 became the first bare-knuckle champion in Merry Olde England. It has ebbed and flowed over the centuries, been bare-fisted and gloved, illegal and legal, celebrated, crime infested, noble, manly, and now womanly, and at one time, when boxing truly mattered, the greatest sport in the world.

The End

The All-Time Best by division

Heavyweight

1. Muhammed Ali
2. Joe Louis
3. Jack Johnson
4. Rocky Marciano
5. Sonny Liston
6. George Foreman
7. Larry Holmes
8. Jack Dempsey
9. Lennox Lewis
10. Mike Tyson
11. Bob Fitzimmons

Light heavyweight

1. Ezzard Charles
2. Archie Moore
3. Bob Foster
4. Sam Langford
5. Gene Tunney
6. Andre Ward
7. Billy Conn
8. Michael Spinks
9. Harold Johnson
10. Jimmy Bivins
11. Tommy Loughran
12. Darius Michalczewski

Middleweights

1. Harry Greb
2. Carlos Monzon
3. Sam Langford
4. Stanley Ketchel
5. Marvelous Marvin Hagler
6. Sugar Ray Robinson
7. Bob Fitzimmons
8. Bernard Hopkins
9. Charley Burley
10. Dick Tiger
11. Tony Zale

Welterweights

1. Sugar Ray Robinson
2. Floyd Mayweather Jr.
3. Henry Armstrong

4. Sugar Ray Leonard
5. Barney Ross
6. Manny Pacquiao
7. Oscar De La Hoya
8. Emile Griffith
9. Joe Walcott
10. Jimmy McLarnin
11. Kid Gavilan

Lightweights

1. Roberto Duran
2. Joe Gans
3. Benny Leonard
4. Aaron Pryor
5. Manny Pacquiao
6. Pernell Whitaker
7. Packy McFarland
8. Henry Armstrong
9. Tony Canzoneri
10. Alexis Arguello
11. Freddie Welsh

Featherweights

1. Willie Pep
2. Abe Attell
3. Henry Armstrong
4. Manny Pacquiao
5. Salvador Sanchez
6. Kid Chocolate
7. George Dixon
8. Sandy Saddler
9. Vicente Saldivar
10. Young Griffo

Bantamweights

1. Eder Jofre
2. Carlos Zarate
3. Panama Al Brown
4. Manual Ortiz
5. Terry McGovern
6. Ruben Oliveres
7. Pete Herman
8. Fighting Harada
9. Kid Williams
10. Jose Becerra

Flyweights

1. Jimmy Wile
2. Pasqual Perez
3. Fidel La Barba
4. Roman Gonzalez
5. Fidel LaBarba
6. Miguel Canto
7. Frankie Genaro
8. Benny Lynch
9. Midget Wolgast
10. Betulio Gonzales

About the Author

Bo Brumble is an artist and writer who lives in Santa Fe, New Mexico. He is a former boxer who fought from 1959–1972. Later in life he was a boxing manager of several professional boxers and ran the South Park Boxing Gym in Seattle. He is a United States Army veteran, a father, and a grandfather. He has been an avid student of boxing history since his early teens.

Blog Address: http://www.brumbleboxing.com

CPSIA information can be obtained
at www.ICGtesting.com
Printed in the USA
FSHW010624010521
80864FS

9 781662 431517